THE IMPACT OF PUBLIC OPINION ON U.S. FOREIGN POLICY SINCE VIETNAM

Constraining the Colossus

Richard Sobel

Harvard University

New York   Oxford

OXFORD UNIVERSITY PRESS

2001

Oxford University Press

Oxford   New York
Athens   Auckland   Bangkok   Bogotá   Buenos Aires   Calcutta
Cape Town   Chennai   Dar es Salaam   Delhi   Florence   Hong Kong   Istanbul
Karachi   Kuala Lumpur   Madrid   Melbourne   Mexico City   Mumbai
Nairobi   Paris   São Paulo   Shanghai   Singapore   Taipei   Tokyo   Toronto   Warsaw

and associated companies in
Berlin   Ibadan

Published by Oxford University Press, Inc.
198 Madison Avenue, New York, New York 10016
http://www.oup-usa.org

Oxford is a registered trademark of Oxford University Press

Library of Congress Cataloging-in-Publication Data

Sobel, Richard, 1949–
     The impact of public opinion on U.S. foreign policy since Vietnam: constraining the
colossus / Richard Sobel.
     p. cm.
     Includes bibliographical references (p.) and index.
     ISBN 0-19-510527-3 (alk. paper) — ISBN 0-19-510528-1 (pbk. : alk. paper)
     1. United States—Foreign relations—1945–1989—Public opinion. 2. United
States—Foreign relations—1989—Public opinion. 3. Public opinion—United
States—History—20th century. 4. Intervention (International law)—Public opinion.   I.
Title.

E744 .S747 2001
327.73—dc21   00-037506

Printing (last digit): 9   8   7   6   5   4   3   2   1

Printed in the United States of America
on acid-free paper

Contents

For Dick Neustadt and Sid Verba
Pioneers and Sages
Bestriding Their Worlds Like a Colossus

List of Tables

Foreword

This study by Richard Sobel is an important substantive and theoretical addition to the literature on the relationship between public opinion and American foreign policy. To understand better the nature of its contribution and to place it in a broader context, it may be useful to review very briefly how the analysis of public opinion and foreign policy has developed during the six decades since the inception of widespread polling on public policy issues.

The first phase, roughly encompassing the three decades between the attack on Pearl Harbor that brought the United States into World War II and the Tet offensive that raised many serious doubts about prospects for American success in the Vietnam War, was originally driven by a single policy concern: What role would the United States play following the end of World War II? More specifically, would it remain actively engaged in world affairs and join a postwar international organization—the United Nations—or would it choose a path of disengagement, as it had done after World War I? Franklin D. Roosevelt, who had served in the Wilson administration and witnessed firsthand the Senate's rejection of the Versailles Treaty, feared that once the guns had stopped firing, the American public would lose interest in the state of international relations and reject a leadership role for the United States. Roosevelt was also the first president to exhibit an active interest in the new science of public opinion polling, perhaps in part because pollster George Gallup had demonstrated in the 1936 presidential election that a small but carefully selected sample of the public could faithfully represent the entire public. Gallup had correctly predicted a Roosevelt landslide victory, whereas the venerable *Literary Digest* survey, based on a very large but wholly unrepresentative sample, had insisted that Republican nominee Alf Landon would oust Roosevelt from the White House. Roosevelt secretly engaged Hadley Cantril, another pioneering public opinion analyst, to conduct surveys throughout the war to assess the state of public sentiments on issues germane to America's postwar role. FDR even took an active part in crafting the specific questions to which the public would be asked to respond.

Although the United States joined the United Nations in 1945 after a resounding 89 to 2 Senate vote in favor of the U.N. treaty, concern about a reversion to a mindless isolationism continued to drive most analyses of public attitudes on international affairs. Although they approached the question from different perspectives, political scientist Gabriel Almond (1950), diplomatic historian Thomas Bailey (1948), journalist Walter Lippmann (1955), and diplomat-historian George Kennan (1951) were among those who came to the same woeful conclusion: The American public, poorly informed about world affairs and indifferent to external events except in times of war or crisis, provides very weak foundations upon which to base the responsible pursuit of vital national interests. Driven by fluctuating moods and lacking any coherent intellectual framework within which to make sense of international events, the public could not be relied on to provide policymakers in Washington with consistent support for an effective international leadership role.

Those who feared the poorly informed and volatile public attitudes assumed that they would be a major and possibly dangerous constraint on policymaking. Almond (1956) warned an audience at the National War College that, "For persons responsible for the making of national security policy these *mood* impacts of the mass public have a highly irrational effect. Often the public opinion is apathetic when it should be concerned, and panicky when it should be calm." However, a classic study of the impact of public opinion by Bernard Cohen (1973) laid to rest some of those fears. His extensive interviews of policymakers in the State Department and elsewhere concluded that those who had attributed a potent role for public opinion, at least in the sense that it established boundaries outside of which only foolhardy policymakers would dare to venture, had simply not established their case. Moreover, Warren Miller and Donald Stokes (1963) demonstrated that, compared with domestic issues, public attitudes on foreign policy questions have far less impact on members of Congress. These studies appeared to mark the end of an era, more or less relegating what had been a thriving area of inquiry to a secondary status. If, at the end of the day, public opinion is largely irrelevant in the larger scheme of things, analysis of its content and structure might be intellectually stimulating but can hardly claim the mantle of urgent policy relevance.

The controversial Vietnam War was the driving force in a second phase of public opinion analysis, encompassing approximately the last three decades of the twentieth century. For many, that conflict raised serious doubts about the standard realist prescription for coping with a feckless public: strengthen executive prerogatives in the conduct of foreign affairs. Each of the three propositions cited above—that public opinion is volatile, lacks coherence, and, in the final analysis, is largely irrelevant to foreign policymaking—came under serious challenge. Longitudinal studies of attitudes on foreign affairs revealed that in fact American public opinion in the aggregate has remained remarkably stable. Benjamin Page and Robert Shapiro (1992) analyzed more than six thousand questions that had been repeated in surveys encompassing a half century. They found that when sharp shifts in public attitudes did take place, they could be explained as reasonable responses rather than random reactions to changing international developments. Although the fact that Americans are poorly informed about foreign affairs has never been seriously challenged, some analysts found that the general public is nevertheless able to use its limited storehouse of information to make reasonably coherent sense of international developments; Samuel Popkin (1991) coined the term "low information rationality" to describe this state of affairs.

The third of the propositions cited above, on the impact of public attitudes, is by far the least well-explored part of the public opinion–foreign policy equation. For that reason this book is an especially welcome contribution. There have been excellent correlational studies by Alan Monroe (1979) and Page and Shapiro (1983) demonstrating that changes in policy often follow shifts in aggregate public attitudes. As impressive as these studies are, they do not resolve beyond reasonable doubt all questions about the impact of public opinion on policy decisions; as every student of Statistics 1 learns, even a high correlation coefficient does not prove causality. V. O. Key's (1961) definition of public opinion as "those opinions held by private persons which governments find it prudent to heed" provides an especially appropriate perspective to any causal analysis of the opinion-policy link. It is thus necessary to go beyond evidence derived from surveys.

Recent years have seen a number of fine studies—for example, Jacobs and Shapiro (1995), Kull and Destler (1999), and Foyle (1999)—that employ interviews and archival research to explore in detail when, how, and with what consequences, if any, public opinion entered into the policymaking process. For more than a decade Richard Sobel (1989, 1993) has made important contributions to this stream of inquiry by skillfully assessing the impact of public opinion on U.S. interventions in Central America during the Cold War. This book, drawing on and significantly expanding his previous research to include two of the most important post–Cold War conflicts, is a major contribution to our understanding of the complex and varied ways that public opinion enters the policy process. In the four case studies that constitute the substantive core of his book, Sobel appropriately focuses on the perspectives of key policymakers in the five administrations that were involved in formulating American policy during the Vietnam War, aid to the "contras" in Nicaragua, the Gulf War, and the civil war in Bosnia. His analysis is greatly strengthened by extensive interviews with officials who were in an excellent position to observe how assessments of public opinion entered into policy discussions within the inner councils of the U.S. government. Four secretaries of defense and three secretaries of state are among the seventeen interviewees whose recollections and insights enrich these fascinating studies. These cases also add further support for the proposition that it is possible to undertake significant research on very recent events.

It is certainly possible that some of Sobel's conclusions about public opinion will require some modification and nuanced adjustments when documentary evidence in archives and presidential libraries becomes available, and when we have access to such sources as the relevant volumes in the *Foreign Relations of the United States* series. Until that time, which lies at least several decades in the future, this is likely to be the standard study of the impact of public opinion on American decisions on Vietnam, contra aid, the Gulf War, and Bosnia. For this contribution, students of American foreign policy decision-making will be grateful.

Ole R. Holsti
Durham, N.C.

Preface

Comprehending the role that public opinion plays in foreign policymaking has long provoked both fascination and frustration. Since before the Vietnam War, the many and varied advances in understanding the complex facets of the topic have still left it theoretically underdeveloped. Since the height of the Vietnam War, scholars, activists, and policymakers have all wondered what role the public actually plays in the policy process. This exploration advances answers to that compelling question.

The Impact of Public Opinion on U.S. Foreign Policy: Constraining the Colossus argues and demonstrates that public opinion constrained but did not set American foreign intervention policy during the generation from the Vietnam War to the Bosnia peacekeeping. The public's attitudes set the parameters within which policymakers operated. Within those limits, the policymakers had relative discretion about which policies to choose. This discretion was wider when conflicts were less salient or when public support was higher. But, in general, the American public constrained what the colossal power of the U.S. could do in foreign interventions.

The climate of opinion against intervention, particularly in the post-Vietnam era, affected decisions as much as specific attitudes about U.S. intervention policies or relative approval of presidential handling of crises. To the extent that the post-Vietnam syndrome was represented in the "Weinberger test," requiring public and congressional support for any U.S. interventions, the opinion climate shaped the impact of public attitudes on decision-making. Opinion shaped policy, too, on contra aid and Bosnia, when in both cases opposition precluded the possibilities of more aggressive policies such as direct U.S. intervention.

While Vietnam set the stage for examining the impact of public opinion, and, notably there, protest on foreign policy, contra aid was the most prominent and lengthy controversy during the post-Vietnam years. As was the case at the end of the Vietnam War, here, too, the public opposed administration policy. The policymakers may have tried to ignore, change, or direct opinion, but public sentiment was undeniably a consistent factor circumscribing their decision-making. The public's opposition to contra aid constrained the administration from pursuing more aggressive or more heavily financed policies. In this case, where congressional votes were a consistent factor, public opinion in congressional districts only loosely constrained representatives' voting, but the legislators were constantly concerned about the potential impact of changing sentiment. By monitoring opinion, the representatives tried to make sure that opinion did not directly constrain their legislative decisions.

The lessons of Vietnam, reiterated in the Powell Doctrine, raised issues of public support for swift, intense, and successful intervention during the Gulf War. But they also warned of the potential constraint that growing public opposition might represent for a protracted conflict. Bosnia as the first major post–Cold War conflict engaging two administrations encountered a climate of opinion first opposing involvement but ultimately permitting limited multilateral engagement.

Public opinion appears to have become more important in foreign policy decision-making since Vietnam, but it has not necessarily had a stronger impact. This paradox has manifested itself in tighter "post-Vietnam" constraints after the Vietnam War and against contra funding, but looser confines during and after the Gulf War. As the post-Vietnam syndrome diminished, especially among some elites, the public became more open to intervention before the Gulf War and continuing into the Bosnia crisis.

Looking back at these cases has clarified these insights into opinion's policy role as developed over a significant period. Looking back, too, at the process of developing these insights has made clear that completing this book has relied on contributions from many individuals and organizations. Besides the insights of scholars like V. O. Key and Ole Holsti, whose works have benefited a generation of scholars, I have learned much from the opportunities to interview several high-level decision-makers themselves, including former Secretaries of State Dean Rusk and George Shultz; former Secretaries of Defense Robert McNamara, Clark Clifford, Melvin Laird, Frank Carlucci, and Richard Cheney; and senators and representatives. Among colleagues and institutions, I would like to acknowledge the assistance of Henry Bienen, Richard Ullman, Michael Doyle, and John Waterbury at the Center for International Studies, Princeton University; Everett Ladd, Don Ferree, and the Roper Center for Public Opinion Research at the University of Connecticut; Marvin Kalb, Pippa Norris, and the Joan Shorenstein Center, Jerry Mechling and the Strategic Computing Program and Roger Porter at the Kennedy School of Government, Robert Putnam and the (Weatherhead) Center for International Affairs, and Graham Allison, Steven Miller, Stephen Walt, and the (Belfer) Center for Science and International Affairs, Harvard University; Badi Foster and the Lincoln Filene Center at Tufts; and Gioia Stevens, Linda Jarkesy, Ben Clark, Scott Burns, Sally James, Susan Monahan, and Lisa Grzan at Oxford University Press. I particularly appreciate the comments of Ole Holsti of Duke University, whose fine foreword opens this book, and of Steve Bloomfield of Harvard on the final manuscript. Thanks also to Pippa Norris at the Kennedy School for her Shakepearean suggestion to choose a subtitle like constraining the colossus to capture a theme of public limitation on American power in the world. That the counsel of Don Stokes, Everett Ladd, and Betty Debs Sobel was not available through the publication of this book is a source of sadness. Dick Neustadt, Sid Verba, and Walter Sobel's stepping in to provide sage advice is a source of appreciation.

In addition, I have been ably assisted by a talented group of research assistants, interns, and friends, particularly from Princeton, Harvard, and Tufts, including Brian Abrams, Sylvie Agudelo, Jeff Ballinger, Michael Bocian, Keith Bradford, Jamal Brathwaite, Jeff Brown, David Callahan, Victoria Canavor, Julie Cho, Jeff Collins, Leanne Doherty, Colin Dueck, Dan Epstein, Melissa Gallagher, John Collins, Erik Gray, Neal Greenfield, Jesse Hawkes, Brad Hevenor, Carolyn Hunt, Elizabeth Huyck, Ron Krebs, Kathryn Lee, Tony Lucero, Roxie Mack, Josh Marshall, Gillian Moore, Song Yee Paik, Eric Paras, Stefanic Rosen, Brooke Rudolf, Dahlia Scheindlen, Sharon Schwartz, Janet Shlaes, Mihaela Smith, and Elizabeth Wahl.

Parts of this analysis were presented in a graduate proseminar at Harvard University, some of whose class members made particular contributions by sharing their research, especially Jenny Kline-Mitchell, Liz Lambert, Kathryn Lee, Gillian Moore, and Mihaela Smith. The Vietnam case contributed to a junior research seminar on social movements, the highlight of which was John Kenneth Galbraith's provocative visit arranged by Sylvia Baldwin.

I would also like to express my appreciation for the opportunity to present earlier versions of Chapter 2 as a series of seminars and lectures at the Olin Institute for Strategic Studies and the Foreign Policy Seminar at the Weatherhead Center for International Affairs at Harvard, the Program in International Policy and Economic Studies at the University of Chicago, the Center of International Studies at Princeton, and the Department of Political Science at Tufts University. My insights into the various cases have been sharpened by the opportunity to draw from and extend beyond, especially through interviews with decision makers, the preliminary analysis of the Nicaragua case in my earlier book on the contra funding controversy. Some of these scholarly insights were reinforced during the opportunity to work as a consultant to the Chicago Council on Foreign Relations on their study of American Public Opinion and U.S. Foreign Policy in 1999. I hope these thanks recognize those and more private contributions in their appropriate proportions. The rest of the responsibility remains mine.

I

INTRODUCTION

CHAPTER 1

Public Opinion in American Foreign Policy

A fundamental premise in our democracy is that government policy reflects the will of the people. In an ideal sense, what the government does should derive from citizen opinion. In actuality, what the government does derives only imperfectly from citizen preferences. Yet the public's beliefs and attitudes do guide and constrain public policy, in foreign as well as domestic affairs.

The Impact of Public Opinion on U.S. Foreign Policy Since Vietnam examines the role that public attitudes have played over the last generation in the making of U.S. foreign policy, particularly decisions about interventions. The study seeks to explain that role in the policy process both on a theoretical level drawn from central cases and from the perspective of actual decision-making. In pursuing this goal, the book focuses on four of the most prominent foreign interventions of the last generation: the Vietnam War, the Nicaraguan contra funding controversy, the Gulf War, and the Bosnia crisis. These cases demonstrate how public opinion affected policy and thereby provide the basis for building an overall theory of public opinion and foreign policymaking.

This book also explores for our democracy the actual role of public opinion in foreign intervention policy. The normative is implicitly part of the empirical analysis of the relationship between public opinion and foreign affairs, because policymakers may represent trustees more than delegates in decision-making in foreign affairs. In this context, by suggesting that public opinion constrains policy, the major empirical theories regarding the influence of public opinion on policy (e.g., Almond, 1950; Cohen, 1973; Key, 1961; Page and Shapiro, 1992; Rosenau, 1961) inherently contain a normative element. In particular, V. O. Key's "system of dikes" theory, that public opinion sets limits on policymakers' discretion, illuminates the democratic process of the citizens directing their leaders.

In developing general insights about the impact of opinion on foreign policy, the study discusses intervention as a particularly significant and forceful type of foreign policy activity. It explores the impact of national public opinion on administration policymakers, and where appropriate, the influence of national and constituent opinion on congressional decision-makers. To set a larger historical context for the particular cases, the book also analyzes how current public opinion interacts with longer term trends or cycles in interventionist or isolationist sentiments (Foster, 1983; Klingberg, 1983; Stimson, 1991). Besides having unique meanings, particular levels of opinion occur within the confines of general climates of opinion toward intervention. In particular, the study explores how contemporary attitudes toward involvement in Vietnam, Nicaragua, the Persian Gulf, and Bosnia fit with long-term trends in attitudes toward intervention or nonintervention (Wittkopf, 1986, 1988). It identifies the dimensions of interventionist sentiments, the expression of attitudes during crises, and how the post-Vietnam syndrome constrained subsequent policy.

INTRODUCTION TO THE CASES

In focusing on the four central interventions in recent American history, the book explores the similarities and differences in the relationship of public opinion to foreign policy. It draws insights from the words of decision-makers in public statements, meeting records, memoirs, and where possible, interviews with the principal actors. The concentration is on the three top constitutionally mandated foreign policy decision-makers: the president, the secretary of state, and the secretary of defense. The contra aid chapter explores other prominent decision-makers, particularly in the Congress. Each case identifies evidence of the decision-maker's awareness of public opinion and the extent to which opinion influenced his (no women had yet held these high posts) policymaking.

The investigation of each intervention consists of two parts. The first identifies the events, policies, and public attitudes at crucial points during the specific controversy. This includes patterns of support, opposition, and presidential approval at key points during each intervention. The second part identifies, whenever possible at particular benchmarks or turning points of the controversies, the decision-makers' awareness of and attentiveness to public opinion, and the influence of these attitudes on governmental action. While it is typically possible to identify the influence of public opinion on the three major decision-makers during each intervention, only when the historical record becomes open or interviewees contribute can the impact at each benchmark be evaluated fully.

The study develops the later cases in the context of the Vietnam War and subsequent U.S. interventions. A long conflict in which more than fifty thousand American soldiers and a million Vietnamese died, the Vietnam War was an intervention that provoked intense expressions of opinion. As this war was often considered the most important national problem of the time (Smith, 1985), it was the most salient issue of its era (Reiter, 1987; RePass, 1971). The Vietnam case shows the extent to which both opinion and protest influenced policy and policy influenced opinion. It focuses on significant benchmarks, including Lyndon Johnson's Gulf of Tonkin escalation in 1964, deescalation after the Tet offensive in early 1968 as well as Richard Nixon's "silent majority" and Vietnamization strategies in 1969, and invasion of Cambodia in 1970. The research draws, in particular, on the comments of Vietnam era policymakers in memoirs and personal interviews about how public opinion entered their decision-making. The case also examines protest as a type of intensely expressed public opinion and the possible influence of demonstrations on the policy process.

During the Nicaraguan conflict of the 1980s, U.S. military forces were not directly involved. The Nicaragua case focuses on opinion's influence on the decisions surrounding aid to the contra rebels, during a period when the "post-Vietnam" syndrome advocating "no more Vietnams" was strong. Opposition opinion placed significant constraints on U.S. policy. The analysis goes beyond previous exploration (Sobel, 1993) by employing the perspectives of highest-level decision-makers in both the administration and, because of its prominence across the crisis, the Congress.

The Gulf War of 1990–91 was the first major post-Vietnam foreign intervention involving the extensive deployment of U.S. troops after the end of the Cold War. Following Iraq's invasion of Kuwait in August 1990, the U.S.-led coalition assembled a force of a half million men and women in the area before initiating the war in early 1991. The rallying of strong initial public support of Desert Shield suggested the diminishing influence of the post-Vietnam syndrome. But decreasing and divided approval and increasing congressional skepticism as the buildup continued during a recession began to restrict the options of the Bush administration. The potential for a sharp decline in public support for Desert Storm if the fighting were prolonged and bloody also constrained the administration to a "100-hour war." Protest against the war grew quickly but had little effect on the administration and was poorly received by a public largely supportive of the U.S. role in the conflict.

Bosnia was the first major post–Cold War conflict in Europe, with eerie similarities to World War II (Ullman, 1996). U.S. involvement was reluctant and limited to nonintervention for three years of first the Bush and then the Clinton administration. Early on, the United States provided humanitarian aid and air patrols; later, in Clinton's first term, American forces took part in allied air strikes. Both administrations consistently refused to send ground troops to fight; instead they each offered to send peacekeepers once the war was settled. Within the context of a public generally approving allied actions, the United States eventually became involved in multilateral cooperation that brought the fighting to an end and led to the Dayton peace agreements in late 1995 (Sobel, 1996).

OVERVIEW OF THE ANALYSIS

The general argument of this book is that public opinion constrains, but does not set, American foreign intervention policy. In other words, the public's attitudes set the limits within which policymakers may operate. Within those parameters of a permissive consensus, decision-makers may operate with less or more political costs and relative discretion about which policies to choose (Key, 1961). That discretion is wider when conflicts are less salient and support is higher.

Moreover, public opinion becomes increasingly salient over time, as shown particularly by Vietnam and its long aftermath. This has manifested itself generally, but not always, in tighter constraints since Vietnam. The limit was particularly clear for Nicaragua and less so for the Gulf War. As the next cycle of interventionism waxed, the post-Vietnam syndrome waned, exerting less force, especially among some elites, during the Bosnia crisis. The cases here demonstrate the overall validity of the constraint theory by showing how it applies to each of the respective interventions across the last generation.

The book uses a simple but powerful methodology. It attempts to determine how public opinion affected the decision-making of the top foreign policy decision-makers in the respective administrations by showing whether they demonstrated awareness of and indicated an impact of public opinion on their decisions. It uses their own words, typically in public statements and memoirs, as prima facie evidence. If decision-makers refer to public opinion or polls, they show a sensitivity to public attitudes. If they discuss the need for public support or discuss the way their decisions are limited by public opinion, they admit an influence of public opinion. If they mention or intimate that they might have done more with higher support, they suggest constraint. In short, they indicate constraint by discussing alternative policies that might have been implemented with greater support or less opposition. Because many decisions-makers explicitly prefer to make decisions without factoring in public sentiment, the analysis of their comments about public opinion is by no means a simple formality. The multiple and consistent references to the constraining nature of public opinion in different sources and by various decision-makers during the crises suggest that opinion did influence each intervention. Although not flawless, this approach is parsimonious and revealing.

The Organization of the Book

This volume contains six major parts: an introduction to the role and theory of public opinion in foreign policymaking, including an examination of trends in interventionist sentiment over time; a Vietnam War case study, a Nicaragua case study, a Gulf War case study, and a Bosnia case study; and conclusions with theoretical and policy implications. Both the Vietnam and Bosnia cases involved two administrations, those of presidents Johnson and Nixon, and Bush and Clinton, respectively. While all of these cases involve some form of intervention, because the respective administrations resisted active involvement of U.S. troops, the Reagan Nicaragua and Bush Bosnia cases also represent noninterventions.

Following this introduction to the elements of the book, Chapter 2 develops the theory of public opinion and foreign policy. It provides an overview of existing theory and presents a synthesis pointing toward the constraint model. Chapter 3 puts contemporary public attitudes about intervention into a historical perspective of cycles of interventionist and noninterventionist sentiment. Interventionist attitudes peaked in the middle of the Vietnam War, subsided afterward, and reemerged in the late twentieth century. After Chapter 4 sets the historical background for Vietnam by discussing the events, policies, and public opinions of the era, Chapter 5 begins the exploration of the roles that public opinion and protest played in the development of U.S. policies of escalation and deescalation in Vietnam from the mid-1960s to the early 1970s. Chapter 5 focuses on the Johnson administration's policy at points during the Gulf of Tonkin escalation in 1964, and the Tet offensive in 1968. Chapter 6 explores for the Nixon administration the moratoriums in 1969 and the Cambodia invasion of 1970. Anticommunism, anti-interventionism, costs, and casualties drove opinion and policy in sometimes conflicting, sometimes overlapping directions. Focusing on the perspectives of decision-makers in memoirs and interviews about how opinion entered their decision-making, the Vietnam chapters also examine the role of protest as a type of intense public sentiment that influences public opinion and the policy process.

The Nicaraguan case in chapters 7 and 8 flows from the Vietnam study because it explores the first major post-Vietnam intervention—albeit indirect and in some ways a nonintervention—during the 1980s. Here constraint is indicated by discussion of alternative policies that might have been implemented with greater support or less opposition. Though anticommunism underlay potential public support for aiding the contra rebels, anti-interventionism and the post-Vietnam syndrome circumscribed what decision-makers could do regarding Nicaragua. As at the end of the Vietnam War, the public opposed intervention in Central America, both in Nicaragua and in El Salvador. Chapter 6 discusses the events, administration policies, public attitudes, and, because of their centrality in this case, congressional actions in their relationships to a changing opinion environment. Chapter 7 focuses on the public impact on administration and congressional decisions surrounding funding for the contras, particularly the resumption of aid to the contras in 1985, congressional votes on $100 million including military aid in mid-1986, and the blocking of additional military aid in 1987.

The Gulf War was the first large-scale direct U.S. intervention after Vietnam. Chapter 9 explores the history of the conflict, Bush administration policy against Iraq, and public attitudes about the conflict from late 1990 to early 1991. It reflects the decline of the post-Vietnam syndrome into a somewhat more interventionist political environment. Chapter 10 explores the relative impacts of public opinion and congressional sentiments on restricting the options of the Bush administration during both Desert Shield and Desert Storm. It explores how the potential decline in public support for a longer war affected policy.

The Bosnia crisis that emerged soon after Desert Storm subsided took a decidedly different direction. Chapter 11 explores the events, policies, and opinion environment during the administrations' involvements in Bosnia from 1992 to 1996. It discusses the initial humanitarian U.S. intervention there, the implications of a potentially higher military profile, and how public attitudes constrained the scope of American involvement, before ultimately providing enough leeway for multilateral action. Chapter 12 examines the impact of public opinion on the Bush administration and then Chapter 13 explores its influence on the Clinton administration policies. In this sense, the investigation explores a case of nonintervention followed by one of intervention.

The concluding Chapter 14 summarizes and reflects on the study's insights into the relationship between public opinion and foreign policymaking. In particular, it draws from comparisons across the cases about how public opinion actually entered the foreign policy decision-making process. In explicating the actual roles of public opinion in a democracy, it supports the constraint model. It identifies the extent to which the role of public opinion has grown or declined in foreign policymaking.

In raising questions for the future scholarship and policy, the study concludes that, typically, public opinion should constrain policy, but policymakers need not always be stymied by public attitudes. When America's fundamental goals are in force or in peril, policymakers may need to educate the public or to risk the public's opprobrium temporarily to pursue enlightened policies for the longer term. The history of the United States before the two world wars suggests that the costs of delaying entrance into the international stage at crucial times may be more devastating than the price of earlier action. In general, however, there should be a dialogue between policymakers and the public about the wisdom of intervention policies.

The significance of this study appears in several guises. First, in building beyond a review of the currently underdeveloped theory, it develops the thesis of the constraining role of public opinion on foreign policy. Second, rather than relying on anecdotal observations or historical summaries about the relative importance of opinion in foreign policymaking, this research bases its conclusions on careful evaluation of evidence about the relationship between opinion and policy at key benchmarks in a variety of pertinent cases. The conclusions in each of the cases are based on a parsimonious, mutually reinforcing method of evaluating evidence of awareness and impact that uses the words of the major decision-makers themselves. Third, the study not only demonstrates that public opinion influences policy but also shows when that influence occurs. This reveals that the major effect of public opinion manifests itself in constraint rather than policy setting.

Furthermore, in investigating how public opinion influences policy, it helps explain when leaders should attempt to bring the public to policy. The study demonstrates the generally increasing role of public opinion in foreign policy, for better or for worse. That public opinion is more important in policymaking is not the same as saying public opinion is always more constraining. Recognition of the level of public support may at times free the hands of policymakers. This exploration of the implications for policymakers and citizens in a democracy suggests how knowledge of the role of public opinion on policy might assist efforts to move the American foreign policy process in a more democratic and effective direction.

CONCLUSION: TOWARD A THEORY OF CONSTRAINT

By delving into theory, events, and public attitudes about Vietnam, Nicaragua, the Gulf War, and the war in Bosnia, this analysis provides valuable insights about public opinion's influences in our foreign relations. It demonstrates the ways in which public opinion has constrained the U.S. foreign policy decision-making process over the last generation. This insight provides an organizing theme for understanding the past interventions and for motivating future investigations of subsequent crises. For scholars, the attentive public, students, and other citizens, the historical material and policy insights here illuminate these complex processes.

As the new century opens soon after America's first post–Cold War interventions, this is an auspicious time to examine in detail a central issue of democratic governance and foreign affairs: how the public influences American foreign policy. In providing evidence on how public opinion constrains foreign policymaking, this book contributes not only to understanding how the nation affects international policy but also to evaluating how well democracy works in the realm of foreign affairs.

CHAPTER 2

The Theory of Public Opinion and Foreign Policy

INTRODUCTION

As a foundation for advancing the understanding of how public opinion influences foreign policy, this chapter summarizes current knowledge about that complex relationship between public attitudes and government action (Davis and Kline, 1988; Kegley and Wittkopf, 1991; Holsti, 1992, 1996; Sobel, 1993). By synthesizing existing insights and "pre-theory" (Key, 1961; Rosenau, 1961) as a basis for extending the knowledge, the chapter also pushes ahead the understanding and theory of opinion and policymaking. The normative prescription that public opinion should play a role in the foreign policy process sets the context for exploring its actual role.

More than a quarter century ago, James Rosenau's pioneering study reported that "we have little reliable knowledge about the role of public opinion in shaping foreign policy" (1961, p. 4). Despite progress since then in understanding the dimensions of attitudes on foreign policy (Chittick and Billingsly, 1989; Hinckley, 1992; Wittkopf, 1990), still today "research in this area remains underdeveloped and ambiguous" (1961, p. 5). In Rosenau's terms, the research is not much beyond the "pretheoretical" developments in the understanding of the flow of public opinion into foreign policymaking.

In short, there has been little progress either in developing the theory of the opinion–foreign policy connection or in explaining the dynamics of the actual impact of public opinion on policy. Theory building is based on the assessment of and advancement beyond the strengths, weaknesses, and interconnections of existing and ongoing literature. By building upon existing insights into how public sentiments set policy limits, this book moves beyond the pretheoretical stage of understanding the "flow of opinion" in foreign policymaking to developing a fuller model of the paths and linkages of actual influence.

Though Rosenau was one of the first scholars to focus on these issues (Rosenau, 1961), "his elaborate taxonomy of 'linkage politics' generated little cumulative research, except for work correlating domestic and international 'conflict behavior'" (Putnam, 1988, p. 430). "Domestic politics and international relations are often somehow entangled," as Putnam notes in a different context, "but our theories have not yet sorted out the puzzling tangle" (Putnam, 1988, p. 427). "Much of the existing literature on relations between domestic and international affairs consists either of ad hoc lists of . . . 'domestic influences' on foreign policy or of generic observations that national and international affairs are somehow 'linked' " (Putnam, 1988, p. 430). "A more adequate account of the domestic determinants of foreign policy and international relations must stress *politics*" beyond officials and institutional arrangements, including political parties, classes, interest groups and legislators, "and even public opinion and elections" (Putnam, 1988, p. 432).

The starting point for extending this analysis is V. O. Key's theory embodied in the metaphor that public opinion constitutes a system of dikes that channel the flow of public policy. Public opinion, in this model, does not set policy but instead is capable of setting the range or limits of policy. In other words, public opinion guides or constrains policymaking. The metaphor of a "system of dikes" that channel policy flow suggests that opinion has a guiding or limiting influence on policy. Support permits or facilitates, while opposition limits or deters, policymaker's discretion. The particular relationships of public opposition versus support constitute the individual "dikes."

Toward a Theory of Public Opinion in Foreign Policy

"Public opinion" implies a predominance—from plurality to supermajority—of sentiment among the entire population as revealed in polls. Yet the public is stratified, and differing publics express their views through various forums, including elections, group participation, party activities, direct communications with representatives, and opinion polls. Individuals who take more activist roles in the political process, who join forces in effective groups, and who command greater resources are typically more influential than the unorganized public (Dahl, 1984). Conflicting groups—interacting in a complex web of relationships—seek to mobilize support for desired outcomes at many decision points (Serafino and Storrs, 1993, p. 123; Truman, 1951).

Foreign policy involves the action of the national government in relations with other countries. Foreign intervention policy involves direct or indirect military or coercive economic involvement in another nation's affairs. Within the presidential administration, principal elected officials, cabinet secretaries, and other upper-level political appointees confirmed by the Senate are typically more responsive to public opinion than nonpolitically appointed career officials, particularly at the middle levels (cf. Cohen, 1973; but see Powlick, 1991).

While the analysis of foreign policymaking typically focuses on the national administration and major national decision-makers, Congress and congressional leaders are also crucial in determining foreign policy, particularly when foreign affairs and defense funding votes become contentious (Destler, Gelb, and Lake, 1984; Pastor, 1993). As the outcome of a central intermediary institution between the public and administration policy, congressional action constitutes both a measure of public opinion and a basis of public policy. Constituents' opinions, themselves sometimes shaped by congressional and presidential leadership, affect representatives' voting patterns, while congressional decisions constrain administration policymaking.

DEMOCRATIC THEORY OF PUBLIC OPINION ON POLICY

There are two major normative models of representation about how public opinion should influence policymakers. The trustee model suggests that representatives should use their best judgment of issues and then vote in the interest of their constituents, not necessarily as the constituents prefer (cf. Burke). The delegate model suggests, alternatively, that representatives vote, and should vote, in response to their constituents' wishes (see Bachrach, 1967; Dahl, 1971). Recent evidence suggests that members of the public feel they should have more input into foreign policymaking (Kull, 1999) and that policymakers misperceive public sentiment toward foreign affairs (Kull and Destler, 1999).

The public's preferences are generally expected to prevail in a democracy. But public opinion need not translate directly into public policy for the government to be democratic. What distinguishes democracy is not that every member of the public has equal influence in the formulation of policy, but that every member has potential access to power and that the political leadership is periodically subject to election (Serafino and Storrs, 1993, p. 124). Leaders' actions are legitimate because those leaders were chosen as the people's representatives in a fair election, not because they necessarily reflect the wishes of the public. The composition and action of representative institutions are more consequential than the general opinions of the populace. Nevertheless, public opinion sets limits on the actions of representatives because public officials want to be reelected (Serafino and Storrs, 1993, p. 124).

An alternate conception sees "delegates" as believing both in the "desirability of public opinion's input influencing policy choices and in the necessity of public support for a successful foreign policy" (Foyle, 1996, p. 145). Delegates act as agent for the public. "Executors" carry out tasks for another person without requiring the active support of him or her. For executors, public input into policy is desirable but not necessary for success. They should rely on their best judgment rather than on active support of the people. "Pragmatists" believe public input is not desirable but is necessary. A pragmatist should try to lead the public to gain their support. "Guardians" find public support neither desirable nor necessary. They pursue the national interest as experts even against the tide of public opinion, which can often be an impediment to policymaking.

Wilsonian liberals believe that public opinion places a popular restraint on "elite choices" (Foyle, 1999). Realist thinking, however, has characterized the role of public opinion for much of the post-World War II thinking. This model is closer to that of delegates. Realists believe that public opinion either restrains policymakers negatively, or else that the policymakers in general lead public opinion toward their chosen policy. Alternately in this model, public opinion may be completely ignored (Foyle, 1996, p. 142).

Elites may respond to public opinion depending upon the relationship between their normative and practical beliefs about the desirability and necessity of public opinion (Foyle, 1996, 1999). This is akin to Key's definition of public opinion as "those opinions held by private persons which governments find prudent to heed" (Key, 1961, p. 14). Decision-makers see and react to public opinion depending on their view of the proper relationship between attitudes and policy decisions. Here the

constraint is as much through the anticipation of later opinion, and electoral outcomes, as of the effect of current opinion on policy. The process works more like the
liberal theory of desirable and necessary public constraint than the realist theory of
opinion as undesirable and unnecessary.

PUBLIC OPINION AND FOREIGN POLICY:
THEORETICAL CONSIDERATIONS

The pioneering conventional wisdom about the role of public opinion in the foreign
policy process maintained that the American public was incapable of holding consistent and stable foreign policy attitudes (Almond, 1950; Rosenau, 1961; cf. Lippmann,
1922). "Foreign policy attitudes among most Americans lack intellectual structure and
factual content" (Almond, 1950, pp. 53, 84, 230–32; cf. Converse, 1964). The public's
"characteristic response to questions of foreign policy is one of indifference"; it reacts
to foreign events with "formless and plastic moods" that frequently change. The
"moodishness" of the American people about foreign policy issues grew out of indifference to foreign policy except during crises. Though some foreign policy crises may
transform indifference to vague apprehension, fatalism, or anger, the mood is still su-
perficial and fluctuating (Wittkopf and McCormick, 1990, 1993, p. 75).
    In foreign policy, the public is divided into three groups: the "mass public" is "nei-
ther interested nor informed" and therefore seldom has any influence over foreign
policy; the "attentive public" is informed but has few means of exerting influence;
and the "elite" is both informed and influential (Almond, 1950, p. 138). Among the
elite are opinion leaders, including media commentators and reporters, leaders of lobbying organizations, and members of Congress, who understand the issue and help
move attitudes (and legislative action) toward specific policies (Lazarsfield, Berelson, and Gaudet, 1968, Page and Shapiro, 1983). The somewhat less involved "attentive public" understands and pays some attention to particular issues and might express an opinion to friends, join a group, or write a letter to their congressperson
(Alder, 1984; Almond, 1950; Devine, 1970; Key, 1961; Rosenau, 1961; LeoGrande,
1993, p. 169; Weissberg, 1976). The opinions of the elite (Levering, 1978; Wittkopf,
1987; Wittkopf and Maggiotto, 1983), of opinion leaders (Rosenau, 1961), of the attentive public (Devine, 1970), of coalitions of minorities (Mueller, 1973), of constituents (Miller and Stokes, 1963), and of pressure groups (Arnson and Brenner,
1993; Truman, 1951) affect politics with different weights.
    "The mass public is uninformed about either the specific foreign policy issues or
foreign affairs in general. . . . Its members pay little, if any, attention to day-to-day
developments in world politics" and "lack structured opinions. . . . Thus their response to foreign policy matters is less one of intellect and more one of emotion"
(Rosenau, 1961, p. 35). The public's "mass immunity" to foreign policy information
occurs because such information has "no immediate utility or meaning" for them (Almond, 1950; LeoGrande, 1993, p. 168). As the American people are uninterested in
and ill-informed about foreign policy, they tend to hold unstable foreign policy attitudes susceptible to elite manipulation (Wittkopf and McCormick, 1993, p. 75).
    The generally uninformed public has been considered a potentially dangerous

source of instability in the foreign policymaking process (LeoGrande, 1993, p. 168; Rosenau, 1961, p. 36). The inattentive mass public is capable of occasional outbursts if sufficiently prodded (Almond, 1960; Rosenau, 1961; Wittkopf and McCormick, 1990). "On the rare occasions when it does awaken from its slumber, the mass public . . . is impulsive, unstable, unreasoning, unpredictable, capable of suddenly shifting direction or of going in several contradictory directions at the same time" (Rosenau, 1961, p. 36). The mass public therefore offers decision-makers no rational guide to policy. Instead, it pushes them "toward emotional responses with no necessary connection to the national interest" (LeoGrande, 1993, pp. 168–69).

Lacking knowledge, the general public could exert little influence over policy formulation. The public was generally "permissive" and would "follow the lead of policy elites if they demonstrate unity and resolve." But the "crude and primarily passive instrument" of public control was prone to mood swings that might suddenly catapult a previously obscure issue to the center of public attention" and worry policymakers (LeoGrande, 1993, p. 168). Since just a small fraction of the public belonged to a foreign policy elite that had the potential to exert influence (Almond, 1950, p. 60), direct public control over foreign policy was virtually impossible. Only a minority of the public has basic information or interest in foreign policy issues: about 25 percent of the public was consistently knowledgeable about foreign affairs; another 45 percent were aware of issues, but uninformed; and 30 percent were entirely unaware of them (Almond, 1950, pp. 82, 92). The public typically considers "the most important issue" facing the United States as one involving domestic matters. Even during international crises, no more than 25 to 30 percent of the public typically considered foreign policy issues to be the most important (LeoGrande, 1993, p. 168).

The relative sizes of the publics vary according to the foundations of the estimates. On the basis of the size of the circulation of prestige newspapers, the attentive public constitutes only about 10 percent of the population; "opinion-makers," roughly equivalent to Almond's "elite," are 1 to 2 percent (Rosenau, 1961, pp. 35, 71–72); and the rest of the population makes up the mass public. On the basis of tests of people's level of information, only about 10 percent of the public is consistently attentive, 25 percent is completely inattentive, and the rest fall somewhere in between (Brewer, 1986, pp. 59–60). On the basis of active participation in the foreign policy process—people who write their congressperson, participate in demonstrations, write letters to the editor—the elite is about 1 percent of the public. The attentive public may be in the 15 to 20 percent range (Crabb and Holt, 1980, pp. 210–12; Kegley and Wittkopf, 1979, p. 305; LeoGrande, 1993, p. 170).

The "mood theory" had been consistently challenged for many years. Drawing on poll data from the late 1940s to the early 1960s, William Caspary first demonstrated that the American people possess a "*strong* and *stable* 'permissive mood' toward international involvement" (1970, p. 546). "Such a mood provides a blank check for foreign policy adventures, not just a responsible support for international organization, genuine foreign assistance, and basic defense measures." In short, the "mood" of the American people is not nearly as unstable and quixotic as Almond implied, although historically it has usually served as an ineffective check on policymakers (Wittkopf and McCormick, 1993, p. 76).

Mass foreign policy beliefs, in fact, have an underlying structure and coherence

(Hurwitz and Peffley, 1987). Specific policy views derive from more general policy orientations, which in turn are related to value preferences. Foreign policy opinions can be structured and maintained even in the face of little information. Individuals utilize "heuristics," or information shortcuts, to make political judgments and to relate preferences toward specific foreign policy issues to general attitudes (Hurwitz and Peffley, 1987). Thus, paradoxically, ordinary citizens hold coherent attitude structures *because* they lack detailed knowledge about foreign policy: "individuals organize information because such organization helps to simplify the world. Thus, lack of information does not *impede* structure and consistency; on the contrary, it *motivates* the development and employment of structure." Individuals try to "cope with an extraordinarily confusing world (with limited resources to pay information costs) by structuring views about specific foreign policies according to their more general and abstract beliefs" (Hurwitz and Peffley, 1987, p. 1114). The elite on the other hand, because they have clearer ideologies, rely less on specific information (Bennett, 1989).

CLIMATES OF OPINION

There are three types of opinion environments that potentially influence policy. The first is the overall "climate of opinion" or general sense of the public mood. The second is presidential popularity or approval, especially in the handling of foreign affairs. The third is specific attitudes toward government policy options.

The climate of opinion refers to what decision-makers perceive as "latent public attitudes" or "manifest but unstructured majorities" (Rosenau, 1961, p. 23). The climate constitutes the general foreign policy decision-making environment that creates "in the policy maker an impression of a public attitude or attitudes," or "by becoming part of the environment and cultural milieu" helps "to shape his own thinking," and then "may consciously affect his official behavior" (Cohen, 1957, p. 29; Wittkopf and McCormick, 1993, p. 74). Policymakers, in fact, often try to create a climate of opinion "more favorable to their contemplated policy, hoping in this way to affect the perceptions of other decision-makers who are either opposed to the projected proposal or not yet persuaded of its wisdom" (Rosenau, 1961, p. 24). Thus the climate of opinion may permeate the decision process through various channels: top-down from decision-makers to opinion-makers, bottom-up from opinion-makers to decision-makers, and intermediate as well (Rosenau, 1961, pp. 19–26). Though the exact mechanism for internalization of the climate of opinion transmission into the policy process remains unclear (Cohen, 1973), the importance of the climate suggests why political leaders, the mass media, and interest groups try to shape public attitudes (Wittkopf and McCormick, 1993, p. 74).

Key's conception of public opinion as a system of dikes that constrain policy flow is a more specific framework of the climate of opinion. The "context" of public opinion can "condition" governmental action (Key, 1961). "That context is not a rigid matrix that fixes a precise form for government action. Nor is it unchangeable." It consists of irregularly distributed opinions that vary in intensity and "convertibility into votes." But that context, as perceived by policymakers, conditions many of their acts that involve "opinion-related decision." "The opinion context may affect the sub-stance of action, the form of action, or the manner of action" (Key, 1961, p. 423).

Presidential Performance and Popular Policy Support

Public approval of the president and his policies, especially among both presidential and congressional constituents, is the second central factor in influencing both ad-ministration and legislative policymakers. Presidential popularity as political capital undergirds congressional support (Edwards, 1981; Neustadt, 1960; Wittkopf, 1988). Such approval, in particular, contributes to a favorable or unfavorable climate of opin-ion (Cohen, 1957; Rosenau, 1961; Wittkopf, 1988)[1] that generally constrains policy. Presidents care about their popularity because it affects their ability to work their will with others involved in the policy process (Wittkopf and McCormick, 1993, p. 92). National policymakers have to think of their "standing with the public outside of Washington." Because policymakers think about it, public standing is a source of in-fluence for them (Kernell, 1986; Neustadt 1980, p. 64). In short, the more popular a president is, the more likely he is to accomplish his political agenda. This is the essence of "the politics of prestige" (Simon and Ostrom, 1988; Wittkopf and Mc-Cormick, 1993, p. 92).

"A president's popularity serves as a transmission belt linking the prevailing cli-mate of opinion to the larger political process by affecting the ability of the president to accomplish his political agenda" (Wittkopf and McCormick, 1993, p. 93). Thus the relationship between opinion and policy is indirect and the opinion-policy nexus is reciprocal; popular presidents are more likely to win support for specific policies than are unpopular presidents. Presidential influence in Congress is stronger when the president's standing in the polls is higher (Bond and Fleisher, 1980; Edwards, 1976; Fleisher and Bond, 1983; Neustadt, 1960; Rivers and Rose, 1985).

Concern for maintaining presidential approval influences administration interven-tion policy (Ostrom and Job, 1986). Popular presidents tend to engage in the use of force short of war because higher popularity levels "free" them from the domestic constraints that would otherwise inhibit resort to force (Ostrom and Job, 1986). His-torically, the American public has rewarded a confrontational foreign and military policy by showing that threats, the actual use of military force, and talking tough, for instance, to the Soviets, won presidents popular approval, while cooperating with the

---

[1]George C. Edwards (1990) usefully summarizes and critiques much of the research on the cor-relates and consequences of presidential popularity. John E. Mueller (1970, 1973) is especially noteworthy in that he seeks explicitly to incorporate foreign policy variables in models of pres-idential performance. See also Hibbs (1982a, 1982b), Hurwitz and Peffley (1987), Kernell (1978), Lanoue (1989), Marra, Ostrom, and Simon (1990), and Ostrom and Simon (1985), Os-trom, Job, Marra, and Simon (1989). Fluctuations in presidential popularity in turn relate to congressional support of presidents' domestic and foreign policies (Bond, Fleisher, and Northrup, 1988; Edwards, 1981, 1985, 1989; but cf. Bond and Fleisher, 1990) and to the out-come of congressional and presidential elections (Abramowitz, 1985; Kernell, 1977; Lewis-Beck and Rice, 1982).

Soviets typically cost them (Ostrom and Simon, 1985). Specific foreign policy events enhance approval or disapproval (Brody, 1991; Marra, Ostrom and Simon, 1990; Ostrom and Simon, 1985). Presidents are more likely to use force during election years (Russett, 1990). However, the public's evaluation of presidential performance is affected by the economy as well as by dramatic foreign and domestic events.

The third type of opinion environment involves specific issue positions. Opinions about intervention are a multidimensional phenomenon, and opinions are divided along various issue dimensions. On the one hand, opinion about foreign policy has both an ideological (abstract) and operational (concrete) spectrum (Free and Cantril, 1968). The American public tends to be ideologically interventionist and operationally anti-interventionist (but see Rosenau, 1990). In principle, people support an aggressive posture, but in practice they are more reluctant to get involved. Once involved, however, the public tends initially to "rally" around the president (Mueller, 1973) and to support interventions in response to presidential leadership as long as the involvement is brief or successful (Brody, 1991).

Consistency or inconsistency appears in the relationship between policy and three types of attitudes: (1) general support or the climate of opinion (e.g., considering sending U.S. troops not a mistake); (2) presidential popularity (e.g., approval of the president's handling of the situation in Vietnam); and (3) policy attitudes (for escalation, maintained level of fighting, or withdrawal). There is considerable scholarship on the movement of public opinion, for instance, during the Vietnam War: some on policymakers' influence on public opinion, but little specifically linking public opinion to policymaking.[2] A review of the history and polls of the Vietnam War indicates that in general public opinion and Vietnam policy were consistent over the various phases of the war (Lunch and Sperlich, 1979; Mueller, 1973).

THE DOMESTIC CLIMATE OF FOREIGN POLICY OPINION AFTER VIETNAM

Until Vietnam, there was a broad-based U.S. consensus about the nation's appropriate role in the world (Chace, 1978; Wittkopf, 1990; Wittkopf and McCormick, 1990). Since then, foreign policy has been the subject of often bitter partisan and ideological dispute (Destler, Gelb, and Lake, 1984). The belief that politics stops at the water's edge has been more myth than reality (McCormick and Wittkopf, 1990), but the extent to which foreign policy has became the object of partisan and ideological disagreement since the 1960s has evoked commentary among scholars, journalists, and policymakers (Wittkopf and McCormick, 1993, p. 77).

Among developments during the 1970s that contributed to the breakdown of the Cold War foreign policy, Vietnam was the primary catalyst, reinforced by détente with the Soviet Union. Along with Watergate, the war challenged the assumptions on

---

[2]Measure of support for war is based on a Gallup poll question, "In view of the developments since we entered the fighting, do you think the U.S. made a mistake sending troops to fight in Vietnam?" (Mueller, 1973, p. 55). The answer "Not a mistake" is interpreted to mean support. See Chapter 3 here for figures.

which the consensus had been built, including the beliefs that American military power alone could achieve American foreign policy objectives; that containment underlay American foreign policy; that American political institutions worked well; and that a preeminent presidency in foreign policy was necessary to cope with the hostile world (Wittkopf and McCormick, 1993).

Over the years of the war, principal decision-makers were aware of public opinion and protest, generally felt that protest should not influence policy, and yet indicated that opinion and protest did influence policy (Johnson, 1971; Nixon, 1978). Early on, Lyndon Johnson relied on the polls showing majority support for his Vietnam approach, but when opinion turned against the war, he eventually modified his policy. Nixon, too, faced a public unhappy with the war. Yet, what he characterized as the "silent majority" undergirded Nixon administration efforts to withdraw at an "honorable" pace.

Presidential approval, both in terms of overall popularity and specific approval of handling a foreign policy problem, affected the relationship between general public opinion and Vietnam policy (Edwards, 1981; Kernell, 1978; Ostrom and Simon, 1975; Wittkopf, 1988). The exploration of the implications for policymakers and citizens in a democracy suggests how knowledge of the role of public opinion on policy might assist efforts to move the American foreign policy process in a more democratic direction. The "attentive public," those knowledgeable about the specifics of policy, may have more strongly influenced Vietnam direction (cf. Devine, 1970). The impact of opinion on policy was stronger than of policy on opinion (Kernell, 1978; Ostrom and Simon, 1985; Page and Shapiro, 1983). Though domestic American opinion was the most important measure of public sentiment, foreign or international opinion played a part.

Early Vietnam-era protest affected military policy, but the impact diminished later (Burstein and Freudenberg, 1978), particularly on Senate votes (Berkowitz, 1973). As vocal and visible expressions of public opinion, protests influenced policy away from more aggressive postures in Vietnam, in particular, by preventing a major escalation against North Vietnam in 1969 (Kissinger, 1979; Nixon, 1978). But protest did not necessarily shorten the war because it may have had the counterproductive effect of sustaining "silent" support for the war and thus indirectly assisting Nixon's policy (Berkowitz, 1973; Mueller, 1973, p. 164).

The Cold War foreign policy consensus dissipated as Americans became divided not only over the question of *whether* the United States should be involved in world affairs—a question that traditionally had divided them along internationalist-isolationist lines—but also *how* it ought to be involved. This transformation then raised questions about the ends of American foreign policy as well as its means (Wittkopf and McCormick, 1993, p. 78).

Internationalist or interventionist sentiment has "two faces," or a cooperative and a militant dimension (Holsti and Rosenau, 1986; Hinckley, 1988b, 1992; Wittkopf, 1990). The American public has been divided among four groups created by the intersection of the two intervention dimensions (whether and how). The elite tends to support involvement of a more cooperative kind, while the general public is equally divided between cooperative and reluctant. Three-quarters of both elite and public have been at least partially internationalist (Wittkopf, 1990, pp. 26, 116).

As differences about ends and means emerged, support for internationalism in U.S. world affairs began to show its different faces. One face is *cooperative internationalism;* the other is *militant internationalism* (Wittkopf, 1990). Attitudes toward communism, the use of American troops abroad, and relations with the Soviet Union distinguished proponents and opponents of these alternative forms of internationalism. They created four distinct foreign policy belief systems: internationalists, isolationists, accommodationists, and hard-liners. Consistent with traditional views of Americans' attitudes toward the role of the United States in world affairs, *internationalists* are those who support active American involvement in international affairs, favoring a combination of conciliatory and conflict strategies reminiscent of the pre-Vietnam internationalist foreign policy paradigm. *Isolationists,* on the other hand, oppose both types of international involvement. Selective internationalists emerged in the 1970s. *Accommodationists* embrace the tenets of cooperative internationalism but reject the elements implicit in militant internationalism, while *hard-liners* manifest the opposite beliefs (Wittkopf and McCormick, 1993, p. 79). The post-Vietnam cleavages in foreign policy belief systems (Holsti and Rosenau, 1984) also extend to the mass public (Wittkopf and Maggiotto, 1983; Wittkopf and McCormick, 1993).[3]

The preferences of accommodationists and hard-liners have closely correlated with liberal and conservative political ideologies and with the lessons drawn from the Vietnam experience (Holsti and Rosenau, 1984; Wittkopf, 1990). As a result, the post-Vietnam climate of opinion has evoked divergent domestic responses to issues related to the involvement of the United States in the affairs of others and especially toward the use of troops abroad (Wittkopf and McCormick, 1993, p. 79). The public prudently supports interventions against outside aggression (Jentleson, 1995) but not in internal civil conflicts except when there are overriding humanitarian components (Jentleson and Britton, 1998).

PATTERNS OF CYCLES

Rather than occurring as independent phenomena, climates of opinion and specific levels of support or opposition exist in the context of general patterns of attitudes toward intervention (cf. Wittkopf, 1987). On a time dimension, current attitudes about foreign policy intervention interact with long-term trends in attitudes toward inter-

---

[3]The cooperative (CI) and militant internationalism (MI) constructs were derived from the quadrennial studies of mass foreign policy attitudes sponsored by the Chicago Council on Foreign Relations (CCFR) beginning in late 1974. See Rielly (1975–99) for discussions of the CCFR surveys and Maggiotto and Wittkopf (1981), Wittkopf (1981, 1986, 1987, 1990), and Wittkopf and Maggioto (1983) for discussions of the CI/MI constructs as they evolved through various of these surveys. Additional evidence for cooperation and militant internationalism as dominant modes of thinking about foreign policy can be found in Hinckley (1988b) and Holsti and Rosenau (1986, 1990).

In the first twenty-nine months of his administration, Reagan met more than twenty-five times with his long-time pollster, Richard Wirthlin (Beal and Hinckley, 1984, pp. 72, 74), who delivered memoranda on over forty public opinion studies to key aides and discussed public opinion polls in more than half of the senior meetings in the White House.

vention or nonintervention (Foster, 1983; Klingberg, 1983). (Chapter 3 discusses the meaning of these cycles in interventionist opinion in relationship to the four major cases of this book.)

Following World War II, as Chapter 3 discusses, isolationism gave way to internationalism as undergirding American foreign policy. The United States sought cooperation with other nations but resorted to intervention, including force, if necessary. As isolationism gradually declined, a new consensus emerged about the U.S. world role reflected in globalism, anticommunism, containment, military might, and interventionism (Kegley and Wittkopf, 1991). The foreign policy consensus reduced differences at home as the nation pursued its mission abroad. Pre-Tet Vietnam was the high point of postwar internationalism. The post-Vietnam era, however, became a less interventionist period (Wittkopf and McCormick, 1993, p. 74). The "post-Vietnam syndrome" since the early 1970s represents the most recent introspective climate of opinion that discouraged interventionist behavior and the use of military forces abroad (see Chapter 3). The 1990s since the Gulf War represent the start of a new era of interventionism.

PRESIDENTIAL LEADERSHIP AND PUBLIC OPINION

As Theodore Roosevelt said, the presidency is a "bully pulpit" for influencing opinion. Every administration takes seriously the job of maintaining or developing public support for its programs. In some cases, the president senses that he has adequate support and that his election gives him a mandate to carry out certain policies (Kelley, 1983). In other cases, where the president lacks public support for his policies, he seeks to exercise presidential leadership to swing opinion to his side (Bass, Bonafede, and Euchner, 1990; Edwards, 1983; Neustadt, 1990; Graber, 1982; Kellerman, 1984; Lowi, 1985; Nelson, 1990; Neustadt, 1990; Serafino and Storrs, 1993, p. 125; Tatalovich and Daynes, 1984).

EXECUTIVE BRANCH INFLUENCES THROUGH AND ON THE MEDIA AND GROUPS

The administration must deal with the public differentiated on the basis of level of activity and attention. The general public has relatively few direct interests, though constituents with foreign policy concerns may influence their representatives. Interest group activity is often considered the democratic expression of public opinion (Truman, 1951; Rosenstone and Hansen, 1993). Pressure groups focus on lobbying specific foreign policy issues. The active involvement of interest groups is thought to remedy the lack of classical democratic control over foreign policy and compensates for mass inattention in serving as the representative of mass opinion (Almond, 1950, pp. 126, 142, 231; LeoGrande, 1993, p. 168). In fact, interest groups often convey elite views (Levering, 1978). Protest is also an expression of public opinion of intense minorities or majorities.

Executive branch attempts to influence public opinion fall into two patterns: first, there are indirect efforts aimed at the media, interest groups, and other opinion leaders; and second, there are more direct efforts aimed at the general public. Despite the president's great advantages in influencing opinion, he faces difficulties, too (Bass, Bonafede, and Euchner, 1990; Margolis and Mauser, 1989; Page and Shapiro, 1984). Presidents try to influence the media, interest, and ethnic groups with the expectation that these groups will then influence the general public (Bonafede, in Bass et al., 1990). Efforts to influence the media are important because TV news commentary from anchor persons, reporters, or commentators has dramatic impact on public opinion; editorials of the elite press have a similar impact (Page, Shapiro, and Dempsey, 1987). Newspaper and television reporters tend to be more politically liberal than the public or other elites (Lichter, Rothman, and Lichter, 1986), and the media tend to reinforce upper-class and upper-middle-class social values and limit the agenda for action (Margolis and Mauser, 1989).

Administration efforts to influence interest groups and ethnic organizations have unclear results. In some cases, it is "preaching to the choir" of groups already in the persuader's camp, though the effort solidifies base support. The net effect of interest groups on public opinion seems in general to be slightly negative (Serafino and Storrs, 1993, p. 126), but "the finding that interest groups tend to have a negative effect on public opinion holds only on the average, and only for direct effects" (Page and Shapiro, 1989, p. 306). In fact, "the public tends to be uninfluenced—or negatively influenced—only by the statements of groups whose interests are perceived to be selfish or narrow or antisocial, while it responds favorably to groups and individuals thought to be concerned with broadly defined public interests" (Page and Shapiro, 1989, p. 306). Environmental groups and general "public interest" groups like Common Cause appear to have had positive effects on public opinion. "Negative effects seem to have come from protestors and demonstrators, corporations and business associations, and some relatively broad groups representing blacks, women, the poor, and organized labor" (Page and Shapiro, 1989, pp. 306–7).

PRESIDENTIAL ADMINISTRATIONS INFLUENCE THE PUBLIC

Presidents appeal directly to the public, particularly by means of nationwide broadcasts, in a strategy of "going public" (Kernell, 1986). The president seeks public support of his policies in hope that the citizens will urge elected representatives to vote for the president's policies. Recent presidents have gone public more often and paid greater attention to public opinion polls than their predecessors (Kernell, 1986; Serafino and Storrs, 1993, p. 126).

A "going public" strategy will be effective only if the president communicates his preferences, if citizens respond favorably with a change of opinion, if the citizens communicate their new views to members of Congress, and if politicians change their positions because of these communications (Kernell, 1986, pp. 150–53). Consequently, even a popular president may have difficulty persuading the public and extracting votes for his policies (cf. Wahlke, 1989; Euchner, in Bass et al., 1990; Serafino and Storrs, 1993, p. 127).

The president may encounter great difficulties in persuading a relatively uninformed public. Even though it might seem that the president could be most successful in persuading people who are least educated, informed, interested, or concerned about the issue, as well as those who lack consistent belief structures, these individuals are least likely to expose themselves to presidential persuasion (Hurwitz, 1989, p. 228). The public's apparent lack of information suggests that foreign policy issues are not salient to most voters, and that the lack of basic information makes exerting influence difficult. But Americans' typical lack of interest in and knowledge about foreign policy is largely irrelevant to whether the American people are able, in the aggregate, to hold *politically relevant foreign policy beliefs* (Wittkopf and McCormick, 1993, p. 76). One need not be informed to have an opinion or to influence decision-makers, however (LeoGrande, 1993, p. 169). Whether knowledgeable or not, the public influenced both Eisenhower and his chief officers in the 1950s at the policy options stages, depending on decision context (Foyle, 1999).

A popular president who makes repeated speeches may achieve a 5 to 10 percentage point change in popular opinion over several months (Page and Shapiro, 1989, p. 306); 40 percent of respondents would change their opinion on use of troops in Central America merely by being told that the president held a contrary opinion (Hurwitz, 1989, p. 234). Support for contra aid generally rose during the 1980s, as Reagan returned repeatedly to the issue, though not to majority levels (Lockerbie and Borrelli, 1990; Sobel, 1993, p. 53). The "rally round the flag" typically increases support following decisive international events, although this sometimes does not happen or is short-lived (Bowen, 1989, pp. 793–801; Brody, 1991; Mueller, 1973, pp. 208–13).

Even a persuaded public does not necessarily convey its views to Congress, nor do members always feel compelled to reflect the public's views. Citizens are unlikely to communicate their views and politicians are unlikely to change their positions, for several reasons. Only voting and expressing political opinions in conversations involve substantial segments of the population. Perhaps 5 percent participate in more demanding activities, such as attending a political meeting, contributing money, or writing to a public official (Ippolito, Walker, and Kolson, 1976, pp. 229–30). Only 16 percent of the population had *ever* attempted to influence the national legislature (Dahl, 1984, p. 102; Serafino and Storrs, 1993, p. 127).

Representatives, moreover, take different views of their relationship to public opinion. There may be considerable consistency between constituents' attitudes and the representatives' *perception* of constituency attitudes, but politicians' perceptions tend to be heavily influenced by contact with the more activist segment of the population (Miller and Stokes, 1963). Among House members, 46 percent characterized themselves as "politicos" who could shift between personal judgment and constituency opinion depending upon the circumstances; 28 percent were "trustees" in their style of representation, relying solely on their own judgment; and only 23 percent chose the "delegate" style of representation under which they would seek to follow the preferences of constituents (cited in Davidson and Oleszek, 1990, p. 129; Serafino and Storrs, 1993, p. 127).

Congressional elections are even less likely than national races to be decided by foreign policy issues. In a 1978 congressional election, for example, only 1 percent of voters cited foreign policy issues as the most important facing the nation, and almost no one cited them as the most important issue in the election (Spanier and Ulsaner, 1989, p. 218). Occasionally, a foreign policy issue—such as Vietnam, the

Panama Canal, the Iranian hostage crisis, or contra aid—seems to have a significant impact on elections (Aldrich, Sullivan, and Borgida, 1989). Congresspersons regard the verdict on the presidential race as a signal of mass preferences which they should heed (Edwards, 1978; Harmon and Brauen, 1979; Martin, 1976; Pritchard, 1986; Schwarz and Fenmore, 1977), and their votes may alter because of "issue evolution"—or changes in events and political conditions. Though voters rarely use the ballot to hold members of Congress accountable for their foreign policy positions, members claim to worry that this is exactly what will happen, and seem to behave as if they believe it is likely to occur.

There is an apparent gap between the empirical results of polls and the intuition of elected politicians (LeoGrande, 1993, p. 172). Only 1 to 2 percent of the variance in the 1968 presidential vote could be attributed to the issue of Vietnam (Page, Shapiro and Brody, 1972). In 1976, domestic issues were more important than foreign policy issues in determining how citizens voted by a 12 to 1 margin (Spanier and Ulsaner, 1989, p. 214). Although commentators regarded the outcome of the 1980 election at least partly the result of Jimmy Carter's foreign policy problems in Iran and Afghanistan, Reagan's vote was increased by only 1 percent due to his issue positions, both domestic and foreign (Markus, 1982). In 1984, Reagan was vulnerable on foreign policy because Central America was the fifth best issue for Walter Mondale, but it added only 2.4 percent to the challenger's total vote (LeoGrande, 1993, p. 171; Spanier and Ulsaner, 1989, p. 217). Salient foreign policy issues do influence the outcomes of some elections, however (Aldrich et al., 1989).

Most issues, however, pass by with constituents taking little notice. "I don't think [constituents] follow your vote except on key emotional issues" (Matthews and Stimson, 1975, p. 47; cf. Skelton in Sobel, 1993, pp. 243–44). "In general, we can conclude that the vote of a congressman or senator for or against foreign aid appropriation or even for a Gulf of Tonkin Resolution will seldom have any impact on his re-election chances" (Hughes, 1978, p. 91; LeoGrande, 1993, p. 172).

The "once conventional wisdom" about the influence of public opinion on foreign policy suggests that "the opinion-policy linkage is a top-down process." An uninterested, ill-informed public is inevitably subject to manipulation by elites who are able to create public support for their policy initiatives where none existed previously (Wittkopf and McCormick, 1993, p. 91). This conventional wisdom is challenged today.

The "climate of opinion" and "system of dikes" theories emphasize that public opinion constrains foreign policy. But the opinion-policy nexus is, in part, reciprocal. Public opinion places limits on what policymakers can do, but leadership matters, too. Largely relying on the media, policymakers influence public opinion through education, leadership, and manipulation (Margolis and Mauser, 1989). Yet even when engineered by government policymakers, public support is considered the foundation of the policy process: the democratic formulation requires that policy depend on public approval, and in order to succeed, the government must experience or engender a favorable climate of opinion (Rosenau, 1961, pp. 23–24).

Since public opinion polls are only one way of measuring the support for a president's policy, the unorganized expressions of opinion are sometimes at odds with public policy. First, public opinion polls may not reflect policy preferences precisely enough to help the policymaker. Second, polls are unlikely to reflect the preferences of the more organized activists who target policymakers and have a greater say in the policy outcome. Third, polls may not reflect the preferences of the party or interest groups that are the main bases for future support and election (Serafino and Storrs, 1993, p. 124). Fourth, politicians may be unaware of or ignore the findings of polls.

THE IMPACT OF OPINION ON POLICY

The connection between opinion and policy, an understanding of which is currently underdeveloped, involves several interrelated aspects. First, opinion and policy may be consistent or "congruent" (Weissberg, 1976) from a number of sources: shared beliefs, values, and preferences among citizens and officials (Weissberg, 1976); the influencing of policy by public opinion; and the influencing of public opinion by policymakers. Second, consistency may lie in either majority agreement with policy outcomes or in corresponding changes in opinion with changes in policy (covariation) (Weissberg, 1976). The consistency or congruence of opinion and policy may be causal when, other things equal, changes in opinion precede changes in policy (Farkas, Shapiro, and Page, 1990). Public opinion facilitates policy when increases in support lead to increases in policy outcomes. Yet corresponding changes reflect a type of constraint when increases in support and in policy outcomes to "satisfactory" levels ("satisfying") contribute to decreases in policy outputs.

Varying levels of support or opposition by groups influential to policymakers produce differing pressures on intervention policy. The influences of attitudes of the elites and the "attentive" publics are typically stronger than those of the general public (Devine, 1970). This is particularly so because political elites and the attentive public concerned with foreign affairs are more knowledgeable and politically connected, and thus more potentially able to influence the policy process. Policymakers in both the administration and Congress typically respond to their respective constituencies as well as to more influential groups. More than simple majority opposition can, however, restrict the actions of constituency-supported presidential policy (cf. Graham, 1989). Both divisions in the public and congressional opposition facilitate the administration's ability to carry out its and its constituents' favored policy. Administration policymakers, moreover, are more likely to undertake covert funding if, despite majority opposition, there is core constituency support (but see Rosenau, 1990).

A number of studies show growing evidence of the impact of public opinion on policy (Foyle, 1999; Graber, 1968; Graham, 1989; Holsti, 1992; 1996, pp. 60–62, 192–200; Jacobs and Shapiro, 1995; Powlick, 1991, 1995; Sobel, 1993; but see Jacobs and Shapiro, 2000, p. 4; Kull, 1999, p. 9; Monroe, 1998, p. 14). The interaction of beliefs about the desirability and necessity of public support influences policymakers (Foyle, 1999). The more immediate the crisis, as is typically the case for interventions, the more likely public opinion will constrain policy (Baum, 1999; Foyle, 1999).

Voting is a relatively direct means of constraint by the mass public. For the public to exercise control over foreign policy through its electoral power, however, three conditions must be met (Campbell et al., 1960, pp. 170–74): (1) voters must be aware of foreign policy issues and informed enough about them to have an opinion; (2) foreign policy issues must be salient enough for voters to give them weight in making their voting decision; and (3) voters must be able to discern differences in the issue positions of the candidates or their parties (LeoGrande, 1993, p. 170). None of these conditions regularly exists for public opinion and foreign policy (Cohen, 1972; Hughes, 1978), and yet attitudes on foreign affairs issues affect voter choice (Aldrich et al., 1989).

Although public opinion should improve policymaking in a democracy, it is hard to trace "direct effects of opinion on decision making, especially in foreign policy" (Cohen, 1973, p. 97). The mass public "through the potentiality of its more active moods, [sets] the outer limits within which decision-makers and opinion-makers feel constrained to operate and interact" (Rosenau, 1961, p. 36). Anticipated positive or negative electoral consequences flowing from citizens' preferences for policy pressure decision-makers in the administration and Congress to consider public sentiment (Arnold, 1990; Foyle, 1999; Miller and Stokes, 1963; Rosenberg, Verba, and Converse, 1970). Public opinion rarely dictates specific policies but does establish the limits of acceptable government action (Key, 1961, pp. 552–53).

Alternatively, the public exercises effective control, not in advance but retrospectively (Key, 1966; cf. Fiorina, 1981). Elections are referendums on performance, and policymakers are held accountable by the electorate if their policies, foreign as well as domestic, fail. "Consequently, although public opinion offers little guidance for policy makers, the Damocles' sword of punishment is always overhead" (LeoGrande, 1993, p. 170). Public opinion is a "slumbering giant" of potential electoral punishment for wayward legislators (Rosenau, 1961). As one congressman said of his constituents, "You have to be as smart in prospect as they are in retrospect" (Hilsman, 1987, p. 170). But, "you have to be very careful and try to judge which ones will blow up into key issues" (Matthews and Stimson, 1975, p. 47). To avoid touching off a negative reaction from constituents, representatives are more likely to modify their positions incrementally (LeoGrande, 1993, p. 170; Matthews and Stimson, 1975, p. 47). There has been little support for the theory of retrospective control in foreign affairs. In the 1956 and 1960 elections, less than 1 percent of the vote was based on foreign policy (Miller, 1967). The classic study of constituency influence found that the correlation between constituent opinions on foreign policy and members' voting records was very low (Miller and Stokes, 1963), and members were generally mistaken about what constituent opinion actually was.

SUMMARY AND CONCLUSION: CONTRIBUTIONS TO THEORY

Although public opinion on foreign affairs has been called unknowledgeable, unstable, "moodish" (Almond, 1950), and of little influence (Cohen, 1973; Miller and Stokes, 1963), today opinion about foreign policy is recognized as possessing relatively high stability (Caspary, 1970; Hurwitz and Peffley, 1987; Page and Shapiro, 1992; Wittkopf, 1988) and significant impact on policy (Devine, 1970; Farkas, Shapiro, and Page, 1990; Page and Shapiro, 1983; Wittkopf, 1988; Sobel, 1993, p. 5). Public opinion on foreign policy is multifaceted and multidimensional. While significant in the political context, it is neither irrelevant nor dominant in setting policy. The climate of opinion and presidential approval are especially effective in setting the limits within which policy must operate. Effective public opinion combines general, attentive, and elite opinion that actually constrain or facilitate policy (cf. Lamert in Kannamer, 1992). Public opinion provides guidelines or "permissive limits" within which elites set policy (Almond, 1950). It affects policy because it is a proxy for the potential outcome of elections.

The starting point for this analysis is Key's theory that public opinion constitutes a system of "dikes" that channel the flow of public policy. Public opinion does not set policy but is capable of setting the range or limits of policy. In short, public opinion constrains policymaking by limiting policy options. Support facilitates, while opposition limits. The particular relationships of public opposition versus support constitute the individual dikes. Policies with relatively greater support and lesser opposition are more likely to be carried out. Support typically ranges lower as options become more aggressive. Lower support of, for example, a military invasion makes an invasion less likely than more strongly supported economic sanctions.

As Putnam notes, "metaphors are not theories," but as Max Black observed, "perhaps every science must start with metaphor and end with algebra: and perhaps without the metaphor there would never have been any algebra" (Putnam, 1988, p. 435). The precise relationship between public opinion and policy depends, among other things, on the "climate of opinion," opinions of influential groups, and where current opinion meets the cycles of interventionism and noninterventionism over time. The agreement of constituent and majority opinion increases the likelihood that policymakers will respond consistently with that opinion. Like the overlap of majority and constituent opinions, the concurrence between current and long-term attitudes reinforces the impact opinion has on policy. On the other hand, conflict between long-term and short-term attitudes make it less likely that public preferences will be carried into policy. The interaction of current opinion about specific forms of intervention with both general trends in interventionist sentiments and opinion on alternative policy options are central constituents of the system of dikes channeling policy.

In the past, public opinion has been considered, at maximum, to constrain policy. Today public opinion, at minimum, constrains policy and, at maximum, sets policy (Nacos, Shapiro, and Isernia, 2000). The influence of public opinion appears to be growing (Hinckley, 1992; but see Monroe, in Kull, 1999, p. 9 on domestic policy). The impact should have grown from Vietnam to Bosnia, but the exact relationship depends in part on interactions with cycles in political climate.

CONCLUSION

This study hypothesizes that in each case public opinion has constrained policy. The cases thus test these propositions about constraints in relationship to how public opinion affected the decisions of the top three constitutional policymakers: the president, the secretary of state and the secretary of defense. The lead chapters in each case identify the key events and policies as well as public opinion at each benchmark. The follow-up chapters identify the impact of public opinion on foreign policy on the basis of the decision-makers' own words.

As our knowledge of the specifics of how public opinion has affected American interventions has grown, so too has the opportunity to develop a more general explanation of the opinion-policy relation. This chapter summarizes and synthesizes current knowledge and advances the theory. The intervention examples and lessons that follow provide the history and insights for more developed insights and the bases for evaluating the constraining role public opinion plays in foreign policymaking. But first an overview of cycles in the history of interventionist attitudes sets the context for the four central cases.

CHAPTER 3

Cycles in American Foreign Policy Opinion

INTRODUCTION

For at least the past century, American attitudes toward foreign policy have shifted periodically between generally interventionist and generally noninterventionist postures. There have been attitude differences between the general public, attentive public and leaders. Besides variations from, for example, socioeconomic and ethnic divisions, there have also been differences among elite groups such as policymakers, journalists, military personnel, academics, and international business people over the role the United States should play in foreign affairs. Although Americans do not express unified opinions on foreign policy questions, public opinion has been characterized by identifiable swings between the two poles of isolationism and internationalism.

Alternations between isolationist and internationalist approaches have typically characterized American foreign policy since the nineteenth century (Foster, 1983; Holmes, 1985; Klingberg, 1983). Periods of about twenty-seven years of "extroversion" during which the United States has expanded and extended its influence have been followed by periods of about twenty-one years of "introversion" in which the country has addressed the results of previous involvement (Klingberg, 1983). Events mark the transitions between these periods, while public opinion defines the periods. This chapter identifies how these tendencies have played out during the twentieth century. Each phase of extroversion in American history tends to occur at a higher level of world involvement than the previous state of introversion (Klingberg, 1983). As time progresses, the differences between extroversion and introversion lessen.

For the twentieth century, periods of extroversion and introversion may be summarized in roughly five alternating periods (see Table 3.1). A brief review of the periods since polling began illuminates the plausibility of the alternations and periodization of the attitudes regarding foreign policy.

CYCLES IN POLLING OPINION: AN OVERVIEW

Since the advent of polling in the 1930s, it has been possible to track isolationist and internationalist trends in public opinion on U.S. involvement abroad. Introversion or noninternationalism describes, for instance, the withdrawing mood more specifically

Table 3.1 PERIODS OF EXTROVERSION AND INTROVERSION

Extroversion (27 years)	Introversion (21 years)
1891–1918 (27)	1918–1940 (21)
1940–1967 (27)	1967–1988 (21)
1988–(2018?)	

Source: Klingberg, 1983, and projection.

than isolationism. While Chittick and Billingsley (1989), Wittkopf (1990), and Hinckley (1992) place isolationism and internationalism into more specific dimensions, the two polar positions still capture overall attitudes toward world affairs. Americans tend to be opponents of U.S. foreign policy when it involves long-term commitment and the expense of troops, arms, or money (Schneider, 1983), but are "followers" into intervention when the country, under presidential authority, undertakes quick and decisive action in foreign affairs (Mueller, 1973). The differing concerns about international problems appear in editorial commentaries, presidential speeches, and party platforms regarding American actions beyond its borders and have been summarized in special public opinion surveys like those conducted by the Chicago Council on Foreign Relations (Rielly, 1975–99).

The century began with an expansionist period when America entered the stage as a major world power during the Spanish American War of 1898. Presidents Roosevelt and Wilson typified this type of internationally active policy. Though reluctant to enter World War I, the United States eventually began fighting in 1917. This internationalist phase ended soon after, however, marked by the U.S. Senate's refusal to participate in Wilson's League of Nations and its rejection of the Versailles Treaty. This was followed by an isolationist period, which ran from 1918 to 1940 (Klingberg, 1983) or from 1921 to 1941 (Foster, 1983). The Great Depression intensified the mood of introversion that is exemplified most clearly in the Neutrality Act of 1935 (Klingberg, 1983). One of the earliest Gallup polls reported in 1936 that 60 percent of those questioned believed the United States could stay out of another world war (Foster, 1983, p. 19). Favoring more help to Britain, in 1940 President Roosevelt tracked public attitudes through Hadley Cantril's work (Roll and Cantril, 1972) to identify what help the public would permit the president to provide Britain. In the months before June 1941, nearly 70 percent of those polled believed that U.S. interests would be seriously at stake in the war. However, this sentiment disappeared instantaneously because of an event that left a permanent mark on the American psyche.

The attack on Pearl Harbor shattered public belief in isolationist policy. Whereas just two decades earlier the idea of the United States entering the League of Nations was unpalatable to Congress, soon after Pearl Harbor the American people welcomed a similar proposal with open arms. Following three years of involvement in World War II, shortly after Roosevelt's 1944 statement favoring the establishment of the United Nations to promote world peace, 72 percent approved of the idea (Survey Research Consultants, 1990, p. 23). This represented a telling shift in public support for the United Nations, despite uncertainties of its ability to guarantee peace. The U.S. public was ready at this point to support international involvement.

While public opinion favored internationalist policies after 1940, questions remained about the type of involvement the United States should pursue and what should be the extent of its commitment to an active foreign involvement. Support for an internationalist policy represented the ascendancy of a widespread feeling that the country should assume an active role in foreign affairs over reservations about the efficacy of such activism in promoting U.S. interests.

Since the end of World War II there have been three movements in the beliefs of Americans regarding foreign policy. A strong consensus that the United States should play an active and interventionist role in global affairs marked the period following the Second World War. Despite a brief period toward the end of the Korean War, support for an internationalist policy predominated during the presidencies of Dwight Eisenhower and John Kennedy. This general agreement for interventionism brought on by the competitive environment of the Cold War dominated the American psyche for over twenty-five years.

The turbulence that surrounded Vietnam ruptured the post–World War II consensus and brought the next phase in American attitudes toward foreign affairs. This period was not one of reverting to overt isolation, but was characterized by a split in opinion regarding the means of implementing foreign policy. Reinforced by the oil and hostage crises of the 1970s, the post-Vietnam era highlighted the differences between and within the opinions of the public and the elites. American society, wary of becoming embroiled in another disaster, grew hesitant of direct intervention but it did not completely withdraw from global affairs. Instead of choosing to combat communism with direct force, it chose the indirect roles of negotiations and détente and financial assistance to opposition groups as revealed in the Nixon and Reagan doctrines. The fear of direct confrontation remained until the end of the 1980s, constraining the policymaking of the executive office, most notably during the Reagan administration.

The presidency of George Bush marked the transition to the third post-war period of American attitudes toward foreign policy. Demonstrated first with the invasion of Panama and then more definitively with the Persian Gulf War of 1991, the post-Vietnam era of nonconfrontation had come to an end. This new phase returned the country to a more active posture on global affairs. Reflected in actions in Somalia, Bosnia, and Iraq, a new American opinion had developed, predicated on multilateralism and often humanitarianism. However, the new motivation for foreign affairs contained remnants of the post-Vietnam syndrome. Americans were still wary of participating in foreign interventions, and those in which Americans did partake were generally short-lived, or postsettlement as in Bosnia.

Contradictions between humanitarian missions and self-interest mark the third period of American opinion on foreign policy. The end of an era of bipolar thinking exposed the complicated nature of foreign policy not only for the elites but for the public as well. Current thinking cannot be understood without considering the trends in public opinion and foreign policy that have brought it to this juncture.

THE END OF ISOLATIONISM AND WORLD WAR II

After World War II there was no strong swing back toward isolationism. In general, the public (and leaders) preferred that America take "an active part" in world affairs.

Table 3.2 ACTIVE PART IN WORLD AFFAIRS, 1945–56

"Do you think it would be best for the future of this country if we take an active part in world affairs, or if we stay out of world affairs?"

Year	Month	Active Part	Stay Out	Don't Know
1945	October	71%	19%	10%
1950	November	72	22	6
1950	December	66	25	9
1952	October	68	23	9
1953	February	73	21	5
1953	September	71	21	8
1954	April	69	25	6
1955	March	72	21	7
1956	November	71	25	4

Source: Gallup polls/NORC. See Table 3.10 for additional 1942–50 data and for details on sources.

More than two-thirds of Americans took an activist posture in the decade after the war ended (Table 3.2).

Buoyed by the moral imperative that had impelled it into the war and confronted by the threat of nuclear destruction and the disintegration of the old balance of power, the United States incurred a greater responsibility for global security. From 1942 to the mid-1950s, from two-thirds to three-fourths of the population thought it best for "the future of this country" if we took "an active part in world affairs." When the North Atlantic Treaty Organization was formed in April 1949, 59 percent of Americans (71 percent of college educated) felt that the United States had "not gone too far" in its involvement in world affairs (Klingberg, 1983). The public recognized that the emerging U.S. superpower had little choice but to assume a leadership role in the global arena.

At the start of the Cold War, with the development of the "Truman Doctrine" in 1947, the goal of containing Soviet expansion through economic or military aid to U.S. allies factored strongly in public opinion. Economic aid was more likely to win public approval than supplying arms or military advisors. Because of fears of becoming embroiled in another war, for example, the public favored sending economic aid to Greece in 1947 (60 percent to 27 percent, NORC), but opposed sending military advisers (54 percent to 37 percent; Gallup). On most questions of economic aid like the Marshall Plan, approval correlated with higher levels of education (Foster, 1983). The public looked with dismay, however, at the "loss" of China to the Communists in 1949.

THE KOREAN WAR

The Korean War challenged internationalist sentiment. The press viewed the June 1950 invasion of South Korea as Soviet-inspired, like the 1948 Czech coup, the blockade of Berlin in 1948–49, and the Communist revolution in China in 1949. Immediately after the attack on South Korea, 81 percent of Americans approved sending military aid to Korea (13 percent opposed, Gallup; Foster, 1983, p. 104). This high approval rate rested on the belief by 57 percent that such aid would help establish peace rather than lead to another world war. In July, 58 percent stressed "Communist aggression" as the cause of the Korean War, although 28 percent could not explain "what the war [was] all about" (Foster, 1983, pp. 104–5). The Chinese entrance into the fighting in November 1950 decreased U.S. popular support, since many Americans believed it would seriously prolong U.S. involvement.

Asked in the early 1950s, "in view of the developments since we entered the fighting, do you think the U.S. made a mistake in deciding to defend South Korea, or not?," two-thirds of Americans initially said it was not a mistake when they rallied in support of the start of the war. The opinion switched over a year to the view that deciding to fight was a mistake (see Table 3.3). Support generally declined as casualties increased significantly (Mueller, 1973). But the perception that it was not a mistake rose again as an armistice settlement loomed toward the end of the war.

Yet the "mistake" question alone obscures the full meaning of public opinion about the war and preferences for different U.S. policy options (Mueller, 1973). Beginning in September 1950, most Americans agreed that the United States was "right" in "sending troops to stop the Communist invasion of South Korea" (NORC; Foster, 1983, pp. 114–15). This sentiment remained a majority throughout the war (see Table 3.4).

The initial impact of the war created a heightened apprehension about the Soviet Union that increased support for United Nations' actions. Involvement of the Chinese in Korea and the perception that the United States was becoming embroiled in another major military effort, however, increased the sense that sending troops had been

Table 3.3 WAS KOREAN WAR A MISTAKE?

"Do you think the United States made a mistake in going into the war in Korea, or not?"			
	Yes (mistake)	No (not a mistake)	No Opinion
1950-August	19%	66%	15%
1950-December	49	39	12
1951-February	49	41	10
1951-March	44	43	13
1951-April	37	45	18
1951-early June	41	42	17
1951-mid June	43	39	18
1951-early August	42	47	11
1952-March	50	37	13
1952-September	41	39	20
1952-early October	46	36	18
1952-late October	42	37	20
1953-January	36	50	14

Source: Gallup polls, in Mueller, 1973, Table 3.1A. Question wording varies.

Table 3.4 WAS IT RIGHT TO SEND TROOPS TO KOREA?

"Do you think the United States was right or wrong in sending American troops to stop
the Communist invasion of South Korea?"

	Right to send troops	Wrong	No opinion
1950-September	81%	13%	6%
1951-January	55	36	9
1951-February	57	32	11
1951-March	60	30	10
1951-April	63	27	10
1951-May	60	30	10
1951-August	60	30	10
1951-November	54	37	9
1952-January	56	34	10
1952-March	50	40	10
1952-July	55	38	7
1953-September	64	28	10

Source: NORC, in Mueller, 1973, Table 3.1B.

wrong. The discrepancy between the results in the two polls (Table 3.3 vs. Table 3.4)
is perhaps best explained by a change in perception. Faced with fighting on a long-
term basis, people were likely to regret the initial decision to become involved in the
war (viewed it as a "mistake"). However, reminded that the United States had undertaken the war to halt Communist expansionism, people maintained that U.S. action
had been justified (right) (Mueller, 1973).

THE EISENHOWER AND KENNEDY ADMINISTRATIONS

With the election of Dwight Eisenhower in 1952 and his promise to go to Korea and
to end U.S. involvement in Korea, popular support for "an active part for the U.S. in
world affairs" rose to 73 percent in February 1953, one of the highest indications of
internationalist sentiment since 1945 (Table 3.2). Approval of the establishment of
the Southeast Asia Treaty Organization and the U.S. role in assisting Guatemala to
set up a "democratic" government reflected the strength of internationalist rhetoric,
particularly among the college-educated. The Berlin crisis in 1948–49 challenged
American commitment to its activist policy, yet even in the face of Krushchev's 1959
"ultimatum" to get out, support for the U.S. commitment to preserve the freedom of
Berlin and to "fight if necessary" remained strong in the public and press. A year later,
in 1961, the Bay of Pigs fiasco in Cuba tested the willingness of Americans to back
presidential foreign policy, but the public did not reject Kennedy because of the military failure. During the Cuban missile crisis of 1962, Kennedy's firm reply to a
threatening message from Krushchev increased presidential approval from 72 percent to 83 percent. The public seemed willing to back almost any foreign policy de-

cision that the president made. Given this environment of support for international intervention during the period, the initial willingness of the American public to become involved in Vietnam is not surprising.

THE VIETNAM CHALLENGE TO INTERNATIONALISM

In the early sixties, Southeast Asia became the major national security concern for the United States. The outbreak of fighting in Laos in 1961 posed a serious dilemma—whether to intervene and face expanded conflict, or to "abandon" another country (after the "loss" of China in 1949) to Communist attack and accept the blow to American prestige. Kennedy's commitment to a neutral Laos was seen as an admirable goal, if feasible in a coalition government with Communists. Others felt South Vietnam was the primary target of Communist aggression in Southeast Asia. The public, in general, had little awareness of the situation. In May 1964, only 37 percent had been "following developments in South Viet-Nam"; of those, 16 percent felt the United States was "doing as well as could be expected," whereas 17 percent felt it was "handling affairs badly" (Gallup). A *Time* cover story heralded U.S. involvement in South Vietnam as an indication of the U.S. decision to defend that country "at all costs."

However, this involvement was never given unconditional support. This was demonstrated in 1963 when concerns surfaced that information on the fighting was being kept from the public. By 1964, with little progress apparent in the war, there was division about what course to take. Conservatives advocated a greater extension of manpower and money including air strikes at North Vietnam; moderates pressed for a political "settlement" that would allow the United States to save face while extricating itself (Mueller, 1973). Clarification of U.S. policy became an issue when defense secretary Robert McNamara announced that U.S. troops would pull out at the end of 1965 regardless of the state of the war (McNamara, 1995). President Lyndon Johnson later issued a contrasting statement that: "we will not pull out because we are not willing to yield that part of the world to communism" (Foster, 1983, p. 261).

The year 1965 marked a change in the U.S. role in Vietnam with the introduction of both retaliatory bombing in February and the arrival of combat troops in March. Public opinion soon split, mirroring the state of indecision and contradiction that policymakers were communicating. The military buildup received majority approval. Two-thirds of Americans (64 percent) felt the United States should "continue present efforts," while a sizable minority (23 percent) advocated negotiations and pulling out (Mueller, 1973, p. 82). In spring 1965, as the no-opinion group diminished, the more extreme alternatives of getting out or expanding the war gained support, "so that the hold-the-line group was flanked by two sizable and contradictory minorities" (Foster, 1983, p. 283) (See Table 3.5).

With renewed bombing of North Vietnam in 1967, the bulk of American opinion continued to hold a middle-of-the-road position of ending the war without "selling out" to the communists. A plurality in July 1967 still felt that the war was "not a mistake" (48 percent vs. 41 percent), but 49 percent opposed any increase in troops (40 percent favored) (Gallup, in Mueller, 1973, p. 55).

The year 1967 was the turning point from extroversion to introversion (Klingberg,

Table 3.5 Preferred Policy in Vietnam

"Which of these three courses do you favor for the U.S. (United States) in Vietnam: carry the war into North Vietnam, at the risk of bringing Red China into the war, negotiate a settlement with the Communists and get out now, or continue to hold the line there to prevent the Communists from taking over South Vietnam?"

	February 1965	March	Early April	Late April 1965
Hold the line	40%	46%	48%	43%
Negotiate and get out	23	35	31	28
Carry war to North	13	12	17	2
Not sure	24	7	4	9
	100%	100%	100%	100%

Source: Harris Surveys, 1965.

1983). In January 1968, when the Viet Cong's surprise Tet offensive brought forcefully to this nation the question of sending more troops, President Johnson marked yet another change in U.S. policy by deciding to deploy only a moderate number of additional troops and to stop most of the bombing of North Vietnam. The two-thirds (64 percent) approval of a bombing halt announced in 1968 with only 26 percent opposed (Gallup) indicated that the U.S. policy of international "activism" had pressed the limits of public support.

The switch from hawkish to dovish sentiment identifies the point around which interventionist sentiment turned to noninterventionist. "Hawks" who wanted to "step up" U.S. military involvement remained in the majority (52 to 61 percent) until after the Tet offensive but ultimately were replaced by "doves," who, by November 1969, wanted to "reduce our military involvement" in Vietnam.

The decline in public support tied to casualties repeated the same downward trend it had shown during the Korean War (Mueller, 1973). Yet despite intense media coverage of the Vietnam conflict, public support did not plunge beneath Korean War levels until U.S. involvement had continued far longer and American casualties were of equal magnitude. In April 1951, after less than a year of war, support for Korea ("was not a mistake") was at 45 percent (Mueller, 1973, p. 45). Total U.S. casualties (killed and wounded) reached about 120,000 in the spring of 1953. It took the Vietnam War until the end of 1967 (over $2\frac{1}{2}$ years of war) for support to drop below 46%, when roughly the same number of casualties had occurred.

Using the answer that it was not a mistake to send U.S. troops to Vietnam as a measure of support ("mistake" meant opposition), support for the war dropped steadily from 1965 to 1973 as opposition rose. Vocal opposition in protest to the war began in 1965 and remained strong until 1970 (Mueller, 1973).

Despite intense media coverage, declining public support for U.S. intervention in Vietnam did not automatically reflect a return to isolationism. Rather, it marked the beginning of a breakdown in the Cold War bipartisan consensus toward internationalism. The issue was not whether the United States should continue to play an active role in world affairs, but what type of role it should play: what combination of mili-

Table 3.6 POLICY PREFERENCES IN VIETNAM: HAWKS AND DOVES

"People are called 'hawks' if they want to step up our military effort in Vietnam. They are called 'doves' if they want to reduce our military effort in Vietnam. How would you describe yourself—as a 'hawk' or a 'dove'?"

	December 1967	Late January 1968	Tet	Early February 1968	Late February 1968
Hawk	52%	56%		61%	58%
Dove	35	28		23	26
No Opinion	13	16		16	16
	March 1968	Bombing Halt	April 1968	Early October 1969	November 1969
Hawk	41		41	44	31
Dove	42		41	42	55
No Opinion	17		18	14	14

Source: Gallup polls, in Mueller, 1973, Table 4.6.

tary action, diplomacy, and economic incentives should be used, and what should be the extent of American commitments to foreign interests (Wittkopf, 1990). For example, while Richard Nixon emphasized the promise to end the Vietnam War in his 1968 presidential campaign, there was still widespread division among the public about what should be the next step in Vietnam: 25 percent thought the United States should "go all out"; 21 percent felt the country should prepare the Vietnamese to fight their own war; and 15 percent felt the country should remain involved until a cease-fire could be obtained (Gallup, April 1969). In March 1970, 21 percent supported withdrawal of all troops immediately, while 25 percent preferred to withdraw all troops within eighteen months (Gallup, March 1970). Almost half (48 percent), however, felt the United States should "withdraw troops but take as many years to do this as are needed to turn the war over to the South Vietnamese." Only 7 percent said "Send more troops to Vietnam and step up the fighting" (Foster, 1983, p. 313). These figures point to a marked decline in public attitudes toward U.S. involvement from the initially high approval rate five years earlier.

The surveys since 1965 about America's role in the world chart fluctuations in opinion during the years since Vietnam. Results over the years since 1965 show a majority activist attitude on the part of the public, although there was a distinct decrease after Vietnam and into the early 1980s.

AFTER VIETNAM—A NEW MOOD OF INTROVERSION

The decline in public support for the Vietnam War signaled the end of a twenty-six-year era of extroversion that had lasted from 1941 to 1967. The years 1967–68 were the turning point in public mood (Holmes, 1985; Klingberg, 1983) not only due to the Tet offensive and Johnson's withdrawal from the presidential race, but also in the af-

Table 3.7 WAS THE VIETNAM WAR A MISTAKE?

"In view of the developments since we entered the fighting, do you think the U.S. made a mistake sending troops to fight in Vietnam?"

	Yes (mistake)	No (not a mistake)	No Opinion
1965-September	24%	60%	15%
1966-March 3	26	59	16
1966-May 5	36	49	15
1966-September 8	35	48	17
1966-November 10	31	52	18
1967-January 26	32	52	16
1967-April 19	37	50	13
1967-July 13	41	48	11
1967-October 6	47	44	10
1967-December 7	45	46	9
1968-February 6	26	59	16
1968-February 27	49	42	9
1968-April	48	40	12
1968-August	53	35	12
1968-October	54	37	9
1969-January	52	39	9
1969-September	58	32	10
1970-January	57	32	10
1970-April	51	34	15
1970-May	56	36	8
1971-January	60	31	9
1971-May	61	28	11
1973-May	60	29	11

Source: Gallup polls, in Mueller, 1973, Table 3.3A.

termath of widespread social conflict and civil violence that contributed to the public's perception of a decline in U.S. prestige at home and abroad. When asked in 1971, "Would it be worth going to war again if the U.S. were invaded?," though 95 percent supported the defense of their own country and 77 percent were also willing to defend Canada, the hypothetical Communist invasion of any other countries evoked a lukewarm response toward defending those countries; Western Europe (47 percent); West Berlin (32 percent); Israel (25 percent); Latin America (21 percent); Taiwan (18 percent).

This decrease in the public's willingness to commit U.S. troops to the defense of its allies was not a revival of prewar American isolationism. Each phase of extroversion or internationalism in American history tends to occur at a higher level of world involvement than the previous state of introversion (or isolationism) (Klingberg, 1983). As time progresses, the difference between extroversion and introversion lessens. The disunity in public opinion during the post-Vietnam years effected a stale-

Table 3.8 ACTIVE PART IN WORLD AFFAIRS, 1965–83

"Do you think it would be best for the future of this country if we take an active part in world affairs, or if we stayed out of world affairs?"

Year	Month	Active Part	Stay Out	Don't Know
1965	June	79%	16%	5%
1973	February	66	31	3
1974	December	67	23	10
1975	February	61	30	4
1976	February	63	32	5
1978	February	64	32	4
1978	November	59	29	12
1980	November	64	33	3
1982	February	61	34	5
1982	October	54	35	12
1983	February	65	31	4

Source: NORC/GSS; CCFR, Nov. 1978, Dec. 1979, October 1982. See Table 3.10 for details.

mate on foreign policy options rather than projecting truly isolationist feeling. There developed widespread divergence about the United States' role in world affairs, but only a small segment of the public became completely isolationist (Watts and Free, 1985) (See Table 3.9).

From 1964 to 1976, Americans showed an increased reluctance to become involved in world affairs, but the shift away from internationalism was slight. With the exception of 1974, the largest segment of public opinion continued to be "predominantly internationalist" and by 1980, this segment contained almost half of those polled.

In contrast, the less than 10 percent "completely isolationist" scarcely changed over sixteen years (see Table 3.9). At the end of 1974, Americans were not in agreement with neoisolationism (Rielly, 1975). While a majority favored the demilitarization of U.S. foreign policy, 86 percent agreed that the United States had a "real responsibility to take an active role in the world." Topping the list of the country's priorities were "keeping the peace" and "promoting our security"—indicating greater

Table 3.9 INTERNATIONALISM VS. ISOLATIONISM

	1964	1968	1972	1974	1976	1980
Completely internationalist	30%	25%	18%	11%	7%	17%
Predominantly internationalist	35	34	38	30	37	44
Mixed	27	32	35	38	33	26
Predominantly isolationist	5	6	5	14	20	11
Completely isolationist	3	3	4	7	3	2

Source: Watts and Free, 1985.

self-interest and cautiousness about foreign intervention. Containing communism ranked in the middle (54 percent terming it "very important"). Only during 1972 and 1974 did isolationism increase, in part due to decreased confidence in the presidency from Watergate and increased fears about the U.S. economy and its dependence on foreign oil. The rise in isolationism was especially evident among those with a low socioeconomic status, attributable in part to the negative impact the Vietnam War had on poorer Americans and government programs that supported them.

In the early 1970s, the introversion that had appeared in the last stages of Vietnam intensified as the United States tried to cope with the results of its extrovert activity during the previous decade and a series of domestic and international crises in the Far East and the Middle East. Such domestic and foreign difficulties forced Americans to recognize new constraints affecting U.S. foreign policy. The Vietnam War had prevented the United States from exerting pressure in other areas of the world and had stimulated inflation to a point where the U.S. economy had become a major source of concern (Klingberg, 1983). The oil crisis of the early 1970s increased Americans' sense of concern about the outside world.

In addition, Congress passed the War Powers Act in 1973 to curb the president's power to involve the United States in military conflicts. Thus in 1976, Gerald Ford and Henry Kissinger found their efforts to intervene in Angola blocked by the Congress. The reduction in defense spending and the increased emphasis on diplomacy and negotiation ("détente") in carrying out U.S. Cold War foreign policy provides other evidence of U.S. introversion.

However, while the public initially favored a policy of negotiation, public support quickly eroded under a growing sense of U.S. weakness and insecurity. Although Jimmy Carter felt by 1977 that Americans were now "free of [their] inordinate fear of communism" (Klingberg, 1983, p. 147), the public was already alarmed by a renewed buildup of Soviet military capacities. From 1974 to 1978, public demand for increased defense spending rose 20 percent, and of those favoring the increase, 69 percent believed the United States was "falling behind" the Soviet Union (Rielly, 1975, p. 6). While the public remained wary of direct involvement abroad, there was a growing inclination toward increased spending on U.S. defenses.

CRISES IN THE MIDDLE EAST AND THE REAGAN PRESIDENCY

In 1979, the Soviet invasion of Afghanistan and the seizure of American hostages by Iranian militants created renewed concern over U.S. power and prestige abroad. Americans were becoming increasingly security conscious without showing a greater willingness to intervene in world affairs. At the end of Carter's term, Americans believed the country was spending too little on defense (GSS, 1978–80). The 1980 election signified that Americans were still more concerned with domestic issues than with foreign policy, but were also concerned about America's declining role in the world. Although a greater proportion of the public believed Carter could keep the United States out of war, Americans were willing to accept the risk of Reagan's strong anticommunist rhetoric because they favored his clear-cut commitment to strengthening both the economy and U.S. defenses.

Yet in attempting to translate campaign promises into foreign policy, Reagan faced constraints. Implementing "Reaganomics" took precedence over any foreign affairs initiative. Moreover, even by the end of 1981, public opinion was shifting from recent approval of increased defense spending toward maintaining current levels (GSS 1981–83). In addition, concern about the military capacity of the Soviet Union waned, diminishing the power of Reagan's anti-Soviet rhetoric.

In 1983 Americans remained convinced that the Vietnam War had been "fundamentally wrong and immoral" (Rielly, 1987). The public was still reluctant to commit troops in hypothetical instances and continued to be extremely selective about which allies it would be willing to defend. The general public, leaders, and the Reagan administration did not share a consensus on foreign policy (Rielly, 1987). Leaders continued to support U.S. interventions abroad, both cooperative and confrontational. The public, however, displayed little enthusiasm for giving U.S. economic or military aid, or selling arms, to other countries, and favored limited cooperation with the Soviet Union (cf. Wittkopf, 1990). The public's increasing sentiment to spend more on domestic social programs and less on defense moved counter to administration policies. The assessment of Reagan's handling of foreign policy crises—including the Afghan invasion, martial law in Poland, unrest in El Salvador, and the Israeli invasion of Lebanon—remained fair to poor. Minor interventions included the one-day air strikes on Libya (1982), and the two-day invasion of Grenada (October 1983).

By 1982, Reagan faced resistance to putting his foreign policy into practice. Indeed, both foreign and domestic constraints forced Reagan to implement the basic policies of his predecessors, combining aggressive rhetoric with diplomatic maneuvers of détente. Faced with a grass-roots nuclear freeze movement, Reagan stressed arms control with the Soviets. He also undertook a mediating rather than militaristic role for the United States in conflicts like the Falklands War. His handling of the Soviet shooting of a Korean jetliner in 1983 and the TWA hijacking in 1985 reassured the public that he was not "trigger-happy." Yet Reagan's initial foreign policy success did not guarantee support for his policies in Central America and the Mideast. The buildup of U.S. military defenses reinforced the public's perception of the Soviet Union as a serious threat. In 1980, only 36 percent felt that "Russia can't be trusted and we will have to rely on increased military strength to counter them in the future"; in 1984, half endorsed this view (see Schneider, 1983, p. 42). Reagan's rhetoric had some effect on public perception.

Thus, the public not only remained skeptical of the communist "threat" posed by the situations in Nicaragua and El Salvador but also became increasingly wary of foreign policy initiatives (see chapters 7 and 8 here). In 1987, "Large gaps continue between public and leadership attitudes, and on many issues between the views of the public and the leadership and those expressed by Reagan administration officials" (Rielly, 1987).

A pattern of tentative support (12 percent "don't know"), followed by extroversion, occurs between the fall of 1982 and the spring of 1983, perhaps in response to the Iran-Iraq War. Another moment when the public was more uncertain was in the fall of 1990, after the Iraqi invasion of Kuwait, but before Congress had come to a decision about its response. After the Gulf War, however, public support of international activity temporarily surged.

If public opinion in those years became as much reaction to events as an influence on policy, this was what the public itself seems to expect. In the fall of 1982, adult Americans expressed the decade's highest rate of uncertainty (12 percent) and the lowest willingness to take an active part in world affairs (54 percent); but at the same time, "opinion leaders" (politicians, academics, journalists, etc.) still were over-whelmingly (98 percent) in favor of America's adopting an active role (see Table 3.10). In early 1985, when support for an active role in world affairs was at its high-est in twenty years (70 percent), only about a third of all people interviewed (35 per-cent) believed that popular involvement in political and social affairs helped control the outcome of world affairs (GSS, 1985).

Public Opinion Constraints on Reagan's Central America Policy

In trying to promote his Central American policies, Reagan met with ongoing resis-tance from the public and many political leaders unwilling to run counter to their con-stituents. In effect, neither Reagan's patriotic rhetoric about the Nicaraguan contras as "freedom fighters," nor his insistence that unrest in Central America resulted from communist insurgency in El Salvador, convinced the public that the situation in Cen-tral America constituted a clear-cut issue of national security. Although Americans were more willing to commit troops to defend Western European allies and Japan than they had been in 1982, their two-to-one opposition to intervention in Central America remained little changed, because they believed such intervention would in-volve a long-term, costly investment of military assistance that could lead to war (Sobel 1989, 1993; see also chapters 7 and 8 here).

Reagan faced formidable constraints in the public sentiment against any such U.S. intervention. The persistent lack of consensus among elites over foreign policy and the widening gap between elite views and administration policy made it difficult for Reagan to manipulate or overlook public sentiment. This dissension was complicated by long-held contradictions in the American public's view of foreign policy: "funda-mental conflict between liberal American ideology and the dictates of U.S. politico-military interests" (Holmes, 1985, p. 6). The general public remained "noninterna-tionalist" rather than isolationist—approving the idea of the United States assuming the role of a powerful world leader but suspicious of specific economic or military in-terventions. While public sentiment tended to "follow" elite or presidential initiative, such support could only be sustained if the action were quick and decisive. In most cases, the public maintained a consistent stance—desiring peace and strength, but es-chewing long-term involvement abroad. In questions about defense of U.S. interests, the word "communism" increased the percentage of public support while mention of "troops" decreased the number of those favoring the intervention (Lockerbie and Borreli, 1990; Sobel, 1993).

These differences underscore the apparently contradictory but self-interested and pragmatic impulses of the American public. "Americans practice a policy that used to be called 'containment'" (Schneider, 1983). They wanted to preserve American prestige abroad and resist communist expansion, but they did not want to make a long-term commitment of economic or military aid; nor did they want to go to war. To prevent a hypothetical communist takeover of an area perceived as "important to U.S. defense interests," Americans approved the use of military force. But if "military force" translated into money or troops, support dwindled rapidly (see Schneider, 1979). For these reasons, the noninternationalist public did not consistently support either conservative or liberal elites but sided with the conservatives on increased defense and with the liberals against direct intervention. The public was predisposed against U.S. involvement in other countries, not on ideological grounds, but out of self-interest and a feeling that what the United States did for the rest of the world was usually "senseless, wasteful, and unappreciated" (Schneider, 1983).

The more educated segment of the public, including academics and policymakers, tended to be more internationalist. The divisions fell along liberal/conservative lines, with the liberals favoring a "global" approach to foreign affairs of using diplomacy and economic aid to promote U.S. interests and the conservatives being more willing to use military force as well as economic incentives (Wittkopf, 1990). The Vietnam War affected the elite opinion the most—not only disrupting the Cold War bipartisan consensus, but also making liberals more suspicious of military intervention as an instrument of foreign policy. The internationalism of elites tended to make them view many parts of the world as "vital" to U.S. interests and prevented them from setting up a realistic set of global priorities (Holmes, 1985). In addition, the educated, attentive segment of the public was easily swayed by domestic and foreign events in "action/reaction decision-making" (Holmes, 1985; Mueller, 1973) and was extremely sensitive to the views of the general public. Elites at this juncture could not achieve consensus in the debate over the proper role of the United States in foreign affairs.

The public during the Reagan years did not consistently or exclusively support either liberal or conservative approaches to foreign policy, and was also at odds with administration policy. While Reagan continued to advocate military buildup, the public was willing only to maintain current defense spending levels and also wanted arms control agreements. While Reagan continued his claims that a Soviet menace existed in Central America, the public was increasingly confident of U.S. military strength against the Soviet Union and more willing to try cooperation instead of confrontation. The public opposed "implementation of the Reagan Doctrine through covert action against communist-oriented regimes in Afghanistan, Angola and Nicaragua" (Rielly, 1987). The continuing dissension among elites made Congress even more susceptible to mass opinion, since the legislature could not agree on a foreign policy of its own. Furthermore, polls for eight years indicated that Americans wanted both public opinion and Congress to play a larger role in the determination of foreign policy with respect to the president (Rielly, 1983, p. 6).

Fundamental public opposition to Reagan's Central America policy remained largely unchanged, though public support or sympathy rose for individuals targeted in the Iran-Contra investigation. The public considered the Iran arms deal an attempt at quick, decisive, "Rambo"-style action that failed. The Iran-contra scandal eroded public confidence in the integrity and competence of its leaders, Reagan in particular. "The long-term trend in public opinion [has not] been right or left but rather anti-establishment, a growing hostility towards political parties and leaders as corrupt, incompetent, and ineffective" (Schneider, 1983, p. 51).

THE PRESIDENCIES OF GEORGE BUSH AND BILL CLINTON

After Reagan, elites and administrations tempered their interventionist tendencies (both militant and cooperative) with some of the general public's inherent caution about U.S. involvement abroad. Under such a compromise, U.S. foreign policy embarked into an era of extroversion, engaging in a higher level of foreign activity than in the past but with a greater likelihood of guaranteeing its people the goals of "peace and strength."

The major foreign policy events of the Bush administration included the military invasion of Panama in 1989 and massive preparation for the Gulf coalition offensive in Iraq in 1990–91. The involvement in Panama was the first time since Vietnam that the United States had risked, though not experienced, the possibility of a long-term intervention in the face of significant opposition. The Gulf War was a major U.S. deployment of half a million troops, though the actual ground war lasted less than a week. To ensure public support, the Bush administration got both UN and congressional resolutions of approval. The sending of U.S. troops to Somalia in 1992 was initially seen as a humanitarian, not a military, intervention, but the humanitarian aid to Somalia included U.S. troops.

For Clinton, the major interventions have been the expanded role in Somalia, the "invasion" of Haiti, and deploying of peacekeepers in Bosnia and Kosovo. Somalia became a military intervention when the mission increased to trying to arrest the leader Mohammed Aidid. This led to the death of eighteen American soldiers and accelerated U.S. withdrawal. Haiti turned out to be a negotiated deployment without armed conflict. Deploying peacekeepers in Bosnia was a more controversial decision. The intervention in Bosnia in late 1995 as part of the NATO force and peacekeeping deployment there in 1995–96 as well as bombing of Serbian forces in Kosovo in 1999 represented significant commitments. None of these represents a willingness to participate in long-term military combat, however (Sobel, 1996)

IN RETROSPECT: CYCLES OVER TIME

From a long-term perspective, the last three decades have confirmed the basic pattern of mood swings that Klingberg posited in 1952: "If America's fourth phase of extroversion should last as long as the previous extrovert phases, it would not end until well into the 1960's" (Table 3.1). American self-confidence, anxiety about nuclear weapons, and the appearance of a bipolar balance of power played an important role in precipitating the next introversion stage, but the intensity of U.S. involvement in foreign affairs precluded a return to the level of U.S. isolationism evinced in the past (Klingberg, 1983).

The United States reached the depth of its latest introversion in the early to mid-1970s with reduction in defense spending, the oil and hostage crises, loss of national esteem, the loss in Vietnam, and Watergate. The next few years saw cautious movement toward extroversion, with Reagan pursuing a middle course between hard-line rhetoric and moderate actions similar to détente.

In large part, Klingberg's predictions have come true, yet he and his theoretical disciples have expressed concern about whether these shifts will continue to the same degree. Analysis of recent decades underscores the continuing divisions that reigned among the American people even when public opinion as a whole was labeled "internationalist" or "isolationist." The breakdown in bipartisan consensus precipitated by Vietnam intensified differences that already existed but had not yet surfaced in public opinion. Yet the more recent stalemate between proponents of different foreign policy measures also contributed to a policy of inward-looking withdrawal.

Klingberg concluded his 1983 assessment with a series of predictions. He foresaw a period of extroversion lasting from 1986/87 to 2013/14, and a partly concurrent period of "deeper idealism," which would last from 1982 to 1998 (1983, p. 171). The participation in international conflicts that America has undertaken since 1986 reflects extroversion but differs from that which typified American attitudes after 1940. Public opinion slowly and cautiously shifted toward extroversion (Rielly, 1987–99). There was "growing appreciation of the importance of foreign affairs . . . combined with a desire for a larger U.S. world role" (Rielly, 1987). At the same time there has been diminished intensity of this mood because of the public's continuing caution about long-term foreign commitments and advocacy of a moderate defense policy. The five-day invasion of Panama in 1989, the five-day ground war in the Gulf in February 1991, and peacekeeping in Bosnia and Kosovo did not per se constitute a commitment to international involvement.

Neither do they reflect a sense of neoisolationism, nor a return to pre–World War II isolationism. America has been wary of taking action in certain areas like Somalia or Bosnia, but the intervention for humanitarian reasons coincides with a phase of "deeper idealism" into which America has supposedly entered. "To those who espouse the application of idealism to international affairs, the role of military force and of the arms race as late as 1983 was shocking, and is unprecedented in an idealist period" (Klingberg, 1983, p. 171). Whether Klingberg's optimistic prediction that "during the next few decades America could make its most creative contributions to mankind" (Klingberg, 1983, p. 174) is yet to be seen.

Only when Reagan felt the United States could intervene swiftly and effectively without miring itself in extended conflict did he use U.S. military strength to achieve foreign policy aims (e.g., Grenada, Libya, and Panama). In the face of other provocations, he adopted a far less aggressive stance (e.g., Iran's attack on the *U.S.S. Stark*). Bush tested the limits of public support first in the Panama invasion and then in the Desert Storm buildup where he claimed the United States had "kicked" the post-Vietnam syndrome.

Klingberg's predicted idealism may have held sway in the nuclear arms race that gave way to negotiation and an arms freeze and the interventions in Haiti and Somalia. But the "role of military force" remained substantial in American intervention in Central America and the Middle East. Since the Gulf intervention was largely practical rather than idealistic (protecting oil rights while ignoring genocide), Klingberg's predictions concerning actual policies, and public opinion, are yet to be confirmed.

The United States began a new extroversion phase sometime during the late 1980s. The current swing toward extroversion may be less pronounced than earlier ones. Just as U.S. shifts toward introversion have occurred at a higher level of U.S. foreign activity in this century, U.S. extroversion may begin to decrease in the face of growing pragmatism and wariness of long-term commitments abroad. The pattern of mood swings should continue, but each shift may be less pronounced as the United States' ability to intervene in world affairs becomes more constrained by resources and public sentiment. The emergence of the United States as a superpower after World War II precluded its return to a true isolationist policy. Increasing internal and external constraints, not long after similar pressures contributed to the decline of the Soviet Union, leaves the only superpower less able to afford the same level of involvement in foreign affairs. Yet the United States eschews leadership in international affairs at its and the world's peril.

Conclusion: Understanding the Cycles

Connecting strands of public opinion regarding U.S. foreign policy in the twentieth century, this chapter identifies cycles of opinion representing introversion (or noninternationalism) and extroversion (or internationalism). The preferences of the American public have alternated between these two sentiments because of the current political and economic climate, national interests, and ethical thinking. Introversions have lasted about twenty-one years, shorter than the extroversions of about twenty-seven years. The events corresponding to each period of introversion and extroversion lead to the question of to what extent public opinion is influencing foreign policy, or policy influencing opinion.

Throughout the twentieth century, American presidents have been generally more willing than the public to undertake foreign involvement. When public opinion accorded with the president, the period was one of extroversion, as during the Eisenhower and Kennedy presidencies. However, when public opinion went against the president's preference for interventionism, policy was limited. This was the case after World War II and during the Reagan administration. Public opinion places constraints on the president's ability to implement foreign policy objectives.

When the twentieth century opened, America was a third of the way through a period of extroversion beginning with the Spanish American War in 1898 and ending after entry into World War I in 1917. The ensuing period of introversion was intensified by the Great Depression. This extreme isolationist policy, however, contributed to catastrophe and to an immediate shift into extroversion. The bombing of Pearl Harbor was an event so large in the American psyche that it forever changed the public's perception of foreign policy. Suddenly, U.S. policy abroad was seen as having a tangible effect on American lives, and the public wanted foreign policy to be active rather than reactive.

With this increased interest in foreign policy, debates regarding the type of role the United States should play intensified as that mid-century period of extroversion wore on. The United Nations was born during these years, as was NATO and the Cold War. The United States had become undeniably the world's only superpower, and it needed to develop clear policies to promote its goals. It needed an adversary, and the Soviet Union fit that role. For a generation the Cold War framed discussions of foreign policy questions in black-and-white terms that the public could both understand and evaluate. The Korean War was supported by a majority of Americans when they were reminded that the aims of U.S. involvement included halting communist expansion. Predictably, public support decreased as casualties increased, but the broader trend toward internationalism lasted through the Eisenhower and Kennedy administrations.

Since World War II there has been general support for U.S. involvement abroad, but there have been divisions over what role the United States should since play. Vietnam had a particularly strong effect on the consciousness of both the public and leaders, but the fear of "another Vietnam" did not simply drive Americans into neoisolationism. Instead, it increased the consciousness of divisions and contradictions that were long present in the public. It made the question of what role the United States should assume in foreign affairs a more sensitive one and contributed to the widening gaps between the foreign policy objectives of the general public, military leaders, and government policymakers. While government may initiate policy, the people set the parameters within which the political leadership may act, and the continuation of any policy is dependent upon public reaction.

It is unclear to what extent cycles in policy can be traced to public opinion. Several recent direct military interventions have begun and ended too quickly for the public to form a clear idea of what is transpiring or to offer much more than a rallying of opinion. In October 1994, 65 percent of adult Americans favored an active role for the United States in international affairs, yet preferred on the whole "pragmatic internationalism" (Rielly, 1995, p. 6). Yet when asked to name the most pressing foreign policy issues, 3 percent or fewer mentioned Bosnia, Somalia, or Rwanda. General opinion did not tally very closely with the opinion of "policy leaders": 60 percent of leaders rated "defending our allies' security" as being a "very important" foreign policy objective, compared with 41 percent of the general public (p. 15). Similar results appeared in 1998 when both the public and leaders supported "guarded engagement" (Rielly, 1999). Both groups, however, are generally more self-interested: a recent report found that "support for many of the more altruistic goals among both the public and leaders has declined to the lowest level in two decades" (Rielly, 1995, pp. 15–16).

In short, attitudes toward U.S. involvement in the world have long demonstrated support, with caveats, for an active U.S. role in world affairs. The 1940s to mid-1960s were largely a period of extroversive involvement in the world. From the height of Vietnam to the end of the Reagan years, Americans were less willing to engage the world. By the start of the Bush administration the United States moved more cautiously into intervention ranging from Panama to the war in Bosnia as the public became more internationalist. The Clinton administration appeared to continue and perhaps expand the cautiously activist trend with a guarded base of public support.

These three eras—post–World War II, post-Vietnam, and the post–Cold War world—do not evoke the simple image of American beliefs vacillating predictably from one side to another. Perhaps there has been a movement toward a new consensus coming out of the confusion of the post–Cold War era. As opinion informs policy, future foreign policy decisions should reflect this movement away from either predominant introversion or extroversion toward a steady, "cautiously active" role.

The ensuing four case studies represent both the general and specific roles of public opinion in foreign intervention policy from Vietnam to Bosnia. Each case of particular policies and opinion rests in the context of general interventionist or noninterventionist opinion. Because of its central place in the postwar era, the Vietnam conflict sets the stage for the wider analysis of the public's role in foreign affairs across the last generation of the twentieth century.

Appendix: Table 3.10 ACTIVE PART IN WORLD AFFAIRS, 1942–99

"Do you think it would be best for the future of this country if we take an active part in world affairs, or if we stay out of world affairs?"

Year	Month	Source	Active Part	Stay Out	Don't Know	Sample Size
1942	February	Gallup	70%	21%	8%	1500*
1943	January	Gallup	76	14	10	1500**
1944	April	Gallup	73	18	9	1500***
1945	October	Gallup	71	19	10	1500
1946	February	Gallup	72	22	6	1500
1946	November	Gallup	78	19	4	1500
1947	March	NORC	68	25	7	532
1947	June	NORC	66	26	8	1273
1947	October	Gallup	65	26	9	1500
1948	March	NORC	70	24	7	1289
1948	June	NORC	70	23	7	1294
1949	September	NORC	67	25	7	1272
1950	January	NORC	63	24	9	1284
1950	May	Gallup	63	23	14	1343
1950	November	Gallup	69	22	9	1352
1950	December	NORC	66	25	9	1252
1952	October	NORC	68	23	9	1291
1953	February	NORC	73	21	5	1291
1953	September	NORC	71	21	8	1262
1954	April	NORC	69	25	6	1207
1955	March	NORC	72	21	7	1225
1956	November	NORC	71	25	4	1287
1965	June	NORC	79	16	5	1469
1973	February	NORC	66	31	3	1504
1974	December	Harris	67	23	10	1513
1975	February	NORC/GSS	61	30	4	1490
1976	February	NORC/GSS	63	32	5	1499
1978	February	NORC/GSS	64	32	4	1532
1978	November	CCFR	59	29	12	1546
1980	November	ABC/CHA	64	33	3	1199
1982	February	NORC/GSS	61	34	5	1506
1982	Oct./Nov.	CCFR	54	35	12	1547

Table 3.10 (CONTINUED)

Year	Month	Source	Active Part	Stay Out	Don't Know	Sample Size
1983	February	NORC/GSS	65	31	4	1599
1985	February	NORC/GSS	70	27	2	1534
1986	January	MOR	67	28	5	1500
1986	February	NORC/GSS	65	32	4	1470
1986	April	SIRC	69	25	6	2427
1986	October	CCFR	64	27	9	1585
1988	February	NORC/GSS	65	32	4	1481
1989	February	NORC/GSS	68	28	4	1537
1990	February	NORC/GSS	69	27	4	1372
1990	Oct/Nov	CCFR	62	28	10	1662
1991	February	NORC/GSS	73	24	2	1517
1991	March	WP	79	15	6	1015
1991	September	Gallup	71	23	6	1005
1993	February	NORC/GSS	67	28	3	1606
1994	January	NORC/GSS	65	32	4	2992
1994	October	CCFR/GAL	65	29	6	1492
1995	November	PSRA	57	37	6	1514
1996	June	PIPA	60	35	6	1227
1996	September	PIPA	66	28	6	1214
1998	October	CCFR	61	28	11	1507
1999	April	Gallup	69	28	3	1014
1999	June	Gallup	61	34	5	1022

Question wordings, 1942–44: *Which of these two things do you think the United States should try to do when the war is over: stay out of world affairs as much as we can, or take an active part in world affairs? **After the war, do you think the United States should stay out of world affairs, or take an active part in world affairs? ***Do you agree with those people who think the United States should take an active part in world affairs, or with those who think we should stay out of world affairs?

Sources: National Opinion Research Center (NORC); NORC/General Social Survey (GSS), 1973–98; Chicago Council on Foreign Relations (CCFR); December 1974 (Harris); CCFR/Gallup: November 1978, October 1982, October 1986, October 1990, October 1994, October 1998; Strategic Information Research Corporation (SIRC), April 1986; Program in International Policy Attitudes (PIPA): June and September 1996; ABC News, March 1991; Gallup Polls, 1942–50, 1991, 1999; Market Opinion Research (MOR), January 1986; Washington Post (WP), March, 1991; Princeton Survey Research Associates (PSRA), November, 1995, as checked by the Roper POLL system.

II

THE VIETNAM CASE
AN END TO INTERVENTIONISM?

LIKE ITS COMPANIONS FOR LATER INTERVENTIONS, THE VIETNAM CASE STUDY EXAM-
ines the relationship of public opinion to U.S. intervention policy. The Vietnam case
in chapters 4 through 6 explores and analyses the links between public opinion,
protest, and the war policies of the Johnson and Nixon administrations. It focuses
on four benchmark decision periods, two for each administration. For Lyndon Johnson these include the decisions to escalate after the Gulf of Tonkin incident in August 1964 and the decision following the Tet offensive in January 1968 to reduce the
Pentagon-suggested troop increase, coupled with Johnson's decision to step down
and cut back the bombing. For Richard Nixon they include the decision to abort the
planned "Duck Hook" decisive strike against North Vietnam in the fall of 1969, and
the decision to escalate and widen the war by invading Cambodia in the spring of
1970. There is also a short discussion of the period of coercive diplomacy in 1972–73.

The decision-makers in the Johnson administration were President Lyndon B.
Johnson, Secretary of State Dean Rusk, and Secretaries of Defense Robert McNamara and Clark Clifford. In the Nixon administration they were President Richard M.
Nixon, National Security Adviser and Secretary of State Henry Kissinger, and Secretary of Defense Melvin Laird.

Chapters 4 through 6 focus on the historical records and the impact of public opinion in foreign policy, using polling data, memoirs, journals, speeches, press statements, declassified documents, and the recollections of policymakers, particularly
when possible in personal interviews. Chapter 4 reviews the key historical events of
the Vietnam War, including public opinion and government policy during the conflict.
Chapter 5 and 6 evaluate the impact of public opinion on foreign policy by concentrating on the statements of major Vietnam-era decision-makers in the Johnson and
Nixon administrations. These recollections include the memoirs of presidents Johnson and Nixon, Secretaries of State Rusk and Kissinger, and Secretaries of Defense
McNamara and Clifford, and interviews with Secretaries Rusk, McNamara, Clifford,
and Laird. When available, there is a brief discussion of the decision-makers' political philosophy in conjunction with possible links to their decision-making. The case
examines evidence of the respective policymaker's awareness of public opinion as
well as of protest for how these did or did not translate into policy. These explorations

tend to support the theory that respective policymakers limited or changed their pre-ferred decisions as an outcome of pressures they felt from the public.

This examination of the relationship between public opinion, protest, and U.S. policy during the Vietnam War has three purposes. First, it contributes to the histori-cal and theoretical understandings of the opinion-policy relationship during the Viet-nam era. Second, it provides a comparison for the analysis of similar dynamics dur-ing subsequent interventions. Third, it identifies how the nexus between public opinion and policy that developed due to Vietnam affected corresponding opinion-policy relations during the later military interventions.

The discussion of each administration concludes with final thoughts on the role the public played in the initiation and then carrying out of Vietnam policies. Then, a general conclusion for the chapters provides the lessons from the Vietnam case and introduces their effect on the decision-making process of the subsequent intervention in Nicaragua.

CHAPTER 4

The Vietnam War: History, Policies, Public Opinion, and Protest

INTRODUCTION

This chapter reviews the major events and policies that constituted U.S military intervention in Vietnam during four benchmark periods from 1964 to 1973 in the Johnson and the Nixon administrations. Two earlier series of decisions prepared the ground for the events and policy decisions covered in this chapter. The first were the decisions of the Truman and Eisenhower administrations to help the French recolonize Vietnam in the aftermath of World War II. These were followed by Eisenhower's decision to replace the French forces after they lost the nine-year war and to bypass the Geneva Convention of 1954 by blocking the 1956 elections in Vietnam. The benchmarks here include Johnson's decision to use the Tonkin Gulf Resolution as authorization for taking steps toward a full-scale American military operation in Vietnam beginning in 1965, and Johnson's March 1968 decision to deescalate the war and retreat from politics in the wake of the Tet offensive. They also include Nixon's decision to abandon the planned "Duck Hook" major offensive against North Vietnam in the fall of 1969 and his decision to widen the war in 1970 by invading Cambodia, in concert with withdrawal of troops, in apparent conflict with the policy of "Vietnamization" and negotiations.

The following two chapters evaluate the four benchmark decisions in conjunction with public support or opposition expressed both in polls and the protest movement on campuses and in the nation's streets and squares. The aim of the analysis is to establish the effect that the preferences of the American public exercised on respective decision-making.

BACKGROUND TO THE VIETNAM WAR

With roots in American intelligence efforts against the Japanese during World War II, U.S. involvement in fighting Vietnamese insurgents began with U.S. financial support to the French colonial regime in the late 1940s and early 1950s. After the North Vietnamese defeated the French in the battle of Dien Bien Phu in 1954, the Eisenhower administration took over the prosecution of the war. The Geneva Conference of 1954 divided the country "temporarily" into North and South. Nationalist Communist Ho Chi Minh led the North; Nationalist anticommunist Ngo Dinh Diem led the South. There was supposed to be an election in 1956 to reunite North and South Vietnam, but with American support Diem blocked it for fear that the communists, led by Ho, would win (Herring, 1986, p. 55). In 1959, the war began in earnest as North Vietnam sent troops south; in 1960 the peasant-based National Liberation Front ("Vietcong") was created in the South (Herring, 1986, p. 68).

The United States feared that if South Vietnam were "lost" to communism as "Red China" had been in 1949, the rest of Asia would follow, in Eisenhower's words, like a row of dominoes. American leaders variously saw the North Vietnamese as puppets of Chinese or Russian attempts to expand communism. The Vietnam War was thus part of U.S. Cold War containment strategy, allied with the hope of "nation building" in Southeast Asia (Herring, 1986, p. 67). The stated U.S. goal was to help secure an independent, noncommunist South Vietnam (Herring, 1986, p. 116). The 1945 Vietnamese declaration of independence was, in fact, modeled on the American version.

Though U.S. casualties began in the late 1950s, U.S. involvement in Vietnam only became visible to the American public in the 1960s when U.S. support for the government of South Vietnam grew into significant economic and military aid against the attacks of North Vietnam and the National Liberation Front (NLF). Like the nationalist Chinese under Chiang Kai-shek, the rulers of the South were entrenched in a system they could not reform. At that point, U.S. policy was in fact focused on the conflict in nearby Laos, which was settled in 1962 by negotiations to form a neutralist, coalition government. U.S. support for the Diem government of South Vietnam increased significantly despite limited popular support here or there as the communist insurgency escalated. At the start of the 1960s, Kennedy administration involvement grew from three thousand to sixteen thousand U.S. troops (Mueller, 1973, p. 28), called military advisers. The number of casualties rose to 2,500 during the period when there were about 400 U.S. deaths (Mueller, 1973, p. 37).

THE BUDDHIST CRISIS AND ASSASSINATION OF DIEM, 1963

The turmoil in the South Vietnamese government, including the Buddhist crisis and assassination of Diem in 1963, brought the first sustained U.S. focus on the problem. The rulers of the South, particularly Diem, a Catholic nationalist in a largely Buddhist nation, were entrenched in an unreformable system of rule. Dissatisfaction with Diem grew among many South Vietnam groups, particularly the Buddhists. On June 16, 1963, a Buddhist monk publicly burned himself to death in downtown Saigon in protest over Diem's religious and political persecution. As a result, over the next several months, demonstrations raged throughout Vietnam. In October 1963, the Kennedy government dissociated itself from Diem, and, fed up with Diem's inability to reform, approved a coup of South Vietnam generals that overthrew the Diem regime and killed Diem (Fitzgerald, 1972, p. 74). Some of Kennedy's former aides have speculated that Kennedy would have reduced America's role in Vietnam after the 1964 U.S. presidential election, but his assassination in November 1963 leaves this unresolved (O'Donnell and Powers, 1972).

Secretary of Defense Robert McNamara supported the new president when John-son took office in November 1963. In a March 2, 1964, conversation, Johnson sought McNamara's advice on bringing the gravity of the Vietnam issue to the American public. Knowledgeable about the "poor morale" and "disunity" on the ground in South Vietnam, McNamara advised the president "to say as little as possible" to the American people about the involvement in Vietnam (Beschloss, 1997, p. 258). His re-peated visits to South Vietnam made him, on the one hand, apprehensive about the deteriorating conditions and, on the other hand, more convinced that escalation was necessary. He recommended to Johnson to "stay as long as it takes . . . to win the battle against communist insurgents" (Karnow, 1983, p. 341).

BENCHMARK 1: JOHNSON'S ESCALATION: THE GULF OF TONKIN RESOLUTION

After Kennedy's assassination, a month after Diem's, and Lyndon Johnson's land-slide election in November 1964 over Barry Goldwater, the United States escalated its involvement in Vietnam. Despite portraying Goldwater as pro-war and promising not to send American "boys" to fight in Southeast Asia, Johnson acted in response to increased gains by the Communist insurgency and deterioration of the South Viet-namese war effort. Johnson feared that the loss of South Vietnam would lead to Com-munist takeovers elsewhere in Asia. After alleged North Vietnam attacks on the U.S. ships *USS Maddox* and *USS Turner Joy* in early August 1964, Congress authorized LBJ to retaliate with the almost unanimous "Gulf of Tonkin Resolution" (House: 416–0, Senate: 88–2). Johnson's popularity soared (Zaroulis and Sullivan, 1984, p. 22; Herring, 1986, p. 123).[1]

In February 1965, the United States introduced U.S. warplanes for sustained bombing of North Vietnam, and then in March sent U.S. combat troops to defend the airfields. An attack on the U.S. troop garrison at Pleiku served as justification for the "Rolling Thunder" bombing campaign against the North. In the words of Johnson's national security adviser McGeorge Bundy, "Pleikus are like street cars." Since at-tacks occur frequently, another would have served equally well as a justification for initiating the bombing (Herring, 1986, p. 129).

From 1964 to the middle of 1965, the public awareness of U.S. policy in Vietnam was low, but in general opinion was supportive of U.S. efforts to provide assistance to the South Vietnamese government. Feeling that U.S. involvement was not a mis-take (61 percent in August 1965; Mueller, 1973, p. 54), while generally approving of help to the South Vietnamese in fighting against Communist overthrow, Americans supported military aid. "The initial reaction was to support the President and the of-ficial policy of intervention" (Mueller 1973, pp. 81–83). Yet pressure from conserva-tives to escalate and a deteriorating military situation contributed to the decision to bomb the North and send U.S. combat troops (Berman, 1982; Burke and Greenstein, 1989; Galbraith, 12/9/99).

---

[1]The first attack on August 1 occurred. The second, supposedly on August 4, did not (Herring, 1986, pp. 119–20).

With the South Vietnamese efforts and American bombing failing to halt the insurgency, by mid-1965 Johnson decided to "Americanize" the war and thus ordered larger numbers of U.S. combat troops to Vietnam. Most of Johnson's advisers, including Secretary of State Dean Rusk and Secretary of Defense Robert McNamara, supported the escalation plans in meetings in May 1965. The domino theory and the need to contain communism in Vietnam were issues viewed with gravity by most policymakers in the Johnson administration. Only Undersecretary of State George Ball opposed the war as an unworthy and losing effort (Ball, interview 1/20/94; Rusk, 9/1/90; McNamara, 1995).

By spring of 1965, "teach-ins" at colleges and universities and demonstrations began the protest campaign against the war. Beginning with roughly 25,000 troops at the start of 1965, with growing draft calls, U.S. forces grew to over 175,000 by the end of the year (Small, 1988, Table 1). By the end of 1966, nearly 400,000 U.S. troops were in South Vietnam; the United States experienced almost 5,000 battle deaths that year (Small, 1988, Table 1). By the end of 1967 there were more than 485,000 U.S. troops and an additional 10,000 battle deaths (Small, 1988, p. 95; Mueller, 1973, p. 28). The "Vietnam Summer" protests and October "March on the Pentagon" increased the administration's awareness of public opposition. The U.S. commitment grew to over half a million U.S. soldiers by 1968. Relying on statistical evidence in "body counts," McNamara asserted to the public and Congress that the United States was winning the war, while privately he harbored doubts that the war was winnable. Starting with 1965, he began to advocate privately the need to start negotiations (McNamara, 1995). He also recognized the Saigon government lacked public support.

Beginning with the first bombing of the North in early 1965 and the buildup of U.S. combat troops after July, the public rallied around the president. In mid-1965 through spring 1966, a "permissive majority" of over 50 percent of Americans generally supported U.S. policy, though support began dropping thereafter (Lunch and Sperlich, 1979, p. 29). Escalation continued through mid-1965 when protest began in earnest. In April, fifteen thousand demonstrated in Washington, D.C., while teachers and professors held the first of many teach-ins at colleges and universities to arouse opposition to the bombing. Although antiescalation sentiment was building, most Americans gave the president's buildup a chance to work. At the start of U.S. involvement in Vietnam, Congress as a whole supported war funding (Gibbons, 1987). By 1966, however, hearings of the Senate Foreign Relations Committee chaired by Senator William Fulbright (D-AR) began to legitimize dissent, particularly among demonstrators and the elite.

Most Americans supported the president from mid-1966 to late 1967 while U.S. troops were increasing to over a half million (Mueller, 1973, pp. 54–55). But the year 1967 marked increasing public protest, with major demonstrations taking place in New York, San Francisco, and other cities. In November 1967, the plurality of 48 percent felt the best policy was to "step up present efforts." A third (34 percent) wanted to "start negotiations, decrease the fighting," 10 percent wanted to "withdraw completely," but 60 percent "would favor United Nations solution even if it includes United States withdrawal" (Mueller, 1973, p. 90). Even though most Americans preferred stronger escalation, approval of the president's policy dropped below 50 percent by July 1967 (Mueller, 1973, p. 54). Aware of the national climate of opinion,

Johnson admitted to his advisers on October 23, 1967: "We've almost lost the war in the last two months in the court of public opinion. . . . We've got to do something about public opinion" (Dallek, 1998, p. 485).

BENCHMARK 2: REEVALUATION AND DEESCALATION: THE TET OFFENSIVE, 1968

Throughout 1967, despite consistent setbacks, the U.S. and South Vietnam governments claimed to the U.S. public that they were winning the war. There was a "light at the end of the tunnel." In late 1967, a group of senior advisers, the "Wise Men," stated that the United States was winning and encouraged further prosecution of the war. In early 1968, however, the Communist Tet offensive during a New Year's cease-fire shattered these claims, along with the credibility of the Johnson administration. The stunning attack featured in the U.S. media, particularly TV, included a simultaneous Communist strike on thirty-six provincial capitals and threatened the U.S. embassy in Saigon. The attacks of the supposedly losing Communists shocked South Vietnam, the United States, and the world. How, asked CBS anchorman Walter Cronkite, could they accomplish this? "I thought we were winning the war" (Herring, 1986, p. 198).

During Tet, three events came to symbolize the war. First, the Saigon chief of police shot a Vietcong suspect before TV cameras. Second, an army lieutenant justified the bombing of Ben Tre by saying, "We had to destroy the town to save it" (Herring, 1986, p. 192). Third, word leaked out in November 1969 that two hundred Vietnamese civilians had been killed at My Lai in a massacre in March 1968 (Mueller, 1973, p. 32).

By effectively repelling the Communist offensive, the United States and South Vietnam forces actually won the battles militarily. But the widespread nature of the surprise attack of a supposedly losing enemy appeared to the U.S. public as a Communist victory. After Tet, public support for the war dropped to 41 percent (Mueller, 1973, p. 55), as protests continued. Even the Wise Men, who the previous fall had advocated continuing the fighting, advised the president to wind down the war (Halberstam, 1972; Issacson, 1997). Johnson's announcement that he would not run again featured a promise to halt the bombing beyond the twenty-first parallel and begin to deescalate the war. As late as the end of Tet, the majority (58 percent) of Americans considered themselves hawks, who wanted to "step up military efforts in Vietnam"; by March, only 41 percent felt hawkish (Mueller, 1973, p. 107).

By fall 1968, presidential approval fell to a wartime low of about 35 percent. Preferences for escalation (34 percent) declined as the preference for ending the fighting increased (56 percent) (Mueller, 1973, p. 42). As "experience mounted steeply in terms of deaths, taxes, and soldiers not home for Christmas," opinion against the war crystallized (Converse and Schuman, 1970, p. 21). A discouraged Lyndon Johnson, almost defeated by antiwar candidate Senator Eugene McCarthy (D-MN) in the New Hampshire primary and challenged by Senator Robert F. Kennedy (D-NY), announced in a March 31, 1968, nationally televised speech that he would not seek reelection. He also announced cutting back the bombing and beginning negotiations with the North Vietnamese in the Paris peace talks. Two-thirds (64 percent) of the American people endorsed the president's decision (Dallek, 1998, p. 570).

BENCHMARK 3: NIXON'S WOULD-BE REESCALATION. DUCK HOOK, MORATORIUMS, AND POLICY OF VIETNAMIZATION

By the time of Johnson's announcement in March 1968, Republican candidate Richard Nixon had concluded that the war could not be won because the public had ceased to support it (Hodgson, 1976, p. 396). During the 1968 presidential campaign, Nixon hinted at a "secret plan" to end the war (Small, 1988). A poll taken on August 21 gave candidate Nixon a sixteen-point edge over the Democratic candidate, Vice President Hubert Humphrey (Dallek, 1998, p. 570). Major demonstrations against the war disrupted the Democratic convention in Chicago in August 1968, creating ill feelings toward the Democrats. In the aftermath of Humphrey's pledge to "stop the bombing of North Vietnam as an acceptable risk for peace" (Dallek, 1998, p. 579), Johnson had felt more inclined to support the Nixon bid rather than his own vice president: "When he [Nixon] gets the nomination, he may prove to be more responsible than the Democrats. He says he is for our position in Vietnam. . . . The GOP may be of more help to us than the Democrats in the next few months" (Dallek, 1998, p. 571). Johnson even admitted to Jim Rowe: "You know that Nixon is following my policies more closely than Humphrey" (Dallek, 1998, p. 580). To help Humphrey in the race, Johnson announced a full bombing halt a week before the election, but coming after Johnson's ambivalent support for the Humphrey campaign, the gesture did not adequately help. By a small margin, 43 to 42 percent, Nixon won the election.

The "plan" Nixon and his national security adviser Henry Kissinger ultimately devised, code named "Duck Hook," was to threaten massive retaliation by the end of the year if the North Vietnamese did not negotiate a settlement (Kissinger, 1979, p. 284). In June 1969, Nixon announced his decision to slowly bring American troops home through a program of "Vietnamizing" the war. With U.S. troops at a peak strength just below 550,000 soldiers, he announced a first withdrawal of 25,000 troops in June 1969. With public negotiations in Paris stalled, Nixon began secret talks with the North Vietnamese through Henry Kissinger. In September, Nixon announced withdrawal of 35,000 more soldiers, followed by another 50,000 at the end of the year (Small, 1988, Table 5).

Beginning in spring 1969, a group of antiwar protesters organized a series of moratoriums, which led to numerous demonstrations across the country. Because it was a grass-roots structure with a mainstream approach, the goals of nationwide campus and community demonstrations on October 14–15 and then protests in Washington on November 13–15 gained significant momentum (Zaroulis and Sullivan, 1985, p. 265). Millions of Americans across the nation peacefully observed the October Vietnam Moratorium Day (Zaroulis and Sullivan, 1985, p. 269). The November demonstration, led by the New Mobilization Committee [New Mobe], brought half a million increasingly middle-class demonstrators to Washington (Zaroulis and Sullivan, 1985, p. 286). Together these public calls to end the war forced Nixon to alter his plan to carry out the threatened Duck Hook attacks (Nixon, 1978, p. 499).

The "Silent Majority" Speech

By denigrating the "vocal minority" of protesters to the "silent majority" of "fellow Americans," Nixon's "Great Silent Majority" speech on November 3, 1969, increased public approval of both his handling of the war and of his policy of phased withdrawal, while diluting the impact of moratorium protests (Berkowitz, 1973; Kissinger, 1979; Nixon, 1978, p. 508; Page and Shapiro, 1983). After the speech, fully three-quarters (77 percent) of Americans approved of Nixon's handling of the war (Nixon, 1978, p. 507). A plurality of 39 percent in December 1969 agreed that the United States should withdraw troops but fight as long as needed to turn the war over to the South Vietnamese government (DeBenedetti, 1990, p. 259; Mueller, 1973, p. 74). A majority (55 percent) considered themselves doves, who wanted to "reduce our military effort in Vietnam" (Mueller, 1973, p. 107). Withdrawing all troops by the end of 1970, regardless of South Vietnamese capabilities, was the choice of 22 percent of the public. Only 11 percent wanted to "step up" the fighting. Opinion and policy both converged through Vietnamization of the war and diverged in escalated air and South Vietnamese ground attacks. Nixon continued the troop withdrawal of 150,000 in April 1970 while intensifying the bombing of North Vietnam, Cambodia, and Laos in his "war for peace" (Herring, 1986, p. 223). Recognition of mobilized public opinion and protest rather than of potential military ineffectiveness constrained the Nixon administration away from U.S. ground escalation to accelerated withdrawal. The Silent Majority speech, however, contributed to enough support to continue the war during the Nixon years (Nixon, 1978, p. 508). By the end of 1969, Nixon announced that a lottery would be established for draft calls, with the ultimate goal of an all-volunteer army by the early 1970s.

BENCHMARK 4: THE SPRING 1970 INVASION OF CAMBODIA

In late April 1970, less than two weeks after announcing the withdrawal of another 150,000 soldiers, Nixon once again escalated the war by sending American and South Vietnamese troops into Cambodia in a failed attempt to find the Communist headquarters (COSVN). U.S. university campuses exploded in protest and a student strike shut down hundreds of colleges. In early May, national guardsmen killed four students at an antiwar protest at Kent State University in Ohio. Under pressure, Nixon withdrew the troops ahead of schedule (Kissinger, 1998, p. 499). During reescalation in Cambodia in mid-1970, the majority of citizens (55 percent, Mueller, 1973, p. 201) approved of the president's actions, though they supported (58 percent) the withdrawal of U.S. troops (Mueller, 1973, p. 95). Presidential popularity, however, was fairly high (50 percent in 1970, Mueller, 1973, p. 201) for a president gradually withdrawing troops. Withdrawal remained the stated goal of the U.S. policy in Vietnam.

By the end of 1970, fewer than 340,000 U.S. troops remained in Vietnam (Mueller, 1973, p. 28), and yearly battle deaths stood at less than 4,000 (Small, 1988, Table 6). Increasing numbers of U.S. senators began to vote for the restriction of war funding (see Burstein and Freudenberg, 1978). These votes served both as a barometer of changing opinion and as a reminder of the ultimate power of Congress to limit funding and restrict the administration's policy. Nixon also reduced draft calls and announced plans to end conscription. In invading Cambodia, the administration acted in spite of anticipated negative public response, yet it accelerated withdrawal in the face of nationwide protest.[2] By September 1970, a majority (55 percent) of the U.S. public preferred withdrawal (Small, 1988, Table 6).

An increasing number of U.S. forces were withdrawn in 1971, so that by the end of the year only 166,000 U.S. troops remained. Nixon escalated the war briefly again in a February 1971 invasion into Laos. By the invasion, the majority (66 percent) of Americans favored a congressional requirement of withdrawal of U.S. troops by the end of 1971 (Mueller, 1973, p. 97). By early 1971, 72 percent favored a congressional requirement of withdrawal by the end of 1971, while 20 percent was opposed to this requirement (Mueller, 1973, p. 97). Spring demonstrations paralyzed Washington during the May Day protests of 1971. By May 1971, fully 61 percent of Americans felt sending troops to Vietnam had been a mistake (Mueller, 1973, p. 55). More Americans supported withdrawal and fewer supported the use of troops. The publication by *The New York Times* and *Washington Post* of the Pentagon Papers in June 1971 highlighted for the nation the failings of previous Vietnam policy. By year's end, only roughly 150,000 American troops remained in Vietnam, with yearly battle deaths down to fewer than 1,500 (Small, 1988, Table 7).

Coercive Diplomacy of 1972–73: Easter and Christmas Bombings of Hanoi

In the spring of 1972, Nixon increased pressure on the North through massive air strikes on Hanoi and the mining of Haiphong harbor in the so-called "Easter bombing." Just prior to the 1972 election with candidate George McGovern advocating peace, Adviser Henry Kissinger stated that "peace is at hand" (Kissinger, 1979, p. 1399). Nixon's last push for a settlement produced the infamous "Christmas bombing" of Hanoi, in December 1972. Just after this bombing and the mining of Haiphong harbor, less than a majority of the citizens (43 percent, Gallup and Harris) approved of the president's handling of the war. As with the Cambodia and Laos invasions, the decision-makers considered the Hanoi operations as part of the process of trying to relieve pressure on the South Vietnamese armies while withdrawing American forces. The massive U.S. bombing culminated in what Nixon called "peace with honor" in the January 1973 Paris Peace Agreement (for which Henry Kissinger

---

[2]Despite the prominence in the media of demonstrations by students, older and working class citizens were generally more opposed to the war than more youthful and affluent groups (Schuman, 1972). Those with lesser social standing, such as blacks and women, tended to be more highly opposed to the war but had a smaller impact as "minorities." In fact, because of the atypical character of protest, both the general public and policymakers perceived demonstrators as outside the mainstream and thus as less powerful threats. As long as older and more established groups were "silent," they could be ignored. But when these likely voters grew more opposed to the war and mobilized, policy leaders increasingly heeded their opinions.

and the North Vietnamese negotiator Le Duc Tho won the Nobel Prize). Three-quarters of Americans then approved of the president's handling of the war.[3]

These escalations, too, were followed by sporadic protests and declining public support. By 1972, the opposition dominated, and public opinion was consistent with the current U.S. policy of withdrawal. For the 1972–73 period of coercive diplomacy, the dropping levels of public support contributed to the strategy of rapidly trying to force the North Vietnamese to come to a negotiated settlement. Troop withdrawals and an end to the draft increased public approval of Nixon's handling of the war, while the 1972 bombing escalations on the North Vietnamese reignited some protest.

By 1973 there was an American consensus for withdrawal of U.S. troops, even when faced with the prospect of a Communist conquest of South Vietnam. After the cease-fire in January 1973, there was stronger American sentiment for maintaining full withdrawal, and almost no support for the reintroduction of American troops in response to North Vietnamese advances in 1974. The last U.S. ground troops had left South Vietnam in March 1973, when U.S. POWs were supposed to be released or ac-counted for. A coalition government was supposed to form in the South, but the war continued with diminishing U.S. financial support for the South Vietnamese govern-ment. The last acts of U.S. disengagement were symbolized by the image of a rescue helicopter flying off the top of the abandoned U.S. embassy in Saigon in April 1975 just before the North Vietnamese took over the South. Many Vietnamese fled by boat as the Communist regime tightened its grip on the entire country.

Though Nixon had promised help for the South if the North violated the truce, Watergate and decreasing congressional support hampered delivery of additional aid. Despite the North Vietnamese invasion of the south in early 1975, the post-Vietnam syndrome of war weariness among the American people and the Congress kept the United States from any further involvement in Vietnam (Bundy, 1998). Though Nixon's successor as president, Gerald Ford, and Henry Kissinger tried to provide additional aid to the beleaguered South Vietnamese, Congress refused.

Subsequent events, moreover, challenged both the domino and containment theories that underlay the war. While Laos and Cambodia also became communist, the rest of Asia remained capitalist. In fact, in an ironic twist in 1979, Vietnam and its former ally China went to war over Vietnamese incursion in Cambodia to put an end to the genocidal Khmer Rouge regime.

THE POST-VIETNAM SYNDROME

In large part, public opposition essentially forced the United States to end a decade of war and withdraw from Vietnam. Congressional votes to restrict U.S. aid had made continued funding of the South Vietnamese government impossible. In the words of the protesters, "No more Vietnams." This so-called "post-Vietnam syndrome" also made later interventions in Angola, Lebanon, and Central America problematic. U.S.

---

[3]On December 4, 1972, 59 percent approved of Nixon's handling of the war (ORC); on January 12, 1973, 43 percent did so; and on January 26, 1973, 75 percent approved (Gallup).

opinion began to echo anti-interventionist, if not isolationist, sentiments. The public's ultimate refusal to support an extension to the U.S. military action in Vietnam was a powerful reminder to policymakers and the military that public support was in the end decisive in determining the duration of military interventionist foreign policy (Weinberger, 1990).

CONCLUSION

In general, Americans supported U.S. policy toward Vietnam at its initial stages. High early support, particularly by military-oriented conservatives, accompanied an aggressive U.S. war. Declining support and growing opposition in the polls and demonstrations accompanied deescalation and withdrawal. Though the high visibility of later protest suggested that opposition was the predominant sentiment and escalation the predominant policy, in fact most Americans supported U.S. policy of early escalation. Only later did the majority of the U.S. public prefer to deescalate and withdraw. The decline in public support more than the deteriorating military situation pushed the Johnson policy in 1968, after four years of Americanized war, in the direction of negotiations and deescalation.

In 1969 recognition of mobilized public opinion and expanding protest constrained the Nixon administration away from escalation toward continued withdrawal. For the Cambodia invasion, the administration acted initially in the face of the potential negative responses, and yet the nationwide protests forced an accelerated withdrawal. For the 1972–73 period of coercive diplomacy, the dropping levels of public support contributed to a strategy of trying quickly to force the North Vietnamese to come to a negotiated settlement. The troop withdrawals and the ending of the draft responded to the decline of public approval. The increased bombing on the North Vietnamese accelerated U.S. progress in the Paris negotiations and indirectly slowed the rate of decline in American public opinion. With the antiwar movement largely reduced after the Cambodia invasion, the threat of demonstrations could only weakly limit administration options. The administration could then undertake the intensified bombings in 1972–73 that they had planned as "Duck Hook" but had to abandon in the face of moratorium protests in fall 1969.

Chapters 5 and 6 examine in greater detail exactly how aware each Vietnam War policymaker in the Johnson and Nixon administrations, respectively, was of public opinion and protest and how he reflected them in his decision-making. Chapter 5 on the Johnson administration begins the exploration of how public opinion and protest affected U.S. Vietnam policy.

CHAPTER 5

Vietnam I: Public Opinion and Protest's Influence on Lyndon Johnson's War

INTRODUCTION

The American military intervention in Vietnam, as conducted by the Johnson and Nixon administrations, took a decade to be brought to an unhappy conclusion. The reasons for this length are many, but in terms of public opinion's influence, the American public's patriotism during most of this period was stronger than its aversion for war or its ability to oppose effectively the government in matters of foreign policy. The two administrations in their turn, sensitive to signs of public disapproval and protest, were also deeply involved in a campaign of rallying the public behind the anticommunist cause and the imperative of an American victory. Anything short of that, the two administrations held, would have severe consequences for world peace and U.S. credibility. Yet despite this intense campaign, President Johnson's decision not to run for office in 1968 was tied to the loss of support he had suffered with the American people. The American public seemed ready to forego victory and bring the troops home.

Nixon's Silent Majority speech and Vietnamization policy, however, bought some additional time for the new administration. Public opinion showed slight majorities for the president's handling of the war. After four more years, U.S. participation in the war had to end because the public had ceased to support it. A close look at the four benchmark decision periods of the Johnson and Nixon administrations sheds light on the extent to which the nature of these decisions was affected during the course of the war by perceptions various policymakers had about the public's support or opposition to the war.

This chapter focuses on the influence of public opinion at two of the four benchmark periods in the Vietnam War: Lyndon Johnson's decisions to begin escalation after the Gulf of Tonkin incident in August 1964 and to initiate deescalation after the Tet offensive in January 1968. The chapter identifies the extent to which policymakers were following public opinion and protest—either voluntarily or by necessity—in setting Vietnam policy. The words of the policymakers themselves provide essential evidence of how that complex historical process actually worked.

THE WORDS OF THE DECISION-MAKERS

Establishing whether public opinion and protest influenced Vietnam-era policymakers begins in discovering the extent to which the principal decision-makers during the Vietnam War were, first, familiar with and, then, constrained by expressions of political attitudes. Public statements, on-the-record interviews, congressional and court testimony, archival documents, memoirs, and published writings provide a record of views of the principals about opinion and protest. Insights from elite interviewing those who actually made the decisions provides strong prima facie case for the influence of public opinion and protest on policy.

Decision-makers' statements about opinion and policy provide two types of insights.[1] First, the leaders' comments about poll results and demonstrations indicate that the officials were aware of public opinion polls and protest. Second, specific comments from memoirs and interviews with the policy elite indicate the relative influence of opinion on their policies.[2]

Most decision-makers during the Vietnam War believed that leaders should lead public opinion, and most tried to lead that opinion toward support for U.S. policies. Most leaders did not generally feel they should follow public opinion or that opposition was wise or principled. Admissions that public opposition constricted the U.S. role usually came in regretful tones that public attitudes were inhibiting the policy of defeating communism. The indications here that opinion affected policy are probably stronger because they were only begrudgingly admitted.

Memoirs or interviews with former Presidents Lyndon Johnson and Richard Nixon, Secretaries of State Dean Rusk and Henry Kissinger, and Secretaries of defense Robert McNamara and Clark Clifford show that these leaders thought public opinion was an important factor in decisions. They were aware of public attitudes of support and opposition across the war. Johnson, of course, was an inveterate poll watcher, at least when the public supported his policies. Nixon, too, was keenly aware of support from the "silent majority." Rusk, Clifford, McNamara, and Kissinger were similarly familiar with poll results and public influences on policymaking. McNamara and Clifford believed that the opposition was reasonable. In terms of overall support, public opinion was in favor of continued involvement in Vietnam in 1965.[3] After a peak of public support at 61 percent in August 1965 (Mueller, 1973, pp. 54–55), support began a slow decline throughout the remainder of American intervention. Finally, beginning

---

[1]Also, available comments reveal the philosophy of the decision-makers about what ought to be the impact of public opinion on policy. This does not mean that the policymakers created policy on the basis of their philosophies or public opinion, but it does suggest that some officials were aware of the normative importance of public opinion in a democracy.

[2]Lyndon Johnson (1971), Dean Rusk (1990), Richard Nixon (1978), Henry Kissinger (1979), Robert McNamara (1995), and Clark Clifford (1991) wrote memoirs. Rusk (9/1/89), McNamara (7/10/90), Clifford (8/13/90) and Laird (2/8/99) provided interviews for this book.

[3]Though generally consistent across the war, public opinion early on appeared to follow policy, whereas by the end of the war, it appeared to lead policy (Lunch and Sperlich, 1979, 32; Page and Shapiro, 1992).

in October 1967, shortly before Secretary McNamara's resignation, polls showed that more people regarded the war in Vietnam as a mistake than did not. Therefore, opposition in the polls was higher than support (Mueller, 1973, p. 89) from 1967 on, approval of presidential handling of the war declining steadily during the Johnson administration. But while it dropped too during the Nixon administration, it occasionally rose during various escalations of negotiations that were part of Nixon's "great silent majority" and "peace with honor" strategies.

PRESIDENT LYNDON B. JOHNSON

Benchmark 1: The Gulf of Tonkin Resolution

In dealing with Vietnam, Lyndon Johnson felt caught between two powerful currents of public opinion. He knew, on the one hand, that those in Washington seen as weak on communism paid a high price, and he vowed, on the other hand, that he would not be the first American president to lose a war. The quintessential politician obsessed with polls and the mood of the Congress, Johnson was keenly aware of public opinion and its potential constraining force on his Vietnam policy. During a cabinet meeting in May of 1964, McGeorge Bundy commented: "It's ninety percent of the people who don't want any part of this [a major war]." To which Johnson replied: "Did you see the poll this morning? Sixty-five percent of them don't know anything about it and of those that do, the majority think we are mishandling it. But they don't know what to do. . . . It's damn easy to get into a war, but it's gonna be awfully hard to ever extricate yourself if you get in" (Beschloss, 1997).[4]

On March 2, 1964, in a conversation with McGeorge Bundy Johnson says: "We haven't got any Congress that will go with us, we haven't got any mothers that will go with us in a war" (Beschloss, 1997, p. 267). This clear demonstration of Johnson's awareness of general public pressure shows Johnson caught between two tides of public opinion. On the one hand, the most vocal opinions then were coming from constituencies advocating escalation. On the other hand, Johnson anticipates potential public opposition to a deepening of the war effort. For Johnson, the debate in 1964 was not, as it would become, between withdrawal and escalation, but rather, how best to present a policy of escalation to the public. A draft resolution to justify escalation was being prepared for Congress as early as June 1964 (Barrett, 1994, pp. 50–54). Johnson and his advisers, however, concerned with reelection, were hesitant to enact this policy until they could rely on public support. Since his Republican opponent, Barry Goldwater, advocated escalation, Johnson chose to present himself as the peace candidate, promising the nation not to send U.S. "boys" to fight a Vietnamese war. Yet Johnson was sensitive to conservative pressures to escalate the war.

The Johnson administration anticipated that direct intervention in Vietnam to protect South Vietnamese government would not resonate with Congress or the public as

---

[4]Telephone conversation between Lyndon Johnson and Richard Russell, May 27, 1964, 10:55. Transcripts of these tapes in Beschloss (1997).

much as a call for self-defense against North Vietnamese aggression. Johnson him-self was skeptical of public awareness of the Vietnam intervention. In a telephone conversation with Richard Russell, Johnson expressed awareness about the public's degree of interest or knowledge about Vietnam: "I don't think people in the country know much about Vietnam, and I think they care a hell of a lot less" (Beschloss, 1997). Since he regarded the majority of the public as uninformed, Johnson saw him-self as the trustee of U.S. policy in Vietnam. This was strengthened by his realist po-litical philosophy, which encouraged a disregard for public opinion when consider-ing important national issues. Johnson was prepared to act despite public opinion: "I have the power, and I aim to use it" (Valenti, 1975, p. 5).

Nevertheless, Johnson was aware that the members of the public who were in-formed on Vietnam generally thought he was mishandling the intervention. With this consciousness of public opinion as a potential constraint on Vietnam policy, Johnson delayed escalation until it could be more positively presented to Congress and the public. This calculated policy shows that the administration was aware of public ap-proval as a factor to be courted and manipulated in an election year, but not a voice to be heeded. Public opinion diminished but did not end the administration's consid-eration of unilateral military escalation in Vietnam.

While public support for escalation was soft, except among conservatives, a direct attack by the North Vietnamese in the Gulf of Tonkin enabled the Johnson adminis-tration to escalate under the guise of self-defense. The attack on a patrol boat in early August 1964 provided the occasion. The Gulf of Tonkin Resolution, passed almost unanimously in August 1964, gave the president power to increase U.S. troops in Vietnam without additional congressional approval, and to legitimize the plans for es-calation. The first air attacks on North Vietnam in early 1965 were presented by the Johnson administration as reactive and defensive strikes, rather than as the product of months of planning. This displays the administration's attempt to galvanize popular support for the war while stemming the underlying dissent that Johnson saw in the polls. Again, Johnson recognized public opinion not as a factor that should impact policy, but rather as a force to sway.

Johnson's Awareness of Public Opinion After the Gulf of Tonkin Resolution

The period after the Gulf of Tonkin Resolution exhibited growing public dissatisfac-tion and protest over the war effort. Johnson noted this in his memoirs:

> From the first time our planes hit the first military target in North Vietnam early in February [1965], we were subjected to an increasingly heavy propaganda barrage from Hanoi, Peking, and Moscow. Every other communist capital joined in. The propaganda message was short and sharp: Stop the Bombing. Soon voices in non-Communist countries joined the chorus. . . . Before long, some American public figures began to repeat the theme." (Johnson, 1971, p. 132)

Johnson and his advisers were growing increasingly concerned about protest and its possible impact on pubic opinion. The Johnson administration consistently began regarding public opinion as an obstacle they needed to circumvent while secretly developing policy. Early public opposition to the war, therefore, had little impact on the direction of the Vietnam policy. Indeed, most polls in 1965 showed greater support of the Vietnam policies than disapproval (Dallek, 1998, p. 280). But Johnson was concerned that the support would not last long. In response to a poll in December 1965 that reported a 71-percent majority in favor of the war, Johnson remarked: "An overwhelming majority for an underwhelming period of time . . . wait and see" (Moyers, 1968, p. 659). Johnson was aware of the momentum that might gather against the war and was concerned about how to deal with it.

Impact of Public Opinion

Johnson wrote of the Gulf of Tonkin period that: "I was convinced that our retreat from this challenge would open the path to World War III" (Johnson, 1971, p. 148). With this motivation, he set out to curb public opposition and see the war through to victory. The focus of his efforts was in how to present his decision for a wider war to the country without indicating a major policy change to either Congress or the public (Dallek, 1998, p. 275). Johnson thought that he could garner support from the people "without having to be too provocative and warlike" (Johnson, 1971, p. 148). To stop the slide in public support, Johnson discussed peace in public while he escalated the war efforts in private.

During 1964, public opinion clearly limited Johnson's policy of escalation, yet not the direction of the policy. In the spring and summer of 1965, with most public opinion polls showing greater approval of the war than disapproval (Dallek, 1998; Mueller, 1973), Johnson authorized the use of ground forces with a planned increase of 150,000 troops by the end of the year. When the year was over, more than 180,000 Americans had been sent into service in Vietnam (Mueller, 1973, p. 28). Johnson wrote that: "My own assessment in 1965 and in 1968 (and today) was that abandoning our pledges and our commitment in Vietnam would generate more and worse controversy at home, not less" (Johnson, 1971, p. 422). But even as he believed this, he was aware of growing public unrest and opposition over his Vietnam policies. Johnson was often tuned in to multiple television sets to gauge the mood of the public and Congress (McNamara, 1995, p. 1), and thus would have been aware of the intensifying public demonstrations and draft-card burnings. He admitted to his advisers on October 23, 1967, that: "We've almost lost the war in the last two months in the court of public opinion. . . . We've got to do something about public opinion" (Dallek, 1998, p. 485). Johnson clearly regarded public opinion, not as a voice to be directly heeded, but rather as a constraint on his Vietnam policy. Though aware of the public disapproval, he expressed little doubt to his advisers that his policy would remain unaltered. In December 1967, Johnson stated in an interview with David Brinkley that: "I am not going to be the first American president to lose a war" (Dallek, 1998, p. 500). Through 1967, public opinion had neither altered Johnson's attitude on the Vietnam intervention nor affected the administration's ultimate goals. It had, however, set the limits within which the administration could act. Nevertheless, Johnson came to see that escalating the war much further in a quest for victory was untenable because of public opposition.

Benchmark 2: The Tet Offensive, 1968

Media reports of the North Vietnamese Tet offensive in early 1968 provoked a backlash of opposition in the United States and led to public calls for deescalation. In March 1968, 56 percent of the public approved a "government-led withdrawal" and 34 percent disapproved (Mueller, 1973, p. 90). Johnson was surprised by the negative impact of the Tet offensive on U.S. public opinion. He remarked that he "did not expect the enemy effort to have the impact on American thinking that it achieved" (Johnson, 1971, p. 384). He blamed both the media and members of Congress for portraying an allied military victory as a major U.S. setback: "The American people and even a number of officials in government, subjected to this daily barrage of bleakness and near panic, began to think that we must have suffered a defeat" (Johnson, 1971, p. 384). To his advisers he observed that "there has been a dramatic shift in public opinion . . . a lot of people are ready to surrender" (Barrett, 1994, p. 145). In response to this rise in public opposition, Johnson felt pressured to act. He instructed his advisers: "I want alternatives examined and . . . recommendations to reconcile the military, diplomatic, economic, congressional, and public opinion problems involved" (Barrett, 1993, p. 127).

Contrary to the shift in public opinion and the concern of Johnson's political advisers, the military advisers continued to recommend an escalation of the war effort after the Tet offensive. At the start of the debate over the reduction of the rate of troop increases, Johnson, encouraged by the reports of General William Westmoreland, observed that he felt generally confident about the situation in Vietnam (Johnson, 1971, p. 392). But he was also "deeply conscious of the criticism we were receiving from the press and from some vocal citizens" (Johnson, 1971, p. 398). Johnson was even concerned with the impact of media reports of the Tet offensive on his own inner circle. "If they [his advisers] had been so deeply influenced by the reports of the Tet offensive, what must the average citizen be thinking?" (Barrett, 1994, p. 145). In his memoirs, Johnson wrote that "I know some of my advisers were thinking of a peace move in terms of public opinion and political consequences" (Johnson, 1971, p. 413). At the end of his presidency he concluded: "I think [my grandchildren] will be proud of two things. What I did for the Negro and seeing it through in Vietnam for all of Asia. The Negro cost me 15 points in the polls and Vietnam cost me 20" (Mueller, 1973, p. 196; Wise, 1968, p. 27).

Impact of Public Opinion

Opinion polls after the Tet offensive showed a rapid drop in public approval of how Johnson was handling the war (Barrett, 1994, p. 113). Thus Johnson, at the recommendation of his advisers, considered a bombing halt and new negotiations to stem the erosion of public support. At the same time, Johnson was worried about the political consequences of scaling down the war effort if the results were detrimental to U.S. goals. "What would happen, I wondered, if we stopped the bombing and the North Vietnamese then launched a major offensive, overran Khe Sanh, and killed thousands of Americans and South Vietnamese? The American people would never forgive me" (Johnson, 1971, p. 408). This question reveals that public opinion not only figured in Johnson's decision-making but also established the boundaries within which he could act.

In March 1968, although Generals Westmoreland and Earle Wheeler recommended an increase in U.S. forces of between 205,000 and 400,000, Johnson approved only 45,000. While Johnson is ambiguous in his memoirs in describing the concerns that determined his decision to deescalate, he counts public opposition as one of four factors that led him to approve only modest troop increases in Vietnam. He acknowledged that "domestic public opinion continued to be discouraged as a result of the Tet offensive and the way events in Vietnam had been presented to the American people in newspapers and on television" (Johnson, 1971, p. 387). At a crucial breakfast meeting on February 28, 1968, Johnson and his advisers debated deescalation. One question on a memo on deescalation read: "What problems would we face with public opinion" (Johnson, 1971, p. 393). He denied, however, that public opinion was the principal motivation behind the bombing halt proposal of March 31.

Impact of Protest

Johnson wrote of this time period that his "biggest worry was not Vietnam itself; it was the divisiveness and pessimism at home" (Johnson, 1971, p. 422). He felt the protest that was contributing to the divisiveness had a negative impact on the war effort. On war protesters, Johnson wrote that he had no doubt that "this dissension prolonged the war, prevented a peaceful settlement on reasonable terms, encouraged our enemies, disheartened our friends—and weakened us as a nation" (Johnson, 1971, p. 530). In retrospect, Johnson was admitting that the war protesters constrained the level of intervention and prevented an escalation that might have won the war. The result, for Johnson, was a dishonorable defeat and a greater number of deaths. The drop in public support played an important role in his decision not to run for president in 1968. Of his withdrawal decision in March 1968, Johnson wrote that "the state of mind and morale on our domestic front was most important" (Johnson, 1971, p. 365).

Conclusion: Johnson

Although he had approved bombing attacks after the Gulf of Tonkin incident and increases in numbers of troops in Vietnam through 1968, Johnson admits that public opinion represented a limit on the rate of early escalation and later on the number of troops he could send. As it turned out, 549,500 troops (Mueller, 1973, p. 31) were short of the number needed to win. The sharp public outcry after the Tet offensive obviously restricted Johnson's policy. Convinced of the importance of winning the war in Vietnam, he was forced to appear conciliatory in order to soften public opposition and maintain sufficient support for the war effort. Johnson acted within the constraints set by public opinion and protest until it was impossible for his administration to advance escalation any further.

However, his withdrawal from politics did not translate into withdrawal from the war (Hodgson, 1976). After his March 31 televised resignation speech, Johnson continued to advocate involvement in Vietnam and the goal of winning the war. In the election of 1968, he approved of Nixon's hawkish stance on Vietnam, even threatening Democratic candidate Hubert Humphrey with reentering the race. Johnson was agitated by Humphrey's claim that stopping the bombing was "an acceptable risk for peace" (Dallek, 1998, p. 579). He later remarked that the speech had cost Humphrey the election, and that Nixon's position on Vietnam was closer to his own than was Humphrey's (Dallek, 1998, p. 571). Johnson believed that withdrawal from Vietnam would have greater public opinion repercussions than escalation. Nevertheless, he clearly experienced the constraining dimensions of public opinion and protest on the Vietnam issue.

Animated by a deep realist political philosophy coupled to a genuine belief that the world and the United States were threatened by the spread of communism in Vietnam, Johnson resorted to policies of unilateral military action against the country of Vietnam and against the broad cooperative internationalist preferences of the American public. During the four years of continuous escalation of the war, Johnson's awareness of public approval, disapproval, or protest remained keen. Negative public opinion, though, was in his view more of a force to be manipulated than to be heeded or listened to. He was not looking for how his preferred policy might be altered to become consistent with public sentiment. Rather he sought to answer how to bring the public to accept the policies that he and his cabinet deemed vital for the country.

Opposition opinion and protests, coupled with presidential ever decreasing approval rates after the Tet offensive, created the atmosphere in which Johnson could no longer escalate the war and had to forego seeking reelection in 1968. His proposal for a bombing halt and an opening to negotiations in Paris, as well as his decision not to seek reelection, brought Richard Nixon to the White House and four more years of war.

SECRETARY OF STATE DEAN RUSK

Johnson's secretary of state Dean Rusk recognized that in a democracy it is very difficult to sustain support for war over a long period of time. He tried not to factor public opinion into his decisions, but recognized that public opinion played a growing role in Vietnam policy (Rusk, 9/1/89, p. 8). While Rusk, along with other Johnson administration officials, initially worried about the hawkish public's response to the United States not intervening in or allowing the fall of South Vietnam, by early 1968 Rusk saw opposition opinion as generally a constraint on the administration's freedom of action in conducting the war.

The administration, Rusk noted in indicating awareness of public opinion, had "strong grass root support for Vietnam until the first half of 1968" (Rusk, 9/1/89, p. 1). What led to the evaporation of that support, said Rusk, was negative news reporting surrounding the Tet offensive. It fed a mounting sense among the public that no clear end to the war was in sight. One of Rusk's two main mistakes in the war was that he "overestimated the patience of the American people" (Rusk, 9/1/89, p. 6). In retrospect, he came to believe that an erosion of support for the U.S. commitment in Vietnam was inevitable, given the natural impatience Americans have about war (Rusk, 1990, p. 497). As assistant secretary of state for Far Eastern Affairs during the Korean War, Rusk had already witnessed the phenomenon of dwindling public support for an Asian land war and the debilitating effects that process had on the executive branch's policy flexibility. He would later say that he and other Johnson administration officials should have "expected" the erosion of public support for the Vietnam War since there had been "the same kind of war weariness at the end of the Korean War" (Rusk, 9/1/89, p. 12). By the time the Johnson administration left office in 1969 Rusk saw little chance of continuing to sustain support for the war "because I thought that, by that time, the American people at the grass roots had pretty well decided we ought to get out" (Rusk, 1990, p. 491). He was thus surprised that the Nixon administration tried to stay in Vietnam as long as it did.

Benchmark 1: Awareness and Impact of Public Opinion Before and After the Gulf of Tonkin Resolution

Although Rusk's stand on the necessity to help the government of South Vietnam was at all times firm, he thought the developments around the Gulf of Tonkin did not warrant an escalation of the American involvement. "I believed we should persevere with our policy of advising and assisting the South Vietnamese and playing for the breaks, rather than risk a major escalation if one could be avoided" (Rusk, 1990, p. 447). Whether the risk factor was thought of in terms of public opinion is not clear. Rusk mentions nowhere, at that point, fear that the American public might oppose a full-scale war in a far off country. His opposition to a sustained retaliatory bombing campaign in late 1964 and early 1965 had more to do with his belief that the war should be a Vietnamese war and that the U.S should only be assisting. He also believed at that time that strategically it made little sense to bomb the North in order to put down the grass-roots resistance in the South. Later on, after the operation Rolling Thunder had started, he began considering the risks and escalation worth taking.

The escalation had to be limited, however, to step by step. "We made a deliberate decision to keep the war as limited as possible and not build up a war fever in the United States. We didn't parade military units through big cities or have beautiful movie stars sell war bonds in factories as we had done during World War II" (Rusk, 1990, p. 456). In his mind, then, an escalation of the war would have electrified the country and, in a nuclear age, too much war exuberance would have been dangerous. He expressed concern about the gradual escalation in terms of fear of too much hawkish support rather than too little general public support. However, the most serious reason Rusk gave for the gradual escalation was fear of the Chinese and the Russians. Only when explaining the restraint the administration felt about using nuclear weapons or about a more aggressive bombing campaign against North Vietnam does Rusk suggest awareness of American opinion. "Our careful selection of bombing targets partially reflected a fear of Soviet and Chinese intervention, but it also reflected the basic humanitarian aspects of American character (Rusk, 1990, p. 458). As far as Rusk was concerned, pressure from the public, negative or positive, only minimally influenced the decisions to escalate and to do so gradually. Principle and fear of a wider war were predominant.

Benchmark 2: Impact of Public Opinion After Tet

The Tet offensive may have been a major military defeat for the Viet Cong and North Vietnamese, but it was also a calamitous political defeat for the United States. Publicly, Rusk joined other administration officials on television in stressing that the failed offensive was a setback for the enemy (Schandler, 1977, p. 84). Privately, however, he saw the event as a turning point that galvanized public opposition to the war and made life for Johnson administration officials infinitely more difficult. In addition, Rusk felt that the North Vietnamese recognized the negative psychological impact that Tet had in the United States and sought to take advantage of growing domestic opposition to the war (Schandler, 1977, p. 184). He believed that the decline in public support for the U.S. commitment in Vietnam affected administration policy on two decisions following Tet: the rejection of General Westmoreland's request for a troop increase in the wake of the Tet offensive and the decision to cut back on bombing and engage the North Vietnamese in negotiations during the spring of 1968.

Following Tet, Rusk supported more U.S. military bombing of North Vietnam (Clifford, 1991, p. 485; Schandler, 1977, p. 92), but he opposed Westmoreland's request for an additional 206,000 troops (Schandler, 1977, p. 183). Rusk did not participate in the Clifford task force that assessed the Westmoreland request, and as was the custom, he did not widely express his views on the matter either on paper or in meetings attended by officials other than Johnson. Rusk later said that he opposed the troop request mainly because he believed "we had enough force in Vietnam to do what was required" (Schandler, 1977, p. 183). Public opinion was not a decisive factor, but "something that had to be taken into account along with other factors" (Rusk, 9/1/89, p. 8). But Rusk believed that Johnson was clearly concerned about public opinion in evaluating the Westmoreland request. According to Rusk, LBJ "felt that there would be a negative response if he had met [Westmoreland's] request" (Rusk 9/1/89, p. 8). The response would be large enough to prevent him from doing it or force him to reverse the decision.

Though the influence of public opinion on Rusk's own views on the Westmoreland troop request is ambiguous, the connection he made between public opinion and a proposed bombing cutback in early 1968 is far clearer (Rusk, 1990, p. 480). In a March 5, 1968, memorandum to Johnson, Rusk supported a partial cutback of the bombing in Vietnam. He argued that the move would offset growing opposition to the war and that if Hanoi did not respond positively the administration would have increased public support with which to conduct the war (Schandler, 1977, pp. 186–87). Clark Clifford would remark later about Rusk's proposal that "his primary motive was clearly to buy time at home for the war effort by showing the American people that we had 'walked the last mile' for peace. . . ." But, "Rusk seemed to be making his proposal primarily as a public-relations move in order to justify an intensification of the war after its failure—the opposite direction I wanted to take" (Clifford, 1991 p. 497).

Rusk offers a different view in his own memoirs, saying that he found himself moving toward Clifford's views on the bombing in early 1968, not simply because of the defense secretary's persuasive argumentation, but also because of the "increasing evidence that Americans were losing heart in the war effort. . . . All my advice to Johnson during this period was based on my view that the American people were tiring of the war, and we needed to get some talks started with North Vietnam as an alternative to further escalation of the war" (Rusk, 1990, pp. 482–84). Rusk writes, however, that Johnson's decision not to run was largely due to concerns about his health, rather than due to loss of popularity (Rusk, 1990, p. 483). In short, the public's attitudes gradually affected Rusk's policy recommendations.

Impact of Protest

Rusk appears to have been only mildly affected by the rising protest over Vietnam. His discussion of awareness of both drew a distinction between public opinion and protest, which he saw as not "necessarily a measure of public opinion" (Rusk, 9/1/89, p. 10). Like most officials in the Johnson and Nixon administrations, Rusk was generally contemptuous of protesters. He commented later that they had "closed minds," were "a little dramatic," and were sometimes manipulated by other politicians. Nonetheless, despite his negative impression of campus activists, he does concede that they limited the Johnson administration's freedom of action by "sen[ding] a message to the authorities in Hanoi" and to a large extent strengthened the hands of the North Vietnamese (Rusk, 9/1/89, p. 11).

Conclusion: Rusk and Minimal Constraint

Not running for elective office, Secretary of State Rusk's concern for public opinion was less pronounced than President Johnson's. This might be the reason he believed that, until the spring of 1968, the administration had "strong grass root support for Vietnam" (Rusk, 9/1/89, p. 1) According to him, therefore, the 1964–68 Vietnam policies had been developed in harmony with the preferences of the American public, If the public had any. Rusk, like Johnson, knew that before the Tonkin Gulf Resolution the public had not focused on Southeast Asia. This allowed the administration to not focus on the public, either.

In retrospect though, Rusk regretted having overestimated the war patience of the American people. He also realized that the grass-roots support he had perceived had turned into war weariness (Rusk, 9/1/89, p. 6). Although he never said it directly, Rusk seemed to imply that the impatience of the American people affected the policies after the Tet offensive. But that any particular policy was diverted due to public pressure, Rusk only acknowledged weakly in his memoir or interviews.

SECRETARY OF DEFENSE ROBERT MCNAMARA

Like other members of the Kennedy and Johnson administrations, Robert McNamara's foreign policy was driven by the belief that an independent Vietnam was crucial to national and world security. He had a strong belief that the United States had a duty to contain communism throughout the globe. In 1961, McNamara and Rusk wrote to Kennedy that:

> the loss of South Vietnam to communism would not only destroy SEATO but would undermine the credibility of American commitments elsewhere. Further, loss of South Vietnam would stimulate bitter domestic controversies in the United States and would be seized upon by extreme elements to divide the country and to harass the administration. (New York Times Staff, 1971, p. 150)

McNamara and Rusk had concluded that, by ignoring its obligation to stop the spread of communism, the U.S. would be susceptible to domestic and international criticism. Public opposition to communism in Vietnam and throughout the world should have given McNamara and the Johnson administration a relatively free hand to escalate the war effort. However, awareness of potential congressional and public opposition led them and the other decision-makers to conceal their policymaking plans from the public. Throughout his term as secretary of defense, McNamara experienced the public's constraining effect on his decision-making.

After he came back from the March 1964 visit to South Vietnam, McNamara advised widening of the war. The atmosphere in Congress at the time was favorable. Most members of Congress were advocating stronger U.S. military intervention to stem the Communist insurgency. In an election year, Johnson and his administration were influenced, not only by the anticommunist rhetoric of Barry Goldwater, but also by more moderate politicians like Senator Richard Russell (D-GA), who urged the president in May 1964 to "get in or out." He advised Johnson that "it would be more consistent with the attitudes of the American people and their general reaction to go in, because they would understand it better" (Beschloss, 1998, p. 368). Nevertheless, anticipation of concern for subsequent public opposition led McNamara and Johnson to pursue a strategy between the two politically unacceptable "in or out" extremes. Sensitive to a possible public outcry, McNamara and Johnson continued the preparation for escalation of U.S. involvement in Vietnam covertly.

Benchmark 1: Public Opinion and the Gulf of Tonkin Resolution

In the spring of 1964, with Johnson concerned about gaining congressional approval for continued escalation, particularly during an election year, his advisers drafted a resolution for Congress that would give the president power to act in Vietnam without further congressional approval. McNamara advised the president to withhold the legislation until the timing for such a resolution was better. Worried that the resolution would not pass, McNamara noted that there was: "dissatisfaction in Congress with what we are now doing. A Congressional resolution before September is unlikely unless the enemy acts suddenly in the area. . . . A press campaign should be launched to avoid building up of public pressure for drastic action" (Glennon, 1992, p. 491–92). More explicitly, McNamara urged the president to "ask for a resolution only when the circumstances are such as to require action, and thereby, force Congressional action" (Glennon, 1992, p. 491). McNamara believed that Congress would not support a resolution unless the North Vietnamese were directly to attack American forces in the region. These statements demonstrate his awareness of potential opposition and his intention to circumvent it in order to achieve the administration's goals. Shortly after these discussions, North Vietnamese ships fired on the U.S. warship USS Maddox in the Gulf of Tonkin. True to McNamara's predictions, Congress quickly approved the "Tonkin Gulf Resolution" with overwhelming support from Congress (House 400–0/Senate 98–2) and the general public.

In June 1965, General Westmoreland proposed a virtual U.S. takeover of the war with a request for large-scale reinforcements of forty-four battalions. After a personal visit to Vietnam, McNamara confided to Johnson that the situation was "worse than a year ago" (Karnow, 1983, p. 425). He recognized the need for additional troops and urged the president to ask Congress for approval to call up U.S. military reserves. McNamara was aware that further escalation would not be possible without support in Congress and among the public. He suggested a bombing halt to give the impression that the United States was doing all it could to end the war. He suggested to President Johnson that "at the same time as we are taking steps to turn the tide in South Vietnam, we would make quiet moves through diplomatic channels . . . to cement support for U.S. policy by the U.S. public, allies and friends, and to keep international opposition at a manageable level" (New York Times Staff, 1971, p. 458). Here, McNamara acknowledged the need for public approval of the decision-making process and showed concern about the need for public support of escalation in Vietnam.

By the end of 1965, McNamara returned from another trip to Vietnam even more skeptical about the possibility of victory. He reported to Johnson that the troop reinforcements "will not guarantee success" (Schandler, 1997, p. 37). For the first time, McNamara suggested privately a compromise solution through negotiations as an alternative to escalation, which he anticipated would create serious repercussions on public attitudes. Therefore, he again suggested a bombing halt to prepare the public for escalating the war. According to McNamara, the purpose of this bombing halt would be to:

> lay a foundation in the mind of the American public and in world opinion for such an enlarged phase of the war. . . . I am seriously concerned about embarking on a markedly higher level of war in Vietnam without having tried, through a pause, to end the war or at least having made it clear to our people that we did our best to end it. (The Defense Department, 1971, p. 623)

For McNamara, concern for public support of escalation established a limit beyond which the administration could not act unless it could lead public opinion in its favor. Accordingly, from this point on McNamara made efforts to emphasize the measures that the government was taking to bring about peace. This stance demonstrates his awareness of potentially dwindling public support for protracted U.S. involvement.

Increasingly doubting strategies of stepping up the military involvement, and aware of diminishing popular support for the war, McNamara recommended to Johnson to limit the U.S. role and stabilize the ground conflict. In reaction to calls for punitive bombing in May 1967, McNamara predicted the negative impact such actions would have on public opinion. He stated that bombing creates "a backfire of revulsion and opposition by killing civilians; it creates serious risks; it may harden the enemy. . . . In addition, an important but hard-to-measure cost is domestic and world opinion. There may be a limit beyond which many Americans and much of the world will not permit the U.S. to go" (New York Times Staff, 1971 pp. 579–80).

On invoking the limits set by the public on the war policies, McNamara no longer seeks ways in which to circumvent the public or educate it in order to change its opposition into support. McNamara himself seems to be using the arguments of the war protesters. He recognizes that the public could constrain further escalating policy and he thinks that the public is right to exercise that force and set limits. On the possible repercussions of indiscriminate bombing, McNamara stated that:

the picture of the world's greatest superpower killing or seriously injuring 1,000 noncombatants a week, while trying to pound a tiny, backwards nation into submission on an issue whose merits are hotly disputed, is not a pretty one. It could conceivably produce a costly distortion in the American national consciousness and in the world image of the U.S. (New York Times Staff, 1971, p. 580)

McNamara addressed the potential domestic and international opposition that could arise as a result of an increased bombing campaign. His references to the issue of Vietnam intervention as "hotly disputed" indicated an awareness of how divisive the debate on Vietnam was becoming. The public opinion on both sides of this "hot" issue were setting the boundaries within which the administration could act.

One of Robert McNamara's final acts before his departure as secretary of defense was to write a memorandum on November 19, 1967, urging President Johnson to limit American involvement in South Vietnam. This memo came shortly after polls showed that public opposition for the war exceeded public support. In the memo, McNamara suggested that "continuation of our present course of action in Southeast Asia would be dangerous, costly in lives, and unsatisfactory to the American people." He stressed that the current Vietnam policy, "while avoiding a national war, will not change Hanoi's mind, so it is not enough to satisfy the American people" (National Security File, Box 75, 18a). He conceded that, though the course of escalation could ultimately prove successful militarily, the public simply would not permit it. McNamara emphasized public opinion as a constraining force: "The American public, frustrated by the slow rate of progress, fearing continued escalation, and doubting that all approaches to peace have been sincerely probed, does not give the appearance of having the will to persist" (National Security File 1967, p. 3). Clearly, despite McNamara's conviction that continued escalation in Vietnam would be the most successful military action, he conceded that supportive public opinion was necessary for continued involvement in Vietnam.

Benchmark 2: Public Opinion and Deescalation After Tet

Concerned with public opinion, McNamara urged the administration toward a compromise settlement. He reminded Johnson of the United States' original goals in Vietnam of providing assistance to the South Vietnam government. He suggested that "the importance of nailing down and understanding the implications of our limited objectives cannot be overemphasized. It relates intimately . . . to U.S. domestic and international opinion as to the justification and the success of our efforts on behalf of Vietnam" (New York Times Staff, 1971, p. 584). While McNamara still supported the initial goals behind intervention in Vietnam, he knew that an impasse had been reached. Dwindling public support for the war meant that escalation with the goal of victory was no longer viable. Although McNamara was still concerned about the U.S. reputation if communism prevailed in Vietnam, he was concerned as well about the United States gaining a reputation as an aggressive power. Furthermore, he believed it was becoming increasingly evident that public opinion would not allow a stepping-up of the war campaign. Although McNamara soon left office, his concerns proved justified in the aftermath of the Tet offensive.

Impact of Protest

While President Johnson and Secretary Rusk were contemptuous of protesters and considered them an impediment in the prosecution of the war, Secretary McNamara viewed protesters in quite a different light. Paradoxically, of the whole administration, McNamara especially was perceived by protesters as "a symbol of America's war machine" (McNamara, 1995, p. 253). Yet he understood their militantism, maybe because he lived with protest in his own home. His daughter Kathy invited her friend Sam Brown, the antiwar leader, home to dinner and to an honest debate with her father, while his son Craig kept the American flag upside down in his dorm room at St. Paul's (Shapley, 1993, pp. 379–81).

While McNamara had a general concern for greater public opposition, public protest in 1965 was not a major factor in McNamara's decision-making. Later, Mc-Namara would defend the war protesters, saying that "they had a right to protest. Our society is strong because we allow rational protest. And they were rational protesters" (McNamara, 4/28/95). When in June 1966 McNamara was received with hostility at Amherst College where he received an honorary degree, his comments did not condemn the students but remarked that the percentage of the summa cum laude graduates wearing the black protest bands was much higher than that of the rest of the student body. He also observed that the more prestigious the college, the more pronounced was the protest (McNamara, 1995, p. 253). Mobbed by Harvard students in a street in Cambridge, he answered Dean John Munro's apologies: "No apology was necessary . . . dissent is both the prerogative and the preservative of free men everywhere" (McNamara, 1995, pp. 256–57).

It was this very freedom, defended by McNamara on behalf of American students in 1966 and later on, which he had believed the United States was fighting for in Vietnam. That is why, among the factors that made him question the justness of the war, was his realization that in South Vietnam the United States was defending a government that was opposed by its people. He expressed repeatedly deep concern about the Buddhist uprisings and "the lack of popular appeal" of the Saigon government (McNamara, 1995, p. 275).

Far from discounting protest, at home or elsewhere, McNamara looked upon it as a sign that people are willing to participate in the decisions that their government is taking in their name. More than any other decision-maker of the Vietnam policies, he also increasingly began to agree with the protesters' objections. He left numerous memos behind attesting to this change in attitude over a period of three years (1965–68), and in November 1967 he offered Johnson his resignation. Antiwar opinion and protest became important to him not because he feared them and felt constrained by them, but perhaps because he came to identify with them.

Conclusion: McNamara

From being a proponent of decisive American involvement in Vietnam the months before the August 1964 Gulf of Tonkin Resolution, by spring of 1965 Robert McNamara adopted a position that negotiation and a peaceful solution were better alternatives. Repeated visits to South Vietnam convinced McNamara that the war could not be won, not because the United States did not have the capability, but because it did not have the support of the people of South Vietnam or the United States. American public opinion and protest became important for him not so much as a compass to guide his policy but as a confirmation that the doubts about the war he had begun to develop early in 1965 had expanded to larger sectors of the population. Vehement expression of the doubts by the best students at the best colleges was a symbol to which the "best and the brightest" could not remain indifferent. The initial constraint from the hawkish sectors of the population, whose access to power and influence and possible verdicts of being soft on communism weighed heavily on Johnson's decision-making, turned to constraint by popular and antiwar sentiment.

SECRETARY OF DEFENSE CLARK CLIFFORD

From the earliest days of America's large-scale commitment in Vietnam, Clark Clifford recognized that maintaining public support would be critical to U.S. success. Though not an official member of the Johnson administration in the first half of 1965 when the initial U.S. escalation was being debated, Clifford was closely involved in deliberations as a personal adviser to President Johnson. Even at this early juncture, Clifford recognized how fragile public support was for fighting a war in Vietnam. His memoirs note that "the support of American public was clearly based on a belief that the conflict would be short in duration; if the war dragged on we all agreed this support would erode" (Clifford, 1991, p. 417). When Clifford formally entered the administration as Robert McNamara's successor as secretary of defense, he played a key role in moving policy toward deescalation.

Benchmark 2: Clifford's Reassessment After the Tet Offensive

By the time Clark Clifford was appointed secretary of defense in early 1968, the fears of declining public support, in the aftermath of Tet, had been realized. Perhaps more than any other presidential adviser, Clifford played a key role in convincing Johnson that his Vietnam policy had to be reversed. This was not just because it was doomed to fail militarily, but also because it had become untenable domestically (Clifford, 1991, pp. 5–7).

Clifford recognized Tet as a public relations disaster. "The impact on the public was enormous," Clifford said in 1991.

> Here they thought things were going well, and thought maybe we were near the end of it, and here the enemy proved to be infinitely stronger. One element that was deeply disturbing to the public was the story that appeared in the *New York Times,* that the military was asking for 206,000 more troops. That really tipped over the bucket with the American public. (Clifford, 8/13/90, pp. 3–4)

Clifford did not believe that biased press accounts of Tet were to blame for the erosion of public support for administration policy. "Tet hurt the administration where it needed support most, with Congress and the American public—not because of the reporting, but because of the event itself, and what it said about the credibility of American leaders" (Clifford, 1991, p. 475).

For Clifford, a veteran of the Washington policy wars, there was never any doubt that the change in public opinion would translate into constraints on administration policy. He identified as indicators of the change in public opinion the shifts in congressmen "which reflected reports they were receiving from their constituencies;" White House mail and telephone calls; changing sentiments in the media; debates on local, state, and federal levels of government; economic concerns over the war; and the unrest at the Chicago Democratic convention (Clifford, 8/13/90, p. 5). Further, he recognized that both Eugene McCarthy and Robert Kennedy were running their 1968 presidential campaigns on strong antiwar platforms (Clifford, 8/13/90, p. 4).

Clifford suggests that the attitudes of the American people were "strongly affecting the policy of our country" (Clifford, 8/13/90, p. 4). "The public was discouraged with [the war]. Young people were alienated by it. There were candle-light parades around the White House. Growing dissatisfaction with it." So, it is "clear to me that the change in attitude by the American public had a great deal to do with the change in attitude on President Johnson's part" (Clifford, 8/13/90, p. 4). Clifford points to Johnson's March 31, 1968, speech, announcing that he would not seek reelection, as a testament to Johnson's sensitivity regarding public opinion. In the face of growing public opposition to the war, Johnson saw that both the U.S. position in Vietnam and his own position as a candidate for reelection had become untenable. The President reached the conclusion, says Clifford, that the public's attitude had changed (Clifford, 8/13/90, p. 4).

Clifford maintains that Johnson was very sensitive to public opinion. He attributes the change in Johnson's policy on the war to the change in the public's attitude on the war, because opinion had changed.

> I think he felt you cannot *force* down the throats of the American people a foreign policy they will not accept. . . . They'll [fail to] be present for the draft, they'll refuse to raise money for it, they will refuse in every way they can to go along with you. And the President who takes that position, despite the warning from the American people, is *practically* guaranteed to be a failure. He's going to fail. (Clifford, 8/13/90, p. 5, emphasis in original)

Three years after the decision to escalate in the spring of 1965, the American people were fed up with the war, and the administration knew it. Television had brought the war right to the living rooms of America. They knew a lot about what was going on. They were sick of it. And they said so (Clifford, 8/13/90, pp. 5–6).

Impact of Protest

Clifford explains that the proliferation of protests was significant because it was indicative of the larger public sentiment. He compares protest to a symptom of a physical ailment:

> It's like getting something wrong with you, I mean another serious ailment, and getting a headache. It isn't the headache that's so important. It's the fact that the headache is a manifestation of something much deeper and more significant. And that's what the protests are—a suggestion that there is a real feeling on the part of the public. (Clifford, 8/13/90, p. 6)

Within a month of his appointment as secretary of defense, Clark Clifford had become the leading opponent of further military escalation in Vietnam. He does not attribute this shift to his reading of public opinion or familiarity with demonstrations. Clifford claims that protest did not "change my attitude" about U.S. involvement in the war. "That was a private decision on my own part." Clifford says that he was "gratified," even "delighted," to see the public response to Tet (Clifford, 8/13/90, p. 7). "I'd opposed it. I'd gone along because the President made the decision" (Clifford, 8/13/90, p. 7).

Clifford had harbored qualms about the Vietnam commitment during the mid-1960s and his doubts about whether the war could be won became overwhelming during intensive study of the situation after becoming secretary of defense. At meetings in March 1968 of the task force on Vietnam policy that Clifford chaired, the new defense secretary posed a stream of questions about whether additional troops could win the war. "Clark Clifford did not find satisfactory answers to these questions," recalled his assistant secretary of defense for public affairs, Phil Goulding. As a result, Clifford became a "vehement proponent of de-escalation during his eleven months in office . . ." (Goulding, 1970, pp. 325–26).

Conclusion: Clifford

In contrast with Johnson and Rusk, but in agreement with McNamara, Clifford did not recognize the antiwar public opinion or protest as a constraint on his preferred policies. This was so because he had been harboring doubts about the war before he came to replace McNamara as secretary of defense. He felt "gratified" and "delighted" about the public response after the Tet offensive. To the degree that he was influenced by opinion, it was not in the direction of altering his preferred policy, but in the direction of being strengthened by it.

CONCLUSION: THE JOHNSON ADMINISTRATION

In the Johnson White House, the Vietnam War policies (1963–69) were crafted in large part without direct reference to "the preferences of the democratic citizenry." The four decision-makers discussed in this chapter suggested often that public opinion played little role in the course of action they took. However, a distinction is in order. While Johnson and Dean Rusk disregarded public opinion out of a consistent realist mindset that compels a leader to lead, shape, or circumvent opinion, McNamara and Clifford had no need to change their policy preferences in response to public opinion because they had begun to doubt the war almost from the very beginning. Clifford, and McNamara later on, insisted that their rejection of the war had been an outgrowth of their own principles rather than a reaction to public pressures. Antiwar opinion only strengthened their own understanding of the situation.

The prosecution of the Vietnam War from August 1964 to October 1968 shows that public sentiments were a factor when the decision to initiate bombing was taken in 1964. Opinion was factored in, but was not decisive, during the subsequent step-by-step escalation. At the height of public protest, President Johnson decided to withdraw from politics and reduce the rate of troop increase from 206,000 asked for by the military to 45,000, which seemed more feasible to the politicians. He had to decide at that time that negotiations needed to replace armed intervention, though he still preferred an American victory. The polls, many opinion leaders and lawmakers, plus the protests in the streets revealed the public's desire for peace, and Johnson, though preferring otherwise, had to respond. Johnson's support of Richard Nixon for the presidency rather than of his own vice president was his last-minute maneuver to seek the victory Nixon was promising in his campaign speeches, and to block a full cessation of bombing and full negotiations (Dallek, 1998, pp. 570–83). Most of the previous attempts to negotiate, as Rusk and others admitted later, had been mainly buying time with the public and preparing the ground for further escalation. Though Johnson would have preferred pursuit of victory, declining public support eroded his policy options severely.

The fact that the war continued for four more years during the Nixon administration suggests that Johnson's preference still echoed within some sectors of the public and leaders. With superior policy maneuvers and opinion-manipulating techniques, the Nixon White House managed to buy the time needed for "Vietnamization" and occasional intensifications of the war in the pursuit of victory. Rather than being tired of the war as such (as the general consensus had been in the Johnson White House), the country was told by the Nixon White House that the public was tired of the way the war had been conducted, the uncertainty about victory, and the prospect that there might not be a victory. Richard Nixon promised to rejuvenate the wary public, as Chapter 6 shows, by pursuing "peace with honor" through a redirected military campaign, Vietnamization, and strategic withdrawals in response to public sentiment.

Vietnam II: Public Opinion and Protest's Influence on Nixon's War

INTRODUCTION

Chapter 6 continues the explorations of the impact of public opinion and protest on U.S. Vietnam policy by looking at the Nixon administration policies after Lyndon Johnson left office. In the fall of 1968, when Richard Nixon ran for the presidency of the United States, he had sent word to President Johnson that a Nixon administration would bring vindication to the Johnson presidency for its stand on Vietnam (Ambrose, 1989, p. 283).[1] In Nixon's interpretation, the majority of the public had not been antiwar but against the uncertainty of not knowing when and how the war would end. The 25 percent of the public who in June 1968 had approved of an "all-out crash effort in the hope of winning the war quickly" (Mueller, 1973, p. 91) or the 34 percent who wanted to "take a stronger stand even if it means invading North Vietnam" (Mueller, 1973, p. 92), represented a sufficient plurality for Nixon to rely on for periodic escalation and widening of the war. This he did for four more years.

Nixon was not alone in this belief. National Security Adviser Henry Kissinger and Secretary of Defense Melvin Laird were in agreement with the new president that what the American people wanted most was a decisive and honorable victory in Vietnam, but not one requiring heavy concentrations of American troops. In the context of this perception, the administration began planning the massive attack on North Vietnam known as "Duck Hook" in 1969, while it also began "Vietnamization" of the war. Separately, the administration undertook the invasion of Cambodia in the spring of 1970, after a fourteen-month period of secret bombing of its countryside. Duck Hook constitutes the first benchmark of the Nixon administration. The Cambodia invasion constitutes the second benchmark.

---

[1] Just before Johnson's speech to the nation that he would not run again and would begin to deescalate the war, Nixon planned to give a speech saying that "there was no way to win the war." He dropped the plans after Johnson's announcement (Hodgson, 1976. p. 396).

PRESIDENT RICHARD NIXON

On entering the White House in January 1969, Richard Nixon interpreted public opin-ion as wanting a U.S. victory in Vietnam, but he also recognized that support for pros-ecuting a costly large-scale land war in Southeast Asia was declining. "Opinion polls showed that a significant percentage of the public favored a military victory in Viet-nam—but only a victory won by delivering a knockout blow that would end the war quickly," Nixon wrote later (Nixon, 1985, p. 101).[2] These conflicting pressures of pub-lic opinion[3] affected U.S. policy at two key benchmarks in the war during the first two years of Nixon's presidency: in late 1969, when Nixon considered a major escalation against North Vietnam; and in the spring of 1970, when the United States and South Vietnamese forces invaded Cambodia. In both cases, Nixon found his hopes for se-curing a quick victory hampered by domestic dissent that he was unable to ignore.

In retrospect, Nixon had a clear philosophy of the role of public opinion in foreign policymaking. In general, he understood that, "Democracies are not well equipped to fight prolonged wars . . . ," because "a democracy fights well only as long as pub-lic opinion supports the war, and public opinion will not continue to support a war that drags on without tangible signs of progress" (Nixon, 1980, p. 115).

In looking at Lyndon Johnson's plight, Nixon felt that "American leaders cannot wage war without the solid support of public opinion, and the American people will go to war only if they are convinced that it is in a just cause. An American President therefore must never commit his troops to battle without getting the people to com-mit themselves to the war" (Nixon, 1985, p. 79). More pragmatically, Nixon insisted that ". . . a democracy fights well only as long as its public opinion supports the war, and public opinion will not continue to support a war that is fought indecisively or that drags on without tangible signs of progress" (Nixon, 1985, p. 79) (cf. 1980, p. 115). In sum, he felt that "wars cannot be waged without the support of the Congress and the people" (Nixon, 1985, p. 224).

Nixon, who commissioned a series of polls on the war, showed a keen awareness of and familiarity with public attitudes. "In November 1967 and February 1968, Gallup polls surveyed public opinion on how the war was going. The proportion who said the United States was losing the war rose from 8 percent before the Tet offensive to 23 percent afterward. The second poll also indicated that 61 percent believed we were either losing ground or standing still in Vietnam" (Nixon, 1985, p. 93). Fur-thermore he distinguished public attitudes from antiwar protests. "Public opinion was not caught up in antiwar sentiments. Unlike many in the antiwar movement, the

---

[2]Jacobs and Shapiro (1995) discuss the use of "presidential polling" in the Nixon White House, but it is not clear to what extent the information affected Vietnam decision-making.

[3]In March 1969, the *New York Times* reported that a third (32 percent) of the public was in favor of escalation. But a quarter (26 percent) wanted to "withdraw completely," 19 percent to "end as soon as possible," 19 percent to "continue present policy," and 21 percent had no opinion (Mueller, 1973, p. 92).

American people did not want to see their country humiliated. But after almost three years of fighting, they were frustrated because no quick end to the war was in sight" (Nixon, 1985, p. 93). In early 1969, Nixon noted, "Opinion polls showed that a significant percentage of the public favored a military victor in Vietnam, ". . . won by . . . a knockout blow that would end the war quickly . . ." (Nixon, 1985, p. 101). Nixon also indicated that public sentiments and protests limited what he could do: "I gave no serious consideration to the nuclear option . . . , [and] rejected the bombing of the dikes" (Nixon, 1985, p. 101).

Benchmark 3: Duck Hook, Moratoriums, and Policy of Vietnamization

During the summer of 1969, Nixon and Kissinger commissioned a series of military options, code named "Duck Hook," for turning the course of the war through escalating against North Vietnam (Hersh, 1983, pp. 118–35). Beginning in August, the administration issued indirect warnings to the North Vietnamese that escalation would occur after November 1 if they didn't make diplomatic concessions (Ambrose, 1989, p. 282; Nixon, 1978, p. 486). Around the same time, the antiwar movement was reaching a new peak of activity. A successful moratorium protest was held October 15, 1969. Another was scheduled for November 14–15, and organizers planned lengthening moratoriums every month until U.S. policy changed. Nixon's memoirs devote considerable attention to the moratoriums.

Since the November 1 deadline passed without significant escalation, the key question is to what degree the successful October 15 moratorium protest, and the promise of another on November 15, influenced the Nixon administration's decision to forgo the escalation. On September 26, 1969, the president said, regarding the antiwar moratorium scheduled for October 15: "under no circumstances will I be affected whatever by it. . . . Faced with the prospect of demonstrations at home that I could not prevent, my only alternative was to try to make it clear to the enemy that the protests would have no effect on my decisions. Otherwise my ultimatum would appear empty" (Nixon, 1978, pp. 493–94). Similarly, in regard to antiwar sentiments in Congress and press reports intensifying in the fall of 1969, "My real concern was that these highly publicized efforts aimed at forcing me to end the war were seriously undermining my behind-the-scenes attempts to do just that" (Nixon, 1978, p. 496).

Nixon argued that he knew by October 14 that the North Vietnamese would not show new flexibility despite his ultimatum. He strongly implied that his decision to forgo escalation by November 1 was determined in large part by the October 15 moratorium:

> I knew that unless I had some indisputably good reason for not carrying out my threat of using increased force when the ultimatum expired on November 1, the Communists would become contemptuous of us and even more difficult to deal with. I knew, however, that after all the protests and the Moratorium, American public opinion would be seriously divided by any military escalation of the war. (Nixon, 1978, p. 497–98)

Nixon appears to have been deeply conflicted over whether to heed the pressures of the antiwar movement. On the one hand, he recognized the perils of taking measures that would antagonize that movement. On the other, he bitterly resisted yielding influence to demonstrators. In a letter to a student in 1969, Nixon addressed the issue of protest in a democracy and reaffirmed his statement that he would not be affected by it:

> If a President—any President—allows his course to be set by those who demonstrate, he would betray the trust of all the rest. Whatever the issue, to allow government policy to be made in the streets would destroy the democratic process. It would give the decision, not to the majority, and not to those with the strongest arguments, but to those with the loudest voices. . . . It would allow every group to test its strength not at the ballot box but through confrontation in the street. (Nixon, 1978, p. 499)

However, Nixon acknowledges that his policy decisions were shaped by the protests: "On the night of October 15 I thought about the irony of this protest for peace. It had, I believed, destroyed whatever small possibility may still have existed of ending the war in 1969" (presumably by making escalation an unacceptable option). "But there was nothing I could do about that now. I would have to adjust my plans accordingly and carry on as best I could" (Nixon, 1978, p. 499).[4]

The "Silent Majority" Speech

While Nixon acknowledges that the October 15 protests "undercut the credibility of the ultimatum" (Nixon, 1978, p. 501),[5] the successful November 3 "Silent Majority" speech gave him new freedom of action in negotiations with the North Vietnamese.

---

[4]Nixon's memoirs significantly overestimate the size of the October 15 moratorium demonstrations: "A quarter of a million people came to Washington for the October 15 Moratorium . . . the demonstrations were generally peaceful" (1978, p. 498). "Opinion within the administration was divided over how to respond. . . . Kissinger urged that I do nothing . . . and let the protest run its course lest I upset our foreign policy strategy. . . . I would not be affected by the protest." Yet Nixon also noted that the demonstrations, or anticipation of their impact, kept the administration from carrying out the threatened Duck Hook escalation and thus removed the chance of ending the war quickly. Kissinger's estimate of the size of the Washington demonstration as 50,000 (1979, p. 291) also exceeded those of antiwar histories of 40,000 (Zaroulis and Sullivan, 1985, p. 269) and 30,000 (DeBenedetti, 1990, p. 256). The [October] "Moratorium Day was peaceably observed by millions of Americans in thousands of cities, towns, and villages across the nation" (Zaroulis and Sullivan, 1984, p. 269). Among "the largest public protest ever on a national scale" (p. 269), the biggest October demonstrations were in New York City (250,000) (DeBenedetti, 1990, p. 255) and Boston (100,000) (DeBenedetti, 1990, p. 255; Kissinger, 1979, p. 291).

[5]While retrospective, Nixon and Kissinger's overestimation of the size of Washington demonstrations, in light of the significant impact they ascribe to the moratorium protest, raises the question of whether they misperceived the magnitude at the time or misremembered the size when writing later. Perhaps Nixon mistook in retrospect the October 15 Washington protests for either the New York ones then or the November mobilization in Washington, which he also estimated as a quarter million (1978, p. 510). Their perceptions and estimates at the time were probably more accurate, but the impact seems to have been significant in any case.

This reduced some of the damage done by his failure to implement the Duck Hook ultimatum. Moreover, the speech also helped to slow the decline of public support that would be needed to continue the waging of the war.

> The November 3 speech was both a milestone and a turning point for my adminis-
> tration. Now, for a time at least, the enemy could no longer count on dissent in Amer-
> ica to give them the victory they could not win on the battlefield. I had the public sup-
> port I needed to continue a policy of waging war in Vietnam and negotiating for
> peace in Paris until we could bring the war to an honorable and successful conclu-
> sion. (Nixon, 1978, p. 508)

In the week after the November 3 speech, Nixon's Gallup poll approval rating rose to 68 percent, the highest since he took office (Nixon, 1978, p. 508).

Despite this boost, Nixon was acutely aware that the public's support could soon decline again. He felt that the speech had "bought me more time" on the war, but not a lot (Nixon, 1978, p. 511). In the months and years ahead, Nixon believed that a key to sustaining his position was to maintain the support of those he had swayed in his November 3 speech. "We must keep our Silent Majority group involved," Nixon wrote to Kissinger at the beginning of 1970 (Ambrose, 1989, p. 325).

Unbeknownst to the antiwar movement, Nixon had decided to abandon the Duck Hook escalation plan of late 1969. The planned attack on North Vietnam early in his presidency was a perilous option particularly because of the antiwar movement's strength demonstrated by the October 15 moratorium (Kissinger, 1979, p. 304; Nixon, 1978, p. 499). Nixon felt he had developed some success in neutralizing the movement in that his public relations efforts and particularly the November 3 speech strength-ened his hand in conducting the war and negotiating with the North Vietnamese.

The Americans protesting the war in Washington on October 15 "had no idea of their impact: they were protesting the policies already adopted by the Nixon Admin-istration and not those under consideration" (Hersh, 1983, pp. 118–35). Though Nixon left the crisis convinced that the protesters had forced him to back down, "the protesters," Hersh concluded, "thought the Moratorium had been largely in vain" (Hersh, 1983, p. 30).

Following the success of the November 3 Silent Majority speech, the Nixon ad-ministration launched a concerted effort to undermine the antiwar movement through speeches and briefings to members of the press and Congress (Hersh, 1983, p. 133). Through the next two years, the Nixon administration would show acute sensitivity toward the antiwar movement. The omnipresence of protesters outside the White House, in America's cities, and on campuses appears to have had a significant psy-chological effect on top officials. The administration's enormous efforts to defuse, defeat, and discredit the antiwar movement are measures of the influence they attrib-uted to public protest.

Benchmark 4: The Cambodia Invasion, Spring 1970

The evidence about public opinion's impact on Nixon's thinking about the invasion of Cambodia in April 1970 points to two conflicting conclusions: First, Nixon did not allow the certainty of adverse public reaction to block his decision to invade. Second, the fact that the adverse reaction was larger than anticipated curtailed the duration and scope of the actual invasion.

Nixon portrays his Cambodia decision as an example of courageous leadership (cf. Nixon, 1962): "I never had any illusions about the shattering effect a decision to go into Cambodia would have on public opinion at home. I knew that opinions among my major foreign policy advisors were deeply divided over the issue of widening the war, and I recognized that it could mean personal and political catastrophe for me and my administration" (Nixon, 1978, p. 556). In his televised speech on April 30 explaining the Cambodia invasion, Nixon advertised his pursuit of the national interest over his own political fortunes:

> Whether I may be a one-term President is insignificant compared to whether by our failure to act in this crisis the United States proves itself unworthy to lead the forces of freedom in this critical period in world history. I would rather be a one-term President and do what I believe is right than to be a two-term President at the cost of seeing America become a second-rate power and to see this Nation accept the first defeat in its proud 190-year history. (Ambrose, 1989, p. 346)

Nixon took a major political risk by his invasion of Cambodia in an attempt to destroy the North Vietnamese headquarters (COSVN). Public opinion and protest appear not to have been a significant constraint in making the decision. However, it seems doubtful that Nixon believed that the Cambodian operation genuinely jeopardized his reelection chances: First, his reelection campaign was still more than two years away, enough time for outrage over Cambodia to die down. Second, Nixon considered ending the war on favorable terms to be key to his reelection bid, and saw the attack on Cambodia as advancing such an end by weakening the enemy. And third, Nixon may have had a correct hunch that the Cambodia operation would spark protests on campuses but nevertheless still be supported by many in the public who still hoped for a victory in Vietnam. In fact, a *Newsweek* poll published in the middle of May 1970 showed that 50 percent of the public backed the Cambodian operation and that Nixon's overall approval rating had not been hurt, staying at 65 percent (Ambrose, 1989, p. 359; Nixon, 1978, p. 578; *Newsweek,* May 1969). Yet in May, 58 percent of the public favored "continued withdrawal even if the South Vietnamese government collapses" and only 13 percent favored "sending in more troops to Vietnam and step up the fighting" (Mueller, 1973, p. 95).

Once the Cambodian operation began, Nixon visited the Pentagon on May 1 and ordered an expansion to hit more North Vietnamese sanctuaries. When the joint chiefs cautioned him about the adverse domestic reaction, Nixon said, "The fact is that we have already taken the heat for this particular operation" (Ambrose, 1989, p. 348). Nixon believed that partial steps got as much heat as full ones (cf. Isaacson, 1993).

By May 5, however, in the wake of the killings at Kent State, protest at hundreds of other campuses, and the uproar in Congress, Nixon had begun to curtail the operation. He met with congressional committees, pledged a removal of all troops in a few weeks, and said that no troops would penetrate more than twenty-one miles into Cambodia. These pledges angered critics on the right and represented a retreat from

Nixon's commitment to give the U.S. military a free hand in the operation. Nixon's pledges to limit the time and the area of operations made it difficult, if not impossible, for the army to destroy the sanctuaries and COSVN (Ambrose, 1989, p. 352). Though Kissinger says the domestic pressures resulted in the "panicky decision" by the administration to withdraw all troops from Cambodia by June 30 (Kissinger, 1979, p. 516), Nixon implied that the June 30 date had been planned all along (Nixon, 1978, p. 578). The president was willing to ignore public opinion in ordering the invasion and widening its goals. After massive protests, however, he moved to limit the operation's scope and set a timetable for withdrawal of U.S. troops.

The reaction to the Cambodian invasion may have shaken Nixon's self-confidence. It reduced some of the gains from the Silent Majority speech and led to a new congressional activism in trying to limit the war. Nixon felt he was running out of time on the domestic front to settle the war on favorable terms (Wicker, 1991, pp. 587–88).

Conclusion: Nixon

During the 1968 campaign, Nixon understood that the country was not calling for an immediate end to the war, but an ultimate resolution of it. Very skillfully, he ran on a platform of ending the war without mentioning directly how he would accomplish it.

With increase in the intensity of the antiwar protest, Nixon had to abandon the Duck Hook plan. But following the relative success of the Silent Majority speech in reducing the rate of decline of public support, Nixon proceeded to intensify the war. Theoretically, he believed that in a democracy policy has to be a reflection of public consent, but practically he also believed that opinion could be changed or circumvented. In responding to protest, he knew that it did not come from the majority of the country and consequently if it could not be neutralized, it could be ignored. In the cases of both the moratoriums and the Cambodia invasion, however, protest could not be ignored. Nixon made it a matter of pride to admit that "Regardless of public opinion and polls, RN [Richard Nixon] will do what his long experience and conviction tells him is right" (Ambrose, 1989, p. 280). Yet even what he felt was right was constrained by public opposition.

NATIONAL SECURITY ADVISER AND
SECRETARY OF STATE HENRY KISSINGER

Like Nixon, Henry Kissinger entered office convinced that America had to get out of Vietnam as quickly as possible. But he was equally convinced that U.S. prestige could not be allowed to suffer seriously in the process. He felt that the American public shared this outlook:

> Clearly, the American people wanted to end the war, but every poll, and indeed Nixon's election (and the Wallace vote), made it equally evident that they saw their country's aims as honorable and did not relish America's humiliation. The new Administration had to respect the concerns of the opponents of the war but also the an-

guish of the families whose sons had suffered and died for their country and who did not want it determined—after the fact—that their sacrifice had been in vain. (Kissinger, 1979, p. 228)

In considering the consequences of defeat in Vietnam, Kissinger was mainly concerned with the international fallout, but also with the negative domestic consequences. Kissinger's fears of these outcomes do not appear as strong as those of Nixon, a professional politician and long-time cold warrior facing reelection. As Kissinger writes in his memoirs, "No foreign policy is stronger than its domestic base" (Kissinger, 1999, p. 470). But he does express his conviction that "An ignominious end in Vietnam would also leave deep scars on our society, fueling impulses for recrimination and deepening the existing crisis of authority" (Kissinger, 1979, p. 1038).[6] In an interview in 1994, Kissinger reflected on qualities that make a good leader: "You have to be close to your public opinion, or you have to reflect your public opinion. When I was secretary of state . . . I had press conferences, I gave a public speech, so that I could bring whatever we were doing to the hinterlands" (Kissinger, 4/7/94). He reflected on public opinion during the Vietnam War:

> I don't really think it was the people that disagreed with the leadership so much as it was the opinion forming groups, the media, the professors, many of the intellectuals. I think the public stuck with the presidents Kennedy, Johnson, and Nixon, in an amazing way, considering all the publicity that was going against it. . . . It was very, very painful to me, because all of the people that I had been close to at Harvard turned against the war. (Kissinger, 4/7/94)

Kissinger appears to have been aware of the constraints placed on policymakers by the antiwar movement. He is, however, more ambiguous in his public statements and memoirs about how exactly public opinion affected his thinking about various decisions on Vietnam. "The public malaise" over the war in 1969, "raised in a profound way the questions of the responsibility of leaders to the public in a democracy. Lucky is the leader, " Kissinger asserted, "whose convictions of what is the national interest coincide with the public mood" (Kissinger, 1979, p. 292). But regarding the "obligation when these perceptions differ," only a "shallow view of democracy would reduce the leader to passivity and have him simply register public opinion. . . . Leaders are responsible not for running public opinion polls but for the consequences of their actions" (Kissinger, 1979, p. 292). Even regarding an unpopular position like possible U.S. insistence on prohibiting further communist infiltration after the cease-fire, that "had next to no public support" in the United States, "we were determined to stick to it" (Kissinger, 1979, p. 1315).

Kissinger considered that the domestic opposition to the Vietnam War was one of the single greatest obstacles to achieving peace with honor. The antiwar activists, said Kissinger, were:

---

[6]The political uproar over the "loss" of China to communism in 1949 were the referents for Kissinger and for Nixon, who, in fact, was a leader of the subsequent anticommunist reaction.

as wrong as they were passionate. Their pressures delayed the end of the war, not accelerated it; their simplifications did not bring closer the peace, of the yearning for which they had no monopoly. Emotion was not a policy. We had to end the war, but in conditions that did not undermine America's power to build the new international order upon which the future of even the most enraged depended. (Kissinger, 1979, p. 510)

More specifically, Kissinger argues that his efforts to negotiate a political settlement with Hanoi were adversely affected by domestic dissent. He recalls that "No meeting with the North Vietnamese was complete without a recitation of the statements of our domestic opposition" (Kissinger, 1979, p. 1041). And he repeatedly portrays the antiwar movement as one of North Vietnam's greatest allies in its quest to impose a communist dictatorship on millions of South Vietnamese: "To end the war honorably we needed to present our enemy with the very margin of uncertainty about our intentions that domestic opponents bent every effort to remove" (Kissinger, 1979, p. 970).[7]

Benchmark 3: Awareness and Impact of Duck Hook on Public Opinion and Protest

In planning for the proposed Duck Hook escalation in 1969, Kissinger was warned by members of his staff of the domestic consequences of such a move. NSC staffer William Watts wrote Kissinger a memo on October 13 warning that if Duck Hook went forward, the United States would be faced with massive riots and student protests. "The nation could be thrown into internal turmoil" (Hersh, 1983, p. 127; Szulc, 1990, p. 155; Isaacson, 1993, p. 247). Kissinger was acutely concerned about the antiwar movement and did everything possible to defuse the October and November moratoriums by trying "to convince the media and Congress that a new peace initiative was in the offing" (Hersh, 1983, p. 127). But no definitive conclusions as to what impact the prospect of domestic upheaval had on Kissinger's thinking appeared to those who did extensive interviews with members of his staff (Hersh, 1983, pp. 130–31; Isaacson, 1993, pp. 247–48; Szulc, 1990, pp. 156–57). Kissinger may have been divided about the wisdom of Duck Hook. His staff analysis suggested that Duck Hook would cause many casualties in North Vietnam, but it would have little impact on the North's ability to continue the war in the South. The basic thrust of the analysis was that since North Vietnam was only a quasi-industrial society, strategic bombing could achieve only limited aims (Hersh, 1983, p. 128; Szulc, 1990, pp. 153–56).

Moreover, though recognizing that Nixon was often able to "rally skillfully" the sentiments of Americans, Kissinger acknowledged that protest circumscribed policy options in 1969 (Kissinger, 1979, p. 298). "We finally rejected the military option" of serious escalation, among other reasons, "because we did not think we could sustain public support for the length of time required to prevail" (Kissinger, 1979, p. 288).

While Nixon's memoirs clearly state that the prospect of increased protests eliminated serious consideration of the escalation option in late 1969, Kissinger's mem-

---

[7]Whether the antiwar movement had any impact on North Vietnam policy is uncertain, but Kissinger felt that it had (Kissinger, 1979; Szulc, 1990).

oirs are not as forthcoming. He does refer to the difficulties in "sustain[ing] public support" (Kissinger, 1979, p. 288) and facing the "domestic pressures dramatized by the Moratorium" (Kissinger, 1979, p. 305). Kissinger does not explain in detail why there was no decision to escalate the war in late 1969 or what his own views were on this issue. And the most conclusive point he makes regarding public opinion during this period is that the success of Nixon's Silent Majority speech of November 3 served to strengthen the administration's position in Vietnam "by tak[ing] his case to the people and receiv[ing] substantial support" (Kissinger, 1979, p. 437).

Benchmark 4: Impact of Public Opinion After the Cambodia Invasion

Again, it is hard to reach clear-cut assessments in regard to Kissinger on the Cambodia "incursion." The record regarding how public opinion affected his decisions on Cambodia is sparse. Kissinger says only that before the invasion he was "painfully conscious of the political upheaval that would certainly follow an attack on the sanctuaries as well as the divisions on my staff" (Kissinger, 1979, p. 493). These two issues were apparently linked: NSC staffers opposed the invasion in part because they believed it would produce widespread domestic unrest (Hersh, 1983, p. 189). Kissinger does note, however, that "Gallup polls showed considerable support for the president's action," with 48 percent support for sending arms and "50 percent approval of the president's handling of the situation" (Kissinger, 1979, p. 512).

On the impact of protest once the invasion was under way, Kissinger expresses his disagreement with Nixon's decision to set a constraining timetable for withdrawal. "I doubt if we would have attracted much more public hostility by extending our stay for the two or three additional months that a careful search needed" (Kissinger, 1979, p. 507). He also says that the "impact of the public protest was to shift discussion from how to make the operation succeed to an elaboration of various restraints" and that in this sense the Cambodia invasion "was a microcosm of our whole effort in Indochina" (Kissinger, 1979, p. 516). Explaining the conflict to college presidents, Kissinger said that protest is considered in decision-making but is not decisive: "We in government have an obligation not only to register what the students say but also to put it into the framework of the longer term" (Kissinger, 1979, p. 1198).

In reflecting on how the Cambodia operation was derailed, Kissinger complained: "There can be no serious national policy when an attempt is made to coerce decisions by an outpouring of emotion and when those in high office are forced to take measures they do not really believe in simply to calm protests in the streets" (Kissinger, 1979, p. 516). These comments reflect his overall view of the impact of the antiwar movement: a demagogic and irrational force that continually hampered efforts to pursue the national interest. While opposed to responding to protest, Kissinger still notes how it limited the administration's options.

Impact of Protest

One testament to the importance of the antiwar movement in Kissinger's thinking is the extent to which he devoted time and energy to worrying about the movement's strength and meeting with its representatives. Clearly, Kissinger believed that neutralizing the antiwar movement was essential if the administration was to achieve its goals in Vietnam. Kissinger met frequently with representatives of the academic community, including student groups. During the months after the Cambodia invasion he met with student activists to try to defend the administration's positions (Kissinger, 1979, p. 1198).[8]

Kissinger dwells in particular on the negative impact of congressional efforts after Cambodia to legislate a withdrawal of all U.S. troops from Vietnam that gained steam in 1970. On the first significant effort, the McGovern–Hatfield amendment that was defeated on September 1, 1970, by 55 to 39, Kissinger writes:

> that thirty-nine Senators sought to prescribe the conduct of peace negotiations, in the face of Administration warnings that they were legislating a debacle, dealt a serious blow to the psychological basis for a coherent strategy. Nor was that vote the end of the amendment. It would come back month after month with constantly increasing support, dramatizing to Hanoi the erosion of our position and thus reducing the North's incentive for serious negotiation. (Kissinger, 1979, p. 971)

In a 1999 interview, Kissinger lays some of the blame for defeat in Vietnam on the congressional leaders who blocked aid to Cambodia. He stated "I think the people who cut off aid to Cambodia, which was [winnable] or which was, at least, stabilizable, have a lot more to answer for" (Kissinger, 3/7/99). Kissinger's memoirs dwell on congressional action against the war, recalling each significant vote and reflecting on how he felt his hands being tied more and more tightly in negotiations with Hanoi. Protesters also should take their share of the blame, according to Kissinger:

> It ended as it ended, because America tore itself apart, domestically. The government has a certain responsibility for it. But the protesters to this day have never admitted the slightest fallibility in their judgment on the matter. The viciousness with which these attacks were conducted and the manner in which the war ended is the reflection on our domestic divisions and not about the original judgments that we made. (Kissinger, 3/7/99)

Kissinger apparently made little distinction between the peace movement and congressional opposition to Vietnam. Instead, he stressed that Congress's view was simply a reflection of public opinion. "The tidal wave of media and student criticism powerfully affected the Congress" (Kissinger, 1979, p. 512). Kissinger's memoirs do not portray Congress as being more or less dovish than the public at large. Yet on most basis decisions and actions such as withdrawal in 1969 (p. 298) or Cambodia (p. 512), Kissinger felt, the administration had majority support. Although in early 1972 "the war was deeply unpopular," Kissinger felt that "however weary the public might be, it was not prepared to join an enemy in defeating an ally" (Kissinger, 1979, p. 1044). While Nixon essentially acknowledges the powerful constraints imposed by public opinion on his decision making in late 1969 and the spring of 1970 invasion of Cam-

---

[8]The author met with Kissinger and a group of students at the White House in the summer of 1970.

bodia, Kissinger's statements and recollections on Vietnam are far more ambiguous. Attempting to assess the impact of public opinion on Henry Kissinger's policy decisions regarding Vietnam is more difficult (Katz, 1997).

Conclusion: Kissinger

Like the president he served, Henry Kissinger came to office with a strong conviction that, in the aggregate, the American public wanted an end to the war but not a humiliating withdrawal. As an architect of the Vietnam operation, he believed the way that peace with victory and honor could take place was through a massive and decisive blow delivered against North Vietnam. Theoretically, he also understood that the support of the public was crucial for such operations, but in its absence, policy could be developed and implemented in secret. Yet he recognized that public opposition and protest both deferred Duck Hook and forced early withdrawal from Cambodia.

With the policy of Vietnamization of the war and neutralization of the American dissent, Nixon and Kissinger were able to keep the American public relatively pacified. These contributed to a reelection of Richard Nixon in 1972 and enough public support to continue the war from 1969 to 1973.

SECRETARY OF DEFENSE MELVIN LAIRD

When Melvin Laird became secretary of defense in 1969, he saw that "public support was on razor's edge for Johnson and his policies in Vietnam" (Laird, 2/8/99). In light of increasing opposition to U.S. involvement in Vietnam, Laird was aware of the delicate nature of public opinion and the obstacles he would face. As the "first professional politician" to hold this title of defense secretary, Laird had served in both the Wisconsin state legislature and the U.S. House of Representatives. A skillful leader and respected Republican, Laird had provided valuable advice during Nixon's 1968 election campaign. As a veteran politician, he played a key role in drawing up the specifications for the next secretary of defense. In response to criticism of the military establishment, Laird replied, "We anticipated that this would happen and for that reason when we started to put the cabinet together I urged the President-elect to appoint a Secretary of Defense from the Congress" (Laird 6/4/1969). Thus from the very start of Nixon's administration, Laird asserted the need for the head of defense to be known and trusted by the public and Capital Hill. This relationship with the American people and Congress is in large part what dictated Laird's appointment. Nixon's decision to place Laird in so important a role was based to some degree on the desire to prevent public disapproval and protest from escalating.

Laird was sensitive to public opinion. Prior to his appointment to the Nixon cabinet, he expressed his view of the obligation of politicians to explore the issues with the American public. He, however, felt a lack of knowledge on the citizenry's part would result in the inability of the U.S. government [to effectively cope] with communism. Through dialogue, an "informed" public would be able to unite behind a coherent policy. "A public strategy arising from public understanding and unity would, I believe, bring us to the sober conclusion that we must declare and wage political war" (Laird, 1962, p. 134). His belief that, while dialogue was necessary for gaining the trust of the American people, policy should be left to the experts remained unaltered during his time as secretary of defense.

Laird placed a high priority on molding public opinion to suit his policies, yet public opinion was an important concern of Laird's. At the beginning as secretary, Laird remarked "the public was probably more concerned about Vietnam in November of 1968 than at any other time. I felt that we had to come forward with a withdrawal program as quickly as possible. . . . Public support . . . continued as long as we were making progress with withdrawal" (Laird, 2/8/99). Spending more time in press conferences and interviews than any other secretary, Laird remained in touch with the public and Congress (Laird, 6/4/69). He was often seen at congressional meetings and discussions, eager to stay connected with his former colleagues.

As a congressman and as secretary of defense, Laird had always placed importance on maintaining an open dialogue with students, as campuses were often the sites of public protest. "I spent more time on college campuses than any other member of Congress, I think" (Laird, 2/8/99). One of his first acts as secretary was to help draft reforms that limited a youth's draft liability to those men who were 19 years old. Secretary Laird elaborated on this decision. "The first decision we made as a result of public opinion was to end the draft as it was being carried out in January of 1969 and that we should go to a lottery immediately and that we should do away with the deferment program because it was not fair. I would say that that was really dictated by public opinion as much as anything else. . . . I think the American public felt that way, too" (Laird, 2/8/99). This action to circumvent the mounting public protest demonstrates his awareness of the need to gain support. While he did not want protest to spread to the general public, he also did not want his policy abroad to be affected. In part, because of his concern with shifting the burden of fighting to the Vietnamese and maintaining the support of the American people, Laird's public comments focus on Vietnamization and deescalation. Moreover, he was excluded from the planning of Duck Hook and escalation (Herring, 1986).

Public Opinion and the Policy of Vietnamization

Laird is credited with developing the basis of the Vietnamization program, a plan to be announced in spring 1969 to train the South Vietnamese for takeover of their own war. In fact he is mainly responsible for the replacement of the term "de-Americanization" with "Vietnamization" (Kissinger, 1979, p. 272), because the policy of troop withdrawal had already been part of the Nixon campaign pledges. It would allow for the withdrawal of United States troops and a lesser military involvement. Laird struggled with President Nixon and Adviser Kissinger on the issue of withdrawal and the Vietnamization schedule. "I think public opinion was having its effect—it didn't have as rapid an effect as I had hoped, but it finally came around" (Laird, 2/8/99). Laird believed in the powerful use of open dialogue to educate and shape opinion: "I'm confident that people, once they fully understand this program, will continue to give us great support because we do have a program for the Vietnamese in that area" (Laird, 12/1/69). Though an adverse reaction often occurred at first on his arrival at college campuses, "once they understand the course of action that we've taken, the change in our policy, we do get support" (Laird, 12/1/69). Laird's outlook is not so much the need to listen to the public, but the necessity of educating the people.

Laird felt the need to reassure the public, in part, from the need to keep up American commitments elsewhere in the world, particularly in NATO. "I felt that we could not sustain our commitments . . . in defense because the public was fed up with Vietnam and I think they showed that in the election, and it was necessary to show that we were going to make progress to get out of there" (Laird, 2/8/99). Laird also felt that it was essential to explain to the American people the resources that were being devoted to the war. This had to be balanced with signs of progress, in order for the Defense Department to maintain a level of support for other important programs. "The commitment was great as far as manpower was concerned and the public was fed up. . . . In order to maintain the Department of Defense budget . . . we had to develop a program that would maintain public support" (Laird, 2/8/99).

In March 1969, Laird received reports of North Vietnamese rocket attacks on Saigon, but Washington was unclear what the next action would be. In press conferences, Laird stressed that "no one should mistake our patience and forbearance as a sign of weakness" (Laird, 3/6/69). When asked if the United States bombing halt was a mistake, he responded, "I would be less than frank with you if I tried to indicate that this was a consensus of the American public opinion." The public, along with Congress, was unable to determine what the correct course of action should be. Whether or not the public was in complete agreement had little impact, however. In Laird's view, the public did not need to know the exact plans for the eventual withdrawal. On April 3, 1969, Laird says, "Certainly we're [moving to 'Vietnamize'] the war as rapidly as we can, but I don't believe it serves our purposes in Paris or at a time when the enemy is conducting an offensive to get into the unilateral withdrawal of troop figures, and I don't think it serves any purpose to discuss those figures today" (Laird, 4/3/69). Even if the public wanted deescalation, many in the Nixon administration did not feel this would be militarily successful. Still, while admitting to an awareness of a time limit, "I think the American people . . . will give us a few more months to try to reach a successful negotiated settlement in Paris" (Laird, 4/3/69). At a time when the enemy was on the offensive, Laird was concerned with the United States being in a weak position.

Benchmark 3: Duck Hook and Moratoriums

Because Laird was not actively involved in making the Duck Hook decisions, there is little evidence of how public opinion about its potential impact or of how the Moratorium protests might have affected his decision making regarding the possible escalation. Nixon's memoirs (1978, p. 495) notes that possible plans for Duck Hook reached Laird and Secretary of State William Rogers through a news leak, which implies that both were not directly consulted on the decisions. Both urged Nixon to consider the low casualty rates recently and the improved South Vietnamese army program as part of Vietnamization, each of which would have had a positive effect on public support.

In providing advice to Nixon about what he should say in the Silent Majority speech, Laird and Rogers again proposed concentrating on hopes for peace (Nixon, 1978, p. 504). Laird again encouraged stressing the prospects for Vietnamization, a program he advocated in order to provide evidence to the public of the scaling back of U.S. involvement.

Benchmark 4: Public Opinion and the Invasion of Cambodia

Because of criticism leveled at his predecessor, Robert McNamara, and the Johnson administration, Laird was quite determined to stay away from the so-called "credibility gap." He reflects on the decision by Nixon and Kissinger, which he advised against, to keep the invasion of Cambodia a secret. Of this decision, Laird said "I felt the public would be up in arms." The public outcry was understandable, according to Laird. "You just can't treat the public that way in our system" (Laird, 2/8/99). Laird and the Nixon administration refused to release specific dates of the withdrawal timetable and sidestepped making promises. "I've stayed away from making forecasts or predictions . . . and as long as I am Secretary of Defense I will stay away from that kind of prediction" (Laird, 3/20/70). Despite the government's desire to control the amount of dialogue with the public, public opinion still placed a constraining limit on the degree to which continuing U.S. involvement in Vietnam would be tolerated, but relatively high presidential approved provided some flexibility.

For the rest of his tenure, Laird reiterated his belief in Vietnamization. He stressed that "the public had to feel that there was some way out and we had to show them we were making progress as far as Southeast Asia was concerned" (Laird, 2/8/99). In response to questions regarding American foreign policy, Laird was quick to describe the president's policy in terms of peace and stability. The Nixon Doctrine, which rested upon the concepts of partnership, maintenance of military strength, and willingness to negotiate, had earned the support of a weary public. In an interview in 1971, Laird said, "We change the public debate, Why Vietnam?, to the application of the Nixon Doctrine of partnership, of strength, and of meaningful negotiations, so that we can achieve this era of peace, this generation of peace, which President Nixon and which I believe all Americans support so strongly" (Laird, 6/13/71). Though he argued that the United States was both fighting a military war in Vietnam and conducting a peaceful negotiation in Paris, a few months later he stated, "I'm not optimistic about the possibilities of negotiation but I do not believe that this is the time to discard the negotiation track" (Laird, 11/14/71). He knew that the consequences would be grave if the United States took a more openly aggressive stance, and that the public looked to these talks as a sign of permanent deescalation. If the United States were to leave talks in Paris, the administration would be vulnerable to wide criticism.

Laird tried at times to downplay the impact of public opinion. When asked, "Are you saying that domestic politics have nothing to do with the withdrawal timetable from Vietnam?," he replied, "That is correct. The withdrawal timetable in Vietnam is based upon our Vietnamization plan; our Vietnamization plan is based upon the capability of the South Vietnamese military force" (Laird, 11/14/71). His attempts at dialogue and changing the public debate from "Why Vietnam?" to "Why Vietnamization?" proved relatively successful. Yet Laird claims that troop withdrawal and Vietnamization were to be unaffected by domestic political concerns. His comments reveal an awareness of public opinion, along with the ability to remain relatively un-influenced. Though he claimed to have based his recommendations on national secu-rity alone, his awareness of public opinion and protest surrounding Vietnamization shows public opinion's impact.

Although public opinion on the Vietnam War was a major factor in the election of 1968, Laird did not feel it was significant in 1972. Though troops were still in Viet-nam and no peace treaty had been signed, Nixon was reelected in 1972. Laird was proved correct in believing that America's involvement in the war "would not be the big political issue so far as the campaign [was] concerned in 1972" (11/14/71). He stated that "the candidate for the Democrats [George McGovern] took a very extreme position. If McGovern had taken a more reasonable position, he could have made an issue out of it [Vietnam]. I don't think Nixon won the election because of Vietnam" (Laird, 2/8/99). However, Laird does attribute part of the Nixon success in 1972 to the Vietnamization program: "If we hadn't made progress on Vietnamization, we wouldn't have won the election" (Laird, 2/8/99).

Impact of Protest

Secretary Laird did not place a clear distinction between public opinion and protest, though he did acknowledge that the general atmosphere was calling for a change. In formulating policy, Laird focused on the attitudes of the country, and did not rely heavily on polls. He said "most polls—and I think sometimes you have to look at them—I think the public supported the positions I was taking on withdrawal. I think I had public support. I felt all along that I had it, because of my understanding of the political climate in America. . . . I did not use the polls, I used my feeling—and I felt the public was fed up" (Laird, 2/8/99). On protesters, Laird said "Public opinion is much more important than a few protesters. . . . I was trying to gauge the over-all opinion of the public. . . . Protesters used very poor judgment, I didn't let that interfere with me and my judgment of public opinion" (Laird, 2/8/99).

In the eyes of the American people, the Nixon administration pursued avenues to peace without placing the United States in a weaker position. Laird perceived support for Vietnamization: "I think public opinion was for my withdrawal program" (Laird, 2/8/99). This does not mean, however, that Laird wanted to allow the military to be vulnerable or communism to spread. Peace was pursued as long as there was no dan-ger to American interests. The ultimate professional politician, Laird contributed to focusing the debate so that his policy could remain intact and unaltered. Though pub-lic opinion had a constraining effect during Laird's residency at the Pentagon, at times he in fact acted in opposition to public sentiment.

Conclusion: Laird

Of the three policymakers, Laird was most directly involved with the creating and sustaining of public support for Vietnam War policies: Having understood that by 1968 the American public favored troop withdrawal and an end to the war, Laird pre-sented the policies of periodic escalation and widening of the war as necessary steps toward the achieving of this very goal. With the language of Vietnamization, negotiation in Paris, and peace without humiliation, he helped to engineer the strategies of four more years of war and to extend the patience of the American public. This ability to continue the war greatly surprised former policymakers in the Johnson administration, like Dean Rusk, who thought that by 1968 the public had become fed up with the war.

CONCLUSION: NIXON ADMINISTRATION

In contrast with the Johnson administration, where McNamara and Clifford distanced themselves from the war on principle and the president decided to step down with the perception that the American public turned against it, the Nixon White House exhibited more unity of purpose and ideology. The three main decision-makers in the Nixon administration believed that the public was more interested in ending the war honorably than in ending it quickly. This perception was behind the policies of Vietnamization, the Cambodia invasion, the prolonged Paris peace negotiations, and the Christmas bombing of 1972. In theory, Nixon, Kissinger, and Laird admitted that public support was essential for success in foreign policy. But while Laird opted for more transparency and public education, Nixon and Kissinger resorted to secret operations in the face of public outcries toward certain policies.

By voting for Nixon in 1972 rather than for the peace candidate George McGovern, the American public confirmed the Nixon administration's reading of its preferences. Despite moratoriums and organized protests, the Vietnam war was not a cutting-edge issue in 1972. The war could continue for three more months until the Paris Peace Agreement, but ultimately the exhaustion of the public's patience called the American part to a halt.

CONCLUSION: THE JOHNSON AND NIXON ADMINISTRATIONS

In sum, though conservative pressure contributed to escalation early in the war, by 1968 Johnson, Rusk, McNamara, and Clifford saw opposition public opinion as limiting their policy options late in the war. The shift in opinion against the war after Tet contributed to a major movement toward deescalation in the Johnson administration policy. Johnson's decision not to run for reelection revealed that the administration felt it no longer had the support to pursue an aggressive policy in Vietnam.

During his first term, Nixon calculated that the public would not tolerate a military defeat in Vietnam and that his own reelection prospects depended in part on ending the war on honorable terms. At the same time, he came to see that the hope for winning the war—though a significant military escalation—was "dependent on the public continuing support for our efforts in Vietnam to the extent that it did for as long as it did" (Nixon, 1978). Potentially escalating the war against North Vietnam was a perilous option early in his presidency because of the antiwar movement's strength demonstrated by the October 15, 1969, moratorium. Nixon felt he had some success in neutralizing the movement through his public relations efforts, and particularly the November 3 Silent Majority speech, which strengthened his hand in conducting the war and negotiating with the North Vietnamese. Nevertheless, the nationwide campus-centered reaction that limited the Cambodia operation in 1970 demonstrated that Nixon was unable to control public sentiment entirely. In short, Nixon stressed how important public support was for his policies and implied that the erosion of support influenced his policies. But he rarely said explicitly that he had to take a particular policy because of public opinion pressure or that he could not do something he wanted because opposition opinion prevented it. He generally tried to lead or circumvent opinion. Kissinger was generally less forthcoming about opinion's role but recognized the power of protest in 1969–70. Political realities tied to public opinion, like protest and congressional action, also deterred until late in the war the implementation of preferred Nixon policies of stronger action against North Vietnam.[9]

The decision-makers' own words reveal that public opinion constrained Vietnam policy across the war. As the shift in opinion around Tet helped drive LBJ to deescalate, declining public support ultimately forced an end to the conflict at the start of Nixon's second term. Protest limited the extent of escalation under both LBJ and Nixon through 1969. But when the antiwar movement subsided in the early 1970s, Nixon could carry out the 1972–73 escalations he threatened in 1969. Though most policymakers would have preferred more latitude, they recognized that public opinion and protest limited the decisions they could take.

Decision-makers in both the Johnson and Nixon administrations stressed the importance of public opinion in policies that affect the lives and the values of the American citizenry. They agreed that, absent public support, any policy is doomed to fail. As theory and practice collide in governing, the reality of the decade of Vietnam War during the Johnson and the Nixon administrations was no exception.

By the end of the Johnson administration, the American public had become fed up with the war and "the administration no longer had the support to pursue an aggressive policy in Vietnam" (Laird, 2/8/99). President Johnson stepped down because the country's aversion for the war had become a disapproval of him and his leadership. Nixon interpreted this message as public dissatisfaction at the length of the war and at the prospect of having it end with no American victory. Capitalizing on this new interpretation of public protest, the Nixon administration (with the blessing of Lyndon Johnson) could escalate and widen the war, while simultaneously amplifying and bettering the Johnson strategies at manipulating and circumventing public opinion.

Melvin Laird makes the same admission as Dean Rusk that the language of peace, negotiation, and deescalation, was necessary to buy time with the public and intensify the attacks. The policies of delaying the escalation from 1969 to 1970 and 1972, of Vietnamization, and of curtailing the draft were part of the same campaign to make the American public change its focus from the war as such to the different potentially winning strategies. The constraint on policy was on the aggressiveness of the campaign, its length, and the way it was presented to the public.

As a result of the second-phase escalation from 1970 to 1973, the number of ca-

---

[9]In an April 9, 1988, "Meet the Press" interview, Nixon said the "biggest mistake" of his presidency was the decision not to bomb and mine North Vietnam in 1969. ("Nixon: I Erred on Viet Bombing," 1988, p. 7).

sualties was higher on both sides, and the destruction of Vietnam and Cambodia by far exceeded anything under the former administration. Intensified public protests were viewed scornfully by the Nixon administration, as they had been by Johnson. While McNamara and Clifford sympathized with the public outrage, the rest of the Vietnam-era decision-makers considered the protests irrational, unpatriotic, and responsible for the prolongation of the war. By 1973, public opposition had essentially forced the United States to withdraw from Vietnam. In 1975, Congress cut off funding to the South Vietnamese government. The "post-Vietnam syndrome," fear of "another Vietnam," informed opposition to U.S. interventions in the 1970s through the 1990s.

If a major part of the Vietnam War policy was to try but ultimately fail to manufacture consent from the American public, it was not surprising the future U.S. intervention in Nicaragua took an indirect path. Having to bypass the public's disapproval of new military interventions because of the "post-Vietnam syndrome," the Reagan administration, as chapters 7 and 8 demonstrate, acted out its Cold-War strategies in the Western Hemisphere by conducting eight years of largely covert operations in the country of Nicaragua.

III

THE NICARAGUA CASE
THE CONTRA FUNDING
CONTROVERSY

THE CASE STUDY IN CHAPTERS 7 AND 8 LOOKS AT AMERICAN AID TO THE NICARAGUAN contras during the Reagan administration. The first part provides an overview of the history that surrounded the debate about giving aid to the contras. It lays out the different sides of the debate over contra aid, the basic flow of events and policy throughout the era, and the public sentiments regarding involvement in Nicaragua at that time. The years 1981 through 1990 were marked by a series of fierce struggles between the administration and Congress over the issue of contra aid. On one hand, staunchly anticommunist, Ronald Reagan felt that the spread of communism in Latin America must be stopped by all means possible. On the other hand, congressional opposition, led mainly by the Democrats, was worried that the United States would get caught in another burdensome civil war like Vietnam. Reagan sought to increase aid to the contras while the congressional opposition sought to limit it. The balance of power shifted back and forth because of the continual contention of moderate Democrats and Republicans concerned with their electoral calculations.

Overall support for Reagan's policies in Nicaragua was generally low. But, by using anticommunist rhetoric and his political clout, Reagan was at times able to convince wavering representatives to side with him. It is in this contending manner that the debate between the president, Congress, and public opinion over American aid to the Nicaraguan rebels progressed until its end in 1990. It is out of this background that the exploration of the impact of public opinion on contra aid policy arises.

Focusing on the actual decision-making process, Chapter 8 explores the perceptions and choices made by members of the Reagan administration and Congress. The chapter generally address three particular benchmarks: the 1985 resumption of aid to the contras, the Congressional refusal and then approval of $100 million in aid in 1986, and the blocking of additional aid in 1987 following the Iran-contra scandal. It identifies the awareness of public opinion by and its potential impact on such influential policymakers such as President Reagan (especially as articulated by his pollster, Richard Wirthlin), Secretary of State George Shultz, Assistant Secretaries of State Elliot Abrams and J. Edward Fox, and Secretaries of Defense Caspar Weinberger and Frank Carlucci. It also explores the awareness about and impact of opinion on Senators Richard Lugar (R-IN) and Claiborne Pell (D-RI), and representatives Ike Skelton (D-MO), Mickey Edwards (R-OK), Bill Richardson (D-NM), and John Spratt (D-NC).

In short, these chapters display the limiting though not defining effect that public opinion had on the policymakers' decisions to give or remove—partially or totally— aid for the contras. These choices, predicated upon the opinions of constituencies, partisan politics, and personal beliefs, convey the manner in which public opinion shaped American policy on contra aid.

CHAPTER 7

Nicaragua: History, Reagan Policies, and Public Opinion

INTRODUCTION

This chapter covers the events, policies, and public opinion that surrounded the giving of U.S. aid to the Nicaraguan contras during the presidency of Ronald Reagan (LeoGrande, 1993; Pastor, 1993). The story of American aid to the contras centered on the conflict between the Reagan administration and its Democratic-led congressional opposition. It was within this debate, where the advantage was constantly shifting from one side to the other, that the United States gave or withheld aid throughout Reagan's two terms in office in the 1980s. Getting "communism" out of Nicaragua was of the utmost importance to Reagan, but his inability to convince the American people of its importance marred his repeated attempts at garnering aid for the contras. The lack of public support limited the scope of Reagan's policies. This continual struggle to gain support from Congress and from the American people for aid for the contras marked the period from 1981 until 1990, into the Bush administration. It influenced the decisions made by the government in both the public and covert spheres.

The history of aid to the contras in Nicaragua running from the start of the Reagan administration in 1981 to the election of the Chamorro government in 1990 is a tale of zealous anticommunism amid congressional and electoral politics. An early act of the Reagan administration in 1981 was to end Carter-era economic assistance to the Sandinista government in Nicaragua that had taken power two years earlier in the overthrow of the Somoza regime. Reagan also secretly authorized Central Intelligence Agency covert operations in the region: these included the establishment of the Nicaraguan Democratic Force (FDN) that came to be known as the "contras." After contra attacks led the Sandinistas to declare a state of national emergency, the first U.S. press stories about the war appeared in early 1982 (Tyler and Woodward, 1982, p. A1).

For 1981, the administration provided $19 million for covert CIA financial and logistical support for the opposition (Gelb, 1982, p. A1). By mid-1982, U.S. support had transformed the contras into an army of four thousand (Brecher and Walcott, 1982, pp. 42–53). By 1983, they would number seven thousand, and by 1986, approximately fifteen thousand contras were at war with the Sandinistas (Brecher and

Walcott, 1982; McNeil, 1988; Oberdorfer, 1983). The U.S. role became more central as the war widened.

Members of Congress opposed U.S. covert support of the contras and entangling this country with the remnants of former Nicaraguan president Anastasio Somoza's national guard. Fearing that efforts to depose the Sandinistas could draw the United States into direct military involvement, Congress limited the scope of the Nicaragua operation to intercepting Sandinista arms shipments to guerrillas fighting the government in El Salvador (Gutman, 1988). A November 1982 *Newsweek* story on how the "secret war" in Nicaragua had grown into a large paramilitary operation prompted congressional proposals to cut funds for the contras (Brecher and Walcott, 1982).[1]

In December 1982, House Intelligence Committee chairman Edward Boland (D-MA) offered an "amendment" that restricted U.S. support for the overthrow of the Sandinistas that the House approved 411 to 0. Though Democrats failed to cut off funding for the covert war (Felton, 1985a, pp. 710–11), the 1983 Intelligence Authorization (PL 97-269) Act prohibited U.S. aid "for the purpose of overthrowing the Government of Nicaragua or provoking a military exchange between Nicaragua and Honduras" (U.S. Congress, 1985). This expressed congressional uneasiness with the contra operation without actually halting it. The Reagan administration interpreted the law as continuing support for the contras.

In January 1983, Mexico, Venezuela, Colombia, and Panama—jointly called the Contadora countries—began searching for a diplomatic settlement to the Central American conflicts in Nicaragua and El Salvador. The Reagan administration continued to give the contras $29 million in covert aid. In March, fifteen hundred contras invaded Nicaragua, as press reports documented the U.S. role (Taubman and Bonner, 1983, pp. A1, A14). Some members of Congress felt that the administration's real aim was to overthrow the Nicaraguan government in violation of the Boland Amendment (Arnson, 1989). Thus, the administration had lost the confidence of activists like Senator Daniel Patrick Moynihan (D-NY) and Representative Boland, who doubted that Congress could control a CIA covert war, and proposed stopping all funding for the contras.

In hopes of heading off the restriction and also winning congressional support for military aid for El Salvador, the administration launched a major campaign to build public support. Reagan addressed a Joint Session of Congress in April 1983, the first time the president had led in making the administration's case. Reagan cast the issue in Cold-War terms of the Cuban-Soviet menace, and blamed Congress for a possible loss of Central America. "Who among us," he asked, "would wish to bear the responsibility for failing to meet our shared obligation?" (Reagan, 1983). Reagan's efforts had some initial success in building support. From April to June 1983, approval of his handling of the situation in Central America jumped four points from 21 to 25 percent (Sobel, 1993, Table 4–24). Approval for Reagan's handling of the Nicaragua

---

[1]The 1974 "Hughes-Ryan" amendment to the Foreign Assistance Act of 1961 and the National Security Act of 1947 require the president to submit to the Intelligence committees a "finding" whenever he initiates a covert operation. The Intelligence committees cannot approve or disapprove the findings, though they can refuse funds for operations they oppose.

situation peaked at 35 percent in mid-1986, but largely remained in the mid 20s afterwards (Gallup in Sobel, 1993, Table 4–24).

Uncomfortable about opposing Reagan's policy without putting something in its place, the Democrats in Congress proposed an overt aid package to answer the administration's claim that the purpose of the covert war was to interdict arms flowing from Nicaragua to guerrilla movements in El Salvador and Guatemala. For the following five years, whenever liberal Democrats tried to stop the financing for the war, their moderate and conservative colleagues insisted on a "politically defensible alternative" (LeoGrande, 1993, p. 32). A compromise provided $24 million for the covert war, less than the administration requested, and prohibited supplements from contingency funds.

From July to December 1983 the United States carried out large-scale joint military maneuvers around Honduras. On October 25, 1983, two days after the bombing of Marine barracks in Beirut killed 241 Americans, the United States invaded Grenada to remove the leftist government. Popular support for the president's actions there prompted a more favorable reappraisal of the administration's Central America policy by the American public. Approval of Reagan's policies in Nicaragua rose from 26 percent before the invasion to 36 percent afterward (Sobel, 1993, Table 4–24). The increased support, however, vanished as quickly as it had appeared. By January of 1984, just two months later, only 28 percent of Americans approved of President Reagan's handling of the situation in Nicaragua (Sobel, 1993, Table 4–24). This was comparable to the preinvasion level.

At the start of 1984, the Kissinger Commission endorsed Reagan's basic Central America policy though not specifically contra aid, and the administration hoped that the commission's report might strengthen the request for more aid. The $24 million in contra aid for 1984 was not enough to continue the war, so in March 1984 the administration made a supplemental request to attach $21 million for the contras to an unrelated appropriation. "The Senate approved the request despite Reagan's indication just before the debate that his aim in Nicaragua was to remove the illegitimate Sandinistas after all" (LeoGrande, 1993, p. 33). But the House voted 241 to 177 to ban the use of funds for military or paramilitary operations to overthrow Nicaragua—the same "Boland Amendment" restriction as before.

Between the Senate and House votes in 1984, the press revealed that the CIA had mined Nicaragua's harbors. Chairman Barry Goldwater (R-AZ), a contra aid supporter, criticized CIA director William Casey for ignoring the law requiring him to notify the committee in advance of significant intelligence operations (Gutman, 1988, pp. 199–200). The administration increased the political damage by refusing to recognize the World Court's hearing of a Nicaraguan complaint about the U.S. mining and contra support. The Congress condemned both the mining and the withdrawal from the Court. Public opinion about the mining was strongly negative: two-thirds disapproval and only 13 percent approval (CBS/New York Times, April). A majority supported Democratic efforts to prohibit mining of Nicaragua's harbors (Harris, May 1984).

In summer 1984, when the Congress considered the supplemental $21 million in contra aid, both Houses refused additional aid, imposing instead a second Boland restriction on any aid. Since the $24 million appropriated in November had been exhausted, the legal expenditure of U.S. contra aid ended. The most the House would accept was a provision for $14 million in military aid that the president could spend only if it was approved after February 1985 by a joint congressional resolution. Thus, this "Boland II" language banned all U.S. aid to the contras.[2] Third countries and private donations coordinated by National Security Council staff member Oliver North (Sobel, 1995a) kept the contras alive. But the administration postponed the fight until after the 1984 U.S. presidential and congressional elections.

In November 1984, Sandinista leader Daniel Ortega was elected president of Nicaragua. Although Nicaragua was not a major issue in the 1984 U.S. campaign, after a landslide victory Reagan launched a bid to resume contra aid. Reagan said his aim was to "remove" the "present structure" of the Nicaraguan government and force the Sandinistas to "say 'uncle'" (LeoGrande, 1993). He called the contras "freedom fighters" and the "moral equal of our founding fathers" (Arnson, 1989, p. 177). In April 1985, Reagan asked for release of the contingent $14 million, promising it for nonmilitary aid only if the Sandinistas agreed to negotiate with the contras. Reagan also proposed a peace plan, cease-fire, church-mediated talks, and internationally supervised elections (Moffett, 1985). The Democratic leadership won a solid victory against the release of the $14 million in military aid. The funding was overwhelmingly defeated by "an odd coalition of Republicans and liberal Democrats," the former against too little aid and the latter against any (LeoGrande, 1993).

Yet the defeat left moderate and conservative Democrats bitter. "The bill included a political compromise to give them 'political cover' in a credible alternative that did not totally abandon the contras." The failure of the democratic compromise in relief aid left many of them "feeling politically vulnerable and willing to vote with the White House next time" (Roberts, 1985b). Since the Republicans needed only two votes to pass a proposal by Minority Leader Robert Michel, the prospects for nonmilitary aid looked good. They looked even better the next day when the press reported that Nicaraguan president Daniel Ortega would soon travel to Moscow (LeoGrande, 1993). Since Reagan had charged that the Sandinistas were Communist puppets, Ortega's trip seemed to prove him right. Many representatives who voted against the contras felt embarrassed; that the purpose of Ortega's trip to Moscow was to obtain badly needed oil was neither "understood nor relevant to the trip's political impact in Washington" (LeoGrande, 1993).

In May 1985, Reagan imposed a trade embargo on Nicaragua, the last element in economic warfare that began with the cut-off of economic aid in 1981. In 1982, Washington had blocked loans to Nicaragua through international financial institutions like the World Bank (Kornbluh, 1987, pp. 123–56). The trade embargo got public support, perhaps because it did not send money or risk U.S. troops. Embargo supporters outnumbered opponents (Harris, 52 percent to 40 percent; Gallup, 46 percent to 37 percent), though CBS/*New York Times* found opponents with a slight plurality of 40 percent to 36 percent.

---

[2]Congress banned the aid, but the administration circumvented the restrictions. The administration also continued to provide covert military aid, uncovered in the Iran-contra scandal, and "political" aid to the contras (Parry and Barger, 1986; Sobel, 1995a).

Benchmark 1: Resumption of Aid to the Contras

The administration attempted to revive contra aid a few weeks later. In mid-1985, the Senate authorized $38 million in nonlethal aid for FY1985 and 1986. "They were not thinking about Nicaragua or El Salvador," said Senator Christopher Dodd (D-CT). "They were thinking about going home and giving a speech to the Veterans of Foreign Wars. The primary concern is that Senators don't want the President to point an accusing finger at them and say, 'You lost Central America'" (Roberts, 1985a).

By then there was no majority coalition for the no aid position (Arnson, 1989). The House rejected extending the Boland ban on military aid. A new aid bill developed in negotiations between the Republican leadership and conservative Democrats headed by Dave McCurdy (D-OK) provided $27 million in nonmilitary aid for the contras not to be delivered by the CIA or Department of Defense. On August 15, 1985, "the legal flow of U.S. aid to the contras resumed for the first time since May 1984," (LeoGrande, 1993). In addition, the contras received $13 million in communications equipment and training provided by the CIA (Serafino, 1989). And, unknown to Congress, arm sales to Iran had begun to provide funds for the contras during 1985 and 1986 (Sobel, 1995a; U.S. Congress, 1987b, pp. 331–40).

Of several House members who changed their votes on contra aid between April and June 1985, seventeen were southern Democrats. Speaker Tip O'Neill explained that "they think Reagan is supreme. They see a wave of people changing parties down there [in the south], office-holders, and they're deeply concerned about that." Speaker Jim Wright, a southern Democrat himself, explained, "Nobody wants to be vulnerable to being portrayed as too favorable to communism" (Shapiro, 1985, pp. 13–14). But the polls did not reveal that southern Democrats needed to be afraid of the contra aid issue because there was little evidence of sharp differences between the north and south on Central America. In 1984 and 1988, southerners approved more highly of Reagan's handling of Nicaragua, but a larger group disapproved. In 1986, southerners were slightly more supportive of contra aid (Gallup: 37 percent in the south, 34 percent elsewhere), though significantly less opposed (45 percent to 55 percent). "By 1987, there was no difference between southern attitudes and the rest of the nation's; contra aid was overwhelmingly opposed everywhere" (LeoGrande, 1993, p. 38).

Southerners' reasons for supporting or opposing contra aid were not particularly distinctive (Market Opinion Research, 1988). Anticommunism and the need to protect U.S. borders from a flow of refugees generated by the Central American wars were not more effective as reason in the South than elsewhere. Among southern contra supporters, 14 percent cited the need to protect U.S. security and borders, (19 percent of others), and 15 percent cited anticommunism (17 percent of others). The U.S. economic embargo on Nicaragua in May 1985 was a source of possible concern for southern Democrats, but southerners supported it by a wide margin (53 percent to 30 percent) (Outside of the South, 42 percent favored, 40 percent opposed). Much to their disappointment, a Democratic leadership-commissioned poll of southern states before the June 1985 vote on contra aid (Brandt, 1985) yielded 62 percent approval for the policy (cf. Lockerbie and Borrelli, 1990). Yet 51 percent of southerners opposed using U.S. troops to remove the Sandinistas to "prevent Communism from spreading in Central America" (Brandt, 1985).

The $27 million approved in June 1985 covered only the first half of FY 1986. In February 1986 the administration asked for $100 million in additional aid, more than twice any previous request. The president called for a repeal of the ban on both lethal military aid and CIA involvement. This fight would be the last major policy battle between President Reagan and retiring Speaker O'Neill. Though O'Neill tried to swing members to the Democrats' side, "Reagan countered by speaking in favor of contra aid almost constantly in early 1986, [including] a nationwide television address on the eve of the congressional votes" (Weinraub, 1986).

The administration's strategy was like the one that had worked in the summer of 1985 of branding opponents of contra aid as soft on communism (cf. Shapiro, 1985). Communications director Patrick Buchanan led the assault in the *Washington Post*: "The national Democratic Party has now become, with Moscow, the co-guarantor of the Brezhnev Doctrine in Central America. . . . With the vote on contra aid, the Democratic Party will reveal whether it stands with Ronald Reagan and the resistance—or Daniel Ortega and the Communists" (Buchanan, 1986).

Benchmark 2: Refusal and Approval at $100 Million in Aid

But Buchanan's hard-line approach backfired. The attempt "at intimidation for narrow partisan advantage" (LeoGrande, 1993, p. 34) was widely criticized as White House McCarthyism. Though Reagan never disavowed Buchanan's attacks, they stopped after Senator Nancy Kassebaum (R-KS), criticized the White House for abandoning "reasoned and rational debate" by presenting the conflict as between "Republicans in white hats and Democrats wrapped in red banners" (Congressional Record, 1986, pp. S2125–26). The administration's approach contributed to the White House losing votes among conservative Democrats and moderate Republicans. On March 20, the aid package lost in the House, 222 to 210.

In mid-1986, Congress investigated reports of corruption in how the contras spent the $27 million in nonmilitary aid from 1985. The General Accounting Office found that over half could not be accounted for. The press reported contra involvement in drug and gun smuggling (Buzenberg, 1986). But the White House need only seven votes from among the sixteen Republicans who had voted against aid in March. In stressing party loyalty, Reagan, whose popularity was at a peak of 68 percent, would remember who voted with him in deciding which Republican candidates to help in the fall elections. The peaking of support for contra aid at 42 percent (Sobel, 1993, p. 25), while not constituting a majority, was adequate to represent some leeway in the national mood for assisting the contras.

The president also needed some moderate Democrats and lowered the harsh, partisan rhetoric (LeoGrande, 1993, p. 41) with a plea for bipartisanship. But "while Reagan spoke of bipartisanship, his allies on the Republican right were publicly targeting Democrats for defeat in 1986 because they opposed contra aid" (LeoGrande, 1993, p. 41). Furthermore, Citizens for Reagan targeted Democratic representative in Florida Buddy MacKay in newspaper ads headlined "Whose Buddy Is He?" The Free Congress PAC promised to use the Nicaragua issue the way it had used the Panama Canal. "There are people who voted against this bill who are going to pay for their vote with their congressional seat this year." This didn't appear to be an idle threat because liberal senators Frank Church (D-ID), Birch Bayh (D-IN), and George Mc-Govern (D-SD) were defeated in 1978 and 1980 "by using their votes on the Panama Canal. It's going to be the same thing all over again" (Taylor, 1986).

On June 25, 1986, the House approved the administration's $100 million package 221 to 209. It also approved (215–212) an amendment prohibiting U.S. personnel from training the contras in Honduras or Costa Rica near the Nicaraguan border. President Reagan was chiefly responsible for the victory in Congress because his lobbying of swing House voters won commitments from eight of the eleven who switched. "When a president gets to the point that he can pinpoint twenty people and work face to face with them, he's hard to stop," noted Tip O'Neill (Frireman, 1986). Just after the vote, however, the World Court voted in favor of the Sandinista complaint against U.S. covert aid to the contras.

Though swing district opinion was more closely divided (Analysis Group, 1987a, 1987b), the opposition to contra aid in national public opinion seemed to make little difference. "If members of Congress were just reacting to the mood of their constituents, it probably wouldn't pass. The nation is opposed to the president's policy," noted Democrat Michael Barnes. "But the possibility that opinion might suddenly change worried members" (LeoGrande 1993, p. 42). Democrats were scared that the Reagan victory could then make them vulnerable. "Democrats live in holy terror that the president will go on the tube and lambaste them for a vote," explained Republican Guy Vander Jagt (R-MI) (Apple, 1986).

The political alignments in the Senate mirrored the House except that the Republicans was the majority party through 1986. About two-thirds of the Democrat senators also opposed contra aid, though a bloc of conservative southerners supported the administration. The Senate vote in March 1986 was close because there were more moderate Republicans opposing contra aid in that body. Moderate Democrats tried unsuccessfully to find a compromise that would get wide support and have a chance to pass. Such attempts were opposed both by liberal Democrats, who refused in principle to vote for contra aid, and by the administration, which saw no need to make any concessions to prevail in the Senate (Roberts, 1986a). Yet when on June 25, the House passed the $100 million in aid and on August 13, the Senate approved it, 53 to 47, the United States was again officially backing the contras. When the bill was signed into law on October 18, 1987, U.S. aid again began to flow to the contras (Serafino, 1987, p. 15).

In two years the Congress had come from the May 1984 cutoff of funds, through a successful administration struggle to restore the program. Though in 1984 and early 1985 opponents had held more than a 60-vote margin over the White House, Reagan gradually eroded the opposition coalition in repeatedly returning to Congress. "The President's landslide reelection victory . . . meant that Democrats were more intimidated by the President's popularity and less inclined to oppose him on issues of importance to him," wrote Victor Johnson, staff director of the House Subcommittee on Western Hemisphere Affairs. "Repeated votes meant that those who found it politically difficult to oppose the Administration were subjected to cumulative political pressure that became intolerable over time" (Johnson, 1989).

The administration had played on the anticommunism theme: the Sandinistas were puppets of Havana and Moscow. They would try to continue exporting revolution to their neighbors. The Sandinistas allegedly violated human rights, committed genocide against the Miskito Indians, drove the Jewish community into exile, smuggled drugs into the United States, got Soviet MiG jet fighters, and let Nicaragua become a base for international terrorism (see, for example, LeoGrande, 1993; Reagan, 1988). The Democrats conceded the criticism of the Sandinistas, but insisted that Reagan's accusations were exaggerated. Yet the United States needed to do something: Reagan promised to get the Sandinistas to behave or get rid of them, without committing American troops. The Democrats offered negotiations, which seemed too soft an alternative.

After the Republicans' losses in the 1986 congressional elections and the breaking of the Iran-contra scandal, the House majority for Reagan's Nicaragua policy disappeared. The administration's apparent violation of the law tainted the policy of aiding the contras. In addition, Reagan could not retain a Republican majority in the Senate, despite personal campaigning, and he started not to seem the electoral threat some Democrats had thought he was. Disapproval of Reagan's handling of Nicaragua policy exceeded approval by more than two to one. By December 1986, for instance, Gallup found approval of the policy stood at only 23 percent, while disapproval was 64 percent (Sobel, 1993, Table 4-24).

On March 11, 1987, the House voted on authorizing release of the last $40 million from the $100 million package. Though a joint resolution could block release of the funds, the vote tested the new balance on the issue. The Democrats "won" 230 to 196. However, the flow of aid continued after March 25, when the Senate voted to release the aid (Congressional Quarterly, 1987, pp. 113, 118).

Benchmark 3: Blocking of Additional Aid, 1987

In summer 1987, the Reagan administration considered asking the Congress for $270 million in aid to the contras for the following year. But the administration had to delay and then reduce requests for military aid during the year to avoid the adverse political atmosphere surrounding the congressional Iran-contra investigation. Revelation of the administration's efforts to trade arms for hostages created a scandal, since the profits from the arms sales were to be devoted to paying for arms for the contras (Sobel, 1995a). The nationally televised testimony to Congress of National Security Council aide Oliver North briefly lifted public approval of aid.

The administration delayed any requests for military aid during 1987 to avoid the congressional Iran-contra investigation, though Oliver North's testimony in mid-July briefly increased support for contra aid. Approval of aid jumped fourteen points to 43 percent in ABC News polls, but a month later, opposition again outnumbered support by two to one (Sobel, 1993, Table 4-12).

Though in early August 1987, House Speaker Jim Wright joined President Reagan in a new diplomatic initiative, their plan was superseded by the Central Americans themselves when on August 7, the five Central American presidents signed the Esquipulas accord based on a draft by Costa Rican president Oscar Arias. In the "Arias Plan," the five presidents pledged to establish democracies, halt support for insurgents, and seek national reconciliation with their opponents. Arias received the Nobel Peace Prize for the plan, which strengthened his and the other proposers' credibility. There was strong U.S. public support for the Esquipulas agreement and a drop in support for contra aid: support for the plan went up to 85 percent while support for contra aid fell from 44 percent in July 1987 to 29 percent in August (Sobel, 1993, Table 4-15).

The diplomatic progress reduced Reagan's chances of winning new military aid. The administration floated the idea of requesting up to $270 million in new aid in September 1987, but withdrew the plan because it lacked support. Instead the administration and the House Democratic leadership agreed on $20.7 million in food and medicine to keep the contras alive while searching for a diplomatic solution to the war (Taylor and Webb, 1988).

By early 1988 the contras ran out of funds and the administration had to ask Congress for more. On February 3, the House voted on President Reagan's request for $36.25 million in aid, including $3.6 million in military assistance (Binkley, 1988; Roberts, 1988); it lost narrowly, 211 to 219. But the Democrats brought their own alternative aid package to the floor for $16 million in food and medicine for the contras and $14.6 million for aid to Nicaraguan children victimized by the war. It was approved initially, 215 to 210 on March 3, but was then defeated on final passage 208 to 216 by "another odd coalition of supporters of the contras" who felt that the plan provided too little and opponents who felt it provided too much (LeoGrande, 1993, p. 46). On March 30, however, Republicans accepted the Democrats' proposal for $17.7 million in nonmilitary aid. In March, Reagan sent troops to Honduras responding to an apparent Sandinista invasion in pursuit of the contras. On March 23, 1988, the Sandinistas and contras signed a cease-fire agreement at Sapoa, ending the war.

In the last Reagan vote on contra aid on May 26, 1988, Henry Hyde (R-IL), offered an amendment to the FY1989 Intelligence Authorization bill to delete a prohibition on military aid to the contras. But it lost, 190 to 214. As the administration ended, the United States was providing limited food and medicine to the contras. Disapproval of Reagan's handling of Nicaragua was twice the level of approval (Gallup, July 1988; 55 percent to 26 percent).

The Bush administration quickly negotiated a bipartisan agreement with the Democratic leadership in the Congress to end the conflict over contra aid. In the March 24, 1989, pact, the administration promised to support the Esquipulas peace process and not apply military pressure on the Sandinistas in the period leading up to the Nicaraguan election in February 1990. On April 13, 1989, Congress approved by 309 to 110 in the House, and 89 to 9 in the Senate, $49.75 in nonmilitary assistance of food and medicine (Felton, 1989). Congress and the president agreed to postpone resolution of the contra issue until after the Nicaraguan election in 1990. The electoral victory over the Sandinistas by a coalition of Nicaraguan opposition groups in February 1990 ended almost a decade's debate over U.S. assistance to the contras. The contras began to disband in May, and had completely disbanded by the end of June 1990.

CONCLUSION: REAGAN'S STRUGGLE

The debate about giving aid to the Nicaraguan contras was a constant struggle between the Reagan administration and Congress. Battling both Congress and the

American people for support, the members of the Reagan administration found themselves in a situation where the advantage constantly shifted back and forth between the president and the Congress. The continual motion was caused by representatives and senators who were pressured, on the one hand, by the threat of being painted as "soft on communism" by the administration and extreme constituents and, on the other hand, by personal doubts about the Reagan plan in Nicaragua. All of this took place within a framework of overall public dissatisfaction with involvement in Central America.

These complex factors created dramatic shifts, from the refusal of all aid to the contras in 1984 to the passage of a $100-million aid package in 1986. Congressional fear of potential public anger over the "loss" of Nicaragua was balanced by the knowledge that current public opinion pointed away from involvement in the region. By constantly assessing the relative effect that voting one way or another would have upon their electoral chances, many representatives were in perpetual motion about Nicaragua. It is from this unsteady and often limiting environment that those who formed policy had to make decisions. With this restrictive climate in mind, Chapter 8 now shifts to the perspectives of the actual policymakers themselves on how public opinion affected their decision-making on contra aid.

Public Opinion's Influence
on Contra Aid Policy

INTRODUCTION

This chapter explores the perspectives of President Ronald Reagan and other decision-makers in the Reagan administration and U.S. Congress about how aware they were about public opinion and its influence upon their actions. Public opinion, party politics, and personal convictions shaped the choices of those who made the policy on giving aid to the Nicaraguan contras in the 1980s. The chapter presents the views of former Secretary of State George Shultz and his undersecretaries, J. Edward Fox and Elliot Abrams. It also contains the views of Secretary of Defense Caspar Weinberger and of Frank Carlucci, who first served as national security adviser and then as secretary of defense. In addition, the chapter draws important insights from Reagan pollster Richard Wirthlin. This look into the thoughts of those who made policy displays a gap between their desires and their ability to affect reality. The administration felt that it could lead public opinion with policy sculpted around the anticommunist beliefs that Reagan held so dearly. This, however, was not the case, as Americans were more influenced by their fear of another Vietnam than their fear of another Cuba and thus consistently opposed intervention in the Nicaragua.

Because of the central role of the Congress in making contra aid policy, the chapter also explores congressional perspectives on such policy in the views of two senators and four congressmen. Senators Richard Lugar (R-IN) and Claiborne Pell (D-RI) were both members of the Foreign Relations Committee. Congressmen Ike Skelton (D-MO), Mickey Edwards (R-OK), Bill Richardson (D-NM), and John Spratt (D-NC) represent a variety of foreign policy backgrounds and perspectives.

This chapter discusses widely how public opinion affected Reagan contra aid policy across the decade. It covers more than the three benchmark periods of the 1985 resumption of aid, Congressional refusal, then approval of $100 million in aid in 1986, and the blocking of further aid in 1987 after the Iran-contra scandal.

On the whole, decision-makers in both the administration and the Congress were aware of public attitudes. A considerable amount of public opposition restricted the administration's plans for sustained and considerable aid to the contras. The congressmen, on the other hand, were less constrained by public opposition or split opinion in their districts; they thus had more latitude for making their decisions.

In short, public opinion had a limited and limiting role in Reagan administration and congressional policymaking.

REAGAN ADMINISTRATION PERSPECTIVES

PRESIDENT RONALD REAGAN

During his administration, President Ronald Reagan found himself caught between two strong currents of opinion about supporting the contras in Nicaragua. On the one hand, Reagan was influenced by strong anticommunist voices within his own administration and the Republican party. Within this Cold-War ideology, the realist Reagan believed strongly that the administration's goals in Central America were too sacred and vital to American national interests to be sacrificed in the face of strong public opposition. On the other hand, throughout his eight years in the White House, polls of the American public showed consistent majority disapproval of aiding the contras. Reagan was not only unable to galvanize public support for his policies for Nicaragua and inspire a concern for the contra "freedom fighters" through his public relations campaign, but was also consistently forced to limit the amount and type of aid that he requested from Congress for the contras.

In his memoirs, President Reagan clearly states his political philosophy toward public opinion and foreign policy:

> You can't have 535 members of the House and Senate administer foreign policy. If the president doesn't do what the people want him to do, they will let him know it. . . . There are some situations in which only the president can and does know all the facts; he should be permitted to lead the nation and make decisions based on what he knows and the trust placed in him by the voters. (Reagan, 1990a, pp. 483–84)

Reagan believed that the president, unlike the Congress, has an inherent constraint on himself, since he is ultimately responsible to the American people for his policies. As Reagan notes, "unlike members of Congress, the president is elected by all the people" (Reagan, 1990a, p. 483). He once lectured Soviet ambassador Anatoly Dobrynin about "the importance of public opinion in our system" (Reagan, 1990a, p. 558). During a press conference in September of 1987, toward the end of his administration, Reagan addressed the general issue of the impact of public opinion polls on his policies. He responded to a reporter who asked whether it was easier to gather congressional support for his programs when support in the polls was high.

> The United States system of government is very responsive to the opinions of the American people. . . . Public opinion polls, while often not on the top of a politician's favorite things, do reflect the mood and feelings of the American people. . . . I don't think, however, that a President's decisions regarding central issues of peace, security, and the economic health of this nation are really determined by the shifts . . . in the opinion polls. (Reagan, 1989)

Although supportive of the role of public opinion in promoting dialogue, these statements indicate Reagan's skepticism about letting public opinion, positive or negative, alter his policy goals. This belief would set the tone throughout his administration on aid to the Nicaraguan contras.

In retrospect, Reagan shows a general skepticism with regard to this opposition. For him, lack of support for his programs indicated a lack of knowledge and sophistication on the part of the American people: "For eight years the press called me the Great Communicator. Well, one of my greatest frustrations during those eight years was my inability to communicate to the American people and to Congress the seriousness of the threat we faced in Central America" (Reagan, 1990a, p. 471). President Reagan prided himself on being a popular president who could communicate with the American people. Intensified by his landslide victory in 1984, this pride led Reagan to believe that he could rally the public around his Nicaragua policies and frustrated him when his attempts failed. Acutely aware of the importance of public support to a successful foreign intervention, he tried in vain to win the American public over to his cause.

In one of his early acts as president in 1981, Reagan withdrew economic assistance to the Sandinista government in Nicaragua. The administration instead authorized funds for covert CIA operations in Central America. As the war in Nicaragua intensified through the 1980s, the role of the United States became increasingly central. In 1982 and 1983, the Reagan administration fought with Congress over the intervention, with many congresspersons expressing reservations about drawing the country into military involvement in Central America. As Reagan notes: "The skirmishes I had with Congress in 1982 and 1983 were minor compared with those that would come later. My battles with Capitol Hill over Central America would continue through my entire presidency" (Reagan, 1990a, p. 478).

As early as January 1982, Reagan was already tailoring his policy in terms of public support. In the first of four decisions concerning Central America, he issued a national security directive to his advisers to "create a public information task force to inform the public and Congress of the critical situation in the area" (Simpson, 1991, p. 53). He demonstrated this concern for informing the public to rouse support throughout his administration. In light of increasing congressional dissent and an intensification of conflict in Nicaragua, in 1983 the administration launched a significant public relations campaign aimed at garnering support for the contra fighters. In a nationwide broadcast before a joint session of Congress on April 27, 1983, Reagan confronted public criticism for his administration's policies and tied the Nicaraguan cause with American national principles and interests.

> I don't believe there's a majority in the Congress or in the country that counsels passivity, resignation, defeatism in the face of this challenge. . . . I don't believe that a majority of the Congress or the country is prepared to stand by passively while the people of Central America are delivered to totalitarianism and we ourselves left vulnerable to new dangers. (Reagan, 1984, p. 605)

Clearly, Reagan regarded the lack of support for his policies as an indication that Americans needed to be awakened to the cause. He believed that support for the contras would come through informing and leading public opinion, since the administration's goals in the region were not only in the best interests of the country, but also adhered to traditional American democratic principles.

The efforts of the Reagan administration to increase public awareness and support for the policy in Nicaragua were only minimally successful. Instead, the campaign to inform the public raised more questions. The issue of public support evoked memories of the Vietnam War. In a July 1983 press conference, UPI's Helen Thomas asked Reagan about military maneuvers off the Nicaraguan coast: "The polls show the American people are not for them, and they fear it may lead to war. . . . Remembering the lessons in Vietnam, does this bother you? And do they have any say?" Reagan responded that "there is no comparison with Vietnam. . . . The American people are disturbed because of the confused pattern that has been presented to them and the constant drumbeat with regard to the . . . suspicion that somehow there is an ulterior purpose in this" (Reagan, 1985, p. 1084).

Reagan later remarked that "after Vietnam, I knew that Americans would be just as reluctant to send their sons to fight in Central America, and I had no intention of asking them to do that" (Reagan, 1995, p. 239). He also blamed the media and Vietnam reporters who tried to "cast Uncle Sam in the role of villain" (Reagan, 1995, p. 480). Although aware of the legacy of the Vietnam War and public opinion, Reagan attributed the lack of support for his policies to confusion and ignorance among the American public. At the same press conference, Reagan was asked if he felt that the American people were ready to support a war in Central America: "I don't think the American people ever wanted a war. . . . Frankly, I don't think they're as aware as perhaps they should be. We've tried to make them aware that this does constitute something of a threat in the hemisphere" (Reagan, 1985, p. 1085). Thus Reagan and his administration regarded public opinion as a force to be courted and a potential constraint on the actions they would be able to take in Nicaragua, but not as something that should affect their policy. When asked directly if he felt that the American people supported his policy in Central America, the President responded that "those that have been informed and understand it do" (Reagan, 1985, p. 1086).

Reagan continued factoring public opinion into foreign policymaking throughout his administration. In a national security memorandum signed in July 1983 outlining the administration's plans for Nicaragua, Reagan directed the secretaries of state and defense to "prepare a coordinated legislative, diplomatic, and public affairs strategy that supports these initiatives" (Simpson, 1991, p. 314). The strategy was to adhere to a "time-phased schedule." Reagan explained that "implementation of these initiatives will be timed to take into account public affairs/legislative factors" (Simpson, 1991, p. 314). Concern for public opinion was affecting the timing of the Reagan administration's policy, although not the content. Reagan was still operating under the belief that public opinion needed to be courted and led on the issue, rather than considered in the policy initiatives. He reflected on the difficulty of courting public opinion to the contra cause in his memoirs; "during the eight years of my presidency I repeatedly expressed my frustration (and sometimes downright exasperation) over my difficulties in convincing the American people and Congress about the seriousness of the threat in Central America" (Reagan, 1990a, p. 574).

In a radio address in August, Reagan confronted the issue of public opinion and his goals in Nicaragua. He stated that "the polls say many Americans are confused about what we're supporting in Central America and about why that region, so close to home and to our strategic trading arteries, is important to us" (Reagan, 1985, p. 1156). Offering a rebuttal to the criticism of his policies and alluding to public protest over the Nicaragua situation, Reagan continued:

> Unfortunately, there have been such distortions about U.S. policy in Central America that the majority of Americans don't know which side we're on. No wonder a great many sincere people write angrily that we should support dialogue . . . or take any number of actions, all of which we're already doing and have been doing for more than two years. (Reagan, 1985, p. 1157)

Two days later, Reagan reassured a group of veterans in a speech in Louisiana that the dissent among the public over the efforts being made to aid the Nicaraguan contras was unfounded. He told them that "in spite of the discouraging hype and hoopla that you often hear, quiet solid progress is being made" (Reagan, 1985, p. 1176). He was not only clearly aware of the lack of support, but more significantly, of vociferous opposition to his policies with regard to Nicaragua. He, however, was not persuaded by the public opposition to change the administration's goals. Abandoning the contra fighters in Nicaragua was not an option. Aware of how public opposition could limit its success in Congress, the administration focused on coaxing public opinion on the issue in order to gain as much support as possible for the activities in Nicaragua.

Public support for Reagan's contra aid policies would peak by the end of 1983 (Gallup in Sobel, 1993, Table 4–14). In the meantime, Reagan alluded to the possibility of circumventing the public altogether, in order to enact a policy that would not be limited by public opinion. At a news conference in October of that year, Reagan was asked whether the American public had a right to be informed of the CIA's actions in Nicaragua. Seemingly contradicting his desire to inform the public of the situation, Reagan responded that he believed "in the right of a country, when it believes that its interests are best served, to practice covert activity. And then, while your people may have a right to know, you can't let your people know without letting the wrong people know, those that are in opposition to what you're doing." Aware of the problems that public opinion created for his Central American policies, Reagan appeared willing to continue the involvement at all costs, regardless of the public's reaction.

In February 1984, Reagan signed a national security directive that endorsed the recommendations of the National Bipartisan Commission on Central America (Kissinger Commission), which outlined economic initiatives against the Communists power in in Nicaragua and the Communist insurgency challenging the government of El Salvador. With an eye on public opinion, Reagan wrote: "It is important that these recommendations . . . be adopted in a diplomatic and security environment that will permit them to succeed." He directed that "due consideration should be given to the net economic impact on Nicaragua, to U.S. public affairs and to Congressional concerns." Reagan also stressed his belief that Communists were acting within America to thwart public opinion against his administration. He noted that the administration's "public diplomacy and information programs/resources should be substantially expanded to counter the intensive Soviet/Cuban/Nicaraguan propaganda campaign"

(Simpson, 1991, p. 384–87). At this period, he may have felt that the resounding lack of public support was more a result of this propaganda than a general public distaste for the administration's policies that needed to be heard.

In March 1984, with the Reagan Central American policy endorsed by the Kissinger Commission, the Reagan administration hoped to gain an additional $21 million dollars for the contras to continue the war. Congress had already approved $24 million in humanitarian aid at the start of 1984 with the stipulation that the money not be used for operations intending to overthrow the Sandinistas. In a radio address in April, Reagan tried to steer opinion back to the anticommunist debate by evoking alarming images of an imminent Soviet attack.

> Much has been made of late regarding our proper role in Central America, and, in particular, toward Nicaragua. Unfortunately, much of the debate has ignored the most relevant facts. Central America has become the stage for a bold attempt by the Soviet Union, Cuba, and Nicaragua to install communism by force throughout this hemisphere. (Reagan, 1986, p. 535)

To the dismay of the Reagan administration, press reports soon revealed evidence that the CIA had mined Nicaragua's harbors. Public opinion on the matter was strongly negative (CBS, 4/23/84) and Reagan's request for additional aid for the contras was subsequently defeated in both Houses.

In light of the growing majority of opposition to aid for the contras, the Reagan administration was unable to execute its policies in the region once the initial appropriation was exhausted. With scant public support, the Reagan administration felt the constraint of public opposition even when attempting to implement an already limited policy. Clearly a weak spot amidst Reagan's high approval ratings, the fight over contra aid was postponed until after the 1984 elections.

Benchmark 1: Resumption of Contra Aid in 1985

Reagan regarded his landslide victory in 1984 as a mandate for his policies in Central America. The administration resumed its attempt to galvanize public support for contra aid.

In fall 1984, Secretary of Defense Caspar Weinberger and Secretary of State George Shultz debated the circumsances under which the U.S. might use force, particularly in Central America. Among Weinberger's "six test" for commitment were the reasonable assurance of support among the American people and Congress (Richard Halloran, 11/29/84, pp. A1, A3). Shultz held that the U.S. must be ready to use its power without public support a prerequisite. Successful policy would generate its own support ("U.S. Must Be Ready," 1984, p. 1)

In a radio address in February, 1985, Reagan pleaded with the American people for support and action. "Now the people of . . . Nicaragua ask for our help. . . . They are our brothers. How can we ignore them? . . . We must help. Congress must understand that the American people support the struggle for democracy in Central America. We can save them . . . , but only if we act now" (Reagan, 1988, pp. 173–74).

In a revitalized attempt to arouse support for the policies in which he strongly believed, Reagan connected the "freedom fighters" in Nicaragua to American founding fathers. By tying his policy toward Nicaragua with American principles, Reagan hoped to awaken the public to the contra cause.

In spite of these efforts, public support remained low. A *Washington Post* interview asked Reagan about the impact of low support on his policies. Indicating an awareness for public dissent, he replied:

> I know this, about what the polls show, and I know what happens up on the Hill. But we've been subjected in this country to a very sophisticated lobbying campaign by a totalitarian government—the Sandinistas. There has been a disinformation program that is virtually worldwide. . . . I don't think the people have heard actually the thing that we're trying to explain or what's going on. (Reagan, 1988, p. 379)

Reagan attributed the low numbers in public opinion polls to a "disinformation network" on the part of the Soviet Union and Cuba. Clearly, although aware of negative public opinion, he did not regard public opposition as a voice to be heeded and factored into foreign policy formulating. In the same interview, Reagan asserted, "as a matter of fact, in spite of the polls, there is more and more private support for the contras" (Reagan, 1988, p. 379). For Reagan, public opposition was, at best, a subversive element that had to be persuaded and, at worst, a clandestine plot that had to be circumvented altogether. Nevertheless, Reagan consistently felt the limitations of public opposition to his policies, and fought against it.

Efforts to court public opinion continued through the end of 1985. In August, Reagan spoke to the public concern over defense spending in Central America: "I realize that the budget pressures have been very severe, and there's a general lack of enthusiasm for foreign aid, and that has made the job more difficult. We have to make the people aware that these programs are the most effective instruments we have for a more secure international environment." In these statements, Reagan continued to depict the strong general disagreement over administration policies as a dangerous obstacle that was impeding progress. He recognized opposition as a force to be overcome.

Benchmark 2: Funding of $100 Million Including Military Aid

In 1986, while playing a strong anti-communist theme and stressing contra aid as a primary foreign policy goal, Reagan successfully lobbied Congress for $100 million in contra aid. After a two-year struggle, military aid to the contras was restored. The administration hardline rhetoric playing the anticommunism theme that the Sandinistas were puppets of Moscow, trying to export revolution to their neighbors, combined with pressure on swing congressional voters, produced the needed 7 votes among 16 Republicans who had voted against aid in March. On March 20, Reagan's nationally televised speech to Congress on CNN stressed the need to restore aid to the contras. The administration campaign played on the public's relative ignorance about Nicaragua (Sobel, 1989) and employed "resonators" like anticommunism that Wirthlin's polling had determined appealed to the public (Kenworthy, 1987, p. 95).

With his popularity at a peak at 68 percent and support for contra aid similarly at a high figure of 42 percent, Reagan's stressing party loyalty and which candidates to help in the fall induced some swing Republicans to go along with the president. He also lowered the partisan rhetoric by calling for bipartisanship. When on June 25, 1986, the House approved the administration's $100 million package 221 to 209, Reagan was chiefly responsible for the victory in Congress from establishing a climate of opinion more favorable to contra aid and lobbying swing voters. Recurring rhetorical flourishes and repeated votes in the Congress subjected those opposed to administration policy but persuadable to cumulative pressure. The national opposition to the president's policy limited what he could achieve, but the peaking of support for contra aid at 42 percent represented some lessoning of contraint in public attitudes on policy possibilities.

Nevertheless, public opinion remained consistently opposed to the administration's policies. After the World Court ruled in June 1986 in favor of the Sandinista government and against aiding the contras and with the breaking of the Iran-contra scandal, support within Congress soon dissipated as well. Reagan addressed this issue in a national security memorandum in February 1987, directing that "a task force will be formed to engage the administration's resources in a campaign of public diplomacy regarding the situation in Central America, the threat to U.S. security and U.S. objectives for the region." In addition to this task force, "a comprehensive action plan to gain sustained Congressional support for the Nicaraguan Democratic Resistance will be developed" (Simpson, 1991, pp. 783–84). Reagan soon brought his concern back in front of the people. In a radio address in the following month, he lobbied Congress and the American people to continue aid for the contras. Addressing the issue of regional conflict and evoking American democratic principles, he stated:

> Nicaraguans want democracy too. Their current rulers broke their promise . . . that they would lead Nicaragua to democracy. And now the Nicaraguan people want them to deliver on that promise. Democracy, progress, and security—those are our goals in Central America, and they're the goals the American people support. . . . How much safer the world will be when the Soviet leaders see Americans standing behind such a firm policy for peace. (Reagan, 1989, pp. 221–22)

Days later, the House attempted to block the remaining $40 million in aid, but was narrowly overturned by the Senate.

Benchmark 3: Proposals for up to $270 Million in Aid

By September 1987, the Reagan administration was considering asking Congress for up to $270 in new aid for the contras. As early as May, Reagan addressed the issue of strong public criticism:

> The debate in this country over Central American policy has been direct and tough and, yes, even heated at times. While such debate is healthy, we all know that a divided America cannot offer the leadership necessary to provide support and confidence to the emerging democracies in Central America. . . . It's now an issue on which all Americans must unite. (Reagan, 1989, p. 454)

Reagan acknowledged his awareness of outspoken public opposition, yet reaffirmed his unwavering support for the contra cause. Rather than taking public opposition to heart, he indicated his hope to unite Americans under support for his policy. Moreover, Reagan was alluding to the importance of American unity and support for foreign interventions. This was the topic of the debate on the use of force between Secretaries Shultz and Weinberger in the fall of 1984 (Weinberger, 1990, pp. 159, 402).

By the summer of 1987, Reagan perceived some public warming to his cause. Preparing for a possible debate over contra aid in Congress in the fall, Reagan intensified his attempts to inspire public support for his programs. During a speech in July, Reagan stated that "the polls now suggest that the American people are waking up to the threat of a Communist powergrab in their own neighborhood." He went even further, predicting that this "increased awareness of the American people . . . will permit us to continue providing weapons and support to those brave individuals who are struggling . . . in their native Nicaragua." Here Reagan is clearly recognizing the significance of American approval for the implementation and success of his policies in Central America. The lower the public support for the contras, the more constrained the administration was in enacting its plans. In the same speech, Reagan declared that "the more people know about what's happening in Central America, the more they support a strong stand for freedom."

The president echoed this sentiment during a radio address later that month. "Some tell me that people in this country just don't care about the freedom fighters, but I don't think that's true. The more people know about the Sandinista Communists, the more they support the freedom fighters." This reveals the skepticism Reagan felt about public opposition. Since he regarded such opposition as ill informed, he stressed the need for public dialogue. Opposition would not change Reagan's mind; rather, it would intensify his efforts to sway public opinion in his favor. In the same address, the president discussed the American people's feelings about Nicaragua, indicating his belief that public opinion was actually in his favor: "In this country, too, we have seen support grow dramatically as the American people learn the facts about Nicaragua. The American people are tired of the off-again-on-again policy in Central America. . . . The American people want the aid to continue."

In September, when he announced his plan to ask for $270 million in contra aid, Reagan perceived that public opinion was now in his favor. At a speech at the end of September, he cited polls in the latest issue of *Public Opinion* magazine and declared broad American support for his policies. He remarked that "the American public recognizes the great danger posed by an aggressive Communist government in Nicaragua and, by a large majority, favors continued aid to the Nicaraguan freedom fighters." On the basis of conclusions drawn from the study, Reagan declared that "aid to the freedom fighters must and will continue. The American people want it—democracy in Nicaragua. We can accept nothing less." The Reagan administration, while consistently resistant to letting public opinion alter its policies toward Nicaragua, was quick to embrace opinion polls that supported its position (Falcoff, 1987).

Yet the Republicans' reverses in the 1986 congressional elections, particularly losing control of the Senate, and the breaking of the Iran-contra scandal dissipated the House majority for contra aid. Disapproval of Reagan's handling of Nicaragua policy (64 percent) exceeded approval (23 percent) by almost three to one by the end of 1986. The administration had delayed requests for military aid during 1987 to avoid the congressional Iran-contra investigation, though North's mid-July testimony briefly increased support for aid to 43 percent before opposition again outnumbered support by two to one. By late in the year, it was clear there was neither public nor Congressional support for anywhere near $270 million in additional aid.

By the end of 1987, the Reagan administration could achieve only a $20.7-million food package for the contras, since diplomatic avenues were making progress in Nicaragua. By early 1988, as the contras ran out of funds, Reagan asked Congress for more. However, this time he requested just $36 million in aid. Ultimately only $17.7 million in humanitarian assistance would be approved. As Reagan was clearly swimming against the tide of public opinion, his remarks became sharper and more critical of his opponents. In a January radio address, he stated: "some say if you're for aid to the freedom fighters in Nicaragua you're against the peace process. Phooey!" (Reagan, 1990, p. 80). In an address to the Veterans of Foreign Wars in March 1988, Reagan said:

> Too many opponents of aid to the freedom fighters claim to be the heir of Franklin Roosevelt, who told us when the odds are stacked against us that America had a rendezvous with destiny and then led us to the fight. Courage hasn't exactly been the watchword of some opponents of aid. . . . Americans have never lacked courage. . . . I can tell you that Americans are full of the spirit of justice, fight and adventure. (Reagan, 1990b, pp. 298–99)

In spite of his impassioned plea to the American people, the support he had hoped for never materialized. Frustrated with the criticism of his policy, he declared at a March White House briefing, "I just don't understand the inability of some people to realize what the Sandinistas are all about" (Reagan, 1990b, p. 335). The president was not accepting the view of the majority of the nation. At a press conference on August 3, 1988, Reagan would discuss the importance of fighting for principles rather than for what is popular in the polls: "I believe that the American people want to prevent that [chaos in Central America]. But on matters of national security, the real issue is not whether it's the popular thing, but whether it's the right thing (Reagan, 1991)."

Such a philosophy would define Reagan's uphill struggle to gather public support for his policies. His concern was always for upholding the policy in which he believed so strongly. His dedication to supporting the contras could not be swayed, no matter how grim the public opinion polls were.

In sum, public opinion affected President Reagan's efforts to fund the contra uprising in Nicaragua throughout the 1980s. Aware of the legacy of Vietnam and the post-Vietnam syndrome, Reagan had already decided that, given domestic and international public attitudes, he could not send troops to Nicaragua. Public opinion had derailed any policy of direct military intervention. Reagan's response to this constraint was to organize and finance a post-Vietnam counter-revolutionary guerrilla movement in Nicaragua to overthrow the Sandinistas. However, the negative sentiment of the public toward involvement in Nicaragua, with roots in a general attitude of noninterventionism among the American people, restricted both military *and* financial assistance to the contras. Reagan's awareness of public and congressional opposition curbed the scope of the aid he wanted to give to the freedom fighters. Opposition forced the Reagan administration to ask for less contra aid than it would have liked and often made it necessary to find new strategies, sometimes covert and illegal, for supporting the contras.

The Reagan administration tried to court public opinion through a public information campaign. In an effort to circumvent public opinion and implement its policies regardless, the administration was instead pushed into covert operations and the Iran-contra arms scandal. Reagan's objective of overthrowing the government in Nicaragua was never changed by public opinion. Considering public opinion from the point of view of the limits of the public's tolerance, the administration felt it had a free hand to enact its policies up to the point when it became apparent that it was pressing the boundaries of public tolerance. At this point, Reagan, rather than reconsidering his own opinion, attempted either to reason with public opinion or to find alternatives to it.

SECRETARY OF STATE GEORGE SHULTZ

Secretary Shultz felt that foreign policy "must not follow public opinion polls" (Shultz, 1995). Nevertheless, his decision-making was influenced by public attitudes. He admits in his memoirs that "Public debate . . . could be a way to sharpen our thinking and strengthen our policy" (Shultz, 1995, p. 646). He also was acutely aware of the legacy of the Vietnam war and public opinion:

> The Vietnam War had left one indisputable legacy: massive press, public, and congressional anxiety that the United States—at all costs—avoid getting mired in 'another Vietnam.' News items datelined from Central America or the Caribbean raised the alarm that this or that country of the region was about to become our next quagmire. (Shultz, 1995, p. 294)

In an interview, Shultz discussed the extent to which Reagan policy was to support the contras against the Nicaraguan regime "to try to create around Nicaragua a much healthier, democratic, and more prosperous area" (Shultz, 7/6/94). He continued: "President Reagan put a tremendous emphasis on contra aid. It was the only subject on which he addressed a joint session of Congress" (Shultz, 7/6/94). Shultz wrote that "the task was to encourage democracy, deny the Communists their goals, and gain greater American public understanding and support for the economic and security assistance that was needed" (Shultz, 1995, p. 291).

Secretary Shultz was aware of public opposition to Reagan policy, and felt the general public was "resisting our policy toward Nicaragua." The public "didn't support it . . . more in some parts of the country than others." But "the closer you got to Central America, the more supportive people were." Shultz was not aware that support for the contras and for the Reagan policy actually grew slightly, through the beginning of the Iran-contra scandal. He acknowledged the importance of congressional support for the contra fighters, writing that otherwise "by the time the 1984 presidential election campaign was in full force, we would confront an avalanche of political opposition at home" (Shultz, 1995, p. 292).

Shultz was aware of public attitudes from reading and hearing "what the Congress says." "I really didn't pay that much attention to polls because I have an aversion to public policy by polling. Rich Wirthlin briefed me from time to time, but his polls were very general." According to Shultz, the polls discussed "support for our foreign policy," and were "not highly specific on issues" (Shultz, 7/6/94). "And I didn't really hear about polls from the State Department people."

Shultz distinguished public opinion from congressional support. The Congress "was my public opinion poll. . . . I think the Congress is very tuned in to opinion in their districts." The administration tried to influence Congress by getting out around the country and speaking.

> I don't know what public attitudes are and I don't think you do. Because polls are subjected to caveats. So in the end the people who have to vote the money are in the Congress, and that's where you need to focus. . . . When it comes to funding, you have to get to Congress to provide the funding. And the Congress is arguing the merits but also reflecting what the constituents are telling them, and what they are telling their constituents. I think the public opinion relationship to policy is very much a two-way street, and it's up to people in the government to figure out what they think is the right course and then sell it to the country. (Shultz, 1995, p. 311)

Shultz summarized the administration's policy in Central America in the following light:

> Here we had a Pentagon that seemed to take any means to avoid the actual use of American military power but every opportunity to display it. We had an administration engaged in a continuous, divisive debate about the use of strength versus diplomacy at a time when we needed both and had neither in Central America. . . . Playing right into this were Bill Clark and Pentagon planners, who now sprung massive U.S. military movements on the world, heightening the worst fears in ways that would only further deprive the United States of the necessary range of options. (Shultz, 1995, p. 311)

These statements reveal Shultz's awareness of the divisiveness of the Nicaragua debate and that he felt constrained by this debate. The public debate deprived the Reagan administration of a range of options.

Shultz worried little about changes in public support. "Any time you decide you're going to make your policy by trying to figure out what public opinion is, you might as well pack up and go home." Though public attitudes "varied by issue and from time to time," people liked and supported President Reagan, and thought he was basically on the right track. . . . The American people supported what we were doing, but half the Republican party in Congress didn't" (Shultz, 7/6/94).

Shultz observed little direct influence of public opinion on decision-making, but felt it was important for the public to influence Congress.

> As a general thing, we had a consciousness in the administration that we had to sell the policy, and a huge effort was made to do it. Otto Reich was in charge of it for a while, and people went out; I and others spoke in different parts of the country trying to develop support. In the end, I always felt that we had to persuade the Congress somehow, by getting public support and persuading them on the merits. I was a nonpolitician, my President was a very good politician. He always liked to say, 'Before they see the light, they have to feel the heat.' Congress had to feel the heat of 'the

public pressure.' Reagan had great confidence that if he felt something was right for the country, he could persuade the American people that it was right, and they would support him. (Shultz, 7/6/94, p. 5)

Benchmark 3: Proposals for up to $270 Million in Aid[1]

In the fall of 1987, after the breaking of the Iran-contra scandal followed by congressional hearings, Secretary Shultz floated the idea of more money for the contras, from about $105 million up to $270 million. The amount was reduced to $20.7 million because as Shultz noted, "we just could see we weren't getting anywhere with Congress . . ." (Shultz, 7/6/99, p. 6)

Though the contras still had some of the $100 million left, Shultz felt that "it was over." The scandal was devastating with the Congress. The public was very disappointed with President Reagan on Iran-contra. Colin Powell, then deputy and later national security adviser, and Shultz went to Congress "but we didn't think there was any more chance of getting it." Shultz tried to restructure policy in the last few months. "We could get non-military aid fairly easily, particularly if the Congress felt that this was the way to get rid of the problem as we were disbanding the contras."

Shultz elaborated on his disappointment in a TV interview on August 16, 1988: "I have to put the finger on a vote in the House of Representatives very much driven by the leadership of the House of Representatives to deny further assistance to the people fighting for freedom and independence in Nicaragua. It just mystifies me why that shouldn't be supported, but the fact is the United States has not been willing to give that support and so people are leaving. It's a tragedy" (Shultz, 8/16/88).

With regard to the 1984 Shultz-Weinberger debate over the proper use of military force, Shultz argued that public support is not always possible for important military interventions. He wrote that "the public must understand before the fact that occasions will come when their government must act before each and every fact is known—and the decisions cannot be tied to the opinion polls" (Shultz, 1995, p. 648). He continued in his rebuttal of Weinberger's criteria: "How would prior 'reasonable assurance' of support from the American people be obtained? By a congressional vote for action against a terrorist group or for a rescue operation for Americans in danger? . . . This was the Vietnam syndrome in spades, carried to an absurd level, and a complete abdication of the duties of leadership" (Shultz, 1995, p. 648).

---

[1]There is not enough pertinent information about Benchmark 1 (1985) in Shultz's memoirs (1995) or his interview (7/6/94) to identify the impact of public opinion on his decisions then. He acknowledged not "hav[ing] a distinct recollection of those events" (7/6/94, p. 6). Little information also exists on Caspar Weinberger's views on the 1985 benchmark.

What little there is for Benchmark 2 (1986) indicates that Shultz felt that getting the $100 million was "certainly a miracle" because the aid request was "a hard sell . . . to the Congress, especially the House of Representatives" (7/6/94, p. 6). "If, however, the administration had had more public approval," Shultz felt, "it would have asked for more aid from Congress." "I think we would have asked for more support for the contras. During the period when we had $100 million . . . [t]he contras became quite effective. . . . If we could have had that level for two or three years, it would have made a difference. We didn't need to have more than that" (Shultz, 7/6/94, p. 6).

In short, Shultz preferred to make good policy and expected the public support to follow. But he recognized that the lack of public approval limited what he and the president could do to support the contras in Nicaragua.

ASSISTANT SECRETARIES OF STATE ELLIOT ABRAMS AND J. EDWARD FOX

Elliott Abrams considered public opinion essentially "a tool" to shift public opinion in the direction of Reagan policy and to bolster congressional support. The polls had a strategic but not a policy-guiding use. Though the people were opposed to contra aid and did not want an American war in Nicaragua, the administration would show polls that "The people don't want a communist Central America." "The polls were purely instrumental . . . [we] pick[ed] the poll result that might persuade the relevant person that day." "Both sides use polls for their use or abuse" (Sobel, 1993, p. 114).

The Reagan administration was "not watching polls to provide a road map."

> The polls were weapons which would occasionally be used against us, and occasionally be used by us. But the polls could not tell us what policy ought to be. We arrived in office with a policy. Over time tactics changed, but the fundamental policy did not change. The operative problem for those of us on the inside was—how do you get Congress to vote the money you want for El Salvador first and later Nicaragua. (Sobel, 1993, p. 106)

Abrams thought "the polls would suggest that the policies did reinforce previous predispositions toward the president's" foreign policies. He was playing to a particular audience. Abrams felt that the relevant audience for decision-makers in Washington was not overall American public opinion but partisan public opinion, including the conservative wing of the Republican party. Moreover, the administration felt that the public was generally against the policy because of the "very well organized groups" on the left, church groups, political groups, and the media (Sobel, 1993, p. 118). But despite other efforts he was not able to move larger pieces of public opinion in his direction. "I would come out on the low end of how important it was to persuade the public as opposed to persuading the Congress" (Sobel, 1993, p. 114). However, Abrams noted, the administration would probably have asked for more money if they had majority public support for contra aid (Sobel, 1993, p. 160).

There was little serious consideration given to direct use of U.S. forces in either El Salvador or Nicaragua. Abrams "was not privy to any conversation in which it was seriously considered by any serious policy maker. . . . Use of American troops directly in either country in terms of a direct military intervention, no. I don't know how much of that was constrained by public opinion. It was just off limits. Therefore, it wasn't going to happen, and people didn't talk about it. It would be pure guesswork as to why it was that it was off limits, although in the case of Panama, President Reagan was quite loath to use American troops" (Sobel, 1993, p. 116).

"Public opinion was clearly opposed to contra aid throughout the Reagan presidency," yet the president got the congressional support he sought about half the time.

Though Congress was split on contra aid, "there were three or four occasions on which Congress voted money, including, the $100 million including military aid. That happened despite the poll data." (Sobel, 1993, p. 114). "We did care what the American public thought," Fox claimed. "But in reality we start off with an assumption that we're trying to educate Congress, and the members are being pulled in other directions because of pressures from public opinion polls." "I don't think that policy makers start with the assumption that referendum is the way to develop policy. You develop policy first, then you try to convince people to support that policy. But you can't adopt a foreign policy by trying to convince the American public alone. You can educate them to a degree" (p. 114). "For the administration," Abrams felt,

> the importance of public opinion was relatively low. It was not a direct constraint. It constrained some members of Congress in their ability to swing with or against us. Public opinion got attention, but Congress got a lot more attention. . . . The real problem was we were in the minority. Had there been a Republican majority in the House and Senate, we'd have gotten the aid, not half the time but all the time. We had the Senate briefly in 1981–86. (Sobel, 1993, pp. 106, 108)

"We have always known that the president gets what is called 'rally around the flag' support. But those kinds of rally points are explained by an innate patriotism and nationalism among the American people. These support their political leaders, but they tend to be short-lived. The interesting question then becomes 'Why didn't the Reagan administration, knowing that is the case, pursue a bolder policy in Central America?'" (Sobel, 1993, p. 117). Over the long run there seems to be a close correspondence between public preferences and public policy.

SECRETARY OF DEFENSE CASPAR WEINBERGER

Upon Secretary Weinberger's resignation from the Defense Department in late 1987, President Reagan hailed Weinberger as "America's finest Secretary of Defense" (Reagan, 1990). In his farewell address, Weinberger reflected on his successes during his seven years as secretary of defense. When he came to office in 1981 "the United States had weakened our own military in the hope, perhaps, that somehow that could soothe the Nation's nerves that had been rent so far apart after Vietnam" (Weinberger, 1990). He referred to the 1970s as a "decade of neglect [that] was fed . . . by a rather insidious idea that somehow American power was immoral. We began by doubting the war in Vietnam, but we ended by doubting ourselves" (Weinberger, 1987). Weinberger was clearly aware of the legacy of the Vietnam War and the significant correlation between public opinion and successful foreign policymaking. His focus, however, was not in allowing public opinion a more active role in the decision-making process in light of the Vietnam debacle, but rather, in restoring the prestige of the American military in the public's eye. Weinberger considered this to be his greatest achievement as secretary of defense. Upon his departure from the Defense Department, he lauded the "renewed respect for the United States throughout the world . . . and [the] clear support for our military that now comes from the American people" (Weinberger, 11/5/87). This dissipation of the Vietnam War legacy in part marks Weinberger's tenure as secretary of defense and the contra funding policies of the Reagan administration.

Like Reagan, Weinberger's world view was defined by Cold-War polarization and a deep preoccupation with deterrence of the Soviet Union, labeled by the administration as the Evil Empire. In a renowned address to the National Press Club in 1984 entitled "The Uses of Military Power," Weinberger argued that "the single-most critical element of a successful democracy is a strong consensus of support and agreement for our basic purposes. Policies formed without a clear understanding of what we hope to achieve will never work. And you help to build that understanding among our citizens" (Weinberger, 1990, p. 433). Weinberger demonstrates an acute understanding of the relationship between public opinion and successful military intervention. In the speech, Weinberger explained how important it is that the public have an understanding of the uses of military forces. According to Weinberger, deterrence of the Soviet Union would only succeed through a "firm commitment . . . and only from a well-informed public can we expect to have that national will and commitment" (Weinberger, 1990, p. 433). Weinberger, in sharp contrast to Secretary Shultz, argued that national power becomes effective only when the national will and military strength are "forged into one instrument" (Weinberger, 1990, p. 434). He asserted that America's adversaries:

> can also take advantage of our open society, and our freedom of speech and opinion to use alarming rhetoric and disinformation to divide and disrupt our unity of purpose. While they would never dare to allow such freedoms to their own people, they are quick to exploit ours by conducting simultaneous military and propaganda campaigns to achieve their ends. They realize that if they can divide our national will at home, it will not be necessary to defeat our forces abroad. (Weinberger, 1990, p. 438)

In light of what he considered to be a dangerous turning point in world history, Weinberger continued to outline "six major steps to be applied when we are weighing the use of U.S. combat forces abroad" (Weinberger, 1990, p. 440). With underlying memories of Vietnam, he advised that the intervention should be vital to our national interest and fought with clearly defined objectives. Significantly, he argued that combat troops should be supported "wholeheartedly and with the clear intention of winning" (Weinberger, 1990, p. 441). His fifth test declared:

> Before the U.S. commits combat forces abroad, there must be some reasonable assurance we will have the support of the American people and their elected representatives in Congress. This support cannot be achieved unless we are candid in making clear the threats we face; the support cannot be sustained without continuing and close consultation. We cannot fight a battle with the Congress at home while asking our troops to win a war overseas. (Weinberger, 1990, p. 442)

He concluded by applying the tests to the situation in Central America. "Policies and principles such as these require decisive leadership . . . and they also require strong and sustained public support" (Weinberger, 1990, p. 444).

The Nicaraguan controversy has been called "a collision" between theory and practice (Sobel, 1993, p. 1). Secretary Weinberger is an embodiment of this collision.

His statements on the role of the public in decision-making clash with the contra policies that the Reagan administration and many conservatives advocated so strongly. Memories of the Vietnam War provoked congressional opposition to the administration's policies throughout the 1980s, as well as dissent among the American people, expressed in public opinion polls. In response to early critics of defense spending, Weinberger wrote that "public support for defense expenditures in a democracy in peacetime is always very shallow" (Weinberger, 1990, p. 70). Such opposition, which constrained the Reagan administration's policy in Central America, prompted what came to be known as the Weinberger Doctrine, in which the secretary of defense emphasized the significance of public and congressional support for military action.

Weinberger, like Reagan, exhibited full awareness that direct American military intervention in Nicaragua would be rejected by the American public. He was cognizant of what he calls a "certain, very basic fact, which our military learned all too well in Vietnam: Military actions not fully supported by the American people cannot succeed" (Weinberger, 1990, p. 361). The dismissal of a military solution in Nicaragua demonstrates an awareness that, in light of the Vietnam failure, the public was a reckoning force curtailing foreign policy. The risks of military intervention involved "the sort of domestic turmoil we experienced during the Vietnam War. . . . Such policies might very well tear at the fabric of our society, endangering the single most critical element of a successful democracy: a strong consensus of support and agreement for our basic purposes" (Weinberger, 1990, p. 437).

Weinberger nevertheless argued vocally about the importance of keeping Nicaragua out of the hands of the Communists. While testifying before the House in the Iran-contra hearings, in response to a congressman's allusion to the public's awareness of the situation in Nicaragua, saying that the public regarded the administration's policy in Nicaragua as "flawed" and the scandal as "terrible," Weinberger stated, "I don't disagree with that for a moment, but what I worry about is that some way that aberration, that one time error will somehow be translated into some kind of additional opposition to the people fighting for their own freedom in Nicaragua" (U.S. Congress, 1987a, p. 182). At the hearings, Weinberger expressed awareness of public opinion, yet emphasized his belief that the cause in Nicaragua was worth supporting.

Toward the end of his testimony, Weinberger was reminded by Congressman Tom Foley of his speech on the uses of military power in a democracy and the Weinberger Doctrine. Foley questioned whether Weinberger's tests for intervention also applied to covert operations. Weinberger responded essentially that covert operations evade public scrutiny: "I think without any question . . . because frequently with clandestine activities, which we have to do in this kind of world, you are not able to have public support. So you certainly need Congressional understanding, Congressional approval wherever it can be obtained" (U.S. Congress, 1987a, p. 215). Weinberger, however, was ultimately skeptical of Congress' ability to conduct foreign policy. He perceived of the elected representatives as impediments in the decision-making process: "Beginning in the 1970s, Congress demanded and assumed a far more active role in the making of foreign policy and in the decision-making process for the employment of military forces abroad than had been thought appropriate before" (Weinberger, 1990, p. 435). Weinberger seems to imply that foreign policy is most effectively executed by the executive branch of government. In June 1986, directing his critics attention to "Nicaragua, an armed and hostile front for Soviet interests in our own hemisphere" Weinberger said that dangers to American national security were growing worse, yet "unfortunately, political expediencies seem to blind Congress to the very real threats faced by this nation" (Buzenberg, 1986, p. 1). Congress, listening to the voices of public opinion, was a constraining factor in the Reagan administration's foreign policymaking.

Benchmark 2: Funding of $100 Million Including Military Aid

Weinberger, aware of public opposition to intervention in Nicaragua, took part in the administration's information campaign to rally American support for its defense policies. A frequent guest on *The MacNeil/Lehrer News Hour,* Weinberger emerged as a strong advocate of defense spending and American military strength. On February 27, 1986, responding to the poll numbers that indicated only 22 percent of the American people actually approved of defense spending increases, Weinberger said:

> Those are certainly not the polls I've seen. . . . There is a poll that says that around 22–25 percent favor an increase in defense spending, and . . . over 50 . . . say that they believe that what we're doing is right. An then there's a small percentage who want things cut. So, if you add the people who want the increase together with the people who feel that the path that we're on is about right . . . you come out with quite a large consensus. (Weinberger, 2/27/86)

These statements reveal Weinberger's views on consensus in policymaking, how he interpreted the polls, and how he molded them to support policies. Later, reflecting on the drop in the polls since 1981, Weinberger stated that the "analysis of poll answers showed . . . we're the victims of our own success." He went on to say that "the people are tired of it, they don't like it. People in democracies don't like to spend money on defense. But it is essential that we do it, and particularly in the kind of world we live in" (Weinberger, 2/27/86).

In October 1986, Weinberger was asked how he planned to get support for contra funding. He replied that "It is important that the people want it. Congress will do ultimately what the people want. . . . It would have to be . . . very clear that this is something the people did want, and that would have to be conveyed to Congress" (Weinberger, 10/28/86). He acknowledged the significance of public opinion in the administration's effort to win aid for the contras and highlighted his views on the role of public opinion in policymaking. In the same interview, Weinberger stated that defense spending "does require public support in areas where public support has been difficult, both in Europe and in the United States. In our kinds of societies, nobody likes to spend money on defense. Everybody likes to hope that you don't need to" (Weinberger, 10/28/86).

Benchmark 3: Proposals for up to $270 Million in Aid

In 1987, Weinberger pressed for congressional approval of a $270-million contra aid package. Opposition to this proposal was widespread among the American people. Responding to this opposition, Weinberger said: "it's very hard for us to understand why there's opposition to this. . . . I don't know why there should be opposition to helping people in their own backyards" (Rood, 1987). This opposition, closely intertwined with the administration's decision-making, was something that Weinberger noted. "I took all of those attacks very seriously, because I knew of the damage they could do by undermining public support for the appropriations we urgently needed; I knew the ammunition they could give those who generally opposed defense spending in any amounts" (Weinberger, 1990, p. 78).

Shortly thereafter, Weinberger resigned from his post as secretary of defense for personal reasons. Reflecting on his tenure in the Defense Department, Weinberger said that "the thing I'm most proud of is the morale and the quality and the preparedness, the pride that our troops have in their own work and in themselves and the realization that . . . the people of the United States have a much greater understanding of the difficulties of these tasks and the quality of the people who perform them" (Weinberger, 11/5/87). Clearly taking pride in his achievements, Weinberger takes credit for restoring the image of the military in the eyes of the American public. In spite of the Defense Department spending being "unpopular," Weinberger felt that he had successfully dealt with the post-Vietnam syndrome.

Secretary of Defense Weinberger had a sophisticated awareness of public opinion and its impact on foreign policy. His understanding of the public opinion dimension of decision-making made him a key leader in the Reagan administration. Strongly advocating peace through strength, Weinberger, like Reagan, was frustrated throughout his tenure by criticism, not only of the administration's policies toward Nicaragua, but also of defense spending in general. Weinberger's policymaking, within the Reagan administration, was clearly defined within the boundaries set by public opinion. More significantly, the Weinberger Doctrine, outlining a litmus test for foreign intervention, arose from Weinberger's consciousness of public opinion. When Weinberger outlined the guidelines for the use of military force with public opinion concerns in the back of his mind, Weinberger imposed a constraint upon himself and the Defense Department.

NATIONAL SECURITY ADVISER AND SECRETARY OF DEFENSE FRANK CARLUCCI

Frank Carlucci did not view his responsibility in the National Security Council or at the Defense Department as one of measuring public opinion, but "as putting together the national security options, getting the process going, helping the President decide on national security grounds, and then seeing that the decision was implemented. . . . But I never considered myself a public opinion expert and never thought that was a fundamental part of my job." Don Regan and then Howard Baker were "supposed to deal with U.S. public opinion" (Carlucci, 6/18/93). Carlucci did, however, have views on public opinion. At a speech in September 1988, Carlucci addressed the perception of the military in the public: "The Congress basically mirrors . . . U.S. public opinion on some of these issues, but that public opinion is not very well informed. And the Secretary of Defense getting on television . . . cannot do the job alone. It really has to be done by all responsible citizens" (Carlucci, 9/28/88).

Like Shultz, Carlucci saw a strong correlation between congressional opinion and public opinion. The relationship between public opinion and Congress is that "the public in general is a little bit more conservative than the Congress. Because of well-known gerrymandering, the Congress, particularly the House, is more liberal than the public. But those people have their ears to the ground . . . almost too closely. They tend to follow more than lead . . . the Congress responds to constituencies and that is a matter of public opinion" (Carlucci, 6/18/93).

Carlucci argued that "it's hard to differentiate between public opinion and Congressional opinion. We looked at the polls and knew we didn't have much public support in the polls. And we tried to interact with the key groups. We were very conscious of the opposition of certain groups, and church groups in particular. But our focus was principally on how we'd get things through the Hill." Carlucci knew "that we weren't going to make much progress on the Hill unless you created a different climate in public opinion" (Calucci, 6/18/93).

While 60 to 70 percent of the public opposed contra aid, most of the votes in Congress were close. Carlucci explained this phenomenon suggesting that "nobody really wants to take on the President, particularly a strong president like Ronald Reagan. So they feel the pressure of public opinion but at the same time they don't want to totally reflect that public opinion. They want to defer, to the degree they can, to a more popular president" (Carlucci, 6/18/93).

In explaining what effect public opinion had in the funding of the contras, Carlucci suggested that "it was very clear right from the outset that one of our problems was public opinion." "But you need to do something, because we don't have the public's support for the policy that we are following. Public support, congressional support, I can't remember the exact figures" (Carlucci, 6/18/93).

However, public opinion impinged on the decision-making "in every case. . . . Everybody pays attention to public opinion. But I'm talking about systematic analysis of public opinion in making the input to the president before he makes a decision." According to Carlucci, public opinion shapes the range of policy options that a given administration can successfully press for. He recognized the constraint that public opinion placed on the administration. He stated that "we couldn't get the level of funding we wanted to get. And that's always the classic case; you don't have enough money to win the war yet you're not willing to back out and lose it, so you're caught right in the middle where the situation continues to deteriorate" (Carlucci, 6/18/93).

Carlucci did not think it was always feasible to have a consensus in order for the president to send troops as part of a military intervention. ". . . the essence of leadership is to lead, and you shouldn't wait for the public consensus to form." "It's part of the job for the President to create public opinion" (Carlucci, 6/18/93). Hence, Carlucci felt that, although public opinion might outline some policy options, it cannot become a deterrent for decisive military action abroad.

Generally Carlucci did not agree with the paradigm of his predecessor at the Defense Department, Caspar Weinberger, that there had to be reasonable expectation of support from Congress and public opinion before an intervention.

> I disagree with it if the implication is that the support has to be there as a precondition. If by "reasonable expectation" you mean that with presidential leadership you

can bring along public and Congressional opinion, then I would agree with it. I don't think anybody wants to engage in an effort that's clearly going to be blocked by the Congress. But if you've got a fighting chance then I think you need to move ahead. You shouldn't insist that the consensus be formed in advance of a presidential decision. Public opinion follows, I think, at least a clear articulation of goals and strategies. (Carlucci, 6/18/93)

Testifying before Congress in 1988, Carlucci was drawn into a discussion of the role of public support in foreign interventions. He stated: "Sustained public support is essential for any military operation, but equally important, as I said in my testimony, is success. And we have to somehow balance those two considerations so we come out with a formula where we can have both" (U.S. Congress, 1988b).

In short, Carlucci tried to make policy without considering public or congressional input. But he recognized that both he and the administration had to act within the limits of public opposition to contra aid policy in administration policy.

REAGAN POLLSTER RICHARD WIRTHLIN

Presidential pollster Richard Wirthlin provided insights into Ronald Reagan's general attitude toward public opinion.

The President has always been interested in public attitudes . . . because he had great suspicion of the legislative branch . . . and its ability to block programs that a president and the people might support. And he used the threat and promise of going to the people when he would be stymied by the legislative process. Even though he enjoyed some modest support increase in 1986, it was not really large enough to use public opinion as a major lever again the major legislative changes he was strongly seeking. (Wirthlin, 5/6/89)

Wirthlin explained that the administration became aware of opinion and it dealt with the differences between opinion and policy on contra funding by measuring saliency of issues—the most important problem facing the United States today. Throughout the Reagan administration, Americans never considered contra aid a highly salient issue. "There were moments when support for aid increased, but never did a strong majority of Americans back some of the more aggressive policies of contra aid. The great concern . . . remained that . . . we could slip into a Vietnam-type of protracted war." The "contra" issue was "one in which the President with full knowledge of opposition, nevertheless steadfastly remained supportive of our actions . . . for the contras" (Wirthlin, 1986). Even though the contra policy lacked public support, Reagan kept pressing for it.

Wirthlin said the real purpose of polls was persuasion. "The cynics and those who superficially view how survey research is used by the executive branch . . . assume that the data is gathered . . . to tell the chief executive officer where he should go to follow the crowd. The opposite case . . . holds: namely, knowing where the crowd wants to go, and knowing where we want to lead, how to persuade the crowd to follow us, rather than lead us" (Wirthlin, 5/6/89).

Wirthlin agreed with Frank Carlucci that the president's role is not to follow public opinion, but rather to create public opinion by choosing carefully from a wide range of possible policies. Wirthlin added that "the President was very successful in changing public attitudes to generate public support on a number of programs which were initially quite unpopular" (Withlin, 5/6/89).

Why was it that President Reagan could not get resonance from patriotic values on support for the contras?

> Values came into conflict. The values touched upon in the issue of aiding the resistance fighters, were patriotism, security, and fear, that if Nicaragua was able to export its revolution . . . we would be inundated with billions of those fleeing the communist insurgency. The value of extending freedom to a group of people who live in a totalitarian country is one that Americans strongly support. But another value that ran in contrast was the belief that we should not overthrow another government, even a totalitarian, communistic state. (Wirthlin, 5/6/89)

How did the administration reconcile public opinion on the handling of the contra affair with the level of approval of the president's handling of his job? Wirthlin said: ". . . the issue of measuring approval was primarily to generate a report card . . . on the President's handling"; it was designed to see the extent to which the president could marshal grass-roots support. Wirthlin met with the president every three to four weeks to review results. Reagan would frequently bring up issues he would like him to follow through on. "We would measure the saliency of an issue, the amount of support or opposition to it; frequently, we would then test scenarios, and also various positions and arguments to understand what kind of communications positions would be most effective in blunting the opposition's message and/or strengthening our own" (Wirthlin, 5/6/89).

Knowledge of the opinion modified policy. Wirthlin accepted that "public opinion surely constrains certain kinds of policy; it doesn't dissuade or reverse alone. The President is willing to undertake issues that may be unpopular, but it [public support] does help" (Wirthlin, 5/6/89). The administration's role is not to govern according to what the polls show but rather to create and guide public opinion according to certain ideals, values, and higher goals. Public opinion, according to Wirthlin, lacks the strength of influencing policy by itself; and polls are instruments for shaping a definite discourse or rhetoric that can undermine the oppositions' arguments against a definite policy supported by the President.

CONGRESSIONAL PERSPECTIVES

Members of Congress provide evidence of how public opinion did and did not influence their decisions about voting on contra aid, particularly the 1985–86 controversies over $27 million and $100 million, respectively. The opinions include those of Republican Senator Richard Lugar from Indiana, who at the time of the contra aid controversy served as the chairman of the Senate Foreign Relations Committee, and Claiborne Pell, a Democrat from Rhode Island, who was also on this committee. Congressmen included Democratic representatives Ike Skelton of Missouri, Bill

Richardson of New Mexico, John Spratt of North Carolina, and Republican Mickey Edwards of Oklahoma.

Richard Lugar perceived public opinion on the $27 million in 1985 and $100 million in 1986 for contra aid as "the majority of Americans were opposed to military assistance to the contras in Nicaragua, as well as troops to any of these countries." A majority of Americans did not want to intervene even to the extent of economic aid. "People became more humanitarian, but there was a strong feeling . . . that many Americans had a sense of fatigue with regard to all of Central American questions." Even if you gave "the softest possible answer, if you send food, humanitarian assistance, a lot of people said no, often a plurality. On the question of military aid, the answer was distinctly no. And the thought of Americans about sending troops was 'off charts' in terms of prohibitive no. Our options were very limited in the face of public opinion." "We would begin to sense when gauging public opinion in constituent grouping, [that] they would say, we're tired of sending money, foreign aid and military aid to the contras. On the other hand, they really didn't want to a Communist government under those circumstances. It was important for our Administration to have some plan and define what we are about" (Lugar, 7/13/90). Thus, as Wirthlin mentioned, values were running opposed to each other: the public did not want to contribute to the contra effort but did want to prevent another Communist beachhead in the neighboring region.

A large part of Lugar's constituents "simply had no idea of what was really happening, nor what the outcome might be. They were alarmed at the fact that a Communist government had a beachhead and the Soviets were supplying them, alarmed with the . . . Vietnam syndrome . . . equating Nicaragua to be . . . another Vietnam" (Lugar, 7/13/90).

Lugar was more aware of national public opinion than opinion in Indiana, because "most polls are national, not state or local" (Lugar, 7/13/90). To find out what Indiana people were thinking, he had to commission a poll:

> Almost all the polling in Indiana is by major political parties. . . . The national polling is pretty extensive. In the course of my work, polls came to me every week on all kinds of subjects. Because I was intensely interested in this, I collected every bit of evidence of how people were feeling and the nuances and the nature of the questions. This was important when arguing with my colleagues generally. (Lugar, 7/13/90)

National polls did play a role and members of Congress wanted to know what the opinion was in order to calculate how risky it would be to assume particular stands.

> I think that is true of each one of us who is a prudent politician on any subject . . . you want to have a reasonable idea of what the parameters are of public tolerance of that point of view . . . how well informed those views are. For example, in the Nicaraguan case [I] came to the conclusion that most views were not well informed. I could see a high correlation of people who were still in Vietnam syndrome mood . . . working out their feeling with regard to Central American issues. (Lugar, 7/13/90)

On the Nicaraguan case, Lugar didn't know whether the influence of public pressure was significant, but "they made themselves known throughout this period. And I visited with a lot of people" (Lugar, 7/13/90). Public attitudes provided the opportunity to take relatively independent stands, particularly on foreign policy. The public's lack of understanding and information, as well as the impression that his support of administration policy had little or no effect on the day-to-day stability and progress of district opinion, left Senator Lugar with leeway in making his decisions.[2]

CONGRESSMAN IKE SKELTON

Congressman Ike Skelton (D-MO) supported President Reagan's contra policy and was the chief Democratic sponsor in 1986 of the Republican-initiated plan to provide $100 million in aid. Skelton blamed Reagan for failing to sell the contra policy effectively to Congress and the American public.

Skelton felt that generally on the issue, "I had a free hand" (Sobel, 1993, p. 243). His mail from a relatively conservative rural district with two military installations "was pretty evenly split 50/50. There was no deep feeling except in a small segment, though it polarized a bit more and became more anti-aid as time went on. I felt pretty much that people trusted me. . . . Public opinion within my district didn't really enter that much in this case. I felt very strongly . . . that we should not allow this communist-oriented regime" to proceed feeding arms to nearby countries, like El Salvador. "I did what I did basically out of concern for this hemisphere and the communist threat that was there" (Sobel, 1993, p. 243).

"If you vote according to popularity all the time, I suppose that will get you re-elected" (Sobel, 1993, p. 243). Skelton "didn't have any major fallout from public opinion on this" (Sobel, 1993, p. 244). He didn't have to pay a political price for his support of contra aid because he was "up front with everyone" (Sobel, 1993, p. 244). "I was known as being for contra aid and relatively active in it" (Sobel, 1993, p. 254). "You can't make a habit of [disagreeing] every week, or you're going to find yourself in deep trouble" (Sobel, 1993, p. 244). Skelton thought that public opinion was not an important factor in his voting. "For those that came from Democratic, somewhat liberal districts, public opinion was probably a slight breeze behind their back in favor of voting against contra aid" (Sobel, 1993, p. 252). "But public opinion would not have changed it" (Sobel, 1993, p. 257).

Skelton mentioned how public opinion was effective. After his amendment passed in June 1986, there was some successful activity by the contras. "Then the so-called Iran-contra specter came along" in early 1987. A vote in February 1988 lost by about

---

[2]Public opinion also mattered in making decisions for Senator Claiborne Pell (D-RI). It influenced the prospects of reelection. Public opinion had less impact in the early stages of a Senate term because voters were less likely to remember congressional decisions made over a year ago. Regarding the decisions in 1985 and 1986 to provide $27 and $100 million in aid to the contras, Senator Pell had "obviously" taken public opinion into account along with his own judgment (Pell, 10/6/90).

eleven votes. Public opinion was running pretty much against "the whole syndrome." "We were on the successful track until some let us down, in or out of the White House." In February if there had been a clean, positive record as was beginning for the contras, "we would have won that vote. . . . But public opinion did cause us to lose a handful of votes in that February vote as a result of the odor" (Sobel, 1993, p. 250). In short, the Iran-contra scandal reversed the movement of public opinion toward support of the contras.

CONGRESSMAN MICKEY EDWARDS

Representative Mickey Edwards (R-OK), as chairman in 1986 of the Leadership Task Force on Central America, successfully offered the amendment in June that provided $100 million to the contras. "I would have supported the contras because I believe our policy was the correct one and was important to the security of our allies in Central America. I don't know . . . whether the majority were for it or not." "Nearly every poll" he "saw showed public disapproval of assistance to the contras," but most of the people he heard from supported contra aid (Sobel, 1993, p. 245).

During 1982–89, his office received about 1,000 letters on that subject—783 supported contra aid, 316 opposed it.

> Two to one in favor of the aid is not nearly as important as that so few people bothered to write. You would think that since I was vice chairman of the Subcommittee on Foreign Operations, active in the contra aid support, co-author of the amendment that provided the $100 million, I would have averaged more than a hundred letters a year on that issue. (Sobel, 1993, p. 246)

Representative Edwards felt that he was not targeted on the issue. "I remember in a couple of town meetings the subject never came up, so I brought it up. But at the couple of town meetings the organized groups did show up to protest, and they were so outrageous that the audience, most of whom really didn't care about the issue, turned on them and told them to shut up." "I didn't find that any of the organized groups were effective at all. They were so extreme that they probably turned off people" (Sobel, 1993, p. 255).

Regarding the effect that public opinion had on support of the contras, Edwards thought "it had very little. . . . The pressure from the public was minimal. What there was not reflective of the public as a whole but of small, well-organized, very vocal groups" (Sobel, 1993, p. 246). If there had been "an outpouring of mail," or the people bringing it up on their own at town meetings were not identifiable activists, "I think we would have responded" (Sobel, 1993, p. 256).

These are issues where a congressman has "to use your own best judgment. . . . [E]ven had it appeared to me that a majority of people in my district did not support contra aid, I still would have supported it" (Sobel, 1993, p. 256).

"Ideology," Edwards noted, "did have a major role in that there were liberals who automatically lined up against the contras, and there were conservatives who automatically lined up against the Sandinistas. . . . Public opinion had a very minor role." There was "a philosophical showdown" in the House on the issue that was "unaffected by the public at large. It was liberals, conservatives, moderates" (Sobel, 1993, p. 249).

There was a surge in public support for the contras during Oliver North's testimony. Congress did "react to the public pressure." In short, in Edward's district public opinion was generally in support of his pro-contra position. Public opinion may have affected other members in Congress.

CONGRESSMAN BILL RICHARDSON

Congressman Bill Richardson (D-NM), a member of the Democratic leadership of the House of Representatives and the House Intelligence Committee, was chairman of the House Hispanic Caucus and active on the issue of contra aid. In his first term he staunchly opposed the contras. But after a 1985 visit with the Sandinista leaders, who ignored Richardson's warning to "clean up their act," he supported nonmilitary aid for the contras one time to give the president the benefit of doubt. From then on, he opposed President Reagan's requests for military aid.

As member of the Whip organization, Richardson was in a leadership position. Contra aid was a leadership issue for the Democrats. "You were closely watched for your position on contra aid" for committee assignments and upward movement in the House. "My posture on contra aid was that we saw the issue in terms of Democratic primaries, of Democratic leadership possibilities and advancement" (Sobel, 1993, p. 249).

Richardson comes from a two-to-one Democratic district, but on the United States–Mexico border. "When President Reagan said that border states should be concerned, this raised the awareness of the issue in New Mexico" (Sobel, 1993, p. 247). Close to 40 percent of the voters are Hispanic, there's "a community of interest" with Latin America.

In 1985 and 1986, his office averaged forty-two letters a week on contra aid; 61 percent were against aid, 39 percent for. In 1985–86, at 288 town meetings, 21 percent of questions were on contra aid and 77 percent of the people at the meetings were against contra aid. Organized groups on the left and right often attended the meetings (Sobel, 1993, p. 248).

Contra aid did not influence public opinion in his congressional district. "It was not a vote cutting issue, one on which you're defeated or elected." However, in a close Democratic primary, this issue might affect the congressional district and state. "When I made that switch on [supporting] humanitarian aid in 1985, I could see a little downward variation in the core liberal support I generally had in most elections." In a Democratic primary, for a core of Democratic voters, "it was a vote cutting issue that could affect the way that individuals voted on you despite support for other issues." (Sobel, 1993, p. 248). Contra aid was an issue on which you don't stray too much. (p. 249). Obviously, I have to listen to these groups right before a primary election (p. 255).

"We also saw it as an issue where we were fairly confident that we wouldn't lose any votes politically out in the hinterlands" (Sobel, 1993, p. 249). The polls were "a lesser factor." "I was thirty-one times against the president, and once for him, and most constituents remember the one time that I was for him. It took me a couple of years from my liberal constituents to recover from that vote" (Sobel, 1993, p. 254). Richardson felt it's the kind of issue he was confident that "whichever way we go, we know we can weather it. Even if there is a tremendous negative opposition to our position, because it's not a vote cutting issues, we are able to weather the contra issue with that trust factor" (Sobel, 1993, p. 254).[3]

CONGRESSMAN JOHN SPRATT

Congressman John Spratt's (D-NC) district was "pro-military, pro-intervention, and anti-Communist." Spratt estimated that 10 percent of his constituency strongly opposed contra aid, 20 percent were strongly in favor, and half of the remaining 70 percent were sufficiently undecided that they were willing to side with President Reagan's pro-contra position. He learned of his constituents' positions on contra aid through mail, phone calls, and personal encounters. Spratt had to contend with the "rather sizable and persistent group which felt strongly that the President was right." "The mail was fairly steady, and personal encounters in the district were rather frequent." Opposed to this pro-contra sector of the constituency was "a group of mainly . . . college and university types, [and] church-affiliated groups." "Those people," he said, "were not just my supporters and friends, but they were people who worked in my campaign. I had a close personal affiliation with them and I did not want to disappoint them" (Spratt, 7/12/90).

Spratt voted for $27 million in humanitarian aid to the contras in 1985, and for $100 million in military and nonmilitary aid in the spring of 1986. He maintained that "the decision itself was made on what I thought to be the right policy." Through field trips, personal contacts, studying, and reading, "I reached my own conclusions about what we should be doing and about what the political alternatives were" (Spratt, 7/12/90).

Spratt did not, however, entirely discount his constituents' influence on his voting record. The minority sector of his constituents on the far right and far left made a difference. "My decision at the margins might have been influenced by public opinion

---

[3]Richardson felt there were two issue areas where opinions affected foreign policy. One of them involved issues important to the several thousand PhDs at the Los Alamos Laboratories. "It's the only [community] that doesn't vote for me," probably because when I started out in the Congress, "I voted for the nuclear freeze. It didn't go over well in Los Alamos. That's a factor for me" (Sobel, 1993, p. 259–60). But he voted his conscience on the freeze issue. "The second is the immigration issue, the relationship with Mexico. We're a border state, and I was actively against the immigration legislation until I found out the only way we could humanely deal with five million undocumented workers . . . was to vote for an immigration bill. We now have the problem of employer sanctions. That issue is foreign policy, because it relates to Mexico. It's a vote cutting issue and so I guided myself carefully in that one, too" (Sobel, 1993, p. 259–60). Here, he voted in the face of perceived opinion.

and having to defend myself" (Spratt, 7/12/90). Thus public opinion's formative influence on Spratt's foreign policy record embodied the threat of questioning and scrutiny. He knew that he would have to defend his position on the contras to his constituents, particularly to the 30 percent who felt strongly about the issue.

Spratt's comments on his vote for the McGurdy bill, "a non-military alternative to the contras," as part of the $100 million legislation in 1986, illuminate his awareness of the necessity of responding to his constituents:

> It was a proposition I could defend to my constituents on the right and the left.
> . . . I told them I agreed with them: that was why I was opposed to funding the contras directly. On the right, I said, "I'm willing to hold the contras in reserve as a threat against the Sandinistas to back up our bargaining position, but I see no use in putting them to the field." (Spratt, 7/12/90)

He did not, however, support the McGurdy bill with the purpose of appeasing both sides: He didn't "formulate my position in order to be responsive to my constituents' views. . . . It was convenient, so I could answer both sides. . . . [But] basically, I thought that kind of approach made the best of the situation" (Spratt, 7/12/90).

In short, John Spratt was aware of the opinions of his constituents on contra aid: their opinions did not determine his voting, but represented possible scrutiny of his decisions. Spratt had the leeway to vote on the position he felt was correct because approximately 50 percent of his constituency were undecided. He felt the large undecided sector would respond favorably to any well-reasoned policy decision.

Two congressmen, Skelton and Edwards, indicated that public opinion did not have much influence, and yet all the senators and representatives included public opinion as a factor. How much would that "slumbering giant" have had to start waking up for them to pay more attention to it? For Democrats particularly, there wasn't a feeling that if you crossed Ronald Reagan on this issue, he would come after you. The several Republican efforts to get Reagan to intensify the debate with his fireside chats didn't succeed.

CONCLUSION: THE LIMITS OF EXECUTIVE AUTHORITY

The Reagan administration was aware of public dissatisfaction with its involvement in Nicaragua. However, at first it believed that it could effectively shape public opinion in support of its policy. This was not the case, as public opinion ultimately limited what shaped American foreign policy toward Nicaragua. First, the general sentiment of the public in the post-Vietnam era prevented Reagan from using a possible strategy of direct military intervention. This restraint meant that the administration could not choose from its full range of options when formulating its policy. Its choices were limited mainly to economic and military aid to the contras. And wary of any kind of intervention, the American people only weakly supported giving economic aid to the contras. General opposition greatly limited the amount of money the administration was able to allocate for its policy. In essence, public opinion's effect upon Reagan's Nicaragua policy was twofold; first in preventing more aggressive military means, and then in limiting the economic and military aid. Public opinion and restricted policy options forced the administration to venture outside the conventional means of policy into covert operations to carry out what it deemed as a vital threat to American security.

Similarly, the congressmen say that public opinion was not very important to them on this issue because the public was basically not informed and their attitudes not developed or coherent enough to be taken seriously on this issue. The congressmen felt opinion could have, but didn't, matter on contra aid. Yet, their behavior was consistent with the expectations that opinion can be aroused on foreign policy issues, as it was in Vietnam, and that it can be effective. And though public opinion may not have been issue specific, it conditioned the way in which the contra aid issues were approached. The amounts of money for contra aid were relatively small (less than $1 billion; Sobel, 1995a), in recognition of the limits of public opinion.

On the whole, both the administration and congressional representatives revealed an awareness of public attitudes. The administration was constrained by significant public opposition, while the congressmen were less constrained, by lower public opposition to contra aid or split opinion in their districts. For the administration, polls were a tool to use as an argument, not a guide for policy. The congressmen had more leeway but still had to watch out for signs of public disenchantment. The relatively split opinion in their districts provided leeway to decide on other factors. Senators were more explicit about the possible electoral influence of contra aid on voters.

Nicaragua provides a clear example of the extent to which public opinion can influence foreign policymakers. The general public disapproval for involvement in Central America greatly aided opposition legislators in their fight to keep America out of Nicaragua by weakening the president's claims that he had a mandate from the people. Without public support to rest on, the administration's continued attempts at establishing significant aid to the contras were ultimately thwarted. Reagan's inability to win over the public resulted in one of the biggest political defeats of his presidency and is one of the best examples of the influence of public opinion on foreign policymaking.

The next case, in chapters 9 and 10, examines the first major foreign policy intervention in the post-Vietnam era, the Gulf War crisis of 1990–91. This presents another example of the constraints placed upon policymakers by the public. However, this time, as the United States moved further away from the legacy of Vietnam, the constraint became a question of how the policy should be carried out rather than if it should be done at all. It is with this new hesitancy that the Bush administration struggled, using both actions and statements throughout the Gulf crisis.

IV

THE PERSIAN GULF CASE
A RETURN TO INTERVENTIONISM?

THE GULF WAR OF THE EARLY 1990S PRESENTS THE NEXT EXAMPLE OF PUBLIC OPIN-ion's relationship with foreign intervention policy. The case study consists of two parts. The first discusses the background of the war, focusing on the chain of events, the Bush administration's policy, and public opinion in 1990 and 1991. This sets the stage for the second part on how public opinion affected the decisions of policymakers themselves.

Focusing on President George Bush, Secretary of State James Baker, and Secretary of Defense Richard Cheney and their reactions to three benchmarks of the crisis, this case study provides insight into the way public opinion affected intervention policy. The benchmarks are the initial decision to deploy troops to the Persian Gulf in August 1990, the decision to reinforce the contingent with combat troops capable of offensive action around the November elections, and the decision to go to war in January of 1991. In what was the biggest commitment of U.S. military power since Vietnam, public opinion had a great influence on the way the administration presented the crisis in 1990–91, the diplomatic strategy the administration used leading up to the invasion, and the way the resulting coalition ultimately fought the war itself.

As the events in the Persian Gulf unfolded in late 1990 and early 1991, the American people's response was one not of overwhelming decisiveness but of unsure skepticism. Following the initial escalation the public was divided until immediately before the invasion. A lack of consensus over issues such as the necessity, likely outcome, and costs of a war with Iraq marked the period leading up to the actual fighting in January of 1991. The administration and the public both displayed remnants of the Vietnam syndrome.

The Bush administration's struggle to overcome this doubt in the American people presents a clear example of public opinion's effect upon foreign policy. The statements of the men who formed foreign policy during the three benchmark periods reflect public attitudes. Their decisions took into account the importance of maintaining the backing of the American people. This understanding had a direct bearing on the way in which crisis policy played out. Realizing the need for garnering public support, the Bush administration tailored its strategy, both in the presentation of the crisis and in the actual plan of the war, to respond to the desires of the public. It was through this attempt at shaping public attitudes that public opinion ultimately shaped policy. Concern for the attitudes of the American people did not change the goals of policy but rather the means by which they were to be attained.

CHAPTER 9

The Gulf War: History, Bush Policies, and Public Opinion

INTRODUCTION

This chapter covers the events, policies, and public opinion in the months that led from the Iraqi invasion of Kuwait in August 1990 to the American invasion of Iraq in January 1991. Public opinion and the progression of events roughly paralleled each other in the Persian Gulf in 1990–91. Following Iraq's invasion of Kuwait in the summer of 1990 and the deployment of troops by President George Bush, the American people supported the policies of the government. As time passed and the American people became both more knowledgeable about the region and concerned about the domestic economy, overall support began to wane.

Questions that had not been asked earlier now came to the fore. Why was the United States in the Gulf and how should it deal with Saddam Hussein? Should economic sanctions against Iraq be given more time to work? What did the United States hope to gain from a conflict? What would be the costs of war? As the public tried to answer these questions the strong base of support began to fade. The administration tried to counter this drop in support by providing its own answers, using deeds, words, and events such as James Baker's meeting with Tariq Aziz, as well as in the continual demonizing of Saddam Hussein to the American people. However, not until the war became imminent did the enormous foundation of public acceptance of the administration's actions return. This hesitancy and doubt by the American public throughout the Gulf War made it not "a defining moment in history" (Atkinson, 1991, p. A1) as Secretary of State James Baker stated, but rather a high point of a declining Bush presidency.

THE CRISIS BEGINS: IRAQ INVADES KUWAIT

On May 3, 1990, Iraqi foreign minister Tariq Aziz criticized unnamed Organization of Petroleum Exporting Countries (OPEC) nations for overproduction of oil. The significance of this complaint became evident on July 16, when Iraq accused its neighbor Kuwait of the theft of $2.4 billion in oil from the Rumalia field on the Iraq-Kuwait border (Blumberg and French, 1994, p. 28). The following day, Iraq officially accused Kuwait and the United Arab Emirates of overproduction and threatened to use force against them (Blumberg, 1994, p. 28).

On July 27, U.S. ambassador April Glaspie met with Iraqi dictator Saddam Hussein, telling him that the United States had "no opinion on the Arab conflicts, like [Iraq's] border conflict with Kuwait" (Blumberg, 1994, p. 28). On August 2, Saddam Hussein surprised the world by sending his troops into Kuwait. Within seven hours, Iraqi troops reached the capital of the small nation. Hussein declared that Kuwait was Iraq's nineteenth province, and renamed it Kuwait City (Taylor, 1998, p. 23). His justification for the intrusion, that Kuwait was violating international agreements by "slant drilling" for Iraqi oil and overproducing to the detriment of other OPEC nations, was widely regarded as specious by world leaders.

Just hours after the invasion, the United States' first action was to send extra warships to the Gulf region. On August 4, United States, the European Community, and Japan imposed an economic blockade on Iraq (Mueller, 1994, p. 15). To U.S. president George Bush and British prime minister Margaret Thatcher, among others, an invasion in an economically vital part of the world was extremely unsettling. Thatcher, who reportedly urged Bush, "Remember, George, this is no time to go wobbly," encouraged a stern Western response (Mueller, 1994, p. 18). Even so, Bush's determined indignation to the invasion of Kuwait was surprising. Bush blasted Iraq's "naked aggression," and declared on August 5, "this aggression will not stand" (Mueller, 1994, p. 15).

Polling organizations and news agencies soon began taking the pulse of the American public concerning involvement in the Gulf. At the time of the blockade in early August, 52 percent of the American public reported that they approved of Bush's handling of the situation in the Middle East, while 16 percent said they disapproved and 32 percent said they didn't know (Gallup in Mueller, 1994, Table 8).

Benchmark 1: The Decision to Deploy Troops to the Gulf

On August 6, the United Nations imposed its own embargo on Iraq. Perhaps fearing a more aggressive Western response, Hussein began taking Westerners living in Iraq and Kuwait as hostages. On August 8, Bush ordered fifty thousand combat troops to the Gulf (Taylor, 1998, p. 23). On August 12, he ordered a naval blockade of Iraq. Support for his handling of the Persian Gulf situation jumped to 80 percent (Gallup in Mueller, 1994, Table 8). Interestingly, those unsure about the president's handling of the situation fell, in that single week of August 9–12, to 8 percent (Gallup in Mueller, 1994, Table 8). Americans were becoming increasingly interested in the Gulf crisis as a television event. By August 12, 83 percent reported that they followed news concerning the Gulf "very closely" or "fairly closely," up from 57 percent a week before (Gallup in Mueller, 1994, Table 46).

Far from backing down, Saddam Hussein escalated. To concentrate efforts on Kuwait, on August 15 Iraq officially ended its bloody eight-year war with Iran by accepting Iranian peace terms (Taylor, 1998, p. 23). On August 22, Iraq announced that hostages would immediately be taken to key military installations for use as "human shields" (Mueller, 1994, p. 15). President Bush responded by drawing "a line in the sand," convincing Saudi Arabian officials that they should allow foreign troops to be stationed on their soil to prevent further aggression on Hussein's part. The Saudis agreed, and Bush called up the U.S. reserves (Mueller, 1994, p. 18).

On August 25, the United Nations formally approved the use of force for the imposition of the embargo against Iraq. On September 11, in the midst of a major call up of U.S. military forces, Bush appeared on national television asking for congressional support in his efforts against Iraq. Hussein, in turn, continued to assert that Kuwait was the nineteenth province of Iraq, and that under no circumstances would his troops leave. Furthermore, he promised that if the recalcitrant West persisted in its efforts against his state, they would experience "the mother of all battles" (Woodward, 1991, p. 297). At the time of Bush's televised appearance, support for his handling of the Gulf crisis stood at 76 percent (Gallup in Mueller, 1994, Table 8). In early September, 21 percent of those polled stated that they felt the Gulf crisis was "the most important problem facing the country today"; this was more than any other single response (Gallup in Mueller, 1994, Table 45). Bush's approval rating as president, which had been 60 percent in the month prior to the invasion, rose to 76 percent (Gallup in Mueller, 1994, Table 1). The two ratings would follow each other closely throughout the crisis.

Desert Shield

In the following weeks, hundreds of thousands of U.S. troops traveled to Saudi Arabia to stand behind Bush's "line in the sand," an operation that would be known as Desert Shield. By October 6, 200,000 U.S. troops, considered a fully adequate complement for defensive operations, were stationed in Saudi Arabia (Taylor, 1998, p. 78). The effect of Bush's speech of September 11 faded, however, and as national debate on the merits of sending forces to the Gulf became more focused, approval of Bush's policies in the Gulf began to slip. By the first week of October, support had dropped to 69 percent (Gallup in Mueller, 1994, Table 8). At mid-month, it was down to 61 percent, while those who disapproved of the president's actions had climbed to 29 percent (Gallup in Mueller, 1994, Table 8). On October 20, organized protests, generally marches and rallies, against involvement in the Gulf took place in at least fifteen U.S. cities (Mueller, 1994, p. 15).

Despite the imposing military force assembled in Saudi Arabia by the United States and other coalition nations, including most notably Britain and France, the American public was, at this point, far from convinced that war with Iraq was necessary or inevitable: President Bush should not rush into military action against Saddam Hussein, but rather give economic and diplomatic sanctions more time (Gallup in Mueller, 1994, Table 72). Thirty-eight percent believed the United States could achieve its objectives solely through economic sanctions and the blockade (NBC/*Wall Street Journal* in Mueller, 1994, Table 68). In October, 69 percent thought that the United States should give the U.N. sanctions two more months to take effect prior to any military action, against 28 percent who opposed giving more time (Harris poll, 1990 Index to International Public Opinion, p. 226). Tellingly, 48 percent of Americans counseled not going to war if the embargo failed, while only 46 percent thought that the United States should go to war at that point (ABC/*Washington*

Post in Mueller, 1994, Table 60). Even in November, 70 percent of Americans felt that the United States should wait before going to war, while 24 percent thought it should not wait (Gallup in Mueller, 1994, Table 71, p. 225). Clearly, the administration had not yet achieved a national consensus on undertaking military action in the Gulf.

National interest in the Gulf situation, while turning more negative toward U.S. involvement, had also declined from early peaks. Despite high support for Bush's policies in September (Rosegrant and Watkins, 1996, p. 27), interest had begun to wane. By mid-October, those considering the Gulf crisis the most important concern for the United States had dipped to 10 percent, ranking it below federal spending and at the same level as unemployment or drugs (Gallup in Mueller, 1994, Table 45).

At this time, domestic politics intervened. October 20 was the day that Bush broke his "no new taxes" 1988 campaign pledge (Mueller, 1994, p. 15). By the time of the tax announcement, support for the president's policies in the Gulf was fairly close to bottoming out, at 61 percent (Gallup in Mueller, 1994, Table 8). An acrimonious debate with Congress over the budget and the breaking of a major campaign promise did not enhance his position. The president's personal approval rating, like his Gulf crisis rating, had fallen rather dramatically from 76 percent in mid-September to 53 percent. There was thus a political imperative for the Bush administration to do something meaningful (Gallup in Mueller, 1994, Table 1). In fact, Bush himself questioned pursuing economic and diplomatic solutions to the Kuwait crisis—"I don't think there's time politically for that strategy" (Mueller, 1994, p. 116). The administration did not plan to wait and find out.

Benchmark 2: The Decision to Reinforce Coalition Troops

On November 8, two days after mid-term elections returned a Democratic Congress, Bush announced that he was increasing troop strength in the Gulf in order to achieve an "adequate offensive military option" (Mueller, 1994, p. 15). He sent 200,000 additional forces and 1,200 tanks to the Gulf (Taylor, 1998, p. 109). This move pushed the total coalition presence to 450,000 troops, sufficient for operations greater than the simple defense of Saudi Arabia. Many political leaders, particularly Democrats in Congress, felt that Bush was moving the country in the direction of war without giving economic sanctions a fair chance to work. About half of Americans apparently agreed. As a result, debate on the Gulf issue became increasingly partisan (Mueller, 1994, p. 20). In mid-November, the percentage of those who felt that Bush was "too quick to get military forces involved" rose nine points from August levels to 47 percent. At the same time, those asserting that Bush had "tried hard enough for diplomatic solutions" fell from 51 percent to 38 percent (*New York Times*/CBS in Mueller, 1994, Table 98).

Furthermore, if the administration hoped that assuming a tough posture against Saddam would reverse sagging support levels, they were incorrect. In the wake of the announcement of troop increase, approval of Bush's handling of the Gulf crisis declined further. By mid-November, 54 percent said that they approved of the way Bush was handling the situation (Gallup in Mueller, 1994, Table 8), down from 75 percent in August, who approved of presidential policies (Rosegrant and Watkins, 1996, p. 27).

Iraq then made an unexpected announcement. All of the hostages would be released, if the United States would not attack. The release would take place during a three-month period beginning at Christmas (Mueller, 1994, p. 15). Bush declared that if Saddam Hussein would not leave Kuwait of his own volition, the United States would "kick his ass out" (Barnes, 1991, p. 9). This fit into the emerging administration strategy, which observers quickly termed Bush's "four nos": "No negotiations, no compromises, no attempts at face saving, and no rewards for aggression" (Drew, 1991, p. 85).

The Iraqis quickly realized the significance of this strategy. "Initially, the Iraqis were interested in the offer of meetings," one senior U.S. administration official noted, "but when they realized we wouldn't negotiate, they backed off" (Mueller, 1994, p. 20). Furthermore, on November 16, Secretary of State James Baker rejected a Soviet proposal to link Iraqi evacuation of Kuwait with Israeli evacuation of Palestine (Taylor, 1998, p. 104). On November 19, 250,000 additional Iraqis moved into Kuwait to reinforce the occupying army, pushing the total number of Iraqi forces toward 400,000 (Taylor, 1998, p. 109). Thus, it became increasingly apparent to the American public that the United States and its partners were moving toward a war with Saddam Hussein. At the end of November, 62 percent felt that the likelihood of war with Iraq had increased in the past few weeks (*Time*/CNN in Mueller, 1994, Table 234). Fully 75 percent of Americans said they felt the United States was going to get involved in a war with Iraq (ABC/*Washington Post* in Mueller, 1994, Table 231). The Bush administration's month-long march to war seemed to close with the international community's approval. On November 29, the United Nations Security Council authorized the use of force against Iraq. Twelve nations voted for the resolution, while Yemen and Cuba voted against it and China abstained (Moore, 1993, p. 34). It formally set a January 15, 1991, deadline for the complete withdrawal of Iraqi troops from Kuwait (Mueller, 1994, p. 16)

ENVISIONING THE WAR

The Bush administration apparently was confident that conventional forces could quickly overwhelm the Iraqis. Bush repeatedly asserted that war with Iraq would not be another Vietnam, a costly, prolonged war with unclear aims and heavy casualties. He set forth before the American people his feelings about U.S. involvement in Iraq: "In our country, I know that there are fears of another Vietnam. Let me assure you, should military actions be required, this will not be another Vietnam. This will not be a protracted, drawn out war" (Thomas, 1990, p. 25). He confidently predicted that the confrontation would be short and decisive, and even told television audiences on December 28 that he hoped that war, once initiated, "would be over in a matter of days" (Mueller, 1994, p. 21).

House Armed Services Committee chairman Les Aspin felt confident enough to tell the American public that "prospects are high for a rapid victory," noting that a likely estimate for American casualties was between three thousand and five thousand, with fewer than one thousand dead (Mueller, 1994, pp. 20, 21). Twenty thousand American casualties, with seven thousand dead, was considered the worst-case scenario (Schmitt, 1991, p. A17).

The public remained unconvinced. Despite the expectation of the majority of Americans that a shooting war would break out (60 percent or more from August 8 through the outbreak of the war), comparatively few thought the United States would be able to escape so painlessly (ABC/*Washington Post* in Mueller, 1994, Table 231). Americans expected to pay a higher price for victory over Saddam's forces. In mid-October, 53 percent predicted that "several thousand" or "tens of thousands" of Americans would die. By early January, this proportion had increased to 62 percent (Gallup in Mueller, 1994, Table 226). In mid-November, 41 percent of poll respondents felt that the United States would achieve victory, but at the price of a long war and heavy casualties. Another 12 percent felt that the United States would eventually withdraw without victory (*Time*/CNN in Mueller, 1994, Table 217). The general impression of the public, however, tended to be that American arms would win, but not easily. For example, 84 percent felt "very confident" or "somewhat confident" in mid-November that the United States would win a war against Iraq (*Los Angeles Times* in Mueller, 1994, Table 216). However, out of this same group of citizens, 62 percent also felt that another Vietnam-type situation was either "very likely" or "somewhat likely" (*Los Angeles Times* in Mueller, 1994, Table 220).

Even days before the deadline, few could believe Bush or Congressman Les Aspin's reassuring predictions. In early January, only 9 percent of Americans expressed confidence that the fighting in Iraq would take "just a few days." A substantial 56 percent felt that the war would take "several months" or "a year or more" (Gallup in Mueller, 1994, Table 224). The impression that this war would resemble Vietnam thus proved difficult to dispel, and in fact would not begin to disappear until the war was well under way. At that point, the majority did not feel that the war would be another Vietnam (ABC/*Washington Post* in Mueller, 1994, Table 221).

WHAT THEY FOUGHT FOR

Many polls during the prewar period attempted to determine what Americans saw as the most important reasons for the U.S. presence in the Gulf. The two that tended to appear at the top of the list were the deterrence of aggression and the preservation of vital oil supplies. In mid-November, 32 percent of respondents said they felt the United States had either sent troops to Saudi Arabia to "stop Iraqi aggression" or because the United States should "defend other countries." At the same time, 39 percent said that oil was the main concern (Gallup in Mueller, 1994, Table 114). James Baker's explanation of "in one word, it's jobs" was met with skepticism (Neuman, 1990).

The administration had portrayed its own set of reasons for going to war, through the press and various publicity campaigns. Bush had compared Saddam Hussein to Hitler (Mueller, 1994, p. 47), and posters were publicized showing the two dictators side by side, with captions reading "Oh, no, he's back." Bush used this comparison as a reason to reject compromises. Baker considered the taking of U.S. hostages as a justification for war, and other officials maintained the need for stability in the Gulf. The most common reason offered by the Bush administration was the need for a "New World Order" in the aftermath of the Cold War, based on "freedom of nations, the rule of law, and justice" (Mueller, 1994). This was to be pursued even if it required crushing dictators, so that the United States could remain the world's leading and only superpower. Finally, the administration also portrayed the war as a means to destroy Iraq's nuclear capabilities (Layne and Carpenter, 1990).

The responses to the question of why the U.S. government was in the Gulf were subject to wider variations than most other opinion-related issues in the Gulf War. They depended on how questions were phrased and which reasons were made available as choices. When the freeing of hostages was listed as a possible reason to go to war, for instance, many Americans considered this to be fair and reasonable (Mueller, 1994, p. 38). When given a choice of several reasons, a majority of Americans saw prevention of Iraq's nuclear capability development as a "good enough reason for the U.S. to take military action." Half agreed with this, 39 percent disagreed it; the other two reasons in the question received only between 30 and 35 percent support (*New York Times*/CBS in Mueller, 1994, Table 134).

Removing Saddam Hussein from power and creating a lasting peace in the Middle East also emerged as reasons the public considered worthwhile for involving U.S. troops in a foreign war. One reason that consistently did not appeal to Americans was the restoration of Kuwait's government, especially when phrased in such fashion as "Returning the Kuwaiti royal family to govern Kuwait" (Americans Tank Security in Mueller, 1994, Table 125). Only 35 percent in a *New York Times*/CBS poll found this an acceptable reason to go to war, against 56 percent who found it unacceptable (Index to International Public Opinion 1990, p. 226). Phrased differently, however, 59 percent of Americans were ready by late November to call the "liberation of Kuwait" worth fighting for (*Time*/CNN in Mueller, 1994, Table 137).

The good reasons to fight differed. For instance, only 29 percent felt that it was worth risking American lives "to protect our oil supplies" (*Los Angeles Times* in Mueller, 1994, Table 127). Yet 58 percent said they thought the United States should engage in combat if Iraq were to control or cut off oil (Gallup in Mueller, 1994, Table 126). Furthermore, while just 12 percent of those polled said that "making sure oil from the Middle East flows freely to the world" should be the most important goal of the United States in Iraq, 26 percent felt that this was Bush's number one reason (Americans Talk Security in Mueller, 1994, Table 125). A source of great frustration for the Bush administration was the feeling that "despite Bush's many protestations about confronting aggression, people most commonly suggested that his primary goal, unlike theirs, was to preserve the free flow of oil" (Mueller, 1994, p. 39). However, most Americans supported his actions, and belief in the rightness of the president's motives would increase as the war drew nearer.

PULLING BACK FROM THE BRINK

On November 30, in the midst of the most intense prewar period of statements and war threats, and concern among the public and politicians to try all means short of war, Bush proposed meetings between the United States and Iraq (Blumberg and French, 1994, p. 34). On December 6, Saddam Hussein released all of the estimated eleven thousand hostages in Iraq and Kuwait (Moore, 1992, p. 86; Mueller, 1994, p.

16). If the Iraqi leader's hope was that this action would pacify Americans, he was mistaken. While 18 percent of Americans did say that the release made them less desirous of going to war with Iraq, another 18 percent said that the freeing of the hostages made an attack on Iraq more attractive to them. President Bush captured the essence of this view, saying, "When you don't have Americans there and if force is required that's just one less worry I've got" (Mueller, 1994, p. 41).

While most observers saw the hostage release as a late effort by an increasingly desperate Hussein to curry favor with Western audiences and avoid a major showdown, the issue of compromise was far from dead. Despite Bush's firm no rewards for aggression policy, a substantial portion of the public felt that compromise would be worthwhile if it meant averting a war. During the second week of November, 58 percent of those polled said that they would choose compromise with Saddam Hussein over starting a war (ICR Research Group in Mueller, 1994, Table 103). One month later, 51 percent of respondents said that they would be willing to accept an agreement "with some concessions" involving control of disputed oil fields (NBC/*Wall Street Journal* in Mueller, 1994, Table 106). Even as the January 15 deadline approached, the statement "Trading [Kuwait)] land for withdrawal would be acceptable" received 47 percent support (*New York Times*/CBS in Mueller, 1994, Table 108). In addition, half of Americans felt that talks between the United States and Iraq would produce a diplomatic solution (ABC/*Washington Post* in Mueller, 1994, Table 110). The public was not yet convinced that American soldiers should be put in danger; nor would it be until hostilities were already under way.

THE THREAT OF WAR

At the time of the hostage release, support for Bush's policies in the Gulf crisis stood at 60 percent (Gallup in Mueller, 1994, Table 8). It remained at about this level until the air war began. In fact, after the release of the hostages, very little seemed to take place to sway Americans one way or the other. Convinced that Bush was making no compromises, the Iraqis offered none (Mueller, 1994, p. 20). The president continued to try to sell the war to the American people. In November, and again on the eve of the war, this included frequent references to the need to destroy Iraq's nuclear and chemical weapons potential; these were justifications that 74 percent of Americans found quite compelling (Associated Press in Mueller, 1994, Table 135D). Bush also spoke often of the Gulf crisis as a great and defining historical moment for America and the international community. "We have before us the opportunity," he announced in a speech on January 16, 1991, "to forge for ourselves and for future generations a new world order, a world where the rule of law, not the rule of the jungle, governs the conduct of nations" (Mueller, 1994, p. 52). Bush soon dropped the New World Order theme when it proved unpopular.

Finally, Bush vilified the Iraqi dictator at every opportunity, even suggesting that Hussein was worse than Hitler (Mueller, 1994, p. 41). Evidence from polls, however, suggests that this was hardly necessary. From the very beginning of the crisis, Saddam Hussein himself helped Bush in his effort to lead America to war. As early as August, Americans were convinced that Hussein truly was a demon, giving him an average rating of 8 on a scale of 100 (Mueller, 1994, Table 33). Hussein's early September television appearances with hostages, referred to as "guests," were probably intended to present the dictator to the world as a "nice guy." Of Americans who reported having seen media coverage of Hussein's "meeting" with the hostages, however, 86 percent claimed that the action had hurt the leader's image (NBC/*Wall Street Journal* in Mueller, 1994, Table 139). Particularly chilling was his supposedly good treatment of a clearly terrified youngster.

As the new year approached the signs were ominous. On December 22, Iraq threatened to use chemical weapons if attacked (Taylor, 1998, p. 124). On January 9, 1991, after Bush promised to "go the extra mile" for peace, last-minute talks between Secretary of State James Baker and Iraqi foreign minister Tariq Aziz failed in Geneva (Mueller, 1994, p. 37). Four days later, similarly urgent talks between U.N. Secretary General Javier Perez de Cuellar and Saddam Hussein also failed. Aziz vowed that if his nation were attacked, it would "absolutely" attack Israel in response.

On January 12, 1991, Congress approved the use of force against Iraq by a vote of 250 to 183 in the House and 52 to 47 in the Senate (Taylor, 1998, p. 140). Democrats remained substantially opposed to the war, and, had the war resolution required a two-thirds majority as does a treaty, the president would have been stymied. With the deadline for Iraq's withdrawal only days away and Hussein showing no signs of withdrawing, war seemed certain. At this time, 86 percent of Americans believed that the United States would get involved in a war with Iraq (ABC/*Washington Post* in Mueller, 1994, Table 231). Furthermore, 89 percent of Americans believed that if war broke out, the United States would win (ABC/*Washington Post* in Mueller, 1994, Table 215). Still, on the eve of the war, support for the president's policies stood at only 62 percent (Gallup in Mueller, 1994, Table 8). That percentage had shown little change since the end of November.

OPERATION DESERT STORM

Benchmark 3: The Decision to Go to War

Operation Desert Shield officially became Operation Desert Storm on January 16, 1991. The coalition immediately undertook a massive strategic bombing campaign intended to cripple Iraq's war-making ability. The strategy proved remarkably successful. Air strikes deep into Iraqi territory quickly paralyzed command, control, and communications for Saddam's armed forces. Coalition fighters flew thousands of sorties against Iraqi missile sites, military targets, and chemical, biological, and nuclear weapons production centers (Blumberg, 1994, p. 35). Iraq put up little effective resistance. Tomahawk cruise missiles performed many of the same bombing tasks as manned aircraft, impressing television audiences worldwide with their apparent accuracy. General Norman Schwarzkopf said in a televised briefing that the air attacks had "plucked the eyes" of Iraq's radar (Taylor, 1998, p. 197). Schwarzkopf's overall goal was to render the Iraqi army 50 percent ineffective before he launched the ground campaign (Taylor, 1998, p. 223). Coalition forces achieved air superiority before the first full day of the war was over. American equipment and technology lived up to its reputation, and the Iraqis proved surprisingly inept on the defensive.

The success of the air campaign was paralleled by the effect of the war on George Bush's approval ratings. No sooner did news of Desert Storm hit CNN than Americans produced a major "rally round the flag" (Mueller, 1994, p. 70). Overnight, approval of the president's handling of the Gulf crisis increased 19 points, from 62 to 81 percent (Gallup in Mueller, 1994, Table 8). His personal approval rating as president also rose 18 points, from 64 to 82 percent (Gallup in Mueller, 1994, Table 1). By starting the war, George Bush became a heroic figure to Americans.

The terminology is instructive. While "Rolling Thunder" had been the name given to the Vietnam-era campaign of "graduated" strategic bombing, the air campaign of Desert Storm was called "Instant Thunder": to denote the fact that there would be no long-term bombing strategy all targets deemed strategically valuable would be destroyed right away. While an organized retreat could have slowed the coalition's advance, or at least made it more costly, the vast majority of Iraqi regiments either surrendered or simply turned and fled.

Those trusting in Bush and his advisers on the handling of the war jumped 20 points, from 67 percent to 87 percent (*Los Angeles Times* in Mueller, 1994, tables 6, 7). Similarly, those feeling that the situation was worth going to war over climbed 25 points from 46 percent to 71 percent (Gallup in Mueller, 1994, Table 40). Those who felt that Bush had done a good job of explaining why U.S. troops were in the Persian Gulf rose 32 points from 50 percent to 82 percent (*Los Angeles Times* in Mueller, 1994, Table 23).

Support remained high throughout the air war. As the television-viewing public saw a steady stream of images from the Gulf, it seemed clear that both success and danger reinforced its determination. On January 17, the Iraqi Scud missiles first struck Israel (Mueller, 1994, p. 67). Eight to ten missiles carrying conventional warheads (but not chemical or biological ones, as had been feared) hit the cities of Tel Aviv and Haifa, injuring twenty civilians (Blumberg, 1994, p. 35). During the night of January 22, a Scud missile fell on a Tel Aviv neighborhood, destroying an apartment complex, killing three civilians, and injuring sixty more (Moore, 1992, pp. 24, 25). While Patriot antiballistic missile batteries supplied by the United States appeared to partially shield the Israelis from these attacks, subsequent analysis called into question the Patriots' efficacy during the crisis. Missile attacks against Israel continued until Iraq was defeated. If the motive for these attacks, as was surmised by U.S. and Israeli leaders alike, was to splinter the U.S.-led coalition by provoking Israel to attack Iraq, the strategy failed when the Israelis agreed under U.S. pressure and reassurances not to enter the war (Moore, 1992, p. 25).

Iraq also fired a number of Scud missiles at Saudi Arabia. One missile was launched against Dhahran on January 17, followed by ten more missiles against Riyadh and Dhahran on January 20. On February 26, one Scud hit a makeshift U.S. barracks in Dhahran, occupied largely by a U.S. quartermaster regiment. The attack killed twenty-eight American soldiers, including the first two women personnel to die in the conflict, and injured eighty-nine (Priest, 1991, p. 833). The attacks continued until the war's conclusion (Moore, 1992, p. 25). This was the largest single loss of life for Americans during the war.

On January 20, Iraqi television broadcast pictures of captured U.S. and coalition airmen who had been injured. These prisoners delivered, in a monotone, the message that Saddam Hussein was treating his captives well and that the coalition war effort against him was unjust. As the Western media quickly reported, these coerced confessions contravened the Geneva Convention's regulations governing the treatment of war prisoners. Support for Bush's handling of the Persian Gulf situation rose another 5 points to 86 percent (Gallup in Mueller, 1994, Table 8).

On January 31, coalition forces pushed back an Iraqi ground assault at Khafji (Mueller, 1994, p. 67). On February 13, the Iraqis showed the world that civilians were being killed by America's bombs in Baghdad. Iraqi television presented graphic pictures of four hundred civilians who had been killed, knowingly, it claimed, by American bombers (Taylor, 1998, p. 223). In fact, the civilians had been housed in an Iraqi communal bunker, even though the safety of civilians could not be guaranteed by Iraq's foes if they were in military facilities; the bunker was a military target for coalition pilots. The United States was quick to respond that, for their own safety, civilians should be kept out of military bunkers. Still, support for Bush's handling of the situation briefly declined from 85 to 79 percent around this time (Gallup in Mueller, 1994, Table 8).

Two days later, on February 15, Iraq made an offer of conditional withdrawal from Kuwait. As Saddam Hussein said, "The Iraqi people will not forgive me for unconditional withdrawal from Kuwait" (Mueller, 1994, p. 21). The United States, however, was not at this point interested in any deals. Already, those approving of Bush's handling of the war had risen to 84 percent (Gallup in Mueller, 1994, Table 8). Furthermore, the air war continued to achieve its objectives of disrupting Iraqi communications infrastructure, destroying military facilities (this destination included suspected nuclear, biological, and chemical weapons centers), and eliminating as many land-based missile launchers as could be discovered. When the Soviet Union offered a peace plan on February 18, Bush quickly rejected it as falling "well short" of U.N. objectives (Mueller, 1994, p. 67).

On February 22, the Iraqis set fire to Kuwaiti oil wells. The new "scorched earth" policy shocked the world. It also created a new hazard for the environment and coalition military planners (Blumberg and French, 1994, p. 38). Ultimately, the burning wells would prove less of an environmental hazard and logistical difficulty than predicted, but they appeared to constitute a major disaster.

CROSSING THE LINE

On February 23, Bush initiated the ground war. The assault on Saddam Hussein's ground forces proved easier than the most optimistic experts had predicted. Apparently expecting that an attack would come only along the Kuwait-Saudi border or from the sea, the Iraqi forces had left their Western flank exposed for hundreds of miles. The coalition's ground units swept right around them, in a strategy that U.S. General Norman H. Schwarzkopf referred to in football terms as a "Hail Mary" (Taylor, 1998, p. 197). Outflanked, outgunned, and rapidly overrun, Iraqi soldiers surrendered in large numbers.

As it turned out, the Iraqi military had never formulated a comprehensive plan for fighting the coalition forces, because it never expected to fight. Many officers fled at the first sign of attack, leaving their units to fend for themselves (Mueller, 1994, p. 155). Those who did stand and fight against the coalition's superior equipment and numbers were generally concentrated not in Kuwait, but in the open desert, where they had the least hope of success (Mueller, 1994, p. 126). Exposed, vulnerable, and lacking air support for their protection, these soldiers were open to attack from coalition aircrafts with long-range weapons. Those who did not abandon their tanks were very often killed in them. As one senior U.S. commander put it, conditions such as open desert, an enemy armed with old and well-known weapons, and a near total lack of military coordination on the Iraqi side made Desert Storm "the perfect war" against "the perfect enemy" (Mueller, 1994, p. 156).

One of the accomplishments of the military was "their humanity in routing their pathetic and terrified, but heavily armed, enemies without killing many of them" (Mueller, 1994, p. 156). The army used its arsenal carefully, and while much enemy equipment was destroyed, there was also "a conscious, and apparently quite successful, effort to avoid the unnecessary killing of troops" (Mueller, 1994, p. 156). The Defense Department determined that, during the ground war, some 86,000 Iraqi troops had surrendered to coalition forces (Mueller, 1994, p. 156). Such a large number of prisoners would typically indicate that there were, as Schwarzkopf put it in a post-war briefing, "a very, very large number of dead" (Mueller, 1994, p. 156). Final estimates, however, suggest that the Iraqi combat deaths numbered several thousand, far below the hundreds of thousands spoken of in early estimates (Mueller, 1994, p. 158); while others estimated anywhere between 35,000 and 100,000 dead (Rosegrant and Watkins, 1996, p. 44).

All of this came as a surprise to American commanders and troops, who had expected their opponent to be highly skilled, motivated, and tenacious. General Schwarzkopf said of the very low U.S. casualty figures, "We certainly didn't expect it to go this way" (Mueller, 1994, p. 154). In his 1992 autobiography, Schwarzkopf declared that in the months before the war he "could conjure up a dozen scenarios in which the Iraqis would make victory extremely costly" (Mueller, 1994, p. 126). What mattered, however, was that Iraqi generals apparently could not conjure up these same scenarios. American battle deaths totaled 95 for the entire war, or less than the 163 American noncombat deaths sustained in the months before the war (Moore, 1992, p. 180). The ground war lasted roughly five days.

President Bush announced a cease-fire on February 27, the same day that coalition tanks recaptured Kuwait City (Blumberg and French, 1994, p. 38). So successful was the ground campaign of the "100-hour war" that, by its final hours, the administration's primary concern was to prevent the slaughter of virtually helpless Iraqi soldiers (Mueller, 1994, p. 157). There was some political justification, too, for the administration's seeking to avoid further wanton destruction. A survey conducted in late December of 1990 showed that, of those favoring military action against Iraq, 64 percent became either unsure or against military action if 100,000 or more Iraqis would be killed or wounded (Mueller, 1994, table 92a). Thus, having pushed Saddam's army in flight back to Iraq, Bush quit while he was ahead. On February 28, Bush suspended the ground war. With Iraq having already agreed to pull its forces out of Kuwait, allied ground forces did not have to go as far as Baghdad.

There was discussion, particularly afterward, of the merits of trying to capture

Saddam Hussein, but the coalition mandate did not authorize such a military mission. In light of the difficulty of finding President Manuel Noriega in smaller Panama, locating and capturing Hussein would likely have been a long, bloody campaign. On March 3, Iraqi leaders accepted the allied terms, formally ending the forty-three-day conflict (Mueller, 1994, pp. 67, 83).

Allied forces also had to enforce two "no-fly" zones in north and south Iraq. The cease-fire agreement's allowing the Iraqis to use helicopters turned out to permit attacks on Kurd rebels in the north, which came back to haunt the Bush administration. The agreement also permitted the U.N. inspection of potential Iraqi nuclear and chemical facilities, which turned out to be the subject of Iraqi evasion later on.

THE MEDIA AND THE WAR

The media played a considerable part in the unfolding of the war in the Persian Gulf. The media responded to the established preferences of their audience and the goals of the government. At the beginning of the Persian Gulf crisis, when public interest in the war rose suddenly, the ratio of news on the Persian Gulf crisis to news on the "other major issue" was roughly 9.2:1 (Gallup in Mueller, 1994, Table 98). However, by early October, when public interest in the Gulf had fallen somewhat, the ratio had fallen to 1:1.7 (Gallup in Mueller, 1994, Table 48). At the time of the war's end, the ratio had jumped to 30:1 (Gallup in Mueller, 1994, Table 48).

The media limited the scope of their coverage. They tended to praise the military, while ignoring episodes of protest. The editors of the *Los Angeles Times* reportedly determined that since support for the war seemed to be running 80 percent to 20 percent, coverage of the war that was 80 percent positive would be "balanced" (Mueller, 1994, p. 75). In many cases, even this amount of attention to the war's negatives was unusual. During the first three weeks of the war, newspapers devoted just 2.7 percent of their space to peace activities, and television news programs only 0.7 percent (LaMay, 1991, p. 50, Lichter, Rothman, and Lichter, 1986, pp. 224, 228). Both the public and politicians were very much opposed to any protests; the media coverage followed this pattern (cf. Hodgson, 1976, on Vietnam protests).

BUSH VICTORIOUS

If going to war had been good for Bush's popularity, winning the war was great. On February 28, support for his handling of the Gulf crisis was at an unprecedented 92 percent (Gallup in Mueller, 1994, Table 8). Bush's approval rating as president had soared to 89 percent, the highest ever during his presidency (Gallup in Mueller, 1994, Table 1). The last president to reach the high 80s had been Harry Truman, at the close of the Second World War soon after FDR's death. Moreover, Americans felt better about nearly every aspect of Bush and his performance as president. Two-thirds even felt that the president was "making progress" in "keeping the nation out of war," compared with only 37 percent before the war (Gallup in Mueller, 1994, Table 5).

Bush bathed in his glory. At the end of February, he addressed Congress in a nationally televised speech accompanied by numerous standing ovations. In a speech in early February 1992, he proudly informed Americans that "We fought for good versus evil. It was that clear to me: right versus wrong, dignity versus oppression. And America stood fast so that liberty could stand tall" (Mueller, 1994, p. 143). Such bold and high-minded rhetoric contributed to unrealistic expectations that precipitated a steep decline in the administration's popularity.

DECLINE AND FALL

Almost as soon as the war was over, Americans began to express diminished confidence in the achievements in the Gulf. One of the biggest problems for President Bush was that Saddam Hussein was still in office. Before and during the war Bush had demonized the Iraqi dictator, even comparing him to Adolf Hitler. The public largely accepted this depiction, but it became problematic when the war ended without the overthrow of Hussein's regime. At the end of the fighting, on February 28, despite general happiness after the victory, 46 percent said that the United States should have continued fighting until Saddam Hussein was removed from power. In early April, this number had risen to 56 percent. By mid-July, it stood at 76 percent (Gallup in Mueller, 1994, Table 164).

Part of the problem may have been the unsettling events in Iraq during the month after the war ended. Possibly fearing further casualties and a Vietnam-style quagmire, and recognizing that the U.N. resolution called for the removal of Iraq from Kuwait and not the overthrow of Hussein, the United States had ended the war without fighting its way to Baghdad. Thus, Saddam Hussein, and not the allied armies, held the capital at the war's end. Although the United States had encouraged (and expected) rebellions against the Iraqi leader, it did little to aid them when they actually occurred. The cease-fire agreement also permitted the Iraqis to fly helicopters, which proved to be powerful weapons against internal opposition. Furthermore, on March 10, the United States declared that it would not involve itself in "Iraqi internal affairs" (Blumberg and French, 1994, p. 39). Thus, the remnants of Hussein's army were able to crush Kurdish and Shiite Muslim rebellions throughout Iraq upon returning from the front. On March 28, loyalist Iraqi troops recaptured the Shiite-held city of Kerbala, and two days later took back Kurdish-held Kirkuk (Blumberg and French, 1994, p. 39). More Iraqis may have died in these suppressed uprisings than in combat with coalition forces (Mueller, 1994, p. 85).

In addition, the plight of the Kurdish people increasingly became a focal point for the American public. Belated U.S. efforts at Kurdish relief, beginning on April 13, did little to reverse the situation (Mueller, 1994, p. 83). Even the imposition by the United States and coalition nations of no-fly zones over Iraqi territory could not prevent massive civilian casualties among the estimated two million refugees (Blumberg and French, 1994, p. 39), particularly because Iraqi helicopters could still fly. The whole episode highlighted the fact that Saddam Hussein was still in control.

Another problem was Bush's often-repeated notion of the New World Order that the Gulf War would create. Bush declared at the end of the war that "ahead of us is the difficult task of pursuing a potentially historic peace" (Mueller, 1994, p. 90). Such notions may actually have sustained support among Americans during the preceding months, but they caused a letdown when it became clear that no stable, lasting peace was emerging in the region. While 63 percent felt in early March that the war would make the Middle East more stable, by mid-July this figure had dropped to 34 percent (ABC/*Washington Post* in Mueller, 1994, Table 259). Just five months after the Iraqi surrender and unconditional withdrawal from Kuwait, only 42 percent said that the Gulf War was a success for the United States (*Los Angeles Times,* 1992, Aug. 12–14).

As America's interest in the war declined after the victory, the media quickly turned to other topics. As Americans turned to more pressing domestic issues, like the recession plaguing the country since late 1990, they quickly left the Gulf War in the past. At the start of February, a record high 37 percent had considered the Gulf crisis "the most important problem facing the country" (Gallup in Mueller, 1994, Table 45). By the end of April, this number had dropped to 1 percent, while the economy as the "most important problem" had jumped from 5 to 30 percent (Gallup in Mueller, 1994, Table 45).

George Bush's efforts to remind Americans of his Gulf War success could not overcome the perception that the president was doing nothing to help the economy. In March 1992, one year after the war's end, 80 percent disapproved of Bush's handling of the economy (Gallup in Mueller, 1994, Table 45). By the end of July, Bush's approval rating as president had fallen to 29 percent (Gallup in Mueller, 1994, Table 1). Though subsequent figures showed, as the Bush campaign had argued, that the recession was over in 1992, the public perceived the economy as weak and blamed Bush. Just twenty months after the stunning military triumphs, the once victorious president was voted out of office in exchange for the governor of a small southern state with no military experience, Bill Clinton.

CONCLUSION: THE END OF THE VIETNAM SYNDROME?

August 1990 through February 1991 was a period of struggle not just between Iraq and the United States but also between President George Bush and the American public. With the exception of the initial deployment of troops in Saudi Arabia and the actual active conflict beginning on January 16, 1991, and ending on February 27, 1991, the American people were mild in their support of Bush and the situation in the Gulf. As the public split over the use of nonmilitary means, casualties, and motivations, Bush could muster only a relatively small consensus for the several months between the original deployment of troops to the Gulf region and the start of the war. Bush's portrayals of Hussein as "Hitler" and the struggle with Iraq as one to preserve a lasting peace were meant to increase public support.

Regardless of the ultimate outcome, Bush's attempts at gaining public support for the war shows his belief in the importance of public opinion. Further evidence of this impact appears in the manner in which the Bush administration planned to carry out the war. The American people were reluctant to become entangled in another long and drawn-out foreign intervention like Vietnam. For this reason Bush and his advisers placed an overwhelming amount of military power in the Gulf to ensure a quick and decisive campaign that would not arouse the public outcry about the quagmire seen in the late 1960s and early 1970s. We now turn to public opinion's effect on the Gulf War decisions made by President Bush and two of his principle advisers, Secretary of State James Baker and Secretary of Defense Richard Cheney in 1990 and 1991.

CHAPTER 10

Public Opinion's Influence on Gulf War Policy

INTRODUCTION

The effect that public attitudes had upon the Bush administration during the Persian Gulf crisis exemplifies the influence of public opinion on foreign policy in the post-Vietnam era. Bush and his advisers had decided on their general plan for war without specific reference to polls. The importance of public opinion was not in forming the idea of war but rather the way in which this ultimate solution was implemented. The concern of the Bush administration about the way that the American public would react to the possibility of war influenced its statement of aims in the Gulf, the diplomatic actions it took, and even the way in which the war was finally fought. Public opinion was a force that said not what to do but how to do it. As Bush and his advisers tried to shape public opinion through its foreign policy, public opinion actually shaped that foreign policy. Public opinion did not specifically determine the destination of the policy, but it had a lot to do with how the administration got there.

The influence of public opinion on U.S. policy toward the Persian Gulf was substantial at each of the three benchmarks. The first benchmark, immediately after Saddam Hussein's invasion of Kuwait on August 2, 1990, was President George Bush's decision to deploy troops to the Gulf in Operation Desert Shield. Sending troops into Saudi Arabia, in August and September of 1990, was the point at which Americans rapidly became interested in the Gulf crisis, and began expressing opinions about the prospect of military involvement. Prior to this, most Americans knew little of the region or of U.S. relations with Iraq. Faced with the knowledge that the American public would not tolerate another long and extended war like Vietnam, Bush realized the importance of quick and decisive action. During August and September 1990, the top policymakers formulated a potential long-term strategy, including a military intervention to remove Hussein's troops from Kuwait. At the time, though, there was little public discussion of a possible war with Iraq.

Bush's commitment to send reinforcements to the Gulf in November 1990, was the second major benchmark. Though he made the decision immediately before the mid-term elections, he announced it on November 8, three days after the vote. This was an escalation of American involvement in the Gulf, and a clear preparation for a greater American military intervention. The decision is crucial for understanding the president's decision-making process during an election. At such a sensitive time, his views of American public opinion are particularly important for understanding how and why he made policy, how it was presented to the public, and the extent of the policymakers' concern with American opinions.

Finally, the period immediately preceding the actual war in early 1991 was the third benchmark. This was a turning point in U.S. leadership, which faced the task of convincing the American public to rally in support of its first full-scale war since Vietnam. The task was not unduly difficult: despite some resistance and protest, the country as a whole accepted the military engagement. Although Bush's overall support level had fallen significantly from its unusually high point of 76 percent in August to 62 percent, a full 89 percent of Americans believed that America would win the war in the Gulf. This section focuses on policymakers' statements in late December 1990 through January 15, 1991, when the deadline for withdrawal from Kuwait expired and the president made the decision to go to war.

This chapter presents and analyzes the comments of three top policymakers and their awareness of public opinion: President Bush, Secretary of State James Baker III, and Secretary of Defense Richard Cheney. At this time, the Bush administration held relatively open discussions about public opinion in various forms, especially using communication with Congress as a medium for presenting its beliefs to the American people. This process affected the speed and clarity of the administration's decisions during the escalation of the Gulf crisis, and the quick pace toward war. The policies maintained from August through January, that "this will not stand," might have given the administration a high expectation of public support, because opinion tends to be more supportive of decisive actions (Sobel, 1996, p. 147). Further, the U.S. national interest in the Gulf, which the administration sought to redefine numerous times, both economically and politically, seemed clear and comprehensible to most Americans and policymakers alike. When the Bosnia crisis began to flare, as Chapter 11 will show, the administration was notably more withdrawn concerning public opinion.

PRESIDENT GEORGE BUSH

Benchmark 1: Troops in the Gulf: August–September 1990

After Iraq invaded Kuwait on August 2, 1990, the first major benchmark of U.S. involvement in the dispute, President Bush made a series of decisions. Only six days later, when he sent troops to Saudi Arabia, support among the American public rose dramatically to 80 percent for his decisive action (Gallup in Mueller, 1994, Table 8). Bush's own comments reflect awareness of this support. He recognized that the newly deployed soldiers had ". . . accepted the challenge . . . with extraordinary dedication to duty." "I want them to know that the American people are behind them 100 percent . . ." (Bush, 1991, p. 1157).

By early September 1990, Bush remained clearly convinced of the American public's support for his policies. In an address to a joint session of Congress on September 11, 1990, he stated, "Let me thank all Americans, especially those here in this Chamber tonight, for your support for our armed forces and for their mission. That support will be even more important in the days to come" (Bush, 1991, p. 1218).

He appealed subtly for continued support as a basis for carrying the war to its conclusions. "There is no substitute for American leadership. In the face of tyranny, let no one doubt American credibility and reliability, . . . [and] our staying power" (Bush, 1991, p. 1219).

Benchmark 2: Mid-Term Elections, Troop Reinforcement: October–November 1990

Bush's call for support was needed because by early October his ratings began to fall even as the troops dug in and the president faced the possibility of sending reinforcement at the second benchmark. Support for his Gulf policies dropped to 69 percent in the first week of October. By mid-October, only 61 percent of Americans supported Bush's policies. Furthermore, Americans did not want to rush toward military action.

Falling poll ratings and the nearing of mid-term elections brought added pressure on Bush to win over the public. At an October 31 exchange with reporters, he defended his policies while simultaneously expressing awareness of public misgivings: "I am concerned about the lives of Americans. . . . So are the American people. . . . I'm simply trying to have the American people understand how strongly I feel about the brutality of Saddam Hussein's policy. . . . I think world opinion is saying he's got to stop it." Bush is reflecting awareness of American opinion, while attempting to guide it through persuasion, and the force of "world opinion." He utilizes public support as a way to send a signal to his opponents that "The American people are concerned . . ." (Bush, 1991, p. 1498).

When asked in a press conference whether the latest escalation of threats following the hostage issue was intended to boost Bush's support for the mid-term elections, Bush fell back on public opinion to defend himself.

> We're talking two separate things: one, a major crisis halfway around the world where we have strong support—Democrats and Republicans, the American people supporting us, the whole world and the United Nations supporting us. . . . Nobody would make a decision based on some political—certainly not me. . . . I'm offended that anybody would even suggest that. (Bush, 1991, p. 1504)

Following the election, which returned a Democratic Congress to power, Bush took the major step of increasing the numbers of troops in Saudi Arabia to create an offensive capability in the Gulf. He also increasingly confronted the American people with the realization that there could be war: "I've been asked why I ordered more troops to the Gulf. I remain hopeful that we can achieve a peaceful solution to the crisis. But if force is required, we . . . will have enough power to get the job done" (Bush, 1991, p. 1720).

Confronted with a blunt question about how to convince the public to put their children at risk on the battlefield, Bush defended his actions:

> People say to do more. How many lives? How many lives can you expend? Each one is precious. . . . You ought to read my mail. It is so heart-moving. Supportive, and yet: Please bring my kid home. Please bring my husband home. It's a tough ques-

tion. But a President has to make the right decision. These are worldwide principles of moral importance. . . . Because of that question that weighs on my mind, I added that language this morning about how this will not be a Vietnam. (Bush, 1991, pp. 1725–26)

In a press session in late November, a reporter accused President Bush of being "afraid of" majority rule in this country, and of not consulting sufficiently with Congress. He responded with assurances of his attention to Congress. The reporter declared that "you won't give the United States people a chance to debate with you." President Bush maintained that congressional discussions were taking place, implying that these represented the people sufficiently: "They're having endless hearings by endless experts up there, each one with a slightly different view. And that's the American way. And that's fine" (Bush, 1991, p. 1727).

Benchmark 3: The Decision to Go to War: December 1990–January 1991

The next benchmark in the crisis was the period from mid-December to the start of the war. This was a critical turning point, when Bush had to weigh the possibilities for a successful war as the withdrawal deadline drew closer. In October, polls had revealed that 48 percent of Americans did not want to go to war even if the sanctions failed. In November the percentage of Americans who thought the United States was escalating too quickly toward war rose, to 47 percent, and only 54 percent approved of Bush's general handling (compared with 80 percent in August). Against the background of this significant reluctance, Bush demonstrated considerable efforts to avoid war. At a December 14 news conference, he repeatedly emphasized his diplomatic efforts: "On November 30th, in offering direct meetings between the United States and Iraq, I offered to go the extra mile for a peaceful solution to the Gulf question. . . . And I will continue now to work for a peaceful solution" (Bush, 1991, p. 1795).

Having restated his diplomatic initiatives to the reporters, Bush portrayed the American public's support for the possibility of offensive action. At this time, 51 percent of Americans would have been prepared to accept a diplomatic settlement with some compromises to the U.S. initial demands (NBC/*Wall Street Journal* in Mueller, 1994, Table 106). Bush stated:

I'm very pleased with the support we've had in Congress [for offensive action]. And I'm very pleased with the level of support from the American people. You see, as these hostages have come home, I think the [American people] have understood . . . much more clearly what's at stake. . . . I think people have said: Wait a minute, this policy deserves support. So, I'm pleased with the support. I think that's being manifested in more support by Congress. (Bush, 1991, p. 1796).

Bush may be reflecting that 18 percent of Americans felt that the release of the hostages made them more inclined to accept the use of force (Mueller, 1994, p. 139).

Reporters confronted Bush with a different side of public opinion, stating that the feedback from their audiences was not supportive of war. Bush did not respond to the comment. In the same session, Bush considered how this support would benefit U.S. policy internationally: "I will be talking to the leaders, continuing to consult. What I told the leaders in the Cabinet Room a few weeks ago: If you want to . . . strongly endorse what I'm doing . . . I welcome that because I think it would send a very strong, clear signal to the world" (Bush, 1991, p. 1796).

He also used the opportunity to discuss American opinion to justify confronting Iraq because of its development of nuclear and unconventional weapons.

> I think Congress and the American people are getting increasingly concerned about his . . . nuclear . . . [and] other unconventional war capabilities. . . . I met with a group of people who were supportive of our policy. And they are emphasizing to me . . . the concern by the American people . . . about his possession of these unconventional weapons and his desire to acquire nuclear weapons. (Bush, 1991, p. 1797)

Finally, several days later, Bush was forced to confront directly the question of U.S. public support for a war. A reporter explained that readers' letters questioned whether Bush saw the American public as supportive of a war. His assessment is revealing:

> I believe the country would support that. But I don't think that support would last if it were a long, drawn-out conflagration. I think support would erode, as it did in the Vietnam . . . conflict. And one of the reasons that I moved this additional force . . . was . . . I would want to be able to assure the parents and the families there is enough force there to minimize the risk to every single American kid and coalition kid. . . . (Bush, 1991, p. 1805)

This statement shows that Bush clearly took public opinion into account in formulating American policy. However, he viewed it as a force that he could manipulate; if he gave the public assurances of maximum safety measures and reinforcement, it would be more likely to support the war. His statements also reflected Bush's realization that Americans were suffering from the post-Vietnam syndrome: 62 percent in January thought that "tens of thousands" could die, and 53 percent saw a long, protracted war, while 62 percent thought that a Vietnam-type war was likely (Mueller, 1994, p. 306). Bush demonstrates his role as a leader responsible to his public in order to justify his policy actions of sending more forces to the Gulf.

In early January, as the United States stood on the brink of war, Americans were not overly confident: despite Bush's reassurances, only 9 percent envisioned a very short war. Bush steadfastly proclaimed American public support in a January 9, 1991, news conference, and continued to insist that he had taken all measures to preserve peace: "I know that there is a good feeling up there [in Congress]. I think people see that the American people are supportive of the policy of this country. I think they see that we have tried the diplomatic track. But I hope they also know that I am firmly determined to see that this aggression not stand. And I think they're backing me . . ." (Bush, 1992, p. 19).

On January 12, Bush claimed that his winning support of Congress (250 to 183 in the House, 52 to 47 in the Senate) through a democratic process justified the impending action. "As a democracy we've debated this issue openly and in good faith. And as president I have held extensive consultation with the Congress. We've now closed ranks behind a clear signal of our determination. . . ." Bush was so confident of American support that he used it to threaten Saddam Hussein: "The action taken by the United States Congress today is a very important step in, hopefully, getting Saddam Hussein to realize what he's up against—the determination of the American people. I have felt the support is there from the people, but I think now with the Congress—the representatives of the people—on record, it makes it much, much clearer to Saddam Hussein." Bush was then asked if he would act quickly, based on American public support: "The polls have shown people support moving fairly quickly after the fifteenth. Would that be your intention?" He did not draw a clear causal link between public opinion and his actions: "I have said . . . without trying to pin it down . . . sooner rather than later" (Bush, 1992, p. 33).

Despite waning public support as the Gulf crisis progressed—from 80 percent in August to 54 percent in November 1990 (Mueller, 1994, Table 8)—Bush viewed Desert Storm as a major accomplishment of his administration:

> I think history will probably look to Desert Storm because of the disparate coalition that we put together. And because the military, when the politicians defined the mission and then got out of the way, fought and won the war and established the moral principle. . . . But what I hope they say is that we did it with honor. We upheld the integrity of the White House. (Bush, 5/28/98)

In spite of declining public support in the polls, Bush perceived the public to be more supportive than Congress for his Gulf policies:

> So I don't know how you measure public opinion at that time. I felt in Desert Storm that we had more support from the people than we did from Congress. I know we did. Because you remember the key vote on the U.N.—I mean, at the Congress—was 53 [52] to 47; almost on party lines. And I say that with no bitterness. But I'm just telling you that's the way it was. Later on, to their credit, they all supported the U.S. once the battle began." (Bush, 5/28/98)

In short, at almost every point, Bush revealed awareness of public opinion about his policies. While his decisions were generally made without specific reference to public attitudes or polls, he took opinion into account in how he presented the decisions to the public. He also recognized the importance of and encouraged the obtaining of public support as key to the effectiveness of carrying out his politics over time.

SECRETARY OF STATE JAMES BAKER III

Benchmark 1: Sending Troops to the Gulf: August–September 1990

James Baker's statements following the August events refer to the American public as a foundation for effective U.S. diplomacy. In general, Baker seemed to believe that the most stable and powerful policy consisted of decisions made in accordance with high public support. As early as August, he writes in his memoirs, the United States was pursuing a policy in the international arena designed to help boost public support at home. "The stronger the [international] coalition, the easier it was to generate consensus at home. Likewise, the more domestic support we had, the more the President was put in a commanding position vis-à-vis other governments" (Baker, 1995, p. 333). Therefore, Baker wrote, the United States pursued an international strategy of gaining U.N. Security Council resolutions, designed to encourage American support: "We believed that the cumulative effect of these resolutions would have the added domestic benefit of eventually thrusting congressional fence-sitters into a politically awkward posture . . ." (Baker, 1995, p. 332).

In a speech to Congress in early September, Baker clearly sought to influence public thinking about the Gulf: "I have come here today to speak to you—and through you to the American people—about the conflict in the Persian Gulf. . . . The President has made it plain we have a straightforward responsibility to the American people: Openly and clearly, we have a duty to state what is at stake. . . . We have a duty to tell our people what our immediate goals are in this conflict. And we have a duty to explain how we plan to achieve those goals . . ." (Baker, 1995).

He also considered this responsibility toward the American public as a valid justification for American actions in the Gulf: "We have a responsibility to assure the American people that a decade from now, their sons and daughters will not be put in jeopardy because we failed to work toward long run solutions to the problems of the Gulf" (Baker, 1990a, p. 23).

Baker seemed to believe that public support was needed in order to carry out administration policies, and he closed his remarks with a request for sustained support: "In this effort, America must lead and our people must understand that. . . . Our efforts will, however, take time, and that is what we ask most of the American people: Stand firm. Be patient. And remain united so that together we can show that aggression does not pay" (Baker, 1990a, p. 24).

Benchmark 1: Mid-Term Elections, Troop Reinforcement: October–November 1990

At a mid-October question-and-answer session between Baker and Foreign Relations Committee members, Baker revealed his views about public opinion when directly confronted with questions of American support: "We learned from the Vietnam experience that the support of the American people as expressed through 535 representatives in Congress is essential. . . . It is important, we think . . . that we have the support of the American people. One way you get that is to have the support of the elected representatives. Therefore, we will consult" (Baker, 1990b, p. 45).

Baker's testimony to the House Foreign Affairs Committee, and the Senate Foreign Relations Committee described Baker's belief that American public support for Bush's Gulf policies remained strong, despite the sharp drop in poll ratings of Bush's general performance from August to September: "It is gratifying that the vast majority of Americans have rallied behind the President in support of both our goals and out strategy in the Persian Gulf. Indeed, most of the world has done so" (Baker, 1990b, p. 45).

Baker's speech at the end of October, following over a week of organized protest rallies and marches against Gulf involvement, does not mention public opinion explicitly. Instead, speaking to the World Affairs Council in Los Angeles, Baker sought to build public support by emphasizing the dangers of inaction:

If the entire world were to be thrust into a deep recession by an Iraqi stranglehold . . . American industry, farmers, and small businesses would be hit especially hard. . . . We understand the concerns of their families, here at home. The courage they have shown in the face of Saddam Hussein's manipulations is great. . . . The American people have not come this long hard way to make the world safe for the likes of Saddam Hussein. (Baker, 1990c, p. 49)

Baker's own recollection of this speech confirms the intention to sway public opinion:

In hopes of conditioning Congress and the public to [the likelihood of war], I used the opportunity of a . . . speech to the Los Angeles World Affairs Council . . . to treat the possible use of force against Iraq. . . . In words carefully chosen for their impact, I said that while the President was exhausting every diplomatic avenue to achieve a peaceful solution, let no one doubt: we will not rule out a possible use of force. . . . (Baker, 1995, p. 335)

Baker's memoirs describe the importance of public presentation of policy decisions for generating public support. His focus was on Congress as representative of the American public, and therefore sensitive to their reactions. On November 8, Bush announced his major decision to send far greater forces to the Gulf. Baker wrote: "The timing was horrible. . . . Congress . . . had [not] been adequately prepared for the news . . . an announcement that would almost by definition start the country thinking seriously about war perhaps ought not be unveiled on Veterans' Day." At this point, Baker still felt that "Congress's disinterest mirrored the public's apathy" (Baker, 1995, p. 332). His negative image was not entirely undergirded by American public opinion polls in early to mid-November, which found that 84 percent were "very confident" of America's victory in a potential war. Nevertheless, Baker stated: "There would be no groundswell from the voters urging Congress to send troops to protect our interests in the Gulf" (Baker, 1995, p. 332).

Baker outlined the problems involved in potentially antagonizing the Congress: "Diplomatic pressure and economic sanctions were hard enough for Congress to endorse . . . marshaling congressional support for a more aggressive policy in the Gulf would be . . . as difficult as passing comprehensive tax reform . . ." (Baker, 1995, p. 330). He revealed how the administration reacted following the congressional outcry. "It took two months of intensive damage control, a United Nations resolution, and a final diplomatic effort by the President, culminating in direct talks between me and the Iraqi Foreign Minister, to persuade legislators to support the option of U.S. military intervention" (Baker, 1995, p. 330). This is clear indication that Baker's incremental policy decisions were powerfully influenced by his perception of American domestic opinion.

Benchmark 3: The Decision to Go to War: December 1990–January 1991

Policymakers faced a public under the influence of Vietnam syndrome, as a result of which, Baker believed, "the President's private resolve to order American forces into combat . . . was conspicuously lacking in support—both in Congress and with the public at large" (Baker, 1995, p. 331). Another difficulty the administration faced at this time, as the United States drew nearer to the realistic possibility of war, was the lack of familiarity of many Americans with the Gulf situation: "Those few Americans who were paying attention could be excused for having missed the shift [to a more aggressive Iraq strategy]. . . . We went from trying to work with Saddam to likening him to Hitler. The apparent contradiction made it more difficult to raise the consciousness of the American people to Saddam's threat" (Baker, 1995, p. 331).

Further, Baker was positive that the administration's disjointed arguments for going to war was hurting possible public support, and he admitted that this was a main reason for his famous "jobs, jobs, jobs" statement. "We were beginning to pay a political price at home as a result of our rhetorical confusion. Public support for Desert Shield was starting to unravel. . . . I was searching for a formulation that drove home the magnitude of the threat to ordinary Americans, and thereby shored up domestic support for a policy . . ." (Baker, 1995, p. 336–37). This comment reveals how perceptions of public opinion affected not only the presentation of policy, but also ultimately the attempt to win essential public support.

Baker saw public support as critical both domestically and internationally. "Realistically, we couldn't have used force in the face of explicit congressional disapproval. Our international coalition would be left to wonder about the durability of America's resolve . . ." (Baker, 1995, p. 337). This implies that domestic opinion affected international efforts. In a later speech on December 5, 1990, he cautioned specifically that American success would depend on public support: "If we are to have any chance of success, I must go to Baghdad with the full support of the Congress and of the American people behind the message of the international community" (Baker, 1995, p. 340).

On November 29, after the mid-term elections, the United States pushed through U.N. Resolution 678, authorizing the international community to force an Iraqi withdrawal by "all necessary means." Despite the decline of political pressures that might have been expected following the elections, Baker recalled great sensitivity to public opinion surrounding the vote: "It [the resolution and the January 15 deadline] helped us particularly with domestic political opinion in the United States. Which was at the beginning . . . very much opposed to the idea of going to war in the Persian Gulf" (Baker, 1/9/96).

The inaccuracy in Baker's statement that at the "beginning" (August) the public was opposed, when in fact public support for Bush was very high then, probably reflects the resistance the administration had met in October. In response to a question on President Bush's feelings about the U.N. resolution:

> . . . We also recognised the importance of doing this . . . in a way that would be supported particularly by the American people. And when the crisis first erupted and particularly in the aftermath of the President's decision to augment our forces back in early November, there was very little public support in the United States for the idea of going to war in the Persian Gulf . . . it was overwhelmingly opposed and one way in which we'd built domestic political support was to bring together an unprecedented international coalition. (Baker, 1/9/96)

As the deadline neared, Baker strongly supported the president's inclination to negotiate with Iraqi Foreign minister Tariq Aziz one more time in January 1991:

> This was . . . not a plot on my part to avoid the war but . . . the meeting with
> Tariq Aziz in Geneva permitted us to achieve congressional support for something
> that the President was determined to do in any event, but how much better that he
> could do it with the support of the American people . . . congressional opposition
> to the use of force pretty well collapsed in the aftermath of my meeting with Tariq
> Aziz so it was clearly the right thing to do at the time. (Baker, 1/9/96)

He thus agreed with Bush on the need to create policy initiatives that demonstrated
peaceful goals in order to win over the public: "Our main purpose in 'going the last
mile' was to show Congress, the American people, and history that we were still looking for ways to avert war. . . . When my meeting in Geneva . . . failed to produce
a breakthrough, opposition in Capitol Hill began to crumble" (Baker, 1995, p. 344).

As a result of the Gulf War, Baker saw American public opinion as fundamentally
changed: "In large measure because Desert Storm was such a resounding success, the
American people and their elected representatives now appear more willing to endorse the application of military power under clearly defined circumstances . . ."
(Baker, 1995, p. 331).

In short, Baker recognized the importance of generating public support in order to
realize the success of administration policies. For Baker, the higher the support the
better, and he spent considerable time and effort in creating and providing rationales
for generating that support as the policy evolved and war approached.

SECRETARY OF DEFENSE RICHARD CHENEY

Richard Cheney's leadership in the Gulf War needs to be viewed in the light of his
political experience as a congressman from Wyoming, and the possibility of his becoming a candidate for the Republican presidential nomination in 1996. As secretary
of defense, Dick Cheney fell under less public scrutiny than the president or the secretary of state. As Chapter 11 will show, throughout his leadership in the Bosnia crisis, his public comments were minimal, and his stated interest in American public
opinion was even less. However, before and during the Gulf War, Cheney was accessible to the press and therefore to the public. Press conferences, interviews, and later
conversations reveal his intense interest and awareness of public opinion during the
Gulf War. Cheney admits that public opinion generally affected his decision-making:
"The mindset that I had—and I think this is true of the President as well and most of
the rest of us—we were trying to figure out what was the right thing to do. . . . Public opinion was then something you had to work on to build support for your position,
but you didn't determine your position based on public opinion" (Cheney, 3/22/99).
"Even if public opinion was against us, we were still going to go" (Cheney, 3/22/99).
Aware of the legacy of Vietnam, he "felt we wanted to 'get right' . . . or 'do better'
. . . in Desert Shield and Desert Storm" (Cheney, 3/22/99).

Benchmark 1: Sending Troops to the Gulf: August–September 1990

As early as August, Cheney felt unambiguous about using force if the situation
seemed to call for it: "I always thought that the commitment to use force if necessary . . . to expel Saddam Hussein from Kuwait was there when the President came

down from Camp David that first week into the crisis and said that this aggression will not stand" (Cheney, 1/9/96, p. 7)

He did not refer to public opinion during the first stages of the situation, concentrating instead on military strategy: "It wasn't really until the end of August that we began to feel fairly comfortable with the size forces we were getting there. That we could respond aggressively if he were to launch an attack. . . . [As the troops built up] through the month of September . . . then you begin to feel that you've achieved your first stage objective which is to be able to defend Saudi Arabia. Then you move into the second phase . . . what are we going to do to get this guy [Hussein] out of Kuwait?" (Cheney, 1/9/96). Regarding the early decision-making process, "In those early, early hours, I don't think we had any information on or spent a lot of time thinking about public opinion. . . . To say that public opinion shaped our decisionmaking at that point would be inaccurate" (Cheney, 3/22/99).

Benchmark 1: Mid-Term Elections, Troop Reinforcement: October–November 1990

As the events in the Gulf progressed, however, public opinion began to play more of a role. "Later on, as we went on down the fall, we were very much aware of public opinion in that it was not united. . . . At the time there was hope that we could resolve it diplomatically" (Cheney, 3/22/99). On October 11, as election politics began to influence the policy discussions, and Bush's poll ratings fell somewhat, the White House held a briefing to try to focus civilian and military leaders in the administration on the next stage. The plan presented by the senior military leadership had two phases: the air war and the ground war. The air-war plan was acceptable, he said, but the ground war was not, because, "we would get bogged down trying to attack the Iraqi fortifications head on, and we'd suffer a lot of casualties, but there weren't many options given the size force we had."

When asked why the force General Schwarzkopf had was considered insufficiently large, Cheney responded with his first indication of how public opinion influenced decision-makers:

> . . . some of out senior military commanders still had doubts about whether or not the same thing would happen to them here that had happened in Vietnam. Now in Vietnam we had a President who refused to deploy reserves. He would never call up the reserves and the National Guard. He didn't want to offend the American people and create a political problem for himself. So the active duty force was forced to fight the war . . . without the kind of support that they'd planned on . . . those senior military commanders had had the experience of a political leadership that was not full square behind the effort and not prepared to make the tough decisions to give them what they needed to do the job. Now that wasn't true of George Bush, we did it very differently . . . when we said "What do you need . . ." they said "Well, we want VII Corps, . . . the 1st Infantry . . . another Marine division and six aircraft carrier battle groups." We said "You got it. . . ." (Cheney, 3/22/99)

Cheney also revealed the early convictions of the Bush administration that the use of force might be necessary, and that the capabilities needed to be developed even as early as mid-October for "a military option."

On October 30, just before the mid-term election, the White House held another military-civilian briefing. President Bush was beginning to respond to public disapproval of the war in his press statements. However, the record of the White House proceedings demonstrates a different attitude:

> I wanted to make certain that they [Powell and Schwarzkopf] had everything they requested [at an October 30 meeting]. I did not want to be in a position where the civilians had denied our military leaders the resources they said they needed to do the job. . . . So they came in with a fairly long shopping list and instead of debating it, I just said "Yes.". . . . We gave them absolutely everything they asked for and then said, "Now you must get on with the job." (Cheney, 1/9/96)

This comment indicates a much earlier plan for going to full-fledged war than President Bush revealed in his statements to the press or the Congress. While Bush was telling the public that all measures were being taken to avoid war, and that he shared the concerns of all Americans who were reluctant to become involved, the military leadership was preparing for battle. The exaggerated size of the "shopping list," however, could have been justified by Bush's statements that he wanted to ensure the utmost safety of all American soldiers.

Cheney noted another aspect of public opinion that constrained the administration during the Gulf conflict. He said: "Every time we made a public statement, we were speaking to different audiences. Audience number one would be Saddam Hussein in Bagdhad. Say you wanted to send a very strong message to Saddam to get out or else, that might play adversely back at home and frighten the American people" (Cheney, 1/9/96).

Benchmark 3: The Decision to Go to War: December 1990–January 1991

When Cheney was asked about the mood of American leadership as the war became imminent around Christmas of 1990, he stated "I think it's difficult to overstate the pressures that the President was under through this period of time." He recapped the American public's views throughout the fall, showing much more attention to detail than Bush's public insistence that support was unambiguous.

> In the fall there was a lot of doubt. The public was not united behind this matter when we started, the Democrats and the Congress were opposed to it. Sam Nunn . . . held hearings after we'd announced . . . that we were going to double the size of the force we'd sent out there. . . . The former Chairman of the Joint Chiefs went up and testified against us on Capital Hill . . . a whole body of opinion in the west . . . raised questions about whether or not we were doing the right thing. (Cheney, 3/22/99)

Cheney correctly assessed the "rally" effect that can take place when troops are sent into a conflict:

> As we got the forces deployed in November and December, we had called up the reserves, people saw that we meant business. By the time we get close to the holidays

the country starts to come together in support of what the President wants to do.
. . . I think it would be fair to say that we were increasingly confident that if it did
in fact come to combat we were increasingly confident we were going to be able to
do it and do it right. (Cheney, 3/22/99)

In discussing the last-minute talks between Secretary of State Baker and Iraqi
Deputy Foreign Minister Tariq Aziz as Bush's effort to "go the extra mile for peace,"
Cheney explained that these talks represented a policy decision that grew out of concern for American public opinion. When asked if they should have taken place, he
replied: ". . . you had different audiences you had to play to. We had the American
public here at home to worry about . . . if you got tough and . . . belliger-
ent . . . then people would get nervous sometimes here at home. Public opinion
would say, 'Well gee, you guys are, you know, too warlike, too eager to go to war.'"

> . . . From very early on in the crisis I operated on the assumption that we were
> going to have to use force . . . it was my job as Secretary of Defense to make cer-
> tain that that was a live option. . . . While the Geneva meeting was controversial
> in some circles . . . it was very helpful here at home in the U.S. because it demon-
> strated conclusively to the public and to the Congress that we in fact were deadly se-
> rious about trying every last option to get him out . . . being able to say to the
> American people and to the press and the Congress, "Look guys we tried everything
> and now we've got no option left but to use military force" really set the stage for the
> kind of unified mission we had behind the effort when we finally had the round up.
> (Cheney, 3/22/99)

The congressional vote on January 12, 1991, approving the use of force was a
turning point for the president and for the country. When asked what the vote meant
to him, Cheney's reply shows the limits of public opinion's influence on his outlook:

> We were absolutely committed to getting Saddam Hussein out of Kuwait one way or
> the other, no matter what we had to do . . . if it had just been the United States and
> Saudi Arabia, without the United Nations, without the authorization of Congress, we
> were prepared to go ahead. I argued in public session before the Congress that we
> did not need Congressional authorization. (Cheney, 1/9/96, p. 7)

Cheney seemed prepared not to forego congressional approval because of the importance of supporting the international coalition. The world's unity over the need to
halt Iraqi aggression was a major point of Bush's public statements justifying U.S. intervention. Bush repeatedly emphasized the importance of the coalition for creating a
New World Order (posited by Bush as a main reason for going to war), and used it as
a means of detracting from the American-Iraqi confrontation. If the international
coalition was a major justification of the war effort to the American people, then
Cheney clearly did not intend to be stopped by public disapproval after a certain point.

Cheney admitted to this discrepancy between his and the president's outlook on
Congress, which Bush often viewed as a representative of the American people:

> The President to his great credit felt very strongly that he wanted the Congress on
> board and he felt we could get them on board. . . . We went to work on them and

that vote in fact prevailed. I think having the Congress vote ultimately was a major plus. . . . If we'd lost the vote in Congress, I would certainly have recommended to the President we go forward anyway. (Cheney, 1/6/96)

Cheney held that Bush ". . . would in fact have gone forward whether Congress had supported the effort or not" (Cheney, 1/9/96).

An interesting aspect of public opinion appeared toward the end of the Gulf War, when the troops' mission had to be revised in light of overwhelming success. Cheney said, "public opinion entered into it by . . . the concern that there was a limit to what we could ask our kids to do" (Cheney, 1/9/96). On February 10, 1991, during a Defense Department briefing while Desert Storm success was being proven, Cheney commented on the significance of public support in ensuring further success. He stated: "I think the support of the American people for the effort has been over-whelming. It has been, frankly, more extensive than I would have anticipated a few months ago. The extent to which the country has sort of pulled together . . . be-hind the forces that have been deployed to the Gulf behind our young men and women in uniform and the President's policy has been truly something to behold." He continued:

> I feel very good about the current state of public support for the effort. I think it's something that's vital in terms of the successful conclusion of the campaign. . . . It's not just a question of the public supporting our forces here in the Gulf. I think it's also a fact that public opinion in the United States, the American people are enor-mously proud of what our men and women have been able to accomplish. (Cheney, 2/10/91)

Clearly, Cheney perceived a surprising and overwhelming mandate for the adminis-tration's policies in the Gulf. Like Baker, Cheney remembered the opposition that the administration experienced in October. Not only did he imply an awareness of how opposition could serve as a potential restraint on his policies, but he also recog-nized the significance of continued support for the "successful conclusion" of the in-tervention. He recognized public opinion as elemental to an effective foreign policy intervention.

In March 1991, Cheney addressed the same issue at a conference for leaders of Jewish organizations, particularly concerned by the Gulf War and Iraqi aggression. He praised President Bush for allowing the military to act "in a way that guaranteed that we would make military judgments based upon how we could have maximum impact upon our adversary at minimum cost in terms of American lives and Ameri-can casualties." He assured the group that

> there was no policy of gradual escalation. There were no artificial political restraints upon targeting. There was no holding back in terms of our military activity. There was the determination to succeed and the provision of the resources we needed to do it, and then the very successful marshaling of world and American public opinion to guarantee that our troops had the kind of support they deserved. (Federal Informa-tion Systems, 3/5/91)

These statements are significant, since Cheney seemed to allude to the failures of the Vietnam War. Aware of public opinion as a potential "political restraint," he recognized that positive public support, in part, enabled the success of the intervention. These remarks also indicate that the way of war that was fought by the coalition forces was, in part, a result of concerns for public opinion.

Cheney also addressed the possibility of influencing public opinion to support the cause. Asked about the use of reservists in order to "guarantee public support," Cheney replied that

> the Guard and Reserve are a vital part of the force today. . . . They play a role in terms of helping us mobilize public opinion when it is time to go to war. I can trace support for the President's policies in the Persian Gulf against Saddam Hussein to that point in time when we called up a large number of Guardsmen and Reservists, and people all across the country, every community was affected, every state was affected. (Cheney, 3/26/92)

In short, aware of the significance of public opinion, Cheney believed that public opinion was a force that could be swayed or "mobilized" in order to ensure the necessary support for a successful military intervention. While as secretary of defense he stressed that decisions were made on their military merits, he also recognized the constraint that the public could put on military options, and the need to engender support for administration policies.

CONCLUSION: BUSH ADMINISTRATION STRATEGY

Bush administration decision-makers displayed considerable attention to public opinion in defining and presenting their policies. Even at the earliest stages of U.S. involvement in the Gulf, all the decision-makers reflected on the role of public opinion in the possible outcomes. This keen interest in the public sentiment was likely related to the fact that from the start, policymakers were dealing with the possibility of full-scale war. For this there is a general consensus among policymakers that they needed significant public support. Top policymakers sought to address the public through the Congress, as evidenced by Bush's televised address to both houses of Congress and Baker's often-repeated statement that he was speaking through Congress to the American people. Both believed that as a vehicle for channeling public sentiment, congressional support was critical.

From the start of the crisis, Bush saw the importance of gaining and maintaining public support. He demonstrated his concern about the fragile nature of public opinion despite the high levels of support surrounding his initial deployment of troops in the Gulf. With the progression of the crisis into the second benchmark period of offensive force buildup, this concern grew with the drop in public support. Bush's policies of diplomacy, aimed at gaining a skeptical public's support, as the war inched closer demonstrated his belief in the necessity of having public backing before a conflict.

Baker shared this belief in the importance of garnering public support. In meetings with the public and Congress, he tried to make the case for a military engagement against Iraq. Baker's conviction that public support was essential for a successful policy appears clearly in his meeting with Tariq Aziz in January 1991. These last-minute talks served little purpose except to show the public that all diplomatic routes had been exhausted and all that was left was the use of force.

Displaying the realist tendency of someone who considered himself a trustee of the American people rather than a delegate, Richard Cheney revealed willingness to overrule Congress' potential lack of support, and pursue military options regardless. These policies, he claimed, had been pursued and prepared from the beginning, and he was steadfastly against backing away from a military solution. His sensitivity to public pressures and American opinion appeared mainly in the effects of these on his method of carrying out policy. This included his insistence upon virtually complete acquiescence to demands made by the military, which he felt would help the public feel secure about the war and distinguish it from Vietnam.

The combination of Cheney's determination to push the administration ahead decisively, and Baker's and Bush's intense focus on rallying public and congressional opinion, helped to maintain adequate public support. The administration's ability to rally an international coalition, which it at times claimed was based on its firm political position at home, encouraged greater support. With the combined support of many Americans and the rest of the world, the war was fought disproportionately by America, with little resistance from the public. Public opinion during the post-Vietnam era was a defining factor for what type of war took place in the Gulf: fast, overwhelming, with minimal casualties. It was one of the defining elements in how the administration chose to present the policy. Further, the increase from the relative lack of knowledge and interest of Americans in the Persian Gulf prior to the event to intense focus on the conflict suggests that the administration did a careful job of leading the public's understanding of the situation toward support for its preferred policy. This contrasted, to a large degree, with the administration's approach to the simmering conflict in Bosnia.

V

THE BOSNIA CASE
FROM NONINTERVENTION
TO INTERVENTION

THE BOSNIA CASE STUDY EXAMINES THE CONNECTIONS BETWEEN AMERICAN PUBLIC opinion and the policies of both the Bush and Clinton administrations after the breakup of Yugoslavia following the end of the Cold War. In particular, it focuses on the fighting in Bosnia from 1992 to 1995. Chapter 11 reviews the historical background, the events on the ground, and the American policy responses to them by the two administrations. Parallel to its examination of the respective events and policies, the chapter looks at the attitudes of the American public as expressed in polls, congressional debates, and the media. The goal of the case study is to establish whether opinion had an impact on policy and if so, how much and what kind. Chapter 12 examines the actual impact of public sentiment on Bush administration policy in 1992 and 1993, while Chapter 13 looks at the impact of opinion on Clinton administration policies from 1993 to 1996.

In the Bush administration, the key decision-makers were, as for the most part in the Gulf War case, President George Bush, Secretaries of State James Baker and Lawrence Eagleburger, and Secretary of Defense Richard Cheney. In the Clinton administration, they were President Bill Clinton, Secretary of State Warren Christopher, and Secretary of Defense William Perry.

For the Bosnia crisis, there are three major benchmarks for the Bush administration and three for the Clinton administration. The first Bush benchmark was the beginning of the fighting in April 1992. The second was the response to the escalation of Serb attacks in early 1992. And the third was the shift to a policy of great engagement in December 1992.

The first Clinton benchmark was the push for NATO airstrikes after the first Sarajevo market massacre in February 1994. The second benchmark was the mid-1995 intensification of U.S. engagement through robust airstrikes. The third benchmark was the Dayton negotiations and accords in late 1995.

Chapters 12 and 13 enlarge and deepen the study of this nexus between opinion and policy by analyzing each major policymaker in the Bush and Clinton administrations separately to establish the particular contribution of public opinion to their respective policymaking. As the Bosnia case took place in the recent past and the sources of evidence are not extensive, the main sources of the views of the decision-makers lie in statements these officials made in public speeches and the media. The chapters pay attention to evidence that reveals the policymaker's awareness of public opinion prior to or during major benchmark decisions; they also explore indications of each decision-maker's inclination or not to factor public attitudes into his policy. The conclusions about each administration contribute to a general synthesis about the link between public attitudes and foreign intervention policy in this final case across the 1990s.

CHAPTER 11

Bosnia: History, Policies, and Public Opinion

Throughout the Cold War, the United States was a steadfast supporter of Yugoslavia for its geopolitical significance. America appreciated Yugoslavia's moderate character and its independence from the Soviet Union (Zimmermann, 1996, p. 6). Few Western governments believed in early 1990 that Yugoslavia, host to the 1984 Sarajevo Winter Olympics and the prototype of a progressive one-party state, would cast aside its economic and political success in return for bloodshed and strife. However, though liberal internally with a participatory economy, Yugoslavia was a fragile federation of Serbia, Bosnia-Herzegovina, Croatia, Macedonia, Montenegro, and Slovenia as well as two autonomous provinces in Serbia—Kosovo, whose population was 90 percent ethnic Albanian, and Vojvodina, a complex mix of Hungarians, Croats, Slovaks, and Rumanians. Two years after the fall of the Berlin Wall, nationalism pushed aside tolerance, and Yugoslavia dissolved into war.

With the breakup of the Soviet Union and the end of the Cold War, Yugoslavia lost much of its security-related relevance to the United States. The international community paid minimal attention in 1987 to Slobodan Milosevic, who rose to the powerful positions of president of the republic and chairman of the League of Communists of Serbia. His influence largely contributed to the development of nationalist conflict in the region.

Bosnian-Serb Milosevic adopted hard-line policies toward any opposition in Serbia and targeted particularly the ethnic Albanians in Kosovo. In 1989 the Milosevic government of Serbia removed the autonomous status of both provinces, Kosovo and Vojvodina, and fired local Albanian officials. Human rights abuses in Kosovo outraged Western diplomats, yet the Milosevic government continued pursuing absolute control over the province. It used the excuse that Kosovo was the "cradle of Serbian civilization," and minimized the role of ethnic Albanians in Kosovo government administration[1] and economic production (Bugajski, 1995, pp. 133–35). The authoritarian regime began systematically denying the basic civil liberties of Kosovo Albanians (Zimmerman, 1996, p. 7). In 1989, American policy toward Yugoslavia focused specifically on human rights issues (Gompert, 1996, p. 124). Overall American pol-

---

[1] During the 1980s and 1990s, the Kosovo Albanians boycotted leadership positions, elections, the educational system, and the political system, which included other ethnic groups, and organized themselves as a state within a state.

icy remained consistent with that of previous decades, supporting a united, independent Yugoslavia that would move unequivocally toward democracy.

The other republics faced serious economic difficulties[2] including over 3,000 percent inflation, bank insolvency, bloated bureaucracy, and unprofitable public sector enterprises (Zimmermann, 1996, p. 45). Federal president Ante Markovic attempted sweeping, liberalizing economic reforms, but Milosevic reallocated federal funds to Serbia to finance his policies in Kosovo and to gain political favor. Markovic was respected by diplomats as an important economic reformer and as a true "democrat," but his authority was undermined by Milosevic's actions.

Markovic desperately needed Western support, and he fought hard for an official visit to Washington in 1989. He met with President Bush and members of congressional committees, hoping to produce economic support from the United States for his democratizing reforms. Congress remained focused on Kosovo and the issue of human rights violations. The meetings indicated that Yugoslavia was "a poor risk" for U.S. economic support, compared with other Eastern European countries, where progress to democracy was not as complicated by nationalism. For this reason, the American policy remained fixed on the narrower issue of Kosovo, without addressing the broader issue of Yugoslavia's future (Zimmermann, 1996, p. 46).

In 1990, democratic initiatives, such as support for alternative pro-Western politicians and sending international observers to elections in all republics, took center stage on the American policy agenda toward Yugoslavia. Deputy Secretary of State Lawrence Eagleburger continued to promote a united Yugoslavia. He conveyed this view to the European governments in early 1990 and warned of impending danger, but they were unconvinced of the urgency of the situation (Zimmermann, 1996, p. 65).

THE EVE OF CRISIS

Throughout 1990, American policy maintained that ideological reform must precede economic aid to Yugoslavia. Congress and the administration focused on forcing the remaining four republics of Bosnia-Herzegovina, Macedonia, Montenegro, and Serbia to hold open elections, which, by December, each republic including Croatia and Slovenia, had conducted. Franjo Tudjman in Croatia and Alija Izetbegovic in Bosnia-Herzegovina were installed as presidents of their republics. Milosevic guaranteed his position as the elected leader of Serbia at great cost to democracy in Serbia and to the federal Yugoslav Central Bank, by appropriating the equivalent of $1.8 billion to finance back wages to workers, perks to political supporters, and campaign materials. Paradoxically, this push for what was considered an advance toward "unity and

---

[2]Susan Woodward's (1995) book *Balkan Tragedy* analyzes in great detail the sources of Yugoslavia's economic woes. The IMF and the World Bank's austerity measures imposed on the Yugoslav government created both unemployment and economic insecurity among the population; these, in turn, contributed to tensions between different ethnic groups. She refutes the theory of old "ethnic hatreds" and proposes the economic fragmentation of the country as the major source of tensions.

democracy" had the opposite effect of increasing the role of independence movements by "sweeping nationalists to power" (Zimmermann, 1996, p. 130).

The U.S. government had "scant sympathy for Slovene and Croat separatists" (Gompert, 1996, p. 124) and ultimately American policy expanded into what became known as President Bush's "unity and democracy" policy. The European Community (EC) called for a cautious approach to independence, hoping to minimize the possibility of violence. Austria and Germany openly supported select politicians in Croatia and Slovenia, thus assisting their independence movements. Germany's support was particularly important, because of its heavy influence in the EC.

The democratically elected leaders of Croatia and Slovenia knew that the Bush administration favored a unitary Yugoslavia. In 1990, the administration sent Deputy Secretary of State Eagleburger to Yugoslavia out of concern over the rise of secessionist tendencies and signs of fascism. Washington seemed to want to "increase the visibility of U.S. support for Markovic," whom it recognized as a democratic reformer (Zimmermann, 1996, p. 58).

U.S. congressional and administration policies still focused exclusively on Kosovo. Congressional support for Kosovo was often in response to ethnic constituencies (Zimmermann, 1996, pp. 130–31). Congressional pressure had thus formed the basis of a relatively confused U.S. policy: Serbs assumed that Congress' numerous resolutions against the Kosovo policy reflected general anti-Serbian sentiment from the administration. An active Croatian lobby recruited Senator Bob Dole as a public supporter of Croatian independence, in direct contradiction with the administration's goal of unity in Yugoslavia. Congress, reacting more directly to U.S. constituencies, intentionally or unintentionally projected support for independence of the republics.

Inconsistency in American policy at this time was compounded by the fact that the Bush administration never indicated an intention to intervene in Yugoslavia in the event of a crisis. Thus the leaders of the region were bold enough to contradict the stated U.S. position. On June 25, 1991, Slovenia and Croatia declared independence, maintaining that they could not remain in a Yugoslavia dominated by Serbia and Milosevic. The Yugoslav People's Army (JNA), largely controlled by the Belgrade regime, attempted to prevent independence, and conflicts between the JNA and Slovenian local police erupted on June 27, 1991; they were followed by similar conflicts in Croatia one day later. Slovenia managed to intimidate the JNA, and Milosevic did not persist in the fight to conquer it; Slovenia thus won independence. Serbs fought with more determination against Croatia because of the importance of the Krajina region, an enclave of Serbs who resisted Croatian independence. During the summer of 1991, Krajinan Croatian-Serbs fighting the Croatian army became engaged in full-scale war. Croatia endured months of fighting, during which Serbs conquered areas dominated by Croatian-Serbs.

Not until the disruptions of June 1991 did Western foreign ministries believe that a violent dissolution of Yugoslavia was on the horizon. The Conference on Security and Cooperation in Europe (CSCE), a multilateral organization and outgrowth of the Helsinki Accords, in conjunction with the EC quickly brokered cease-fires. Until this time, the United States had been trying to persuade Europe that a crisis was fomenting in Yugoslavia. Following this turning point between June 1991 and January 1992, Washington explicitly encouraged European leaders to take command of the Yugoslav crisis. This was not unproblematic, given divided European views on the preferred future of Yugoslavia. Nevertheless, Europe seemed eager to control the situation without strong American input (Rosegrant and Watkins, 1996, p. 5). The foreign minister of Luxembourg declared famously that "This is the hour of Europe." European policy initiatives included resolutions by EC foreign ministers, the Hague peace conferences, and the September 25, 1991, U.N. Security Council Resolution 713 calling for a complete arms embargo on former Yugoslavia, followed by the December 15, 1991, Resolution 724 sending U.N. observers to the region. The European Community also placed trade sanctions and an oil embargo on the whole of former Yugoslavia.[3]

Throughout the breakup, in fact, American officials deferred to the Europeans' attempt to seek a solution to the growing crisis. With the Gulf War just over in March 1991 and American presidential elections around the corner, America welcomed the EC's request to defer the handling of the conflict to the Europeans, limiting American responsibility (Gompert, 1996, pp. 127–28). President Bush's attempt to allow Europe to take charge also reflected American interest, or lack thereof: In January 1993, only 1 percent of Americans polled believed that Bosnia was the most important issue in American politics.[4] Especially at the early stages, a majority of Americans did not know how to evaluate the president's handling of the situation, indicating little real understanding or interest (Sobel, 1996, p. 146). This also reflects the administration's notably inconsistent positions, which caused public opinion to vacillate in confusion (Sobel, 1996, p. 149). Of those who favored American involvement throughout the crisis, a majority believed that Europe should work closely with the United States at all stages. In sum, to the extent that the American public followed the events in former Yugoslavia, they perceived a complicated situation that was difficult to evaluate and untangle. Americans felt that it was largely a European issue that had little direct U.S. interest. Nevertheless, the American public supported various forms of aid to prevent humanitarian disaster: 54 percent by the summer of 1992 (*Los Angeles Times* in Sobel, 1996, Table 6-6) supported U.S. troop contribution to humanitarian efforts, against 33 percent who disapproved. At the same time, 80 percent, and a plurality throughout the war, supported U.N. or joint U.S./U.N. efforts (Harris in Sobel, 1996, Table 6-10).

The Outbreak of War

From July 1991, chaos reigned in Serbian-dominated Croatia as the Serbs seized control of over one-quarter of Croatian territory. On December 24, 1991, the Parliament of the Republic of Bosnia-Herzegovina requested recognition of independence from

---

[3]U.N. Security Council Resolution 749, adopted on April 7, 1992, authorized the deployment of peacekeeping troops. The Resolution received U.S. support, but the U.S. government was unwilling to provide troops for the peacekeeping force deployed soon after.

[4]Americans rarely elect candidates to the presidency on account of their foreign policy successes or failures. In *Unvanquished: A U.S.–U.N. Saga,* former U.N. Secretary General Boutros Boutros-Ghali mentions that the latest *Wall Street Journal*/NBC poll put foreign policy "dead last in a list of sixteen issues that would affect the American public's vote for president" (Boutros-Ghali, 1999, p. 289).

the European Community. At the same time, the Serbs in Bosnia declared their own autonomy, claiming that the Bosnian government no longer represented Serbian interests. Contrary to British, French, and American policies, as well as to the general European view, Germany began to push for recognition of the independent republics, especially Croatia. Its forceful action in this direction contributed to European governments following Germany's lead (Zimmermann, 1996, pp. 176–77).

Nevertheless, after three months the European Community concluded that, because of the great risk of ethnic conflict in Bosnia, the EC would not recognize Bosnia-Herzegovina (Johnston, 1993, p. 6). The Bush administration was becoming increasingly wary of involvement. Anticipating the 1992 elections, the administration felt that the issue was politically dangerous; this attitude was manifested by the administration's lack of coherent, decisive action throughout 1992 (Zimmermann, 1996, p. 215). Nevertheless, some American diplomats in the region began efforts to consider recognizing the independence movements.

In the fall of 1991, the EC and the United States provided negotiators, Lord Peter Carrington, former U.S. Secretary of State Cyrus Vance, and the Dutch diplomat Henri Wejnaedts, who had negotiated for a cease-fire in Croatia. On January 2, 1992, a cease-fire was reached, and the United Nations agreed to deploy a small number of military peacekeeping monitors to oversee the initiative. The United States did not contribute troops to this force, which consisted of about 38,000 international troops (Center for Policy Analysis, 1994).

In response to the EC's decision, on February 29, 1992, the Bosnian government held a referendum on independence. Nearly all voters turned out in favor of independence, but Bosnian Serbs boycotted the referendum.[5] Almost immediately, fighting began between JNA forces loyal to Belgrade and the Bosnian-Serb militia; and between Bosnian Croats supported by Croatian paramilitary units and Bosnian Muslims. Fighting intensified throughout the region (Johnston, 1993, p. 7).

Benchmark 1: Fighting Breaks Out in Bosnia

Immediately following EC recognition of Bosnia-Herzegovina on April 6, 1992, fighting broke out in Bosnia-Herzegovina. After a protracted diplomatic push, and the decision by the National Security Council and the State Department that Bosnia met its criteria for democracy, the American government recognized Bosnia-Herzegovina on April 7. Bosnia was admitted to the United Nations not long afterward. These events touched off war in Bosnia. The Republic of Bosnian Serbs (Republika Srpska) organized a militia with the assistance of the JNA. These irregular forces stormed towns along the Drina River, and by the fall of 1992, they had captured 70 percent of Bosnia. The Serb militia's initiative culminated in the siege of Sarajevo. The president of Bosnia-Herzegovina, Alija Izetbegovic, began to call repeatedly for U.S. and European intervention, to no avail.

---

[5]According to the 1991 census in the Republic of Bosnia-Herzegovina, the ethnic composition of the Republic was: 43.6 percent Muslim, 31.4 percent Serb, 17.3 percent Croat, 5.5 percent "Yugoslav," and 2.2 percent "other." The total population of Bosnia-Herzegovina was 4.2 million people.

During this time, the American State Department repeatedly criticized the Serbian army and sought through public statements to deter violence (Zimmermann, 1996, p. 150). The American public tended to support American intervention through U.N. peacekeeping activity. During July 1992, while the conflict was escalating into full-scale war, 80 percent of Americans supported U.N. peacekeeping operations (Sobel, 1996, p. 147). But at no time from 1991 to 1992 did the American government consider using force against the Serbian army (Rosegrant and Watkins, 1996).

President Bush continued with the view that the war was a European problem, and American opinion did not display much sentiment otherwise. In September, although a majority of Americans were aware of the issues in Bosnia, only 37 percent stated that they followed the situation fairly or very closely (Princeton Survey Research in Sobel, 1996, Table 6-1). America's comfortably distanced position then began to erode. "The hour of Europe" was short-lived. In September 1991, Europeans asked the U.N. Security Council to take the initiative in the crisis (Hoffman, 1996, p. 98). The United Nations deployed a force of peacekeepers to Croatia in March 1992, to which again the United States did not contribute forces. The U.N. sanctions imposed in September 1991 were also intended to curb the Serbian forces.

AMERICA DISENGAGED

After the United States officially recognized Bosnia-Herzegovina, some within the U.S. government hoped that this stance would necessitate direct American involvement in conflict-resolution efforts (Zimmermann, 1996, p. 192). Their hopes were short-lived, however, as higher level policymakers continued their reliance upon European initiatives. The State Department gradually put more pressure on the Serbs, implicating them for initiating the violence, but only through threats of isolation. The United States also demonstrated a willingness to consider recognition of the republics upon evidence of progress toward democracy. Polls from August 1992 showed equal percentages of approval and disapproval of Bush's handling of the situation. The approval rating then began to rise steadily, perhaps as Americans perceived the Bush administration's policy becoming more decisive (Princeton Survey Research, in Sobel, 1996, p. 162).

In the first stages of the war, the Bosnian government requested extension of the U.N. peacekeeping (UNPROFOR) mandate to the Republic and asked that the arms embargo be lifted in order for the Bosnians to protect themselves. This initiative was advocated by the U.S. Congress throughout the war, and was espoused by George Bush during his final days in office.

While the Serbs in Croatia "jeopardized the success of UNPROFOR by refusing to demobilize their forces" (Johnston, 1993, p. 7), the U.N. Security Council called for expanding the UNPROFOR mandate to Bosnia to keep the only international airport open during the Serbian siege of Sarajevo. The United Nations then set up several Bosnian cities, including Sarajevo, Sbrebrenica, and Zepa, as "safe havens."

The Serbs assaulted U.N. personnel and disregarded U.N. proclamations, and by the end of May 1992, the United Nations moved its headquarters from Sarajevo in

Bosnia to Zagreb in Croatia in an effort to diminish its humiliation by the Serbs. On May 31, 1992, the Security Council adopted Resolution 757, imposing sanctions on Serbia and Montenegro (known collectively as the Federal Republic of Yugoslavia or FRY), freezing foreign assets of the government and private individuals, prohibiting exports from FRY, restricting imports to food and some medicines, and ceasing international air traffic.

During the siege of Sarajevo, the fate of the city was broadcast into the homes of millions of Europeans and Americans for the first time since the 1984 Winter Olympic Games. Starving children, bullet-marred buildings, and internment camps provided the backdrop for news coverage of the war, and the parties chiefly blamed were the JNA and Serbian militia groups with headquarters in Serbia proper. American public opinion gradually became more tolerant of various forms of potential U.S. involvement. Whereas in July 1992 45 percent of Americans disapproved of U.S. air strikes, as opposed to 35 percent who approved, by August approval rose to 53 percent and disapproval dropped to 33 percent (Gallup in Sobel, 1996, Table 6-5). This support remained high throughout 1992. A mid-August *Los Angeles Times* poll also showed the highest percentage of approval yet for the United States' contributing forces to humanitarian and peacekeeping missions: 54 percent, compared with 33 percent disapproval (Sobel, 1996, Table 6-6). Yet, public opinion showed consistent opposition to of "active involvement" and "peacemaking" activities (Sobel, 1996, Table 6-7).

American diplomats in former Yugoslavia began to press for greater American activity, but the Bush administration still maintained that the Europeans should take the initiative to bring peace to Bosnia—after all, Bosnia was in Europe's backyard. Extremely conscious of the November elections, Bush reiterated that American troops would not be engaged in the conflict, citing the desire to keep America from becoming involved in another Vietnam crisis (Gompert, 1996, pp. 128–29). When polled a few months later, the American public did not seem to fear protracted defeat, but actually envisioned a quick, Gulf-War-like victory (Sobel, 1996, p. 146).

Establishing an ethnically homogeneous "Greater Serbia" became the goal of Serb politicians and fighters (Gompert, 1996, p. 131). To achieve this and other political ends, Serb forces drove non-Serbs from their homes to designated areas, raped women in order to increase the number of Serbs,[6] and led thousands of boys and men away from their homes to their deaths. American newspapers began using the term "ethnic cleansing" to describe Serbian war tactics. By June 1992, U.S. senators began to broach the possibilities of using force to counter the siege, to "put some teeth" into the U.N. sanctions (*Congressional Quarterly,* 1992). In August public opinion clearly favored U.S. contribution to air strikes. Approval was generally limited to joint efforts in multilateral operations. Former U.S. ambassador to Yugoslavia Warren Zimmermann maintains that such air strikes in July 1992 could have preempted much of the successive fighting and caused a settlement to be negotiated soon after (Zimmermann, 1996).

---

[6]Though rapes took place roughly equally among the fighting groups (Woodward, 1995), Serb "transgressions" exceeded the others (Ullman, 1996, p. 212).

Benchmark 2: Increased Violence

Abuses of human rights were rampant throughout the war,[7] but the shocks from broadcasts into American and European homes were greatest during the first year. A refugee crisis developed from the Serb practice of "ethnic cleansing." The U.N. High Commissioner for Refugees (UNHCR) and the Red Cross estimated that by the end of July 1992, 2.5 million people from the former Yugoslavia (including Croatia) were displaced, and 10,000 Bosnian citizens each day were fleeing their homes (Johnston, 1993, p. 8). Outside of former Yugoslavia, refugees fled in large numbers to Germany (200,000), Austria (50,000), Hungary (50,000), Sweden (44,000), and in smaller numbers to other European countries. Reports and pictures in July and August 1992 of gaunt and abused Muslim men in Serb concentration campus began to feed the pressure for stronger U.S. action (Gutman, 1992).

The refugee crisis heightened European attention, but brought no direct intervention. Human rights abuses became the focus of newspaper articles and TV reports about the situation in Bosnia. The seige and snipper killings in Sarajevo attracted world attention. Increasing sensitivity to these abuses contributed to greater American responsiveness. A short time later, three-fifths of Americans believed that the United States should use military force if the atrocities could not be prevented by any other means (Sobel, 1996, p. 146). A former official of the National Security Council countered that "Notwithstanding the public outcry over televised Bosnian horrors, the Bush administration was convinced that the American public, seeing no vital interests at stake, would not support the level of commitment and casualties that might be required for an intervention to succeed" (Gompert, 1996, p. 132). Americans did express fears about putting troops at risk, and despite the growing approval of troop activity from 1992 to 1994, this approval remained in the minority. Americans typically disapproved of using U.S. troops for ground combat against Serbs (Sobel, 1996, p. 148). Furthermore, the Department of Defense, especially Chairman Colin Powell of the Joint Chiefs of Staff, believed that military action to resolve the conflict was ill-advised (Quinn-Judge, 1994, p. 1).

The Muslim Bosnian government continued to request that the arms embargo be lifted. While the Europeans contended that lifting the arms embargo would place U.N. troops at greater risk, the Organization of Islamic States advocated using force against the Serbian army and militia forces. On August 4, 1992, the Islamic Conference Organization, invoking Article 42 of the U.N. Charter, supported the use of force against the Serbs and lifting of the arms embargo.[8]

The U.N. Security Council replied on August 13, 1992, by approving Resolution 770 to secure transport of humanitarian aid in Bosnia. The United Kingdom offered 1,800 troops for the effort. Although American public support regarding intervention

---

[7]For the extent, see Kissinger (1996), and the U.N. Security Council resolutions between 1992 and 1994.

[8]At the time, diplomats and observers reported the appearance of foreign arms and troops in Bosnia, but these reports were unconfirmed until February 1996, when the *Washington Post* and Agence-France Presse reported that the government of Saudi Arabia had channeled over $300 million in arms to the Bosnian Muslims (Agence-France Press, 1996, p. 1).

was high for sending in U.N. peacekeepers (80 percent), the United States provided no troops for this humanitarian relief effort. Instead, the U.S. government financed humanitarian aid to be provided by nongovernmental organizations and transport for the aid to Bosnia. At least this would ensure the delivery of aid, responding to the public outcry over the humanitarian conditions in Bosnia. Internationally assisted humanitarian organizations then began delivering food and other provisions throughout Bosnia.

In the summer of 1992, the London Conference convened to seek a solution to the crisis chaired by David Owen and Cyrus Vance. UNPROFOR troops escorting humanitarian aid convoys came under Serb fire, leading the U.N. Security Council to pass Resolution 781, banning all Serb military flights over Bosnia. It also passed Resolution 787, calling on member-states to stop and search shipping vessels in the Adriatic Sea and on the Danube to ensure implementation of U.N. sanctions. The Vance-Owen planned proposed in early 1993 would have divided Bosnia into 10 autonomous provinces relatively independent of the central government. Though receiving over two-fifths of the land, the Serbs would get less than the almost three-fourth of Bosnia they had conquered. The Vance-Owen plan in spring 1993 fell apart when the United States provided little support and Serbs insisted that Sarajevo fall into their territory.[9]

By January 1993, 58 percent of Americans believed that military force should be used to protect humanitarian relief and prevent atrocities (Sobel, 1996, p. 146). Interestingly, the skepticism expressed by Americans regarding involvement was not necessarily a reaction to fears of long-term entanglement. Fewer Americans believed that American involvement would turn into a protracted defeat than saw a swift victory as in the Gulf War (Sobel, 1996, p. 146).

NEW AMERICAN ADMINISTRATION, THE BOSNIA CRISIS WORSENS[10]

During the American presidential campaign, candidate Bill Clinton took a strong stand against the Bosnian Serbs and promised, if elected, to support the Bosnian Mus-

---

[9]According to U.N. secretary general Boutros Boutros-Ghali (1999) and Susan Woodward (1995), the Vance-Owen plan failed because the United States killed it: "In its first weeks in office, the Clinton administration had administered a death blow to a Vance-Owen plan that would have given the Serbs 43 percent of the territory of a unified state. In 1995 at Dayton, the administration took pride in an agreement that, after nearly three more years of horror and slaughter, gave the Serbs 49 percent in a state partitioned into two entities" (Boutros-Ghali, 1999, p. 247).

[10]According to the observations made by Boutros Boutros-Ghali, the Bosnia situation worsened because of the new administration: "The new Clinton team seemed to want to have little to do with him [Cyrus Vance] and even less to do with David Owen. Worse, the chances of peace were being thrown away, as Clinton and Christopher, using strong language, attacked the Vance-Owen plan as appeasement of the Serbs. They were wrong. . . . To the world outside the United States, the Clinton administration's approach made sense only as the product of some obscure Machiavellian calculation" (Boutros-Ghali, 1999, p. 69).

lims. Yet, despite his campaign pledges, the main tenets of American policy did not change with Clinton's inauguration as president. Clinton already believed that there was not enough support in Congress or among the people to allow the deployment of American troops in Bosnia (Rosegrant and Watkins, 1996a; p. 6), although public approval for deployment of troops with humanitarian missions was at times as high as 80 percent (Sobel, 1996). However, Clinton did pledge to contribute 25,000 troops to a NATO-led force in the event of a peace agreement. The central factor was peace; if there was peace to keep, Clinton would consider sending troops. He would only send them as part of a NATO command force, however.

Immediately following his inauguration, Clinton called for tighter sanctions against Serbia, conflict prevention measures in Kosovo and Macedonia, and enforcement of the no-fly zone over Bosnia. If necessary, Clinton added, the United States would join the United Nations, NATO, and others to enforce a resolution. Simultaneously, the Serbs seized the strategic town of Srebrenica, which was primarily inhabited by Bosnian-Muslims, and the press revealed some of the most repugnant human rights abuses. On April 16, 1993, the U.N. Security Council passed Resolution 819, returning Srebrenica to the Muslims with the assistance of U.N. personnel. All the while, the Clinton administration was trying to develop a strategy to support the president's statements that the United States would not stand for ethnic cleansing, while taking into account the different concerns of the Defense Department, State Department, National Security Council officials, and the Central Intelligence Agency. Long hours of meeting represented protracted agonizing over Bosnia: "it wasn't policy-making. It was group therapy . . ." (Drew, 1995, p. 150).[11]

In May 1993, Secretary of State Warren Christopher went to Europe in an attempt to persuade America's allies to back a policy of "lift and strike": lift the arms embargo against the Muslims and use multilateral military air strikes against Serb installations. The Europeans dismissed Christopher's plan, mostly out of fear of expanding the war by infusing more weapons into the conflict and out of concern for the safety of European troops on the ground with a broader war and air strikes. The United States again declined to send troops for the UNPROFOR peacekeeping mission. With no troops in this force, the United States had little to counter the European argument.

Americans clearly favored the lift-and-strike plan: 58 percent polled in May supported lifting the arms embargo, while only 26 percent did not (Kull, 1993, p. 174). Americans further favored NATO air strikes against the Serbs by an even greater margin: in August 1993, 61 percent approved of air strikes (CBS). This support remained consistent throughout April 1994 (54 percent). High approval ratings depended on efforts being undertaken jointly with Europeans; there was little support for unilateral American strikes.

While Christopher was traveling, Clinton began to back off of his policy, in part because of the secretary of state's poor reception in Europe and partly after reading Robert Kaplan's *Balkan Ghosts* about the historical origins of ethnic conflict in the Balkans (Drew, 1995, p. 157). Nevertheless, "lift and strike" became the official

---

[11]For a detailed account of the development of Clinton administration policy in Bosnia, see Drew, 1995, chapter 10.

stance of the U.S. government. Congress began increasing the pressure for U.S. action to support the Muslims. Therefore, U.S. policy shifted markedly between the presidents. Under the new Clinton administration the United States explicitly favored the Bosnian Muslims, whom the Congress, perhaps on behalf of their constituencies, perceived as the true victims.

The administration was now balancing contradictory sentiments: one coming from domestic opinion, willing to undertake action to help the Bosnian Muslims; the other coming from Europe, flatly rejecting American proposals for them to do so. After the disastrous Christopher mission, American policy retained two components: protect Muslims and provide humanitarian relief, but the lift and strike policy, although official, stagnated.

The United States kept a low profile, while the United Nations and NATO began to create policies that would protect Bosnian Muslims without intervention. Less than one month after the mission, Security Council Resolution 824 created six "safe havens" for Bosnian-Muslims in Bihac, Gorazde, Sarajevo, Srebrenica, Tuzla, and Zepa, and the Defense Department began air drops of food into Bosnia. Throughout 1993, European initiatives, supported by the Clinton administration, focused on bringing Bosnian Muslims, Croats, and Serbs to the negotiating table. On June 4, 1993, UNPROFOR troops were dispatched to protect civilian populations in the safe havens (U.N. Resolution 836). Meanwhile, until June 17, 1993, Lord David Owen and former Secretary of State Vance pursued their peace plan, which was declared a "failure" by Lord Owen when Serbs and Croats presented an alternative plan to divide Bosnia into three constituent nations (30 percent would go to Bosnian Muslims, which was roughly the proportion they controlled at the time).

Beginning in April 1993, NATO had been enforcing U.N. no-fly zones declared in October 1992, and in August under U.S. pressure the alliance threatened air strikes against the Bosnian Serbs. Yet the Serbs' siege of Sarajevo continued. As Croats and Bosnian government troops began fighting in areas not controlled by the Serbs and Serbs continued assaulting U.N. personnel, the humanitarian situation worsened. In August, four U.S. State Department officials resigned in protest over the lack of U.S. action in helping to prevent the genocidal violence. By the end of 1993, the U.S. government again pledged its participation in a peacekeeping force if all three parties accepted a peace plan. International policy continued to be ineffectual in stopping the war. Similar to its views on air strikes, Americans by this time clearly favored U.N./NATO/allied[12] troop action in a peacekeeping operation: 76 percent in May 1993 approved such actions (PIPA, 1994), 72 percent in February 1994 (PIPA, 1994), but this support was clearly for multilateral action. There was consistently high approval for military action with the same coalition, from July 1992 to May 1993, after which approval declined somewhat.

---

[12]Americans have recently favored cooperative internationalism. Yet the allies, the United Nations, and the United States found relatively little to cooperate about mainly "because the U.S. was so deeply involved politically and so deeply determined not to be involved militarily" (Boutros-Ghali, 1999, p. 247) and because it insisted on suggesting military strikes, despite the objections of the European allies.

Benchmark 4: The First Sarajevo Market Massacre

On February 6, 1994, a mortar shell exploded in the central Sarajevo market, killing sixty-eight people and injuring more than two hundred.[13] Evidence pointed to the Serbs, who were entrenched in the hillsides surrounding Sarajevo, as the culprits. Again, the horrors of the Bosnian war were broadcast into homes throughout the West. The U.S. government, finally taking decisive leadership, responded by demanding that Serbs pull heavy weapons away from Sarajevo or turn them over to U.N. personnel. If the Serbs failed to respond, according to Secretary of Defense William Perry, NATO would conduct air strikes (Lippmann, 1994, p. A20). Concerned over possible retaliation against their troops, the Europeans cautiously endorsed the American scheme, but raised additional concerns about civilian populations caught in the bombing raids and the possibility that NATO engagement would embolden the Bosnian Muslims to keep fighting (*Economist,* 1994, p. 15).

Britain and France now began pressuring America to become more involved in the Bosnian crisis. The U.S. response was to focus intently on forging a relationship between the Croats and Bosnian Muslims to expand military support and provide a foundation for maintaining a unitary Bosnia. Building on the Vance-Owen plan, American ambassador Charles Redman mediated the negotiations, which culminated in Washington, D.C. on March 18, 1994, with the signing of the constitution and a framework agreement for the Federation of Bosnian Muslims and Croats. President Tudjman of Croatia, President Izetbegovic of Bosnia-Herzegovina, Prime Minister Haris Silajdzic of Bosnia, and Bosnian-Croat representative Kresimir Zubak signed the agreements (U.S. Department of State, 1994, p. 2). This U.S.-initiated move was considered a breakthrough and was followed by greater efforts by some European countries toward a settlement.

It is not surprising that February 1994 saw a peak of U.S. public support for military and peacekeeping activity; but still strictly for multilateral action.[14] Three-quarters (PIPA) favored peacekeeping activity with U.S. troop involvement, with only 25 percent disapproval. U.S. military activity, undertaken with the allies, was publicly supported by a margin of 20 percent (ABC). American public support for coalition peacekeeping (U.N./NATO/allies), which had fallen somewhat in March 1993, rose again through April, and reached a high of 63 percent approval by mid-April (PIPA in Kull and Ramsey, 1994, p. 173). Meanwhile, public approval for military action increased steadily, outweighing disapproval by April (56 percent approval, PIPA in Kull and Ramsey, 1994, p. 173). Upon this strong basis of public support, the Clinton administration pushed NATO to issue the ultimatum of an air

---

[13]The evidence that the February 1994 mortar attack was Serb is somewhat inconclusive. Boutros-Ghali "told Christopher that Akashi reported that the mortar round that had exploded in the Sarajevo market on Saturday might had been fired by Bosnian Muslims in order to induce a NATO intervention. Christopher replied that he had seen many intelligence reports and that they went 'both ways'" (Boutros-Ghali, 1999, p. 145).

[14]American public attitudes for unilateral action against the Serbs never rose beyond 27 percent (January, 1993, ABC). Even in February 1994, approval for unilateral action hovered at only 17 percent, while disapproval was high at 79 percent (Sobel, 1996, Table 6.9).

strike. In late May, NATO undertook its first offensive action ever, and shot down four Bosnian-Serb planes.

America Engaged

Through the end of 1994, the American Congress continued to pass nonbinding resolutions to lift the arms embargo on the Bosnian Muslims so they could protect themselves. The Europeans, particularly the British and French, continued to thwart lifting the arms embargo, adding concern over prolonging the war with additional arms to their argument that it would put their troops at greater risk. The U.S. and European governments found themselves indirectly contributing to the de facto partitioning of Bosnia, through perpetuation of the conflict (Gompert, 1996, p. 139). The Russians now became players, and while traditional sympathies between the Orthodox Russians and Orthodox Serbs played a role in the Russian policy position, key Russian officials also put pressure on the Serbs.

Finally, not long after the March 1994 agreement in Washington, a Contact Group was formed from among European nations (France, Britain, Germany, Russia) and the United States. The agreement they negotiated was ultimately rejected, but its near-acceptance offered some measure of hope for progress. This process also brought out the first notable break in Serbian positions: Slobodan Milosevic supported the agreement, but Radovan Karadzic was obstinately opposed.

In 1991, the United Nations established the International War Crimes Tribunal. Modeled after World War II precedents, this tribunal was chaired by eminent South African judge Richard Goldstone and was headquartered in the Hague. However, for the first year of operations, there was little financing and staff. Nevertheless, in 1994 the tribunal made its first indictment, and later indicted Karadzic and Radko Mladic, political and military leaders of the Bosnian Serbs, and leaders of Serb militias operating in Bosnia (Chayes and Chayes, 1996, p. 213).

Throughout the end of 1994 and the first half of 1995, the events in the former Yugoslavia continued to be a game between NATO and the Serbs: the Serbs harassed safe areas, such as Gorazde and Sarajevo, but received only "slaps on the wrists" (Rosegrant and Watkins, 1996a). NATO reacted with the heavily bureaucratized decision to carry out an air strike, which caused only limited damage to the Serbs (Rosegrant and Watkins, 1996a, p. 9). Throughout this period, U.S. policy remained elusive, but American support for U.S. troops aiding U.N. peacekeepers remained steadily high, and rose somewhat around June. (PSR reported between 66 percent and 78 percent approved U.S. troops aiding U.N. missions.) The new head of the State Department's European and Canadian Affairs, Richard Holbrooke, argued for a tougher U.S. policy, but Clinton refused to commit ground troops.

Benchmark 5: The Intensification of U.S. Engagement

In May 1995 another turning point occurred. To head off impending NATO air strikes, Serb forces took U.N. soldiers hostage. American support for U.S. air strikes, which had fluctuated from a range of 30 percent to 60 percent, now rose through June

1995 to as high as 71 percent (CBS in Sobel, 1995, p. 167). Americans began to pay significantly more attention to Bosnia as well: a peak of 75 percent reported watching the situation fairly or very closely in June (NBC in Sobel, 1995). This was significantly more than at any time from 1992 onward. Only 6 percent reported that they did not follow the events in Bosnia at all.

The taking of U.N. hostages was decisive. Not only were U.N. forces humiliated and rendered ineffective on international television, but the Serbs also completely stripped NATO of its military effectiveness. One response was Britain's and France's deployment of a 12,500-strong "rapid reaction force." Another response came after the French inauguration of its new president, Jacques Chirac, who immediately took a forceful line in Europe by urging immediate action. This apparently was a strong influence on President Clinton in early 1995 toward a more aggressive policy: "Chirac and Clinton spoke a lot at that point on Bosnia," noted one National Security Council official (Rosegrant and Watkins, 1996a, p. 12).

Western policy seems to have played directly into the hands of the Serbian regimes in Belgrade and Pale, the unofficial capital of the Bosnian-Serb Republic. The international community was not able to protect the safe havens or stop Serbian aggression against the Muslims. Serbs around Sarajevo continued to fire at civilians in the city. President Clinton insisted that NATO begin a fierce bombing campaign to protect the remaining safe havens, and European allies concurred.

Against this background, another crisis on the ground finally pushed the American policy, and international action, to a new pace. On July 9, while Dutch U.N. commanders called desperately for immediate NATO air strikes, Serb tank forces rolled by the helpless peacekeepers and captured the safe area of Srebrenica, followed by Zepa two weeks later. Not long after, the international press revealed that Serbs had massacred up to seven thousand Bosnian Muslims during these takeovers.

The international community was shaken. UNPROFOR was clearly ineffective, perhaps even causing damage to the situation by displaying the West's inability to act forcefully. The United States and Europe prepared to withdraw UNPROFOR, but this left Clinton in a dilemma: Should he send U.S. troops into Bosnia to help in the retreat of U.N. troops when he had refused to send them to help the Muslims? Elections were again on the horizon, just over one year away, and deploying troops for this reason could have caused a publicity disaster in foreign policy (Rosegrant and Watkins, 1996a, p. 13), where Clinton was typically considered weak. The alternative was to negotiate a settlement and send in U.S. troops to enforce an agreement.

President Clinton came under greater pressure from within the administration, from the U.N. ambassador Madeleine Albright and national security adviser Anthony Lake (as well as the lingering symbol of the four diplomats who had resigned their positions in 1993) to seek a diplomatic but decisive solution. In July, NATO took a tougher line, promising preemptive, disproportionate air strikes if the Serbs threatened Gorazde. This strong backing of military force paved the way for the United States to begin a new round of negotiations. The Congress was clearly in favor of a more aggressive approach: in August both Houses voted to lift the arms embargo if UNPROFOR should withdraw.

August cemented the United States' new policy. The first market massacre in February 1994 illustrated the role of the Serbs in the war. After a second attack on Sarajevo's central market on August 28, 1994, that killed thirty-seven and wounded eighty-five persons, there was less ambiguity that the Serbs were perpetrators. NATO issued an ultimatum to the Serbs to stop shelling Sarajevo, cease offensive action in the remaining safe havens, withdraw heavy weapons from around Sarajevo, and open roads into the capital (U.S. Department of State, 1994, p. 1). Serbs refused, and in August for the first time, NATO began heavy air strikes against the Serbs. Many of these missions were flown by American personnel stationed at American military bases in Italy and on ships in the Adriatic Sea.

Benchmark 6: The Dayton Negotiations

The heavy action took a toll. By August 31, when the new negotiating team led by Richard Holbrooke entered Belgrade, the Serbs were practically cooperative (Rosegrant and Watkins, 1996a, p. 19). NATO increased its action during September, as negotiations got under way. The Contact Group, whose settlement had been rejected in 1994, with the addition of Dutch negotiators forged another agreement. On September 26, 1995, the Bosnian, Croatian, and Serbian representatives agreed to maintain Bosnia as a single state, with 51 percent of the territory under the control of the Bosnian-Croat Federation and 49 percent under the control of the Bosnian-Serb republic, Repubiika Srpska; to establish constitutional structures; and to plan democratic elections. On October 12, 1995, a cease-fire took effect.

AMERICA DETERMINED

The cease-fire paved the way for "Proximity Peace Talks," conducted from November 1 to 21, 1995, at Wright-Patterson Air Force Base outside of Dayton, Ohio. Bosnians, Croats, Serbs, and representatives of the Contact Group, led by the American assistant secretary of state for European affairs, Richard Holbrooke, established the framework known as the Dayton Peace Agreement, with mutual agreements on constitutional, boundary, military, police, political, and election issues. According to the November 21 Dayton agreement, Bosnia was divided into two entities: the Federation of Bosnian Muslims and Croats holding 51 percent of the territory, and Republika Srpska, the Bosnian-Serb republic, with control over 49 percent of the country.

Throughout the negotiation process the press had been focused on President Clinton's promise to provide American military troops if a peace agreement could be reached. Some members of Congress, both Democrats and Republicans, had rejected the proposal immediately, citing the need to protect American military personnel from involvement in the Bosnia conflict. Others, led by the Republican Senate majority leader Robert Dole, were supportive of the president's initiative, so long as the peace agreement called for maintaining a multiethnic Bosnian state. In a December 14, 1995, vote, the Senate approved the deployment of twenty thousand U.S. troops to Bosnia by 60 votes in favor to 39 opposed.

In December 1995, more Americans were watching the events in the former Yugoslavia than at any point previously (73 percent "closely"). On December 14, 1995, the Contact Group heads of state, including Bill Clinton, and the presidents of

Bosnia, Croatia, and Serbia signed the D^yton Peace Agreement in Paris. In the following week, the North Atlantic Council, NATO's political arm, approved deployment of the Implementation Force (IFOR). NATO forces were formally ordered to deploy in Bosnia, and UNPROFOR transferred authority to IFOR. In December, President Clinton deployed twenty thousand American troops to Bosnia as part of the sixty thousand troop mission.

At this point, polls of the American people's opinion on troop deployment varied. Interestingly, support was not significantly higher in December 1995, after the agreement had been reached, than at other times. Approval for U.N./NATO/allied peacekeeping troops actually dropped in November (ABC), down to 38 percent, from its peak of 87 percent in April 1995 (Sobel, 1996, Table 6.10). In spite of concerns of the Congress, the United States decisively pursued deployment of troops and implementation of the Dayton Accords. Despite American support for the War Crimes Tribunal, indicted war criminals remained free in Bosnia, since IFOR did not have a mandate to seek those indicted.

Preparations for multiparty elections were pursued with similar zeal by the American administration, including a special mission by former negotiator Richard Holbrooke to ensure that Radovan Karadzic abandoned his political leadership of the Bosnian Serbs. International financial institutions and bilateral reconstruction support was pledged in April 1996, and a U.S. contribution of $282 million was included in the international contribution of $1.8 billion. On June 17, 1996, the United Nations lifted the arms embargo on Bosnia, after over four years of requests. In concern for potential election irregularities by populations voting away from their prewar residences, local elections were scheduled for November, while parliamentary elections took place on September 14, 1996, according to the Dayton agreement.

The presidential and parliamentary elections reconfirmed the leadership roles of the same political parties that waged war against each other for almost four years. President Izetbegovic retained the position of president of Bosnia-Herzegovina, and representatives of the Croatian Democratic Union, the Serb Democratic party, and the Party for Democratic Action were overwhelmingly elected to the Parliament of Bosnia-Herzegovina, the federation Parliament, and the presidency and Parliament of Republika Srpska.

The Dayton process had no date for total withdrawal of IFOR or for the implementation of international civilian leadership. The September 1996 elections were supposed to begin the process of transferring administration of Bosnia-Herzegovina to local administration, but the process was slow because of difficulties for refugees returning to their prewar homes and political disputes between officials of Republika Srpska and the Federation. As a result of these problems, local elections were delayed until 1997, and civilian election administrators requested an extension of the mandate in Bosnia. Though the ethnic communities in Bosnia were to follow the principles of the Dayton agreement, an extended mandate for IFOR, including possible American participation in a longer-term mission, could have led to long-term international military engagement to maintain the cease-fire in Bosnia.

Chapters 12 and 13 turn to an analysis of the influence of public opinion on the Bosnia policy of the key decision-makers. First, Chapter 12 discusses the Bush administration. Then Chapter 13 explores the Clinton administration.

Bosnia I: Public Opinion's Influence on Bush's Nonintervention Policy

INTRODUCTION

At different points since 1990, American policy toward the former Yugoslavia reflected and rejected public opinion. As chapters 12 and 13 show, policy did not clearly reflect relatively supportive public opinion nor did major shifts in public opinion typically precipitate policy changes. Americans were notably reluctant to undertake an active involvement in the Bosnia situation, but were open to humanitarian assistance.

This chapter examines to what extent Bush administration policymakers were aware of the attitudes of the American people and responded to those attitudes in policy decisions. It asks whether their perceptions of public views accurately reflected the American people's beliefs and concerns regarding Bosnia and how the decisionmakers reacted to the perceptions. Analyzing benchmarks of the conflict illuminates these questions. At each benchmark, the chapters explore the relevant statements of the most important policymakers of the Bush and Clinton administrations. Thus, Chapter 12 looks at President George Bush, Secretary of State James Baker, Deputy Secretary of State (later Secretary of State) Lawrence Eagleburger, and Secretary of Defense Richard Cheney. Chapter 13 examines President Bill Clinton, Secretary of State Warren Christopher, and Secretary of Defense William Perry.

The discussion uses differing sources to identify policymakers' views of public opinion. Frequently, policymakers presented their views in congressional hearings, which some considered a form of connection with the public and useful indicators of public sentiment, yet they are not direct evidence, as in poll data. Press exchanges also reveal occasional evidence of policymakers' sense of public opinion and its influence. Memoirs and public statements provide direct evidence of policymaking views of public opinion and its influence. Bush and Baker have written memoirs. Cheney provided an interview. Together, the responses of policymakers suggest their assessment of public opinion and its impact on their decision-making.

There were three major Bosnia benchmarks during the Bush administration. Fighting broke out in Bosnia in April 1992,[1] the first benchmark event considered

---

[1]The European Community (EC) and the United States recognized the independence and sovereignty of Bosnia-Herzegovina as a unitary state under the control of the Muslim government of Alija Izetbegovic on April 6 and 7, respectively.

here, but U.S. policy avoided direct involvement. The administration sought to lead public opinion in order to quell potential protests over American inaction as the world became aware of "ethnic cleansing" and other atrocities. At other times, the administration seemed convinced that its disengaged policy followed the American public's preferences. The latter part of Bush's term included the formative years of the Bosnia crisis, and of American policy. This policy contributed to European policy and later American policy. What were the connections between the formation of American policy and the opinions of the American people?

During the earlier phases of the war in the Balkans, American policymakers made decisions that constituted a hands-off policy toward the region. During the first benchmark phase beginning in mid-1992, George Bush opted for a policy of noninvolvement. While advocating the unity of a democratic, multiethnic Yugoslavia, he hoped and encouraged European governments to take control of the situation. His public statements and memoirs reveal some attentiveness to what he perceived as the American public's interest in the potential U.S. role. His perceptions only roughly correspond to the American people's actual views.

The next benchmark during Bush's term was the late summer and early fall of 1992. Reports of horrifying mass violence against civilians led the American public to pay more attention to the crisis. Bush's relative inaction contributed to the voters' view of him they would see when they went to the polls in November.

Toward the end of his term, Bush's policies shifted toward engagement, representing the third policy benchmark. During the presidential campaign, his opponent, Bill Clinton, attacked his strategies in Bosnia as weak. With the campaign lost and his popularity plummeting, Bush took a final, forceful stance. In December, Bush and French president Mitterrand agreed on military enforcement of the U.N.-declared no-fly zone.

Many thought this would be an initiative of the incoming president, who had campaigned for more aggressive action in Bosnia. However, Clinton's first term consisted not of decisive engagement but of lofty rhetoric and meandering, inconsistent involvement. To what extent was Clinton reacting to public opinion regarding Bosnia as it had developed over the two years prior to his term? Was his administration aware of public opinions as it formulated its Bosnia policies during its first term? These questions will be examined in Chapter 13.

PRESIDENT BUSH AND THE BOSNIAN WAR: MISSED OPPORTUNITIES FOR DECISIVE LEADERSHIP

Benchmark 1: Fighting Breaks Out

The American government had steadfastly supported a unitary Yugoslavia before Slovenian and Croatian independence, and had relied on European initiatives to bring about a cease-fire in Croatia. When fighting began in Bosnia on April 7, 1992, American policy continued to follow Europe's stated intent to lead.[2] Bush preferred to

---

[2]The American administration had anticipated fighting as both Baker and Eagleburger made statements about the danger resulting from the break-up of Yugoslavia. But when on April 6,

maintain that the United States should promote a united Yugoslavia. He wanted to take few risks by committing American forces to an unstable environment.

The policy of noninvolvement may have conveniently followed the sentiments of the American public, which during the first half of 1992 seemed largely uninterested. European leaders may have realized that the events of the previous year, such as Slovenia's and Croatia's declarations of independence; recognition by Europe, the United States, and the United Nations; and the outbreak of war in Croatia, did not capture America's attention. In September 1992, only 37 percent of Americans followed the Bosnian situation at all closely (Sobel, 1996, Table 6.1). The American public believed that the conflict was largely a European problem, and was not even the most important foreign policy issue. (Sobel, 1996, Table 6.3). Although a small Croatian-American lobby prompted some congressional recommendations urging an active U.S. pro-Croatian independence stance, most Americans did not become seriously interested at this time. Lobbying helped to push policy discussions between Congress and the White House, while the majority opinion as perceived by Bush supported his insistence on noninvolvement.

The first significant challenge to Bush's policies came with the outbreak of war in April 1992. This conflagration quickly precipitated a humanitarian crisis around "ethnic cleansing" and indiscriminate shelling of civilian targets. U.S. media began raising an American obligation to respond, threatening Bush's distanced approach. In July and August press conferences, reporters noted the ineffectiveness of European actions, questioned the possibilities for greater American leadership, and bluntly raised the issue of moral responsibility in public questioning: "If it is confirmed that there are death camps there, would the United States have a moral obligation to do whatever is necessary to stop that?" The president answered: "I feel a moral obligation to see that these camps are inspected. . . . I think all of the American people feel, and I'm sure it's true of other peoples around the world, that we must have access to these camps . . . we must stop the killing" (Bush, 1992, p. 1318).

Bush soon realized that his perception of the American public as resistant to military engagement could be used to support disengagement. The administration began to claim that the American public did not support U.S. intervention in the conflict, in order to explain the absence of American troops in the U.N.-led peacekeeping initiatives, and the lack of direct U.S. leadership. A July 10 interview on the *MacNeil/Lehrer NewsHour* demonstrates this: "I think people are reluctant to get bogged down in a kind of . . . guerrilla warfare. And I also think that the main objective now [is] humanitarian relief. . . . I think it's a reluctance on the part of the people to go storming into a situation that is very complicated from a military standpoint. And also we think diplomatic pressure, sanctions, and humanitarian relief is the answer right now" (Bush, 7/10/92).

By August 1992, public support appeared in public opinion polls, where approval for U.S./U.N. air strikes against the Serbs rose (Sobel, 1996, Table 6-5), and polls showed higher numbers supporting humanitarian relief efforts. In domestic and in-

---

1992, the EC recognized the independence of Bosnia-Herzegovina, the United States followed suit the day after.

ternational press, columnists publicized the humanitarian disasters. Most notably in an op-ed piece in *The New York Times,* Margaret Thatcher urged Bush to end the arms embargo on the Bosnian Muslims. Candidate Bill Clinton began attacking Bush's unwillingness to take stronger measures against the Serbs.

Bush began justifying to the American people his policy of nonengagement, as it received increasing criticism. At a press conference on August 8, 1992, the president remarked on how the complicated nature of the crisis limited possible U.S. responses: ". . . I've reviewed today with Secretary Cheney, [and] . . . Eagleburger . . . the complexity. . . . [T]he American people must not be misled into thinking there is some quick and easy military answer to this highly complex question." (Bush, 1993b, p. 1327) Bush's continued emphasis on the complexity of the situation, and the ancient intractability of the conflict, seemed intended to reinforce the public's resolve not to become involved: "Now, the war in Bosnia-Herzegovina and Croatia is a complex, convoluted conflict that grows out of age-old innocents being spilled over century-old feuds. The lines between enemies and even friends are jumbled and fragmented.[3] Let no one think there is an easy or a simple solution to this tragedy. The violence will not end overnight . . ." (Bush, 1993b, p. 1327). Bush defended his ability to make decisions and not get involved by succumbing to electoral pressure: "We are not going to get . . . sandbagged down in some guerrilla warfare. . . . I owe it to the military not to make some rash decision based on politics" (Bush, 1993b, pp. 92–93).

Bush stressed that concern for the public response would not direct his policy. "This is not a political matter. This is something that a commander-in-chief and a president has to deal with, and I plan to do it. . . . I'm getting swiped at politically, but I will not make one decision based on American politics, election politics '92" (Bush, 1993b, p. 1328). He repeatedly emphasized that there was no electoral influence on his policies: "Absolutely no. This is not a political matter. This is a matter of humanitarian concern." (Bush, 1993b, p. 1326).

Later on August 16, 1992, when the decision of whether to send peacekeeping troops became central, Bush implicitly made comparisons with Vietnam: policymakers and the public feared a similar protracted entanglement in Bosnia. Bush's public remarks seem to invoke the fear of a lengthy involvement with no exit strategy: "The violence will not end overnight, whatever . . . means the international community brings to bear" (Bush, 1993b, pp. 1315–16). He continued: "Everyone has been reluctant . . . to use force. There are a lot of voices out there in the United States that say, use force. But they don't have the responsibility for sending somebody else's son or somebody else's daughter into harm's way, and I do. . . . I don't want to see the U.S. bogged down in any way into some guerrilla warfare. We lived through that crisis" (Bush, 1993b, p. 1320).

Despite Bush's portrayal of the conflict as inappropriate for American involve-

---

[3]Many officials both in the United States and Europe stated that there were no innocent parties in the Bosnian War. The Bush administration excused its lack of military involvement despite access to intelligence about the severe nature of the conflict to which the American press and public were not privy.

ment, support grew during the summer of 1992 for an American role in humanitarian relief. Press reports focused primarily on the humanitarian crisis, as rumors and reports began to spread about World War II–like concentration camps, mass killings, and lawless civilian terrorization, including the killing of children and mass rape. Congress remained split on the implications of the humanitarian crisis for potential American involvement. The same percentage of Americans who had opposed American military troop action supported humanitarian relief activities, even if American troops were involved: half in August approved of U.S. troops contributing to humanitarian and peacekeeping activities, and 33 percent disapproved (*Los Angeles Times* in Sobel, Table 6-6); 54 percent disapproved of U.S. troops' active involvement or peacemaking (NBC, 8/10/92). This shows that resistance to troop participation depends on their missions. The American public has often favored multilateral peacekeeping missions (Rielly, 1999).

Bush's statements in early July showed greater concern with humanitarian issues, while maintaining the validity of his distanced policy: "The U.S. role has been to say . . . we want to help . . . on a humanitarian basis. And that's the role we're in. We are not in a forward-leaning role . . . of saying our objective is to bring lasting peace to this troubled land. . . . I think the immediate goal should be relief effort to the people that are suffering" (Bush, 1993b, p. 1066).

Benchmark 2: Greater Reports of Violence

In an August exchange with reporters, Bush referred more explicitly to the American dismay over the humanitarian crisis in Bosnia: "Like all Americans, I am outraged and horrified at the terrible violence shattering the lives of innocent men, women, and children in Bosnia. The aggressors and extremists pursue a . . . vile policy, of ethnic cleansing, deliberately murdering innocent civilians, driving others from their homes. . . . This is, without a doubt, a true humanitarian nightmare" (Bush, 8/8/1992). Bush used the remainder of the press conference to outline and justify American noninvolvement.

Two days later a reporter asked Bush about his meeting with Lawrence Eagleburger, Brent Scowcroft, and Dick Cheney after the United Nations had reported on camps in the region that were presumed to be death camps. Bush stated: "I will try to keep the American people filled in as we go along on this, trying to help solve these tremendous humanitarian problems there" (Bush, 1993b, p. 1326). Bush continued to emphasize the point that politics should not play into decision-making in order to deflect criticism from his rival:

> A lot of people are suggesting . . . in my view, reckless use of force. . . . I haven't conducted myself that way . . . and I'm not going to start now for election reasons. . . . When it comes to serious foreign policy initiative, I'm going . . . to keep it out of the political arena . . . it is too very, very important that we conduct ourselves . . . without political leanings. . . . I'm going to keep on these foreign policy issues and try to keep them out of the political arena, the jockeying, the instant statement. . . . I am not going to get engaged in the political arena when we are trying to do something that really has a tremendous humanitarian aspect. (Bush, 1993b, p. 1321)

In short, Bush defended his policy by responding to public opinion. Despite public criticism, the challenges he faced in Bosnia would transcend the criticism that arose out of domestic political squabbles.

By the end of his term, Bush found himself at odds with public opinion that called for greater response to the growing crisis on a humanitarian basis. He responded to the public's concern over humanitarian aid instead of undertaking forceful Bosnia policy that might have altered the course of the war.

During the fall Bush took small steps under domestic and foreign pressure. On October 2, 1992, he affirmed the policy of U.S. participation in enforcing the no-fly zones. His decision on the use of force to secure the zones, however, was not made until December 1992, when Bush took the lead in promoting U.N. enforcement of the zone. In October, he stated merely that the United States would "participate in enforcement measures" (Bush, 1992, p. 1739). Bush also continued his focus on humanitarian aid, on which, notably, U.S. public opinion was most united: "All Americans and people of compassion everywhere, remain deeply troubled by the cruel war in Bosnia. . . . The U.S. has been working . . . to . . . alleviate the human misery . . ." (Bush, 1993b, p. 1738).

In October 1992, perhaps to deflect pressure on other fronts, Bush reemphasized that he would not put troops into the region without the endorsement of Secretary Cheney and Chairman of the Joint Chiefs of Staff Colin Powell.[4] This contradicted his earlier attitude, but did not eliminate the possibility that these two might one day agree to send troops. Since Powell at that time was stringently opposed to such a step, Bush could be fairly well assured that he was not implying that troops should be sent.

Bush responded to heavy election campaign criticism of inaction, while reinforcing his commitment not to send troops, with explicit references to Vietnam:

> I'm not considering sending American kids into this very complicated, ethnic, historically ethnic battle out there. As long as I'm president, I'm not going to put American forces into a troubled situation unless I can see what the mission is. . . . Vietnam we didn't [win]. And the horrible problems . . . cannot be solved by putting the 82nd Airborne Division into Bosnia. . . . It does not lend itself . . . to put American kids on the ground . . . down into an area that looks like Dien Bien Phu. (Bush, 1993b, p. 2083)

Benchmark 3: More Active Engagement

The transition between Bush's and Clinton's policy was a classic case of domestic influences on foreign policy. The Bush administration reached a benchmark of policymaking in Bosnia by reacting to electoral politics. The results were the reverse of what might have been expected: during the campaign, Bush had repeatedly insisted

---

[4]Cheney, Powell, and other national security officers and military advisers opposed the use of force in Yugoslavia because the Serbian forces were more effective than the Iraqis were and the American public had a reputation for having almost no tolerance for casualties on its side. A war on the ground in Yugoslavia would have meant many casualties, which were avoided by restricting involvement to air attack.

that he would not take action on the basis of Clinton's criticism of his being "soft" in Bosnia. For most of 1992, Bush seemed convinced that the American public was far more concerned with humanitarian issues and largely unconcerned with actual protection or peacekeeping. Thus he both followed and reinforced this attitude.

During winter 1992–93, public opinion resonated with Bush's new actions. The vast majority of Americans believed that other European countries must help with any activity in Bosnia; Bush moved ahead with high focus on his partnerships with Europe. Public opinion polls several months later showed 61 percent approval for enforcing the zones and 31 percent disapproval (Sobel, 1996, Table 6-12) American support for sending U.S. troops for humanitarian missions was high: 67 percent approved (26 percent disapproved) through January (Sobel, 1996, Table 6.6).

With less fear of public recriminations after the elections, Bush began to take a more active stance in the region. In early January, in one of his final gestures as president, Bush initiated the enforcement of the no-fly zone policy, declared in October 1992. No country had been inclined to enforce until January, when François Mitterrand and Bush met to agree on enforcement. The leaders "stressed a shared approach to the Balkan conflict" (Binder, 1993).

Conclusion: Bush

In some respects President Bush's Bosnia policies reflected the American public's preferences, and in others they did not. As polling has shown consistently, the American public, in the aggregate, prefers policies of negotiation to military intervention in solving international conflicts. If military solutions are necessary, the American public prefers humanitarian, cooperative, and multilateral interventions under the auspices of the United Nations (Rielly, 1991–99).

In refraining for more than one year from striking Serbian forces in Bosnia or Yugoslavia, President Bush's policies were a reflection of the American public's desires. His repeated policy statements, although not acknowledging influence exerted on him by the public, echoed public preferences. Likewise, the frequent mention Bush and most of his advisers made about the cost to the American people in lives or money, also echoed the public's low tolerance for sacrificing lives for causes that do not affect them personally.

When President Bush "aborted a plan nearly agreed on between the Bosnian ethnic groups that would have created a loose confederation amounting to partition" (Kissinger, 1996, p. O1), he decided against this negotiated settlement that the American public would have supported and that might have avoided the war and the humanitarian disaster. Opposite public sentiment, he also decided against sending peacekeeping troops on two occasions. Refraining from sending peacemaking troops, however, fell well within what the American public tolerated.

The reasons for not getting involved in a war in Yugoslavia are less clear, though. The Vietnam syndrome, invoked often by Bush and members of his cabinet, suggested that they were aware that a war in Yugoslavia would not be a quick affair and that the American public was not willing to bear the cost. In this respect one could say that this awareness made Bush reject any major use of force.

SECRETARY OF STATE JAMES A. BAKER III

James Baker was integral in formulating U.S. policy during the formative stages of the conflict. His involvement took place during the potentially preventive stage and ended shortly after the first benchmark, the outbreak of war in April 1992. In mid-July, Baker was appointed the chief of staff for President Bush's reelection campaign, and former Deputy Secretary of State Lawrence Eagleburger became acting secretary of state.

In 1991 Baker warned against the break-up of former Yugoslavia (Baker, 1995, p. 5), but he generally opposed American intervention and involvement in the Bosnian conflict. He perceived the problem as gloomy and intractable, and believed that only overwhelming and perhaps long-term military force could affect the situation (Baker, 1995, p. 635). For Americans to play this role would have cost significant lives, resources, and time, and Baker did not feel that the American public would support such involvement: "There was never any thought at that time of using U.S. ground troops in Yugoslavia—the American people would never have supported it" (Baker, 1995, pp. 634–35). Here, the salient reason for not using ground troops was the lack of support of the American people. Thus, in order to articulate and justify his policy publicly, Baker drew upon his perception of American public opinion, at a time when his basic approach of noninvolvement was being called into question.

During this preliminary stage of the conflict, Baker acknowledged that American public support would have been needed to take the initiative for early intervention. While his attitude may have reflected the public's relative lack of overall interest in Bosnia (only 37 percent followed the conflict in September 1992; Sobel, 1996, Table 6-12), it may also have been an excuse to justify his strategy of noninvolvement that had been formulated on other issues. Baker's summary of his policy reveals underlying policy goals:

> President Bush's decision that our national interest did not require the United States of America to fight its fourth war in Europe in this century, with the loss of America's sons and daughters that would have ensued, was absolutely the right one. We cannot and should not be expected to be, the world's policeman, and the necessary support by the American people for the degree of force that would have been required in Bosnia could never have been built or maintained. (Baker, 1995, p. 651)

Baker argued that Americans were not supportive of U.S. intervention in the war in Bosnia, and with the large number of troops necessary for military intervention, the minimal public support that there was would die (Gompert, 1996, p. 128). According to an NBC poll taken on August 10, 1992, 54 percent of Americans were opposed to active military involvement of U.S. troops in Bosnia, while 33 percent supported American involvement and 18 percent were unsure (Sobel, 1996, Table 6-7).

Baker frowned on the use of U.S. ground troops. "But the critical question facing us was, in fact, what role we should take in trying to negotiate a peace process" (Baker, 1995) because the use of troops would not have been supported by the public.

Clearly, American public opinion was a factor for Baker's policy response that the United States should not get involved. Later, Baker displayed a forceful strategy for influencing public opinion. This implies that while other factors were more important in shaping policy, public opinion was important for implementing policy. Nevertheless, the fact that the secretary of state saw the importance of gaining public sentiment shows his belief that public opinion was a crucial aspect of major policy decisions.

Benchmark 1: Fighting Breaks Out

At the start of the war, Baker became aware of a human rights disaster when on April 14, Haris Silajdzic, Bosnia's foreign minister, informed him of the beginning stages of a serious humanitarian crisis. Without lessening his commitment to military non-involvement, Baker responded by seeking to secure public support for a new approach: "[I] asked Margaret Tutwiler to talk to the foreign minister about the importance of using Western mass media to build support in Europe and North American for the Bosnia cause. I also had her talk to her contacts at the four television networks, the *Washington Post,* and the *New York Times* to try to get more attention focused on the story" (Baker, 1995, p. 644).

Baker's concern for the humanitarian aspect of the crisis led him to take the initiative in building public support to help his and other governments create a new policy, instead of justifying decisions already made. Once Baker had spread awareness of the traumatic situation in Bosnia in April, public opinion became strongly in favor of action to ease the humanitarian situation. Opinion polls reported that 80 percent approved of participation of U.N./NATO/allied peacekeeping forces (Harris) and 54 percent approved U.S. participation in peacekeeping and humanitarian missions (Sobel, 1996, Tables 6-10, 6-6).

When Baker felt that public opinion had responded to his media tactics, he used the response to promote his policy overseas: "That Friday, May 22 [1992] . . . I met with Prime Minister Major at 10 Downing Street. 'We're seeing mounting public concern and criticism over impotent Western inaction in the face of a true humanitarian nightmare,' . . . I asked Major to get the EC to move more aggressively against Serbia. . . . 'Can the United Kingdom join in immediately?'" (Baker, 1995, p. 645).

Baker then took further action to affect public opinion: "Following my meeting with Major, I used a press availability to turn up the rhetoric. Stating publicly for the first time that the situation in Bosnia was 'a humanitarian nightmare' and 'is unconscionable,' I announced the unilateral political and diplomatic measures the United States would take" (Baker, 1995, p. 464).

And at a CSCE conference directly afterward, Baker recalls: "I used the conference's concluding press conference the next day to put the spotlight on European indifference, even inaction" (Baker, 1995, p. 647). In late June, Baker was pushing for a new policy direction that would consider the use of force under strictly multilateral settings, and exclusively for humanitarian purposes. The policy shift may have responded to the major trends of public opinion throughout the summer of 1992: Americans at this point favored humanitarian assistance to the besieged communities in the region (54 percent approval, 33 percent disapproval; Sobel, 1996, Table 6-6), and disapproved of unilateral action while favoring multilateral action (81 percent, 8/11/92; Sobel, 1996, Table 6-3).

In light of this background, he formulated the "game-plan" that represented the Bush administration's response to the war. The game-plan combined sanctions enforcement, cutting of oil pipelines, and demonstration of willingness to conduct multilateral air strikes, all in order to ensure the delivery of humanitarian aid. The plan successfully followed American interest in humanitarian relief, and adhered to the administration's conviction that the public would not support direct or forceful engagement. With the president's support, as well as that of Canada, Turkey, Russia, and Germany, Baker's game-plan became his last contribution to the situation in Bosnia, as Baker left his office to lead the Bush campaign (Baker, 1995, pp. 649–51).

Conclusion: Baker

Somewhat more outspoken than Bush, Baker had warned against the partition of Yugoslavia. "The two republics [Slovenia and Croatia] should not break away, nor should Serbia or any other country challenge existing borders" (Rosegrant and Wattkins, 1996a, p. 5). Eight months later, his administration gave recognition not only to Slovenia and Croatia but to Bosnia-Herzegovina as well.

As in the case of President Bush, Baker's policy of "noninvolvement" both reflected and rejected public attitudes. The avoidance of the 1991 negotiated settlement and the refraining from sending peacekeeping troops on two occasions in 1992 were policies with weak backing from the American public. The policy of rejecting a unilateral punitive attack on former Yugoslavia was anchored in the preferences of the American public. The Bush administration understood, from the intelligence it possessed, that a military attack on the country of Yugoslavia, in Vietnam fashion, could be costly and long and felt that the American public would not support the involvement.

Deputy Secretary of State/Secretary of State Lawrence Eagleburger

Benchmark 2: Greater Reports of Violence

In August 1992, at the London Conference of European States regarding Bosnia, newly elevated Secretary of State Lawrence Eagleburger used every opportunity to raise awareness about the urgency of Yugoslavia's crisis. His long address at the conference was an extensive articulation of the U.S. government's outlook, assumptions, and subsequent approaches to the conflict. His address was a major policy statement at a time when the issue was becoming increasingly important to the American public because of the reports of humanitarian disaster. American support for U.S. involvement in humanitarian efforts had risen over the summer.

Eagleburger confirmed the view that the conflict had ancient ethnic roots: "The friends of the peoples of the former Yugoslavia must acknowledge that history did not begin there yesterday, and that the tragedy now unfolding has ancient and complicated roots" (Eagleburger, 1992a, p. 1). These complexities were often exploited to exacerbate the violence.

At the conclusion of the London Conference, Eagleburger seemed proud of the U.S. pledge to give $40 million aid for refugees and humanitarian assistance. He insisted on the effectiveness of the conference for influencing the situation: "We will see fairly quickly, I believe, a substantial diminution in the shelling with regard to Sarajevo . . . hopefully as a result of the agreements in this conference . . . [aid flights] will be increased, that should provide some additional support to their view that this conference has begun to change things" (Eagleburger, 1992a, p. 10).

However, upon his return to the United States, Eagleburger confronted a far less optimistic press. His remarks displayed sensitivity to, and frustration with, public sentiment regarding U.S. policy at this defining period of the conflict. To a remark that the U.S. press saw the London Conference as mere talk but minimal action, Eagleburger responded:

> I don't happen to think that's true . . . unless you start from an assumption that this is a conflict that can be ended one way or another by some application of outside force. . . . I am, in fact, horrified by what I see in the press in the United States and in Britain . . . about all of these arm-chair strategists and generals who are prepared to say we must use some form of force: they aren't the ones that have to worry about the Americans getting killed if we get into a situation . . . from which we cannot easily extract ourselves. (Eagleburger, 1992a, p. 11)

He took pains to address the media over the highly publicized resignation of George Kenney, a foreign service officer, in protest against what Kenney perceived as nonaction by the American government (Kenney, 1992, pp. 33–34). In an August 28 television broadcast, Eagleburger defended the Bush administration's approach:

> I come back to saying . . . it from that perspective as against a perspective that George Bush, Jim Baker, and indeed . . . Dick Cheney [secretary of defense] and General Powell [chairman of the Joint Chiefs of Staff] have to worry about, which is the degree to which the United States involves itself militarily in a process for which there is no clear purpose and no clear end. Because . . . in my judgment, Kenney is also saying military involvement on our part was, in the end, essential. . . . That process leads you into the kind of situation that got us into Vietnam. And I'm not prepared to accept arguments that there must be something between the kind of involvement of Vietnam and doing nothing, that the *New York Times* and the *Washington Post* keep blabbing about. . . . (Eagleburger, 8/28/92)

Eagleburger's reference to Vietnam clearly alludes to the severe repercussions in public opinion that resulted from protracted, unsuccessful involvement. He recalled this scenario as a warning to the American public against greater U.S. involvement in Bosnia, while presupposing their lack of support for involvement, in order to justify current policy.

Thus he found himself distinctly at odds with the public sentiment that had been expressed through the press: Eagleburger discredited parallels with Iraq, the situation that Baker had heralded as an exemplary success especially in terms of public opinion.

The comparisons between Iraq and Bosnia it seems to me are totally incorrect. The proper comparison with regard to Iraq . . . is the fact that the president stopped at a point . . . He didn't go chasing after Saddam Hussein throughout all of Iraq and getting us tied down; that there is a fundamental difference between the kind of activity that went on in Iraq, including the Iraqi invasion of another country . . . and . . . inter-ethnic conflict . . . it is massively mixed up; it is in territory that is extremely difficult to fight in. (Eagleburger, 11/28/92)

Eagleburger used Vietnam as a paradigm for comparison rather than Iraq in order to portray the Bosnian conflict to his public audience as a situation that warranted nonengagement. This paradigm would be reversed later as leaders in 1995 insisted that American involvement had clear goals and strategies and would never become another Vietnam.

In late November, after first steps toward a policy shift, Eagleburger maintained his justification of why force could not be used in the former Yugoslavia by the United States: "The fact of the matter is that in the case of what was Yugoslavia it . . . ought to be clear to everyone that the use of force as a means of bringing that war to an end would require far more in the way of troops and far more in the way of commitment and far more precisely on the question of how you extract people" (Eagleburger, 11/28/92). When confronted with the fact that the conflict was producing one million refugees, and presented with a *New York Times* article that portrayed gruesome humanitarian affronts, Eagleburger responded to the press' sentiment by holding firm: "The issue is . . . how you bring it to a halt . . . if you presuppose the use of military force. . . . The ability to accomplish your objective . . . in the former Yugoslav case . . . it becomes much more complicated than that, and therefore, the conditions are different." He did, however, admit to the possible use of force in Kosovo. "I can't predict whether there's going to be an explosion in the Kosovo . . . were there to be that kind of an explosion, I think we would have to look at it differently" (Eagleburger, 11/28/92).

Benchmark 3: More Active Engagement

In December, as Bush's term was nearing its end, U.S. policy shifts prompted very different justifications and explanations from Eagleburger. As the United States began to consider more direct action and slightly deeper involvement, Eagleburger shifted in a news conference at Geneva on December 17, 1992. Eagleburger responded to the sentiment as expressed by Elie Wiesel, in such a way that brought him toward a discussion of the new U.S. policy: "He [Wiesel] really impressed me as the question of how much longer we could go on without focusing on the fact that . . . there is . . . a humanitarian tragedy. . . . I just decided, after talking with Elie Wiesel and thinking about it a bit, I decided it was time we started naming names" (Eagleburger, 1992b, p. 924).

In a December interview, Eagleburger elaborated on his perception of how public opinion influenced the administration's policy. When asked if domestic (election) politics had prevented earlier American action in Bosnia over the summer of 1992, Eagleburger responded: "No . . . to the degree I think this issue has cut politically in the course of the last month, it . . . has cut slightly in favor of those who would like to get tougher. So I don't think that's the issue. I don't think it ever has been" (Eagleburger, 12/20/92).

When asked about the future of American policy if the conflict should worsen in 1993, Eagleburger replied: ". . . I don't know how you deal with it unless . . . [you] put in several hundred thousand ground troops—U.S. or whatever. . . . I don't think the American people are prepared to accept that. I think it would be a terrible idea because you don't know how you'd get out, you don't know what your objectives are" (Eagleburger, 12/20/92).

Later, commenting on the Clinton administration, Eagleburger elaborated on his view of the relationship between the president and Congress, and on the role of public opinion in Bosnia. Regarding Clinton's policy, he stated: "As to the use of force, particularly in the Bosnian case, I think the president should have consulted sooner and more specifically [with Congress], but he got away with a bare minimum . . . because the Congress didn't want to have to be responsible one way or the other" (Eagleburger, 1/30/96). When asked about how public opinion could influence presidential policymaking, he replied: "If you take Bosnia right now, and you do a poll of the American people, there is a fairly strong majority against the deployment of troops. But do you see any rioting in the streets, or any real impact that makes the president worry? No. Now, if we begin to suffer losses . . . it can become a political issue." He concluded: "When Bush decided not to go into Bosnia . . . we thought this was a European problem, . . . the vision of Vietnam was in our heads . . . the Vietnam syndrome would apply . . . and there's an increasing scream for us to get out" (Eagleburger, 1992a, p. 247).

Conclusion: Eagleburger

Following his predecessor, Eagleburger made policy decisions from awareness of three factors. First, the conflict in Yugoslavia had no innocent parties. Second, American use of force would have had to take sides in a Vietnam fashion, to be massive, to be unilateral, and to last long because the Serbs, not unlike the Vietnamese, had the determination and capability to fight. And third, the American public would not be supportive of any of the above.

Eagleburger's reading of the public sentiment about use of military force appeared accurate. Whether his policies were an intended reflection of the public's will is more difficult to establish. More plausible would be that his knowledge of what an American attack on Yugoslavia would entail shaped his convictions rather than fear of a public backlash. When they can be sure of a quick victory, American policymakers can count on public support, if not initially, at least after acting forcefully.

SECRETARY OF DEFENSE RICHARD CHENEY

In general, former congressman and Secretary of Defense Richard Cheney made few public remarks about Bosnia policymaking during his tenure, instead emphasizing his role in executing the president's own foreign policy. Cheney was not as outspoken on the issue of Bosnia as he had been during Desert Storm making it difficult to assess changes in his positions between the three benchmark. Toward the end of 1992, with the election on the horizon, Cheney made several speeches praising President Bush's foreign policy and addressing criticism that the president could not handle domestic affairs. During President Bush's run for reelection, at the time when Bosnia was becoming a more important international issue, Cheney perceived foreign policy to be an issue that concerned few Americans. The electoral contest that pitted Bush against then Governor Clinton was heavily focused on domestic politics, and the president was receiving a great deal of criticism over his handling of domestic issues. At a briefing in October 1992, Cheney remarked "if we listen to the pundits and the public opinion polls, nobody gives a damn about foreign policy and national security. If you look at it, it's down to 1 or 2 percent in the polls in terms of what people rate as important considerations facing the country this day" (Cheney, 10/1/92). During a later interview, Cheney remarked in retrospect:

> This was in the aftermath of Desert Storm. The public had been mixed, frankly, on Desert Storm until it was a success. . . . This was not a burning issue in terms of the American public. If you were to go out . . . and ask, in a poll of the American people, what was an important issue, I don't think Bosnia would have placed very high on that list. Once in a while some event would elevate it in the public consciousness . . . but it was not the kind of thing a large number of Americans were deeply involved in, in my opinion, or concerned about. (Cheney, 3/22/99)

This perception may in part explain why Cheney and the Bush administration were reluctant to become involved in a foreign policy intervention in the Balkans, even after their successes in the Persian Gulf. Cheney preferred to make decisions based on his own convictions and his sense of foreign policy, rather than on the polls. Cheney's decisions were nevertheless shaped and constrained by the mood of the American people. His general attitude on leadership can be summarized in the following statement:

> We didn't make decisions based on polls. On the campaign there would have been polls, but I didn't ordinarily see those polls. I would have seen stuff that was generally available in the press: *Wall Street Journal,* NBC. We would not have been doing any polling in the defense department. We honored the tradition that the defense department stayed out of partisan politics. (Cheney, 3/22/99)

While Cheney would not admit to a link between Bosnia policy and public opinion, his decisions were formulated amidst a climate that constrained the breadth of decisions that he could actually make.

At a briefing in 1992, Cheney was asked about the "possibility of the United States stopping aggression in Bosnia as it did in Kuwait." Cheney replied: "We've looked at the situation in Bosnia. We are continuing to wrestle with it within the government and within the Alliance. It's different than Kuwait. . . . The problem isn't one of lack of involvement. I mean, we care very much about what happens there." He reminded the audience that "In Kuwait . . . we also had a situation where our strategic interests were immediately threatened," concluding "I am a reluctant warrior in Yugoslavia" (Cheney, 10/1/92).

Cheney did not consult the polls when formulating policy in the Balkans. Instead, he relied on his own convictions and the opinion of his staff within the Defense Department. To him, Bosnia became an issue in the election only when the press wanted it to. "The press . . . helped determine whether or not Bosnia was prominent on the radar screen. I don't recall seeing any polls" (Cheney, 3/22/99). Cheney displayed an awareness on public attitudes on Bosnia, but does not admit that these attitudes played a part in the decision-making process:

> My general impression is that what we had was growing concern on the part of the public about what was going on in Bosnia that was sort of fanned by press coverage. It wasn't so much an ongoing burning issue for the American people, but occasionally something would happen in Bosnia, particularly a tragic event, an explosion of mortar going off in a marketplace, that would get television coverage. And if it got television coverage, that would . . . elevate it in terms of public knowledge. (Cheney, 3/22/99)

After the November elections, Cheney was somewhat more candid regarding the situation in Bosnia. In an interview in December, Cheney remarked with regard to Bosnia,

> I think there's a growing consensus that the no-fly zone does indeed have to be enforced, but there has been a lot of discussion in terms of trying to decide exactly what that means, how you would do it, what the consequences might be for forces on the ground, working within the alliance. . . . Many of them [allies] have been reluctant in part out of a concern that enforcing the no-fly zone might lead to retribution against the U.N. peacekeeping forces and the humanitarian effort that's already underway in Bosnia. (Cheney, 12/20/92)

Elaborating on his reservations, Cheney stated: "I feel very strongly about avoiding the commitment of U.S. ground forces into the Yugoslav crisis. I don't think it's appropriate and . . . I think it's important when we do something like that we need to know what our mission is. It needs to be achievable by military means at a cost that's acceptable from the standpoint of the United States" (Cheney, 12/20/92). Cheney was aware of the fact that a Gulf War–style intervention would be impossible in the Balkans and that ground troops might be too much to ask from the American public. In part out of fear of such a prolonged entanglement that would be unacceptable to the American people, Cheney and the Bush administration chose a more distant posture on the Bosnian crisis.

Cheney did not reveal strong sentiment about public opinion and U.S. policy in Bosnia. With regard to decision-making, Cheney drew no connections between policy and public opinion: "I argued against U.S. intervention. That was basically a matter of conviction on my part, based on my conversation with people inside the department. It didn't have much to do with public opinion. It was more a matter of our stating a position on it and trying to persuade people that it was the correct position" (Cheney, 3/22/99). The lack of policy-related statements during his tenure as secretary of defense that address public attitudes makes an assessment of his view difficult. He became more vocal on the issue as a critic of President Clinton's policy.

Nevertheless, indications of his sensitivity to public opinion do appear. In an interview after Clinton's inauguration in January 1993, Cheney emphasized his view that ground troops would be a mistake: "As long as we can contain it, it's very important not to have U.S. forces on the ground over there. . . . I feel very strongly that it would be difficult to define what our military mission was; that you'd have to commit a very large force. It wouldn't be clear what constituted victory and, once you got out, probably the situation would immediately return to its unsettled state" (Cheney, 1/27/93). Cheney is clearly sensitive to a prolonged ground war in the Balkans. Most likely, Cheney believed that a war fought like Vietnam—without a clearly defined, easily obtainable objective—would be impossible to present to the American public. This perception had pushed the administration toward a swift intervention in the Gulf a couple of years earlier.

In an interview two days later, Cheney elaborated on this sentiment:

> I believe very strongly that . . . the idea of putting a large number of U.S. forces on the ground in Bosnia, I think was a bad idea and still is a bad idea. It's not clear what their military mission would be. It would take probably hundreds of thousands of troops to pacify that part of Yugoslavia. It's not clear how you would get them out when it is over with or that it could be done at an acceptable cost in terms of U.S. casualties. (Cheney, 1/29/93)

Speaking of an "acceptable cost" is evidence of Cheney's need for a policy that would not exacerbate the public's disapproval. While no longer in office, Cheney reveals a feeling of constraint from domestic politics on foreign policy. Although he regretted the humanitarian tragedies in Bosnia, there was a limit to the amount of support Cheney and the administration could offer. And that limit seems to be dictated by what the American public would be willing to accept when faced with a military involvement in a place they know little about. Yes, if it is quick, and cost free. He was aware, whether overtly or not, that there was a limited range of options that the Bush administration could employ in Bosnia, because he could not see how a military involvement could be quick and cost free.

In February 1993, Cheney responded to criticism that "more should have been done while the Bush administration was watching this happen." He responded "There's always this great desire to do something. People watch the television coverage of the tragedy in Bosnia, and it generates a demand for action of some kind" (Cheney, 2/26/93). Somewhat skeptical about the full awareness of the American people, Cheney may have perceived a shift in public opinion since his tenure. After all, President Clinton was strongly critical of Bush's inaction in Bosnia. Nevertheless, although Cheney admitted that the people wanted an involvement of "some kind," he declined to say whether this demand was an endorsement of the policies of the Bush administration or a call for increased involvement. In retrospect, Cheney emphasized the importance and conviction of his own foreign policy perspective on Bosnia during his tenure, remarking: "We were prepared to argue based on what we thought was right and not what public opinion necessarily supported" (Cheney, 3/22/99).

In an interview in the summer of 1993, he elaborated on his perspective:

I don't think that advocates of U.S. military force to end the bloodshed in Bosnia have properly considered what would be entailed. . . . You need an objective that you can define in military terms . . . if you say, "Go in an stop the bloodshed in Bosnia," that's not sufficiently clear to build a mission around. Does that mean you're going to put a U.S. soldier between every Bosnian Serb and Bosnian Muslim . . . ? You also need to know what constitutes victory. How would you define it? How would you know when you had achieved it? . . . how do you get out? (Cheney, summer 1993, p.15).

Like Bush and Baker, Cheney was apprehensive about intervention leading to a Vietnam-like entanglement and sought to assure his audience that he would avoid such a situation: "Is there any reason to expect that an age-old conflict based on animosities that go back for hundreds of years is going to be ameliorated or ended by the temporary presence of U.S. military force? I don't think so. . . . I was, and still am, very reluctant to see us rely on U.S. forces to solve Bosnia's problems." During an interview in 1995, Cheney criticized President Clinton's Bosnia policy and speculated on the issue of congressional approval for further involvement: "In the end, the president will make the decision and Congress always has the ability to cut off funds, for example, and shut down the operation, but he'd be far better off if he had the support of the Congress and could explain it to the Congress so that he could explain it to the American people" (Cheney, 10/22/95).

At a time when Cheney was considering seeking his party's nomination for president in 1996, this statement highlights his awareness of public opinion as a crucial force in executing an effective foreign policy. The public's lack of interest in foreign affairs was one of the factors in Cheney's leaving politics (Cheney, 3/22/99). His relative silence about public sentiment on Bosnia during his tenure contrasts with his outspokenness on the subject of the Gulf War.

Conclusion: Cheney

On the surface, Secretary Cheney's repeated statements about the lack of importance of public opinion suggest that his decisions were made out of personal convictions, not out of constraints public preferences place upon him. His convictions, however, coincided with what the American public in the aggregate preferred about the military involvement in former Yugoslavia.

At closer scrutiny, Cheney's personal convictions had not been formed in a vacuum. They were an outgrowth of his knowledge and expertise in matters of military involvements and awareness of the American public's reactions toward them going back to his congressional years. Cheney's expertise led him to conclude that a military attack on Yugoslavia would be costly in terms of American lives. His awareness of public opinion advised him that the American public would not back such a mission. "I am a reluctant warrior in Yugoslavia" reflected both his own views and those of the American public. He was not, however, a reluctant negotiator, peacekeeper, or humanitarian helper. Cheney also showed keen awareness of the media's role in creating public perceptions and opinion. Awareness of this helped shape Cheney's convictions about what to do or not to do in the former Yugoslavia.

Conclusion: The Bush Administration

Despite great confusion about what was taking place in Yugoslavia or about the administration's policies toward the events there, the American public maintained a remarkably consistent attitude from April 1992, when the war in Bosnia started, to January 1993, when Bush was replaced by Clinton: yes to multilateral humanitarian or peacekeeping missions under the auspices of the United Nations, and no to massive and decisive use of American military force against Serb forces in Yugoslavia. The policies of the Bush administration reflected quite well the preferences of the American public. Using frequent Vietnam analogies, the policymakers in the Bush administration rejected the option of all-out war, not from following the polls, they said, but on principle and judgment. They understood that military action against Serb forces would not be short and cost free and that a public would not have accepted a Vietnam-like reality.

In its turn, the American public, with little knowledge of history or military strategy, still feared that a military attack on Yugoslavia could lead to protracted warfare, which it did not want to fight. Consequently, as far as the policy of eliminating the military peacemaking alternative as an option, the Bush administration was well in tune with the preferences of the citizenry. There were few demonstrations protesting this policy.

More complex, contradictory, and confusing were the affirmative policies of the administration, preceding the war and during the war. From public statements that promoted a unified Yugoslavia (Eagleburger in 1990 and Baker in 1991), and that warned Europe against the dangers of splitting Yugoslavia into independent republics, by April 1992 the Bush administration came to recognize the independence of not only Croatia and Slovenia but Bosnia-Herzegovina as well.

Despite the American public's strong support for using American troops for humanitarian purposes (80 percent in favor), the Bush administration refrained from sending U.S. peacekeeping troops on two occasions, in February 1992 and in August 1992. Although members of the administration acknowledged awareness that the public was more concerned with humanitarian issues and less inclined to go to war against Yugoslavia, no American troops were sent to the UNPROFOR contingent in Bosnia. This was also a point of contention with Europe, which later rejected Clinton's proposal for "lift and strike" on the grounds that the United States can easily suggest such strategies knowing that it has no forces on the ground and under the strikes.

While the Bush administration seemed reluctant to respond to public opinion on Bosnia in an electoral climate, its members were sensitive to the attitudes of the American people. Criticized for focusing too much on foreign policy, Bush repeatedly assured the American people that there would be no prolonged intervention in Bosnia. Considering how outspoken he often was on other policy matters, Eagleburger made relatively few comments on the issue. Nevertheless, he reveals an awareness of the importance of public support and the legacy of public opinion and foreign policy left over from the Vietnam War. Secretary of Defense Richard Cheney made few public comments about Bosnia policymaking, an important contrast to his vocalness on the Gulf War.

That Bush policymakers did not speak as publicly or at length about their perceptions of public opinion does not mean that they were not affected by it. Rather, policymakers wanted to keep policymaking out of the public eye, because they feared that the American people and politicians would criticize their policies.

The administration could not count on public outrage over the humanitarian atrocities committed over the summer of 1992 continuing. Ultimately, the administration was fighting a losing battle with time: the longer the situation went unaltered, the less chance there was of the tensions blowing over, and the worse the human devastation became. The more Americans learned about the brutalization of the civilian populations, the more they, the Congress, and the press seemed to support forms of intervention. The press often took on the role of pressuring for greater U.S. action toward Bosnia during April through December 1992.

Determined not to become entangled, the Bush administration increasingly expressed approaches at variance with humanitarian public opinion. During the early months, prior to the summer of 1992, the administration took a wait-and-see attitude, and eventually was forced to shift its policy directions, though this move did not save the Bush presidency. Sharp criticism from his opponent, Governor Clinton, on Bosnia did nothing to improve Bush's image. The public favored more aggressive humanitarian policies while still retaining the military options. Chapter 13 turns now to the Clinton administration's response to public attitudes about Bosnia.

Bosnia II: Public Opinion's Influence on Clinton's Intervention Policy

INTRODUCTION

As the Clinton administration became aware of public opinion, the preferences of the American public began to affect Bosnia policies. Because those policies were made relatively recently and most of the internal discussions are still not on the public record, Chapter 13 incorporates the decision-makers' public statements in the media or in front of Congress as well as their senses of public opinion during benchmark periods. The major decision-makers were President Bill Clinton, Secretary of State Warren Christopher, and Secretary of Defense William Perry.

The Clinton administration's central involvement in the crisis in Bosnia began with the Clinton presidency in January 1993 and continued beyond the Dayton Accords in November–December 1995, with the deployment of U.S. peacekeepers as part of a NATO force. Reviewing candidate Clinton's campaign speeches criticizing the Bush administration for its weak approach to the problem would suggest that the new administration would pursue a more resolute policy. In reality, for reasons that had to do with weak public support and a categorical opposition to the use of military force from the European allies and some U.S. leaders, the Clinton campaign rhetoric long remained unmatched by the Clinton policies.

From the outset Clinton began with a faltering Bosnia policy that proposed what became known as "lift and strike," a plan that Secretary of State Warren Christopher sought unsuccessfully to sell to the European community in the spring of 1993. The Europeans, whose troops were stationed on the ground in Bosnia, fearing that a wider war would endanger their forces if the arms embargo was lifted, rejected the plan. After this attempt, the administration took a low profile in Bosnia, becoming involved again only in February 1994.

The first benchmark of Clinton's term was the step of pushing for NATO air strikes following the killing of civilians at a Sarajevo marketplace in February 1994. NATO had recently taken its first military action in shooting down four Serbian planes earlier in the month. In the wake of the massacre, the United States pursued forceful NATO action; after false starts, NATO undertook its first air strikes in April mainly with American F-16s. Serbs retaliated by taking U.N. peacekeepers hostage, and the situation again stagnated until the summer of 1995.

America's policy of belated but intense engagement in mid-1995 is the second crucial policy benchmark of Clinton's Bosnia activity. Both the Clinton administration and the U.S. Congress felt compelled by pressures at home and abroad to take decisive leadership in ending the conflict using diplomacy as well as force. During this phase, the administration participated in robust air strikes and contemplated what had previously been the most sensitive issues to American citizens: the use of American ground troops and active American involvement in peacekeeping and military activities. The Dayton negotiations, and eventually the Accords, formed a turning point in American policy and in the war itself, and are the third major benchmark.

At each stage, this chapter assesses the policymakers' awareness of public opinion. It also tries to determine from their words to what extent these opinions were taken into account when they devised policy and how much opinions influenced the ultimate decisions. While politicians comment directly on polls, or reveal their reasoning in the policymaking process, often their statements indirectly refer to the American people and their sentiments. The Clinton administration made relatively few such statements. This stance contrasts markedly with that of the Bush administration, in Bosnia and particularly in the Gulf War.

The Clinton administration only rarely discussed public opinion in public statements. Clinton's statements reveal some concern with American opinion, but this is infrequently based on factual evidence of American opinions. Nevertheless, his perception of public opinion is an important aspect of connecting his foreign policy decisions with his knowledge of the attitudes of the American public. His general statements regarding foreign policy and America's role in the coming decades also reveal a great deal about his awareness of public opinion.

PRESIDENT BILL CLINTON

Benchmark 1: NATO's Action in Bosnia: February–April 1994

Bill Clinton criticized the Bush administration's inaction in the former Yugoslavia during the presidential campaign in 1992. Clinton implied that as president, he would take quick and decisive measures in the region, such as lifting the arms embargo: "We may have to use military force. I would begin with air power against the Serbs, to try and restore the basic conditions of humanity" (Ullmann, 1992).

During the spring of 1993, Clinton's new secretary of state Warren Christopher attempted unsuccessfully to sell the lift-and-strike plan to European allies in an ill-fated trip in May. Like Bush, he balked at sending ground troops, and as the lift-and-strike plan faded, so did American activity in the region. Thus, for the first year of his presidency, Clinton's policy did not shift markedly from Bush's actions.

Clinton's policy began to change after the first Sarajevo marketplace bombing in February 1994. Following this massacre, the United States and the European nations felt compelled to take more serious action. When Serb planes continued to violate the exclusion zone, NATO shot down four in February in its first-ever military strike. Though Clinton had new impetus at this point to pursue lifting the arms embargo and carrying out air strikes, in some public statements he held out hope for successful political negotiations to end the conflict. "I have approved an effort to try to reach a settlement, hoping that the shock of this incident will perhaps make all parties more willing to bring this matter to a close" (Clinton, 1995, p. 186).

This statement was not fully consistent with his general advocacy of NATO force through air strikes, but might have been intended to show that he first sought all peaceful means (like President Bush before the Gulf War, that he had "gone the extra mile") on the eve of America's push for military action. However, Clinton seemed to believe that the U.S. public generally supported such strikes. When asked if he had decided against air strikes, Clinton answered: "No, there's more reluctance on the part of some of the Europeans than there is on the part of the United States, because they do have troops on the ground (Clinton, 1995, p. 186). Clinton denied using polls to determine his policy, yet admitted to awareness of public opinion by looking at them. In 1994, he stated: "I can tell you categorically that I do not use polls to decide what position to take. I have used polling information to try to make sure I understand where the American people are, what they know, what they don't know" (Reeves, 1994).

Clinton repeatedly mentioned concern for European fears of retribution against U.N. troops on the ground in the press conference on February 6. He used this point in response to a congressional criticism of his repeated threats to use air strikes, without subsequent action. "The United States . . . in the absence of an attack on our people, does not have the authority to unilaterally undertake airstrikes. . . . It's very well for these members of Congress to say that; they don't have any constituents on the ground there" (Clinton, 1995, p. 182). Clinton thus wavered after promoting air strikes and NATO action by defending not taking such action in February.

On February 9, Clinton addressed the World Jewish Congress, which had lobbied for a more forceful U.S. policy in Bosnia. Answering to the clear advocacy of force, Clinton said: ". . . But I also think that today we will begin to reinvigorate the negotiations to try to help to bring a permanent end to the bloodshed and aggression. If you listen to what the parties say they want, [they want] an agreement that all might be able to live with" (Clinton, 1995, p. 217). He thus stressed political solutions even as NATO's decision on air strikes was expected momentarily. Clinton even used the European concern for the safety of European ground troops to explain to his critics why air strikes might not take place.

The American public at this time was growing increasingly supportive of air strikes and military action, on a multilateral basis. Three-quarters of Americans favored U.N. peacekeeping activity with U.S. participation (PIPA in Sobel, 1996, Table 6-10). According to an ABC poll, 57 percent in March 1994 approved of U.S. military action, specifically air strikes, undertaken jointly with Europeans (Sobel, 1996, Table 6-9), and approval for military action continued to rise during the spring of 1994. (Gallup and CBS polls showed 54 percent to 65 percent approved in April 1994, Sobel, 1996, Table 6-5.) Clinton's cautious statements that defended political settlements even as NATO was poised to carry out its first military action indicated to the public that he did not want to rush into air strikes. Clinton either was unaware of increasing support, or else did not heed it in his addresses to the public, in which he shied away from advocating military action. However, several days later Clinton appeared more forceful. "Like people everywhere, I was outraged by the brutal killing of innocent civilians in the Sarajevo market. The events reinforce the belief that I have that more must be done to stop the shelling of Sarajevo and the murder of innocents" (Clinton, 1995, p. 218).

Clinton promoted more forceful tactics by showing his attentiveness to congressional opinion:

> I have been meeting . . . with leaders of both parties in Congress, and I stressed to them that our contribution to resolving the Bosnia conflict will be proportionate to our interests. . . . The actions that I have proposed and that NATO has approved today demonstrate that our Nation and the international community cannot and will not stand idly by in the face of a conflict that affects our interests, offends our consciences, and disrupts the peace. (Clinton, 1995, p. 219)

Still wary of committing ground troops, Clinton insisted that there would be no troops in this mission. However, he acknowledged the risks of the NATO mission: "There is no such thing as a risk-free operation. I don't want to mislead the American people on that. However, we believe that the risks are minimal" (Clinton, 1995, p. 220). Clinton's mention of the "American people" reflects his concern with their reactions, and the need to direct his comments to the public.

On February 17, the deadline for Serb withdrawal of heavy artillery was nearing and the United States and NATO were faced with carrying out air strikes. When asked how he had "prepared the American people psychologically for the possibility of military conflict," Clinton mentioned the public's sentiments in his answer: "The American people, I think, understand what is at stake here and understand our interest in not permitting thousands of people's lives to be destroyed and in working for a peaceful agreement." In discussing the pending mission in his weekly radio address, Clinton stated that "Europe must bear most of the responsibility for solving this problem and indeed, it has." He reassured the audience that "I have not sent American ground units into Bosnia. And I will not send American ground forces to impose a settlement . . ." (Clinton, 1995, p. 280). Polls from February show a slight rise in the touchy issue of peacemaking, or "imposing" a settlement: ABC and Yankelovitch polls showed peak support of 47 percent and 40 percent approval, respectively, for active involvement of U.S. troops (Sobel, 1996, Table 6-7). Clinton shows little awareness of shifting sentiments.

He then appealed to American unity on the new, more active role he had initiated:

> I have consulted with leaders from both parties in the Congress and asked for their support in this effort. I want us all to stand united behind our forces if they need to conduct air strikes and united in our determination to do our part in bringing an end to this dangerous conflict. Now, with our interests at stake and with our allies united at our side, let us show the world our leadership once again. (Clinton, 1995, pp. 284–85)

On February 21, 1994, the ultimatum against the Serbian shelling of Sarajevo went into effect, but NATO air strikes were initially avoided when the Serbs pulled most of their heavy weaponry out of the 20-mile zone surrounding Sarajevo. In April, however, NATO carried out its first bombing of ground targets, in response to Serb attacks on the safe area of Gorazde. In a press interview the next month, Clinton assessed his Bosnia policy by elaborating on U.S. interests for the audience: "We don't want the conflict to spread to other countries . . . that would involve us badly. Secondly, if we can stop the slaughter of innocents . . . this ethnic cleansing . . . we ought to try it. . . ." He then characterized his vision of America's role in the conflict: "I think the United States should participate. That's part of our role. We did that in Somalia and it worked real well . . . now we're virtually completely out. And the mission worked well" (Clinton, 5/20/94). Clinton defended a general view of American foreign policy by appealing to what would later be perceived by many as the Somalia public opinion disaster. Clinton shows relative lack of awareness of or attention to popular perceptions of American foreign policy.

Benchmark 2: NATO Action: May–August 1995

The second major benchmark event in the conflict began in May 1995, when the international community again threatened the Serbs with robust NATO air strikes. Serbs thwarted the air strikes by taking U.N. soldiers hostage at the target sites. In July, the Serbs overran the safe heavens of Zepa and Srebrenica. These events prompted major U.N., NATO, and U.S. efforts to end the fighting by using significant force. As the Clinton administration examined the option of greater involvement, awareness of public opinion began to factor into public statements more explicitly.

Clinton spoke directly to the American people to inform them of the events and of relevance of public support. In June 1995, in reaction to the U.N. hostage taking, he said:

> I have made it very clear to the American people . . . that actions like this could occur because of the vulnerability of the U.N. peacekeepers. If our allies decide to stay, we want to support them, but within the very careful limits. . . . We will use [ground forces] only if, first, there is a genuine peace . . . and no fighting and the United States is part of policing that peace. That's exactly what we've been doing in the Middle East since the late 1970s without incident. It's worked so well that I imagine most Americans don't even recall that we still have forces there. (Clinton, 1996a, p. 805)

Clinton was confronted with an increasingly complicated situation on the ground. His statements regarding possible American troop involvement in a Bosnia peacekeeping force became more frequent and they displayed his perception that Americans disapproved of the idea. "I determined that the role of the United States should be to vigorously support the diplomatic search for peace . . . our interests were in doing what we could, short of putting in ground forces. . . . I determined that we certainly should not have ground forces there, not as part of the military conflict nor as a part of the United Nations peacekeeping mission . . ." (Clinton, 1996a, p. 804).

In fact up to 78 percent of Americans in June 1995 approved of U.S. troops aiding U.N. missions (PSR, 6/1/95; Sobel, 1996, Table 6-8). Americans supported troop activity undertaken to aid international forces when they remained under American command. The majority infrequently resisted sending American troops in this context (Sobel, 1996, Table 6-8).

Clinton also seemed to respond to the sense that Americans did not approve of his general policy in Bosnia: "I know it's frustrating to everyone, as it is to me, that we can't completely solve all the world's problems and that more progress toward peace hasn't been made in Bosnia" (Clinton, 1996a, p. 804). Polls assessing presidential handling of the situation in Bosnia showed 33 percent to 41 percent approval (CBS 6/4/95; NBC, 6/2/95, respectively), within the average range of support over a three-year period (Sobel, 1998, p. 262).

Clinton did express the belief that Americans concurred with some of his goals for greater action in Bosnia: "We have troops in Macedonia because we are determined not to have a Balkan War. We don't want this thing to spread across the Balkans, and I think most Americans would understand that" (Clinton, 1996a, p. 810); but he also emphasized that U.S. ground troops would never take part in ground combat in Bosnia: "I don't think we should have ground troops there in combat or in the peace-keeping force. If they stop fighting, they want us to help police it like we have in the Middle East; that's something we would consider doing" (Clinton, 1996a).

During this period, as the Clinton administration was strengthening its involvement, Clinton was in the position of publicizing the U.S. outlook as it became more engaged. Reporters who mediated between public opinion and policymakers, by representing the public at press conferences to the president and then by conveying the president's views back to the people, often presented the president with the difficulties of convincing Americans of the need for action. Reporters were possibly the most frequent contact policymakers had with public attitudes, besides Congress.

During an interview in June 1995, President Clinton addressed the political risk involved with intervention in the Balkans:

> A lot of people are bewildered almost by all the things that are going on in the world; there's some political risk in everything. But you have to do what you think is right. I'd ask the United States to remember that we went into Haiti with a multinational force that restored the Aristide government and democracy, but we were able to hand it off to a U.N. force with even more nations involved. I think most Americans know that there are going to be problems all around the world that affect United States citizens, and it's better to have a larger number of nations working on those problems and a larger number of nations paying for the solutions to those problems. (Clinton, 1996a, p. 941).

Clinton emphasized the American intention to take only strictly multilateral action. Polls showed that throughout the conflict, Americans thought that action should be multilateral. In April of 1995, a PIPA poll had reported 87 percent approval (the highest point throughout the conflict) for U.N./NATO/allied intervention for peacekeeping efforts (Sobel, 1996, Table 6-10), while approval for unilateral U.S. action was still a majority but significantly lower, at 52 percent (PIPA, 4/19/95).

Reporters further questioned whether U.S. leadership or prestige had suffered through the Bosnia quandary. The president replied with a comment on America's role in the conflict and in the world in general: "A lot of people still say, 'Well America ought to fix it'" (Clinton, 1996b, p. 1158). He seemed to believe that some Americans felt a need for a more interventionist American role in the post–Cold War world, while others felt critical of too much engagement.

Clinton's goal in relation to public opinion was to convince the public to support what he considered necessary action; he seems to be responding to the impression that the public was not inclined toward such support:

> I would ask the American people . . . to think about . . . [whether] it is appropriate for other countries to take the lead, and they have troops on the ground . . . and we don't, then we have to be willing to accept the fact that we may not be able to dictate the ultimate outcome of the situation. But I would caution the American people that that does not mean they should give up on the U.N. (Clinton, 1996b, p. 1159).

Benchmark 3: Dayton Peace Accords: November–December 1995

By December 1995, Clinton believed that the deployment of American troops envisioned in the Dayton agreements would be accepted by the American people. A December news conference indicates Clinton's sense of American public support: "I think our people [in IFOR] are doing a very good job. Every day I worry about [casualties], but I think they're showing their training . . . and the integrity of the plan in the way that they are working to minimize casualties and maximize the effectiveness of the mission" (Clinton, 1996b, pp. 1918–19).

When Clinton was asked if he believed that Americans understood the reason for the mission, he replied: "We have a very clear and limited mission. In fact, I want to make sure that all of our folks know that the parties actually asked our military people to fashion the agreement that was initiated in Dayton so that there would be a limited, defined, strictly military mission" (Clinton, 1996b, p. 1920). Yet, as the troops were being deployed, public support fell somewhat. This was an unusual trend at a time when support generally climbs because of a "rally" effect. The Dayton Accords were signed on November 21, and at that time, public support for the president's handling of the situation was between 40 and 44 percent (ABC, 11/10/95, 11/29/95). However, in December, when troops were actually sent, approval remained at 42 percent (Sobel, 1998b, p. 263). It rose to a majority in January.

At a news conference in late December, Clinton revealed strong awareness of public opinion and its potential influence on policymaking. A reporter questioned the political implications of the Bosnia crisis for his presidency, and the relationship between electoral politics in 1996 and Bosnia policy. President Clinton answered:

> If you look at recent American history, the evidence is that the success of the Bosnia operation may not have much to do with the election in 1996, but the failure of the Bosnia operation or the sustaining of significant casualties could have a great deal to do with it in a negative way. . . . The conventional political wisdom is ". . . There's no upside and tons of downside." (Clinton, 1996b, p. 1922)

He continued:

> When you take a job . . . you have to do the job once I became convinced we could train for this mission, that we could define the mission in the peace agreement, that we could minimize the risks to our troops, then the decision to me was not so diffi-

cult, no matter what the political downside, because . . . you have to ask yourself which decision would you rather defend 10 years from now when you're not in office, if it goes wrong? . . . I would rather explain why we tried to do that than why, because of the short-term political problems, we permitted the war to resume, it expanded, NATO's alliance was destroyed, and the influence of the United States was compromised for 10 years. The political risk is part of the price you pay for being president. So even though I wanted to go there and say to the American people I believe this mission is on the right track and, most importantly, to support the troops and to reassure their families, I'm taking the advice of the military commanders [not to visit the troops over Christmas]. (Clinton, 1996b, p. 1922)

Clinton also recognized concrete elements that contribute to public opinion, such as the highly damaging influence of casualties in battle on public support. His view that casualty rates were a more powerful influence than electoral politics indicates that he considered them likely to affect the public's level of support for sustaining the peacekeeping mission.

Clinton concluded a speech to Congress on November 11, 1995 with a strong intention to solicit congressional support:

As the peace process moves forward, I will continue to consult closely with Congress. If a peace agreement is reached, I will request an expression of support in Congress for committing United States troops to a NATO implementation force. Our foreign policy works best when we work together. I want the widest possible support for peace. . . . But now it would be premature to request an expression of support. . . . Our conscience as a nation devoted to freedom and tolerance demands [that we do our part] to end. . . . this mindless slaughter. Our enduring interest in the security and stability of Europe demands it. . . . I am determined to do everything I can to see that America meets that challenge. (Clinton, 1996a, p. 1702)

Conclusion: Clinton

Despite his statements on the campaign trail in 1992 about taking more forceful action if he were in the White House, once he became president Bill Clinton[6] began to realize that his preferred policy was not easily achievable. After he identified President Milosevic as a new Hitler and the Serbian people as the new Nazis (Woodward, 1995), he saw himself unable to stop them for almost three years. This was so because he would have had to involve the United States in combat, absorb casualties, and suffer politically, because he felt the American people had little tolerance for sacrifices of this nature.

Rather than being inactive between January 1993 and May 1995, Clinton tried to put pressure on the allies and the United Nations to agree to military action against

---

[6]According to Foyle (1999, pp. 193–97), Clinton does not derive his policies from public opinion but by the promises he's made, and he adjusts timing and shape to anticipated public reaction. Clinton says he does "not use polls to decide what positions to take" in foreign policy but to understand the American people and develop arguments and explanations for what he feels are the best positions (Foyle, 1999, p. 195).

Yugoslavia and the Bosnian Serbs. U.N. commander of UNPROFOR, General Sir Michael Rose, insisted until January 1995 "on viewing all parties as equally responsible for the conflict" (Rosegrant and Watkins, 1996a, p. 9). In not resorting to military action against Yugoslavia, Clinton was in agreement with the general preferences of the American public. While not a neutral broker, neither did he heed public preferences when he decided that a cooperative peacekeeping mission with the allies under the auspices of the United Nations was not acceptable to the United States. Clinton's policies were, however, generally limited despite the leeway he had in pursuing them. As in the Bush case, Clinton's preferred policy for waging a war against Serb forces was constrained by the political costs he knew he might have to pay, due both in part to lack of U.S. public approval and especially support for unilaterally directed military action.

SECRETARY OF STATE WARREN CHRISTOPHER

Benchmark 1: NATO Action in Bosnia: February–April 1994

Following the bombing of the Sarajevo marketplace in February 1994, the U.S. stance shifted toward involvement in Bosnia. With possible U.S. and U.N. military engagement imminent, administration statements shifted in support of the new policy direction. A speech by Secretary of State Warren Christopher reflected the shift in public statements by the administration on Bosnia as it began to prepare the public for the deployment of American troops there (Christopher, 2/24/94b).

Christopher's comments on public opinion were generally in response to direct questioning; he rarely mentioned American opinion unprompted. In a media session with the Bosnian prime minister Haris Silajdzic, he stated that support would have to be enlisted, but did not imply real concern that support would be lacking:

> I think, if it's a viable agreement that would bring an end to the fighting, the administration would make a very strong case to the Congress and the American people that that was a worthy subject of peacekeeping. . . . If we made the recommendation, we would certainly . . . try very hard to persuade the American people and the Congress to carry it out. (Christopher, 2/24/94b)

Christopher also emphasized his intention to solicit this support: "In this particular situation, and without waiving any of the president's prerogatives, we would not go forward without consultation with and the concurrence of Congress" (Christopher, 2/24/94b).

News reports conveyed the relevance of generally perceived public support to Christopher: "Christopher told Congress the Bosnian Muslims have made it clear American willingness to participate is key to any peace plan. Several senators said their constituents would be very uneasy about U.S. troops in Bosnia. The administration has a lot more persuading to do" (Christopher, 2/24/94b).

Given Christopher's tendency not to discuss public opinion unprompted, he was more likely to address public sentiment when speaking with Congress or when considering American constituent support. Congressional leaders in turn often expressed

the opinions of their constituents and "the American people" when confronting
Christopher. At a congressional hearing on February 23, 1994, Christopher addressed
the importance of educating the public on the Bosnia conflict:

> I want to emphasize that the expertise and support of this committee is absolutely es-
> sential to me and to the administration as we chart a new course for the post–Cold
> War era. . . . I want to address events undoubtedly on the mind of the committee
> and the American people by reviewing where we stand on Bosnia. Congress and the
> American people should now have a clear understanding of our national interests
> that have guided our actions. . . . (Christopher, 1994a)

While the hearing continued to discuss the actual possibilities for American troop
participation, Senator Richard Lugar (R-IN) commented: "I'm not certain the American people understand the potential for American involvement right now, and it
seems to me important that you explain that and likewise the procedure that might be
followed before those troops get to Bosnia."
Secretary Christopher answered:

> Without giving up any of the president's prerogatives . . . the Congress will be
> fully consulted and its approval sought before U.S. forces are put into Bosnia. The
> situation has reached the point where I feel quite safe in saying to you that we would
> come to Congress for that. . . . I think we've learned . . . that before going into
> that kind of an endeavor, we would set some high standards and we would certainly
> consult fully with the Congress. (Christopher, 1994a)

Both senators and Christopher were concerned in February 1994 with the need to
sway public opinion should troops be called. The presumption that opinion would
need to be swayed implied their belief that the public was essentially unsupportive of
U.S. troop involvement. Senator Nancy Kassebaum (R-KS) made the following
point:

> I would suggest to you that it's terribly important . . . for this debate to begin and
> for Congress to be engaged. Nothing could be . . . a greater setback than to assume
> there's going to be support for our participation with troops on the ground and then
> to find that that might not be there . . . the Administration is going to have to make
> the case to the American people, and we're going to have to be engaged in that so
> that we'll not be caught in a difficult situation. . . . I think this is going to have to
> be understood and support built for that.

Christopher replied: "I understand that. I think the people of the country probably
are getting a much better idea what our interests [are] there . . . we need to prepare
not only the Congress but the American people for such a decision" (Christopher,
1994a).
Prior to NATO's first strike, Christopher was directly confronted with the threat
of unsupportive public opinion. Senator Patrick Leahy (D-VT) remarked to
Christopher:

> One national poll I saw . . . asked were you in favor of foreign aid to any country,
> and 75 percent of Americans said no. So we have to make a case for it . . . we need

both consultations with the Congress . . . but we also need a firm mandate from the Congress. If you don't have that I can assure you that ground forces could go in, they would be [sic] . . . perhaps deaths of American troops, and everybody's going to be saying "Wait a minute, that's not what we understood" . . . if the Congress gave that kind of support . . . then you would have the support on a long-term basis. Without it, failure to ensure a strong base of congressional support . . . could set the U.S. up for a major embarrassment. [Christopher did not respond before the next senator began speaking on other subjects.] (Christopher, 1994b)

Benchmark 2: U.N. Hostage Crisis: May–August 1995

During the summer of 1995, the United States began a policy of engagement. Following the hostage crisis, the situation escalated over the summer, until in August NATO, at American urging, carried out the most intensive air strikes ever. Relatively reticent during this period, Christopher's testimonies in Congress focused intensely on U.S. policy and its relationship to allied policies, as well as the role of American action in the conflict. In July 1995, Christopher remarked in an interview: "I am convinced that unilateral action by the United States to lift the arms embargo . . . is unwise, imprudent, would lead to an escalating spiral of violence and ultimately to the Americanization of the conflict in Bosnia. That is why we have so strongly opposed the amendment being put forward today by Senator Dole" (Christopher, 7/19/95).

Christopher further believed that "Of course in the long run we all understand that there must be a negotiated settlement to put an end to the fighting" (Christopher, 7/19/95). Thus Christopher's overall policy statement was clear in his forcefully advocating negotiation tactics over military solutions. His stance against Senator Dole is notable because of Christopher's view on Congress' role: "Congress is in many senses only a mirror of the American people, so we need to have a better mirror to reach out" (Christopher, 1/15/97). As a response to a question at a speech at Harvard, Christopher also indicated his perception of public attitudes on Bosnia: "With respect to Bosnia, it never was an issue that rose very high in the polls. There was a very strong attitude in some parts of the country, and certainly in the press" (Christopher, 1/15/97).

Christopher implied an awareness of resistance to his diplomatic measures. In September, following intense negotiations in the wake of August's bombings, he commented on America's role:

> Today's agreement demonstrates that when the world confronts intractable problems, American leadership is absolutely essential. As I've emphasized time and again . . . it's pure illusion to think that America can lead if we're not willing to spend what we must to maintain our diplomatic capability around the world . . . the actions that this Subcommittee has taken are just not responsible actions. . . . I'll continue to make this case for adequate funding for our diplomatic activities. (Christopher, 9/8/95)

Again, Christopher pits himself directly against Congress, although he sees it as representative of the American people. This contrasts with a general stance that public opinion is important: "The role of public opinion, always has an influence on American foreign policy, and I think it ought to . . . after all this is a democracy, and those who say somehow that foreign policy ought to be abstracted from the views of the American people simply miss the point . . ." (Christopher, 1/15/97).

Benchmark 3: Dayton Accords: November–December 1995

Christopher's statements during the signing of the Dayton Accords were optimistic about the ability of the agreements to promote lasting peace. He saw the Bosnia crisis much more as an issue that defined the post–Cold War order and America's role in Europe, than as an issue involving any domestic controversy.

Christopher addressed the issue of international troop deployment, and warned that such action would be contingent upon American support, which would depend on the fruitfulness of the conference: "The American people and the United States Congress are asking serious and appropriate questions about U.S. participation in the implementation force. They will watch very closely for signs that the parties are finally ready to lay down their arms and begin a lasting, stable peace. The United States will not send troops where there is no peace to keep" (Christopher, 1995, p. 3)

After the agreements were initialed on November 21, Christopher's remarks to the American press indicated concern over the public debate:

> There will be considerable national debate commencing in the United States. It is important that the people of America remember the . . . terrible images of the last four years of people dying . . . hungry . . . in camps. Those are the things that we should have in our mind when we engage on this national debate which will determine whether the United States continues to play its leadership role in the world. (Christopher, 1995a)

In speeches to European and NATO leaders, Christopher mentioned American public support as a reassurance. Like President Clinton, he expressed confidence in American public support immediately following the signing of the Accords, in a December 5 statement to NATO foreign and defense ministers:

> NATO has approved a detailed operational plan to implement the agreement. This plan meets two tests that President Clinton laid out in his address to the American people. First the mission is precisely defined with clear, realistic goals that can be achieved in a finite period of time. Second, our troops will have the strength and authority to protect themselves and to fulfill their mission. I am confident this plan will have the support of the American people and our Congress. (Christopher, 12/5/95)

Conclusion: Christopher

Secretary of State Christopher's more than two years of tireless efforts to persuade both the allies and the U.S. Congress to accept the lift-and-strike plan remained futile. Open about his belief that the public had a legitimate right to influence policy, he was equally candid about his awareness that the American public had not focused on the Bosnia crisis and that it would not agree with an "Americanization" of this European crisis. That is why the lift-and-strike plan had to happen on a multilateral basis.

In this respect Christopher was guided in the actions he could take by both domestic and international pressures.

Christopher had a more nuanced if not more accurate understanding of the Balkan conflict than President Clinton. Christopher believed that it was "an intractable 'problem from hell' that no one can be expected to solve . . . less as a moral tragedy . . . and more as a tribal feud that no outsider could hope to settle (Christopher, 3/28/93). He walked a fine line between the pressures from a minority of vocal Americans led by Senator Dole who favored military action, and the rest of the population who would have opposed such policy in case it was conducted unilaterally and involved American casualties. And while he tried hard to sell the lift-and-strike policy, he continued to express preference for negotiated solutions over military action and be thus in tune with the preferences of the citizenry.

SECRETARY OF DEFENSE WILLIAM PERRY

Benchmark 1: NATO Action in Bosnia: February–April 1994

In a March 1994 Washington speech, Secretary of Defense William Perry commented on the U.S. military policy on Bosnia's safe areas, and was criticized by *The Washington Post* for being too revealing (3/13/94). In a letter to the *Post*, Perry cited pride in keeping American audiences informed of U.S. policy:

> It's surprising that the *Post*'s editorial should take me to task for being explicit about our objectives in Bosnia and the conditions that govern our use of military force. Being clear about our objectives and the means we will use to secure them is the best guard against mission creep. It is also what we owe the American people and Congress when we employ this country's armed forces to achieve limited political objectives. (Perry, 1994)

Later in March, Perry was questioned on his views of deploying American troops in the event of a cease-fire. He again displayed sensitivity to, if not agreement with, popular concerns, expressed by Congress. Asked if the United States was prepared to send in troops to help maintain a peace, Perry answered: "If that's a real peace agreement, we're prepared to go in and help sustain it. We will need to go to the Congress and get their support for it" (Perry, 3/28/94).

He also closely observed Congress. Asked if there was resistance, particularly in Congress, to turning the control of U.S. combat troops over to the United Nations, he replied: "I think whatever resistance in Congress there is . . . they simply see the importance of having adequate command and control" (Perry, 3/28/94).

Immediately before the first set of NATO air strikes in April 1994, Perry commented on *Meet the Press* that the United States under no circumstances intended to carry out air strikes. His remarks created a slight public furor, in part because they seemed to conflict with comments by the president, and in part because they conflicted with other official statements. Perry had stated that if the Serbs invaded Gorazde, the United States would "not enter the war to stop that from happening" (Perry, 4/3/94). However, the next day Clinton stated that the United States was still "looking at what our options are." Several days later, National Security Adviser Anthony Lake stated that "Neither the president nor any of his senior advisers rules out the use of air power to help stop attacks such as those on Gorazde." Various media figures expressed incredulity and public dismay at Perry's determination not to carry out air strikes: "I have to go back . . . to the *Meet the Press* interview, when you talked about not intervening to stop the fall of Gorazde. . . . What did change that it was appropriate?" Perry's answer can be seen as a response to three weeks of similar outcries in the press:

> I did say we would use air power, but air power under these very limited authorizations that we have in the United Nations? What I did say . . . is that we would not enter the war. I was in favor of, and strongly in favor of the use of air power to assist in the peacekeeping operations, but I was not in favor of air power, and we had no authority to use air power, as a combatant in the war. (Perry, 4/26/94).

Perry's expansion of his view of America's role at this turning point showed sensitivity to public opinion. The interviewer asked what America's exit strategy would entail: "Tell the American people about how we're going to get out of there." Perry answered:

> I think it's important that we're not in there. We are not a combatant in the war in Bosnia. There are many people who think we are, and there are other people who urge that we become a combatant in the war, but we have strongly resisted that, precisely because it's not clear what the exit strategy is if we are a combatant in the war. [If] we wanted to determine that outcome of that war and force the outcome to military action, we would have to enter as a combatant in the war and we would have to enter with substantial ground combatant forces. We're not prepared to recommend that. I don't believe the American people are prepared to accept that. (Perry, 4/26/94)

Benchmark 2: NATO Actions in Bosnia: June–August 1995

Prior to the June 1995 incident in which U.N. hostages were taken by Serbs, U.S. policy had yet to shift to serious engagement; government officials were still defending nonintervention. Perry relied on his perception of U.S. public opinion to justify nonintervention, in March 1995, remarking "Now many people, while sympathizing with the Bosnia Muslims, find the situation too confusing, too complicated and too frustrating. They say that Bosnia is a tragedy, but not our tragedy. They say that we should wash our hands of the whole situation" (Perry, 1995, p. A26). Perry described why the United States should continue to seek solutions to the war, but maintained that it should not intervene, despite some people's opinions:

> We have not succeeded in achieving a peace settlement. People find this frustrating. I find this frustrating. Many are further frustrated that our policies have not assisted the Bosnia people in their struggle to reverse the Serb gains and to punish those who participate in "ethnic cleansing." The active measures that have been proposed for that purpose send the United States headlong down a slippery slope. At the bottom of that slope will be American troops in ground combat. Nearly everyone accepts that sending American troops is a non-starter. There is no support for this idea among

the public or in Congress. American casualties undoubtedly would be high. . . .
(Perry, 3/9/1995)

He elaborated on these views in an interview on the *MacNeil/Lehrer News Hour* in
July 1995:

> Understand that to try to really change the situation in there we'd have to send in
> hundreds of thousands of ground troops. I am not prepared. I do not believe the Con-
> gress or the American people are prepared to send large numbers of ground troops
> into Bosnia to become a combatant in this war. The alternative of simply withdraw-
> ing the UNPROFOR will either lead to humanitarian catastrophe, which will make
> what we're seeing today seem pale by comparison, or it will lead to the introduction
> of U.S. troops to stop that. (Perry, 7/13/95)

Clearly, public opinion was a factor in his formulation of Clinton foreign policy toward Bosnia.

Benchmark 3: Dayton Accords: November–December 1995

Perry's statements around the Dayton agreements did not significantly address the
nature of American public opinion. He commented on America's role in the world, in
the context of a long-term foreign policy vision, instead: "It is both ironic and won-
derful that the largest military operation in NATO's history will be to forge a peace.
. . . All the qualities that [NATO] developed . . . unity of command, discipline
and a shared vision of a secure Europe . . . will make us effective in peace" (Perry,
12/5/95).

When offering comments to a domestic audience in a late November Department
of Defense briefing, Perry elaborated significantly on the reasons for sending troops.
He did not indicate particular awareness of public opinion, but offered extensive efforts to persuade the audience to accept the reasoning of the Department of Defense.
"Why are we asking you to go to Bosnia? I believe that the reasons are compelling,
and I want to share with you why I find them so compelling. I believe that you will
find them compelling also." He also assumed agreement on the U.S. interests: "The
United States does have vital political, economic, and security interests in Europe.
For many audiences I would stop to explain that, but . . . you know very well what
our interests in Europe are" (Perry, 11/24/95).

Perry then emphasized the need for American support: "In order to seize this opportunity for peace, we must make an American commitment to participate. None of
the parties . . . would have been willing to sign the peace agreement without an
American commitment." He also answered criticisms of specific details of his policy:
"Some have argued that we could get by with a force half this size. But if we err, it
will be on the side of sending in too many." In this statement he noted public criticism, and explained why he intended to override it. Perry appealed for American
support: "The American people will be asking the question, 'Who will go for us?'
And I expect the First Armored Division will answer, 'Here I am. Send me'" (Perry,
11/24/95).

In assessing the outcome of Dayton's troop deployments, Perry faced criticism from Congress and elsewhere that the mission was dragging and could not be completed in the time that the agreements specified. In a speech in July 1996, Perry addressed this criticism: "I very well remember the mood at that time right after we had the agreement, but before we sent our forces in. I testified probably five or six times to the Congress. Many of the skeptics in the Congress, in the public, in the media, predicted that the peace would not hold and that IFOR would never succeed" (Perry, 7/12/96). He later addressed current criticism:

> [On] all of those . . . very important and substantial debates, . . . we've got nearly all of those right in our assessment. . . . The one judgment . . . that we conduct all these military missions spelled out in the annex in 12 months was right . . . what I failed to assess properly at that time was the importance of having the civil functions . . . getting done in the same time frame, they have lagged behind. . . . And so my judgment now is that we need to provide more time and that's why I recommended to the president that he agree . . . to put a new force in there. . . . (Perry, 11/15/96)

Clearly, Perry met public criticism with strong statements of policy despite the policy's divergence from that opinion.

Toward the end of his tenure as secretary of defense, Perry commented on the most difficult aspect of his term:

> The hardest thing any secretary of defense has to do is sign the deployment orders to send troops into dangerous situations. . . . I signed the deployment into Bosnia, we sent about 30,000 troops into that theater, more than 20,000 initially into Bosnia. People were saying that we were going to have thousands of casualties a week . . . we never believed that. (Perry, 12/19/96)

This retrospective statement demonstrates that Secretary of State Perry was aware of public attitudes on the Bosnia issue. While these attitudes alone did not determine his policymaking, they certainly played a role in the boundaries within which the Clinton administration could act.

Conclusion: Perry

Secretary William Perry believed in shaping policy that was in tune with public preferences and congressional and international approval. His public statements that the United States would not resort to military action in Yugoslavia echoed what he perceived the public wanted but also expressed his own preferences. While he did not often refer directly to public attitudes, they appeared as a factor in his decisions. Usually, policymakers invoke the preferences of the public to strengthen their own stand on issues in front of the same public, as in McNamara's appeal to President Johnson to stop the war by reminding him of what the American public felt about it. When Clinton policymakers' preferences were at odds with those of the public, they usually refrained from mentioning public opinion unless asked about it.

CONCLUSION: THE CLINTON ADMINISTRATION

Although candidate Clinton expressed disapproval of George Bush's weak Bosnia policies, President Clinton continued them. Not even the portrayal of the Serbs as Nazis, or the use of "genocide," "appeasement," and "concentration camp" imagery made the allies or the American public want to start a war against Yugoslavia. Tensions between the United States and the European Community increased after Clinton came to the White House and started undermining the Vance-Owen plan, which the Europeans had seen as a beginning of the end of the war: they then saw this American act as a contribution to the escalation of the war (Woodward, 1995, p. 306). More remarkable, if not unwarranted, was Clinton's insistence on selling the lift-and-strike plan for more than a year afterward, despite knowledge that the Europeans would consider military strikes unacceptable. Whereas Warren Christopher and William Perry used the will of the American people and or Congress in explaining their cautious policy, President Clinton was more frustrated by the constraints put on his plan by the allies than by the American public. Had the allies agreed with lift and strike, he knew from precedent that the American public would at least give initial support.

Clinton's campaign statements responded to the American public's concern that the United States take clear action to prevent genocide. Despite his promises, his initial floundering in office indicated uncertainty, after the failure of Christopher's lift-and-strike plan, about the consistency of the long-term support of the American people.

The Clinton administration then encountered the same consideration that had deterred Bush from taking decisive action: the situation was complicated, multilayered, and held little U.S. national interest that was clear and accessible to the average citizen. After the first benchmark discussed here, the marketplace massacre in February 1994, the United States and the international community were pushed toward stronger action.

Clinton was extremely careful in his public references to American opinion. His statements explicitly sought to address the concerns of citizens, Congress, and the international community. The Clinton administration was far more concerned with cultivating a relationship with various audiences and used congressional hearings; press conversations; candid conversations, particularly in Perry's case; and personal appeals, particularly in Clinton's case. Faced with domestic criticism, the charge of being novice and ineffective in foreign policy, Clinton and his secretaries ultimately appeared interested in winning public support, but often displayed lack of awareness of public opinion. It may not be coincidental that the most intense engagement in bombing that began following the second benchmark (August 1995) was initiated in the year before second-term elections.

Clinton shifted his views on public opinion and its role in policy debates. He justified his actions in February 1994 and June 1995 by seeking to rally public support for his policies. In December 1995, he displayed both confidence in American existing public support and, paradoxically, the sense that he was morally obliged to take action that might overrule public disapproval, if his decisions had to diverge from public opinion.

Bush, too, had responded to charges of ineffectiveness in Bosnia, but he only decided to take more forceful action after the elections were over, fearing perhaps more damage to his public image. Despite controversy over American troop activity in Bosnia, Clinton may have been aware that public sentiment could be more damaging to his image if he remained disengaged than if the United States became involved.

Both presidents seemed likely to try to influence public opinion toward supporting their basic approaches while policy was being formulated, before moments of crisis. During crises, policymakers appeared to make policy relatively decisively, and then seek public support for it by emphasizing the greater likelihood of success given public support.

In the case of the Clinton administration, its seeming lesser awareness of public opinion is consistent with the observation that his administration was unresponsive to public opinion (Jacobs and Shapiro, 2000). "Interviews with individuals tied to the Clinton administration suggested that public opinion did not generally drive the formulation of specific social policies" (p. 3). Stan Greenberg, Clinton's pollster in 1993 and 1994, stated, "'His [Clinton's] tendency is to develop policy removed from politics.'" This agrees with Clinton's own statements about not using polls in policymaking.

CONCLUSION: BOSNIA CASE STUDY

The American policies toward the Bosnia crisis are extremely important in the study of opinion-foreign policy relationships as they complete the picture that began to emerge during the Vietnam War. The American public praises the principles of cooperative internationalism, negotiation, and a strong role for the United Nations in solving local problems in the world; yet most American policymakers prefer and at times advocate militant internationalism, even at the expense of creating tensions within the United States or with the United Nations. Instead of decisive and short action, policies have to be channeled, in V.O. Key's terms, between the two banks of public opinion and of multilateral action.

Despite the twenty years that divide the Vietnam War from the Bosnia intervention, the similarities between the policies of the earlier war and the latter intervention point to a continuation in the foreign policy decision-making process and its relationship with the American public. First, two administrations each, one Republican and one Democrat, conducted each policy. Second, both continued the other's policy despite Republican Nixon's running on a platform of offering a different policy from Democrat Johnson and Democrat Clinton's platform criticizing Republican Bush. Whether a Republican succeeded a Democrat or the other way around, mattered little.

Third, the four administrations preferred more military engagement than the public was willing to accept and were thus closer to each other than they were to the American public. The administrations were stopped from preferred policies (more decisive bombing in Vietnam and military action against Yugoslavia) first by the international community (fear of Russian or Chinese involvement in the case of Vietnam and the EC and the United Nations in the case of Bosnia) and then by a climate of opinion in the country that was not supportive. Fourth, the four administrations showed intermittent reluctance to cooperate with United Nations' efforts, public attitudes lessened the likelihood especially of unilaterial military actions; this was because more cooperative policies tended to have stronger support from the American people. Moreover, the administrations at times employed covert diplomacy or actions that undercut peace plans, extending the wars and alienating world and American opinion.

Policymakers in both the Bush and Clinton administrations showed awareness if not accurate perceptions of public attitudes about intervention in Bosnia. The public constrained the Bush and early Clinton administration to relative inaction. It permitted only relatively robust air strikes but not combat troops when the situation on the ground improved for the Muslim-Croat coalition and the atrocities compelled the allies into action. The limited public support restricted the mission to peacekeeping that ultimately proved to be successful and publicly supported. The concluding chapter of this book looks back at the lessons of Bosnia and at the preceding interventions in Vietnam, Nicaragua, and the Gulf.

VI

CONCLUSION

Extending the Theory of Public Opinion in American Foreign Policy: Public Opinion as Intervention Constraint

The Impact of Public Opinion on U.S. Foreign Policy Since Vietnam examines the role that public attitudes have played over the last generation in the making of U.S. foreign policy. The study explains the place of opinion in the policy process, particularly decisions about U.S. interventions, both on a theoretical level and from the perspective of actual decision-makers. In pursuing its goals, the book focuses on four of the most prominent foreign interventions of the last generation: the Vietnam War, the Nicaraguan contra funding controversy, the Gulf War, and the war in Bosnia. By demonstrating how public opinion affected policy, the cases provide the basis for the building of an overall theory of public opinion in foreign policymaking.

This concluding chapter summarizes and reflects on the insights the book provides into the relationship between public opinion and foreign policymaking. In particular, it draws conclusions from comparisons across the cases about how public opinion actually entered into the foreign policy decision-making process in military interventions. Further, it explores the impact of national public opinion on administration policymakers, and for the Nicaragua case, the influence of national and constituent opinion on congressional decision-makers. In short, it evaluates the actual roles of public opinion in the foreign policy of our democracy.

Through the combination of analytic approaches, the investigation of these four controversies advances the knowledge of and the theories about public opinion in foreign interventions. Reviews of the major empirical theories of the influence of public opinion set the basis for Key's system of dikes theory, which generally holds that public opinion sets limits or constraints on the discretion that policymakers have in choosing from among possible policy options. The decline of public support established, for instance, how long the United States could continue intervention in Vietnam. Protest as a type of public opinion set limits on how extreme, for example, could be the options from which the Johnson and Nixon administration policymakers could choose.

In developing general insights about opinion's impact on foreign policy, the study explores foreign policy attitudes as shaped by the climate of opinion, overall presidential approval, and public preferences for specific policies. The examination of the actual role of public opinion in foreign intervention policy shows that both administration and congressional policymakers saw themselves more typically as trustees of good government than as delegates of the people. Despite minimizing the importance of public opinion, officials were aware of public attitudes and recognized the central importance of public support for their policies. Both recognized existing or anticipated constraints in public opinion on their decisions.

To set a larger historical context for the particular cases, the book also investigates how current public opinion interacts with longer term trends or cycles in interventionist or isolationist sentiments. Rather than having unique meanings, particular levels of opinion occur within the general climate of attitudes of interventionism or noninterventionism. In particular, contemporary attitudes toward involvement in Vietnam, against intervention in Nicaragua, and for and against actions in the Persian Gulf and Bosnia fit with long-term trends in attitudes toward intervention or nonintervention. Each era was both influenced by and contributed to the adjacent cycles in internationalism and noninterventionism.

Though the Vietnam War began during an interventionist era, it soon contributed to and was influenced by sentiments toward withdrawal. The contra funding controversy was constrained by the "post-Vietnam syndrome." Attitudes during the Gulf War and war in Bosnia were both influenced by the post-Vietnam syndrome and contributed to attitudes more supportive of later successful interventions. Anticommunism and humanitarianism drove interventionism, while isolationism, the post-Vietnam syndrome, costs, and casualties drove anti-interventionism. Generally, opinion influenced policy, though policymakers also affected opinion, particularly through the media.

The significance of this study appears in several guises. First, the research bases its conclusions on careful evaluation of prominent cases, pertinent evidence, and appropriate multiple and mutually reinforcing sources of information. The analysis is based on the words by the major decision-makers themselves in speeches, public statements, memos, memoirs, minutes, and interviews. Because they are given public scrutiny and reflect sensitivity to public sentiment, public statements often reveal more than private papers, although private papers reveal personal thoughts and concerns often kept from the public. Leaders may not think about public opinion explicitly in their daily decisions or may try to deny any influence, but they find that public attitudes are an unavoidable and consistent factor in their decision-making processes. Second, the study demonstrates not only that public opinion influences policy but also that the major effects of public opinion typically manifest themselves in constraint rather than in policy setting.

Third, the study shows the generally increasing role of public opinion in, if not always on, foreign policymaking and how that change has occurred over time. For better or worse, the public voice grows louder, and sensitivity to that volume increases, though not always more responsively. The exploration of the implications for policymakers and citizens in a democracy suggests that knowledge of the role of public opinion on policy might assist efforts to move the American foreign policy process in a more democratic direction. The coincidence of empirical evidence of how public opinion affects foreign policymaking with normative ideas about how public opinion should affect policy may create more effective decision making.

REVIEW OF THE CASES

In focusing on the relationship of public opinion to foreign policy in the four central military interventions in recent history, the book draws insights from the words of principal decision-makers. Major cabinet officers, confirmed by the Senate, in the State Department and Department of Defense (as well as the National Security Council) inform the president, who ultimately decides policy. To fill out the historical record, the Nicaragua chapter explore other prominent decision-makers, particularly representatives and senators for the contra funding controversy when Congress was central to funding decisions, as it was for the vote to go to war in the Gulf.

In short, for each major crisis and decision-maker, the study identifies, from the decision-maker's own words, to what extent he was aware of public opinion at key benchmarks during the controversy. Then it attempts to ascertain whether public opinion, and in the case of Vietnam, protest, influenced the policymaker's decisions.

The Vietnam War

The opening case examines the complexities of the Vietnam War and how public opinion and protest affected the development of U.S. escalatory and deescalatory policies from the 1960s to the early 1970s. It focuses on U.S. policy at the specific benchmarks of the Johnson decision to escalate the war in 1964 after the Tonkin Gulf incident, the period after the Tet offensive, and the 1969 moratorium and the Nixon administration's planned Duck Hook escalation and the 1970 Cambodia invasion. During the war, support dropped and opposition rose, though presidential approval depended on the perceived success of current policy. Yet opinion and policy were generally consistent because, as opinion changed, so did the policy. The Vietnam case shows that both opinion influenced policy and policy influenced opinion. Johnson was the consummate poll reader who cited the polls he kept in his pocket when they favored him and tried to ignore them when they opposed him. Johnson's decisions to escalate in 1965 were abetted by conservative pressure, while his post-Tet decisions to deescalate in 1968 were constrained by both declining public support and increasing protest. Dean Rusk underestimated the extent to which the American public was impatient to end the war, while Robert McNamara felt, and perhaps later accepted, the constraints of protest and declining public support against his rational evaluation of policy options. When it was clear the public and elite opposed further involvement in Vietnam, McNamara's successor, Clark Clifford, overturned Johnson's opposition to beginning to deescalate the war.

Aware of public opposition in the ongoing moratorium protests, Richard Nixon's strategies in 1969 were constrained to Vietnamization rather than escalation by declining public support and increasing protest, especially around the time of the moratoriums. But his "silent majority" speech in November 1969 created leeway for continuing the war, and the threat and actuality of protests as intense forms of public expression constrained the extremity of policy options away from intensive bombing or even invasion of the North. The surge in protest on campuses after the Cambodia invasions accelerated the exit of allied forces.

First as national security adviser, and then as secretary of state, Henry Kissinger was hamstrung by public opposition to his policy. Though he railed against the anti-war movement, he ultimately had to accommodate to it. (William Rogers' role as secretary of state was largely focused elsewhere.) As a former congressman and practicing politician, Melvin Laird recognized the declining public support in his advocacy of Vietnamization as a way of deescalating the war and reducing public pressure for a quick end. The decline of the antiwar movement permitted the escalatory bombings in 1972 that led to an armistice in 1973. The U.S. role in the war ended when the public's patience ultimately ran out.

The Contra Funding Controversy

The examination of the Nicaraguan case flows from the Vietnam study because it focuses on the first major, albeit indirect, post-Vietnam intervention during the 1980s. Nicaragua was a case of both nonintervention and intervention constrained by public opposition. Although U.S. combat forces were not directly involved, U.S. funding sustained the contras. Interviews with high-level decision-makers in both the Reagan administration and Congress reveal influences at the top unknown to previous exploration of the issues (Sobel, 1993). The post-Vietnam syndrome, public opposition, and congressional resistance circumscribed what policymakers could do in Nicaragua. As at the end of the Vietnam War, despite continuing anticommunist sentiment, the public opposed intervention in Central America.

Specifically, public opinion constraints appeared in limits to the amount of money or potential personnel the administration could allocate to the contras. The failure of President Reagan to persuade the public to support administration policy demonstrates the limits of leadership even for a popularly perceived president who attempts to change public opinion on a controversial issue. Administration policymakers acknowledged that opinion limited the scope of their contra aid policy, but they largely attempted to ignore public opposition. Recognizing that they lacked general public support, the leaders were unwilling to change their goals to meet the public preference for nonintervention. Instead they sought public approval as a potential "tool" with which they could act as trustees of the people in choosing a different foreign policy direction from that which the American public preferred.

Ronald Reagan was well aware of public opinion and that it forced his administration to ask for less funding for the contras than he would have liked. Yet he continued to press for a policy that the public rejected. George Shultz was also aware of public opposition, but he felt that correct and successful policy would produce its own constituency. Taking lessons from Vietnam, and recognizing public opposition Caspar Weinberger took into account public attitudes and felt that the support of the Congress and the public was essential to carrying out intervention policy. The Shultz-Weinberger debate in November 1984 on the bases for U.S. intervention policy set the terms for discussions of the role of opinion in this and later foreign interventions. Shultz's deputies Elliot Abrams and Ed Fox revealed how opinion was a tool toward a chosen policy. Reagan pollster Richard Wirthlin reveals how extensively poll evidence entered the policy process.

Public opinion also loosely influenced the Congress, which represented public preferences by voting largely according to ideology, partisanship, and presidential popularity. Public opinion influenced members of Congress, but not particularly how they voted on contra aid. Legislators were not especially worried about public opinion in their districts but were afraid of what public sentiment might become, particularly during an election campaign. Representatives carefully monitored public opinion to be sure that their voting decisions were not too directly constrained. Despite consistent public opposition to the Reagan policy of aiding the contras, Congress typically reflected district public opinion in voting for only limited assistance and opposing direct involvement. Senators Lugar and Pell acknowledged that electoral consequences sensitized them to the public attitudes. Congressmen Skelton and Spratt felt they were trusted by their constituencies but they carefully monitored public support in their districts to make sure that they were not more clearly constrained. Presidential lobbying of Congress ultimately provided the few swing votes on close funding decisions.

The Gulf War

The Gulf War was the first major post-Vietnam direct U.S. intervention. In response to Iraq's invasion of Kuwait in August 1990, the United States led coalition forces into the Middle East and ultimately initiated an air and ground war in January and February 1991. Strong initial public support of Desert Shield indicated a decline of the post-Vietnam syndrome. But decreasing and divided support and increasing congressional questioning as the buildup to war continued during a recession began to restrict the Bush administration's options in the direction of negotiations. Administration attention and communication that reflected sensitivity to domestic political support also sent mixed messages to Mideast leaders. The potential for a sharp decline in public support for a prolonged Desert Storm campaign constrained the administration to a "100-hour war." Protest against the war grew quickly but had little effect on the administration and was poorly received by a public largely supportive of the U.S.'s role in the conflict.

George Bush was aware that there was more public support for the war than there was in Congress, but he promised that politics would not affect his policies. The lessons of Vietnam encouraged his undertaking a massive but short intervention to circumvent the dynamics of potentially dropping public support. James Baker recognized at the start of the war that there was not yet public support for an intervention, but he contributed to its rise as the war approached. Like Melvin Laird, Dick Cheney, a former congressman and later White House chief of staff, knowledgeable about public opinion, revealed little in his public statements about his own awareness of public opinion or its impact on his decisions; but in interviews both men acknowledged the public's constraining role in interventions. Cheney's deft use of the media suggested an awareness of the need to keep the public on the administration's side.

Bosnia

Bosnia was the first extended post–Cold War conflict. In a sense, it was both an example of nonintervention, during most of the Bush and the early Clinton administration, and of more forceful intervention that began during the middle of the Clinton presidency. The public opposed unilateral U.S. intervention but supported humanitarian, indirect, and multilateral involvement. Because of their perceptions of public opposition, U.S. leaders consistently refused to send ground troops to fight but offered to send peacekeepers once the war was settled. Eventually the United States became involved in fairly popular multilateral air strikes that brought the fighting to an end.

Perceptions of public opposition, first in the Bush administration and then in the Clinton administration, restrained Bosnia policy. U.S. involvement was limited and reluctant for three years across both administrations. At first, the United States provided humanitarian aid and patrolled the no-fly zone, for both of which there was strong support. Eventually it took part in aggressive allied air strikes of which the public approved in a multilateral context. Finally, it sent peacekeeping troops, a measure for which there had been strong public support earlier. As deployment approached, this support gradually reduced to minority levels until it became clear to a majority again that the involvement was relatively riskless and successful.

George Bush was aware of public opposition but promised not to let politics interfere with his concerns for humanitarian intervention. Always the political animal, James Baker felt there was not enough U.S. public support to intervene more forcefully. Lawrence Eagleburger was little aware of public sentiments and felt little constrained by them. Dick Cheney held his counsel in public on this issue but later revealed his sensitivity to public sentiment.

Bill Clinton indicated some awareness of more forceful public sentiment in his interventionist campaign statements. When in office, he weakened his policy as he felt the constraint of public opposition. Though Warren Christopher was aware of public opinion and felt it should have a role in policymaking, he perceived the public to be more opposed to involvement than it really was. William Perry indicated less awareness or influence by public opinion, and he was generally opposed to intervention for pragmatic reasons.

SOME REFLECTIONS

Aggressive conservative pressures and general anticommunism permitted U.S. involvement in Vietnam until casualties and costs that contrasted with administration promises of success destroyed public support. Despite continuing anticommunist sentiments and approval of a communicative president who strongly supported Nicaragua involvement, during the early post-Vietnam era the American public generally preferred to avoid interventions. Those specific attitudes on policy contributed to the climate of opinion that constrained the administration's efforts. Both administration members and congressional representatives were aware of public opposition, and even when they sought to avoid it, they acknowledged its apparent or potential effects. What is "effective" public opinion that actually influences policy depends on the opinion context and the centrality of groups holding specific attitudes (Kull and Destler, 1999).

In short, decision-makers were constantly aware of public opinion and were by necessity constrained in the timing, extent, and direction of their actions. Presidents follow the polls for both governing and electoral purposes. Secretaries of state are often more aggressive than the public would require and typically less aware of public opinion until it runs counter to their policies. Secretaries of defense tend, in general, to be less aware of and less constrained by public attitudes, yet often less interventionist than their state department counterparts.

Even four compelling cases do not make a theory, but the consistencies in research findings suggest that constraint is the revealing theoretical model. The testimony of principal decision-makers through interviews, memoirs, and public statements advances empirical theory for public opinion that also emphasizes constraint and indirect control. Rather than constraint being the maximum effect that opinion may have on policy, public opinion increasingly influences the nature and presentation of policy (Nacos, Shapiro, and Isernia, 2000). When intensely focused, public opinion may essentially set policy (Graham, 1989). That its influence extends further into the different stages of development of policy actions is increasingly apparent.

EXTENDING THE THEORY

The theoretical models developed here about the constraining nexus between public opinion and policy relations in foreign affairs identified in U.S. cases require further development. While the U.S. foreign policy process merits comprehensive scrutiny because of the centrality of the United States as a world power and of American politics in political theory, a wider perspective is needed. Ole Holsti suggests that three factors are central for fuller theoretical flowering: the examination of multiple cases, a cross-national context, and repeated question wordings (Holsti, 1996, pp. 191–92). There is a "need for public opinion research in which evidence about the United States is placed in a broader comparative context": the nature of public opinion, the channels by which it "enters the policy process," and its impact vary "across countries and political system" (Holsti, 1996, p. 204). "By far the least well developed of the areas of public opinion research has been the opinion-policy linkage" Holsti notes (p. 196). Further, "In order to develop and test competing hypotheses about opinion-policy linkages, there is no alternative to carefully crafted case studies, employing interviews and archival research, designed to uncover how decision makers perceive public opinion; feel themselves motivated or constrained" (p. 59). While America's central role in the international system requires close examination of its foreign policy process, comparative analysis is necessary to avoid generalizing from a single, largely American, perspective.

As Thomas Risse-Kappen notes for France, West Germany, the United States, and Japan, the impact of public opinion is "significantly affected by the domestic institutions and coalition building processes among elites" (Holsti, 1996, p. 205). Since the wordings of questions and context affect results in public opinion surveys, it is essential to repeat the same questions at regular intervals. Though typically independent surveys undertake different probes, "the development of even a handful of standard foreign and defense policy questions that would be included in all such surveys is highly desirable" (Holsti, 1996, p. 208; Sobel, 1995b).

By focusing on the processes of the making of overt decisions on intervention, commentaries have understated the ways public opinion influenced administration decisions to fund the contras covertly against congressional wishes, or similarly to arm the Bosnian Muslims, despite an arms embargo. The important implications of hiding policy from public opinion and Congress require the scrutiny of the theory and practice of covert action in a democratic society (Maxwell, 1994).

Further cases need to assess the impact of public opinion on foreign policy by focusing on important distinctions: the types of involvement, from humanitarian relief to military conflict. Also key are the stages of the policy process from initial discussion to implementation, the decision context surrounding foreign policy of the time, and the policymakers' beliefs about and sensitivity to public opinion (Holsti, 1996, p. 197; Foyle, 1999). Moreover, public opinion constrains policy, but so does the international system. Two-level game theory adds an important dimension here by looking explicitly at the reciprocal impact involving domestic politics and the international system (Putnam, 1988).

CONCLUSION: BEYOND CONSTRAINT

In short, public opinion has constrained the U.S. foreign policy decision-making process over the last generation. By delving into theory, events, and interpretations of the Vietnam, Nicaragua, Gulf, and Bosnia interventions and obtaining the views of active decision-makers, this analysis provides valuable insights about public opinion's influences in U.S. foreign relations for scholars, policymakers, and citizens engaged by the historical material and policy recommendations illuminating these complex processes.

The issues of public support and opposition to U.S. interventions remain pressing ones for American domestic politics and foreign policy. Public opinion is increasingly recognized as a central factor in the decisions about U.S. foreign relations. The voice of the people speaks during intervention debates, and, in this collision of public attitudes with national security, policy continues to be of fundamental concern for citizens and policymakers. The reality that public opinion constrains foreign intervention policy contributes both to the development of theory about opinion in foreign interventions and to the advance of democracy in the realm of foreign affairs.

Public opinion may constrain policy, but policymakers need not always be constrained by public attitudes. There are times when leaders should heed opinion, times when they should lead opinion, and times when they should proceed despite opinion. Those times depend on American norms and history, because U.S. policy needs to follow the fundamental principles of the nation and the goals of democracy and world peace. The history of the United States before the two world wars suggests that when presidents delay in entering the world stage at crucial times, the costs of such dalliance may be far more devastating than the price of earlier action. When America's fundamental goals are in evidence or in peril, policymakers should educate the public; but leadership may need to risk the public's opprobrium temporarily to pursue enlightened policies and develop public support for the longer term.

The beginning of the new century, a decade after the Cold War's end, is an auspicious time to examine in detail a central issue of democratic governance and international affairs: how public opinion influences U.S. foreign policy. In providing evidence about how opinion affected past foreign interventions in the context of our normative ideals, this study helps readers to comprehend how America makes its foreign policy and also to evaluate how well democracy works here in the realm of foreign affairs.

Interviews, Statements, and Questions

Baker, James. *Frontline.* Original airing, 9 January 1996.

Ball, George. Interview by author. Princeton, N.J. 20 January 1994.

Bush, George. *MacNeil/Lehrer NewsHour.* 10 July 1992.

Bush, George. *MacNeil/Lehrer NewsHour.* 19 July 1996.

Bush, George. Question by author. Kennedy School, Harvard University, 28 May 1998.

Carlucci, Frank. Federal Information Services. 28 September 1988.

Carlucci, Frank. Interview by author. Washington, D.C. 18 June 1993.

Cheney, Richard. Federal Information Services. 10 February 1991.

Cheney, Richard. Defense Department Briefing. 26 March 1992.

Cheney, Richard. Defense Department Briefing. 1 October 1992.

Cheney, Richard. *Face the Nation,* with Bob Schieffer. 20 December 1992.

Cheney, Richard. Interview by Larry King. 27 January 1993.

Cheney, Richard. Interview by Adam Heyerson in *Policy Review,* summer, 1993.

Cheney, Richard. *CBS This Morning,* with Harry Smith. 29 January 1993.

Cheney, Richard. CNN interview, with Donna Kelley. 26 February 1993.

Cheney, Richard. *Face the Nation,* with Bob Schieffer. 22 October 1995.

Cheney, Richard. *Frontline.* Original airing, 9 January, 1996.

Cheney, Richard. Telephone interview by author. 22 March 1999.

Christopher, Warren. *Face the Nation,* with Bob Schieffer. 28 March 1993.

Christopher, Warren. Interview with Anne Garrels, *NPR Morning Edition.* 24 February 1994a.

Christopher, Warren. Media Photo Opportunity. Federal News Service. 24 February 1994b.

Christopher, Warren. State Department Press Briefing. Washington, D.C. 8 September 1995.

Christopher, Warren. Doorstep Interview. Washington, D.C. 19 July 1995.

Christopher, Warren. Statement to NATO Members. Brussels, Belgium. 5 December 1995.

Christopher, Warren. Question by Author. Kennedy School, Harvard University. 15 January 1997.

Clifford, Clark. Interview by author. Washington, D.C. 13 August 1990.

Clinton, William J. Interview. Federal News Service. 20 May 1994.

Eagleburger, Lawrence. *MacNeil/Lehrer NewsHour.* 28 November 1992.

Eagleburger, Lawrence. Interview by CNN. 20 December 1992.

Eagleburger, Lawrence. Interview by J. Peter Scoblic. Reuters. 30 January 1996.

Galbraith, J. Kenneth. Presentation to Government 90, Harvard University. 9 December 1999.

Kissinger, Henry. Interview by Leslie Stahl. *60 Minutes.* 7 March 1999.

Laird, Melvin. Press Conference in Saigon. 6 March 1969.

Laird, Melvin. *CBS Morning News,* with John Hart. Washington, D.C. 3 April 1969.

Laird, Melvin. Interview by Richard Starnes. *Washington Daily News.* 4 June 1969 (published 6/13/69).

Laird, Melvin. Press Conference, Pentagon, Washington, D.C. 1 December 1969.

Laird, Melvin. Metromedia Radio News, Dan Blackburn, Washington, D.C. 20 March 1970.

Laird, Melvin. Interview by Julius Duscha. Washington, D.C. 29 March 1971.

Laird, Melvin. *Face the Nation,* with George Herman, Washington, D.C. 13 June 1971.

Laird, Melvin. *Meet the Press.* 14 November 1971.

Laird, Melvin. Telephone interview by author. 8 February 1999.

Lake, Anthony. Interview by author. Northampton, Mass. 22 May 1987.

Lugar, Richard. Interview by author. Washington, D.C. 13 July 1990.

McNamara, Robert. Interview by author. Amherst, Mass. 20 February 1987.

McNamara, Robert. Telephone interview by author. 10 July 1990.

McNamara, Robert. Kennedy School, Harvard University, Cambridge, Mass. 28 April 1995.

Nixon, Richard. *Meet the Press.* 7 March 1988.

Oberdorfer, Donald. Interview by author. Princeton, N.J. 20 January 1994.

Pell, Claiborne. Telephone interview by author. 6 October 1990.

Perry, William. *MacNeil/Lehrer NewsHour,* 28 March 1994.

Perry, William. *Meet the Press* 3 April 1994.

Perry, William. *NPR NewsHour.* 26 April 1994.

Perry, William. Speech. 9 March 1995.

Perry, William. *MacNeil/Lehrer NewsHour,* 13 July 1995.

Perry, William. Defense Department Briefing. 24 November 1995.

Perry, William. Defense Department Briefing. 5 December 1995.

Perry, William. Defense Department Briefing. 11 July 1996.

Perry, William. *NewsHour with Jim Lehrer.* 15 November 1996.

Perry, William. *NewsHour with Jim Lehrer.* 19 December 1996.

Reagan, Ronald. A Reagan Interview. *Washington Post.* 2 April 1985.

Rusk, Dean. Interview by author. Athens, Ga. 1 September 1989.

Shultz, George. Interview by author. Cummington, Mass. 6 July 1994.

Shultz, George. *MacNeil/Lehrer NewsHour.* 16 August 1988.

Spratt, John. Interview by author. Washington, D.C. 12 July 1990.

Weinberger, Casper. *MacNeil/Lehrer NewsHour.* 27 February 1986.

Weinberger, Casper. *MacNeil/Lehrer NewsHour.* 28 October 1986.

Weinberger, Casper. *MacNeil/Lehrer NewsHour.* 5 November 1987.

Wirthlin, Richard. Interview by author. Storrs, Conn. 6 May 1989.

Bibliography

Abramowitz, Alan I. 1985. Economic conditions, presidential popularity, and voting behavior in midterm congressional elections. *Journal of Politics* 47: 31–43.

Adelman, Kenneth L. 1981. Speaking of America: Public diplomacy in our times. *Foreign Affairs* 59: 914–36.

Agence France Presse. 1996. Saudi Arms Programme for Bosnia Had Tacit U.S. Backing. Washington, D.C., 2 February.

Alder, Kenneth P. 1984. Polling the attentive public. *Annals of the American Academy of Political and Social Science* 472: 143–54.

Aldrich, John H., John L. Sullivan, and Eugene Borgida. 1989. Foreign affairs and issue voting: Do presidential candidates waltz before a blind audience? *American Political Science Review* 83: 123–41.

Almond, Gabriel A. 1950. *The American People and Foreign Policy.* New York: Praeger.

Almond, Gabriel A. 1956. Public opinion and national security. *Public Opinion Quarterly* 20: 373–78.

Ambrose Stephen. 1989. *Nixon: The Triumph of a Politician.* New York: Simon & Schuster.

American Friends Service Committee. 1985. *Humanitarian Aid to Nicaragua.* Philadelphia: American Friends Service Committee.

Americans Talk Security. 1989. *Compendium.* Boston: Americans Talk Security.

The Analysis Group. 1987a. Summary of attitudes toward contra aid. Washington, D.C. Mimeo.

The Analysis Group. 1987b. Contra aid: American antipathy to foreign engagement. Washington, D.C. Mimeo.

Annals of the American Academy of Political and Social Science. 1984. Polling and the Democratic Consensus. 472 (March).

Apple, R. W. Jr. 1986. Mudslinging over contras. *New York Times,* 12 March: A5.

Arnold, R. Douglas. 1990. *The Logic of Congressional Action.* New Haven, Conn.: Yale University Press.

Arnson, Cynthia J. 1988. The Reagan administration, Congress, and Central America: The search for consensus. In *Crisis in Central America.* Edited by Nora Hamilton et al. Boulder, Colo.: Westview Press.

Arnson, Cynthia J. 1989. *Crossroads: Congress, the Reagan Administration, and Central America.* New York: Pantheon.

Arnson, Cynthia J., and Philip Brenner. 1993. The limits of lobbying: Interest groups, Congress, and aid to the contras. In *Public Opinion in U.S. Foreign Policy: The Controversy Over Contra Aid.* Edited by Richard Sobel. Lanham, Md.: Rowman & Littlefield.

Asher, Herbert B., and Herbert F. Weisberg. 1978. Voting change in Congress: Some dynamic perspectives on an evolutionary process. *American Journal of Political Science* 22: 391–425.

Atkinson, Rick. 1991. "A defining moment in history": As midnight deadline approaches, stakes for U.S. are enormous. *Washington Post,* 15 January: A1.

Bachrach, Peter. 1967. *Theory of Democratic Elitism: A Critique.* Boston: Little, Brown.

Bailey, Thomas A. 1964 [1948]. *The Man on the Street: The Impact of American Public Opinion on Foreign Policy.* Gloucester, Mass.: Peter Smith.

Baker, James A. 1990a. "The Persian Gulf Crisis in a Global Perspective," Testimony on the Persian Gulf Crisis, to the House Foreign Affairs Committee. In *Foreign Policy Bulletin,* September/October 1990. September 4.

Baker, James A. 1990b. Excerpts from Q&A Following Secretary Baker's Statement, Senate Foreign Relations Committee, *Foreign Policy Bulletin,* November/December, 17 October.

Baker, James A. 1990c. Why America Is in the Gulf. Address to the Los Angeles World Affairs Council, 29 October. *Foreign Policy Bulletin,* November/December. 29 October.

Baker, James A. 1995. *The Politics of Diplomacy: Revolution, War and Peace 1989–1992.* New York: Putnam.

Ball, George. 1982. *The Past Has Another Pattern: Memoirs.* New York: Norton.

Barnes, Fred. 1991. The Hauk Factor. *New Republic,* 28 January: 8–9.

Barnouw, Erik. 1978. *The Sponsor.* New York: Oxford University Press.

Barrett, David M. 1994. *Uncertain Warriors: Lyndon Johnson and his Vietnam Advisers.* Lawrence, Kansas: University Press of Kansas.

Bass, Harold F. Jr., Dom Bonafede, and Charles C. Euchner. 1990. *The Presidents and the Public.* Washington, D.C.: Congressional Quarterly.

Baum, Matt. 1999. The opinionated public: How the mass media raised America's interest in war. Paper presented at the American Political Science Association Meetings, Atlanta, Ga., August.

Beal, Richard S., and Ronald H. Hinckley. 1984. Presidential decision making and opinion polls. *Annals of the American Academy of Political and Social Science* 472: 72–84.

Bennett, W. Lance. 1989. Marginalizing the majority: Conditioning public opinion. In *Manipulating Public Opinion: Essays on Public Opinion as a Dependent Variable.* Edited by Michael Margolis and Gary A. Mausar. Pacific Grove, Calif.: Brooks/Cole.

Berkowitz, William. 1973. The Impact of Anti-Vietnam Demonstrations upon National Public Opinion and Military Indicators. *Social Science Research,* 2(1): 1–14.

Berman, Larry. 1982. *Planning a Tragedy: The Americanization of the War in Vietnam.* New York: Norton.

Bernstein, Robert A. 1989. *Elections, Representation, and Congressional Voting Behavior: The Myth of Constituency Control.* Englewood Cliffs, N.J.: Prentice-Hall.

Berry, Jeffrey M. 1989. *The Interest Group Society.* 2d ed. Glenview, Ill.: Scott, Foresman.

Beschloss, Michael R. 1997. *Taking Charge: The Johnson White House Tapes, 1963–1964.* New York: Simon & Schuster.

Binder, David. 1993. Bosnia's bitter enemies sit down and talk in Geneva. *New York Times,* 4 January.

Binkley, Joel. 1988. White House seeks $36 million in aid for the contras. *New York Times,* 27 January: A1.

Blachman, Morris J., and Kenneth E. Sharpe. 1987–88. Central American traps: Challenging the Reagan agenda. *World Policy Journal* 5: 1–28.

Blumberg, Herbert, and Christopher French. 1994. *The Persian Gulf War: Views from the Social and Behavioral Sciences.* Lanham, Md: University Press of America.

Bollinger, William, and Daniel Lund. 1988. Gallup in Central America: Mixing the polls and propaganda. *The Nation* 246(18): 635.

Bonafede, Dom. 1990. Presidents and the news media. In *The Presidents and the Public.* Edited by Harold F. Bass Jr., Dom Bonafede, and Charles C. Euchner. Washington, D.C.: Congressional Quarterly.

Bond, Jon R., and Richard Fleisher. 1990. *The President in the Legislative Arena.* Chicago: University of Chicago Press.

Bond, Jon R., and Richard Fleisher. 1980. The limits of presidential popularity as a source of influence in the House. *Legislative Studies Quarterly* 5: 69–78.

Bond, Jon R., Richard Fleisher, and Michael Northrup. 1988. Public opinion and presidential support. *The Annals* 499: 47–63.

Boutros-Ghali, Boutros. 1999. *Unvanquished: A U.S.–U.N. Saga.* New York: Random House.

Bowen, Gordon L. 1989. Presidential action and public opinion about U.S. Nicaraguan policy: Limits to the "rally round the flag" syndrome. *PS: Political Science & Politics* 22: 793–801.

Boyd, Gerald M. 1986a. Reagan sees a "moral obligation" by U.S. to aid Nicaraguan rebels. *New York Times,* 11 March: 1.

Boyd, Gerald M. 1986b. Reagan asks arms aid for Nicaraguan rebels. *New York Times,* February 19: 7.

Brandt, Thomas D. 1985. Reagan fails to sell Latin policy at home or abroad, O'Neill says. *Washington Times,* June 6.

Brecher, John, and John Walcott. 1982. The secret war in Nicaragua. *Newsweek,* November 8: 42–53.

Brenner, Philip, and William M. LeoGrande. 1985. *Congress and the not-so-secret war against Nicaragua: A preliminary analysis.* Washington, D.C.: American University, typescript.

Brenner, Philip, and William M. LeoGrande. 1991. Congress and Nicaragua: The limits of alternative policymaking. In *Divided Democracy.* Edited by J. Thurber. Washington, D.C.: Congressional Quarterly.

Brewer, Thomas L. 1986. *American Foreign Policy: A Contemporary Introduction.* 2d ed. Englewood Cliffs, N.J.: Prentice-Hall.

Brzezinski, Zbigniew K. 1984. The three requirements for a bipartisan foreign policy. *Washington Quarterly White Paper.* Washington, D.C.: Center for Strategic and International Studies, Georgetown University.

Brody, Richard A. 1991. *Assessing the President: The Media, Elite Opinion, and Public Support.* Stanford, Calif.: Stanford University Press.

Buchanan, Patrick. 1986. The contras need our help. *Washington Post,* 5 March: 19A.

Bugajski, Janusz. 1995. *Nations in Turmoil.* Boulder, Colo.: Westview Press.

Bullock, Charles S. III. 1985. Congressional roll call voting in a two party south. *Social Science Quarterly* 66: 789–804.

Bundy, William. 1998. *A Tangled Web: the Making of Foreign Policy in Nixon Presidency.* New York: Hill & Wang.

Burke, John P., and Fred I. Greenstein. 1989. *How Presidents Test Reality: Decisions on Vietnam.* New York: Russell Sage Foundation.

Burstein, Paul, and William Freudenberg. 1978. Changing public policy: The impact of public opinion, anti-war demonstrations and war costs on Senate voting and Vietnam War motions. *American Journal of Sociology* 84(1): 99–122.

Bush, George. 1991. *Public Papers of the Presidents of the United States: George Bush 1990 Book II.* Washington, D.C.: United States Government Printing Office.

Bush, George. 1992. *Public Papers of the Presidents of the United States: George Bush 1991 Book I.* Washington, D.C.: United States Government Printing Office.

Bush, George. 1993a. *Public Papers of the President of the United States: George Bush 1992 Book I.* Washington, D.C.: United States Government Printing Office.

Bush, George. 1993b. *Public Papers of the President of the United States: George Bush 1992–93 Book II.* Washington, D.C.: United States Government Printing Office.

Bush, George (and Brent Scowcroft). 1998. *A World Transformed.* New York: Knopf. Distributed by Random House.

Buzenberg, William. 1986. Who got the $27 million intended for the contras? *New York Times,* 19 June: A27.

Campbell, Angus, Philip Converse, Warren Miller, and Donald Stokes. 1960. *The American Voter.* New York: John Wiley.

Cannon, Lori, and Tom Kenworthy. 1988. Reagan again vows support for contras. *Washington Post,* 23 March: A23.

Carson, Richard T., and Joe A. Oppenheimer. 1984. A method of estimating the personal ideology of political representatives. *American Political Science Review* 78: 163–78.

Caspary, William R. 1970. The "mood theory": A study of public opinion and foreign policy. *American Political Science Review* 64: 536–54.

Center for Policy Analysis. 1994. George Mason University, Fairfax, Va. November 30.

Chace, James. 1978. Is a foreign policy consensus possible? *Foreign Affairs* 57: 1–16.

Chappell, Henry W. Jr., and William R. Keech. 1985. A new view of political accountability for economic performance. *American Political Science Review* 79: 10–27.

Chardy, Alfonso. 1987. NSC oversaw campaign to sway contra aid vote. *Miami Herald,* 19 July: 18A.

Chayes, Antonia Handler, and Abram Chayes. 1996. *After the End.* In *The World and Yugoslavia's Wars.* Edited by Richard H. Ullman. New York: Council on Foreign Relations.

Chittick, William O., and Keith R. Billingsley. 1989. The structure of elite foreign policy beliefs. *Western Political Quarterly* 42: 201–24.

Chomsky, Noam. 1989. *Necessary Illusions: Thought Control in Democratic Societies.* Boston: South End Press.

Christopher, Warren. 1994a. Hearings of the Senate Foreign Relations Committee. Washington, D.C.: United States Government Printing Office. 23 February.

Christopher, Warren. 1994b. Hearing of the Foreign Operations Subcommittee of the Senate Appropriations Committee. *Federal News Service,* March 2.

Christopher, Warren. 1995. The Dayton Peace Agreement: Building Peace with Justice. *U.S. Department of State Dispatch Supplement,* 21 November. 6(5): 16–17.

Cigler, Allan J., and Burdett A. Loomis, eds. 1986. *Interest Group Politics.* 2d ed. Washington, D.C.: Congressional Quarterly.

Clausen, Aage R. 1973. *How Congressmen Decide: A Policy Focus.* New York: St. Martin's.

Clifford, Clark, with Richard Holbrooke. 1991. *Counsel to the President: A Memoir.* New York: Random House.

Clines, Francis X., and Steven R. Weisman. 1984. An interview with President Reagan on campaign issues. *New York Times,* 29 March: B11

Clinton, William J. 1995. *Public Papers of the Presidents of the United States William Jefferson Clinton 1994 Book I.* Washington, D.C.: United States Government Printing Office.

Clinton, Willam J. 1996a. *Public Papers of the Presidents of the United States: William Jefferson Clinton 1995 Book I.* Washington, D.C.: United States Government Printing Office.

Clinton, William J. 1996b. *Public Papers of the Presidents of the United States: William Jefferson Clinton 1995 Book II.* Washington, D.C.: United States Government Printing Office.

Clymer, Adam. 1983. Poll finds Americans don't know U.S. positions on Central America. *New York Times,* 1 July: A1.

Clymer, Adam. 1985. Most Americans in survey oppose aid for overthrow of Sandinistas. *New York Times,* 5 June: A8.

Coalition for a New Foreign and Military Policy and Commission on U.S.-Central American Relations. 1985. *Central America 1985: Basic information and legislative history on U.S.-Central American relations.* Washington, D.C.: Coalition for a New Foreign and Military Policy and Commission on U.S.-Central American Relations.

Cohen, William S., and George J. Mitchell. 1989. *Men of Zeal: A Candid Inside Story of the Iran-Contra Hearings.* New York: Penguin Books.

Cohen, Bernard C. 1957. *The Political Process and Foreign Policy: The Making of the Japanese Peace Settlement.* Princeton, N.J.: Princeton University Press.

Cohen, Bernard C. 1973. *The Public's Impact on Foreign Policy.* Boston: Little, Brown.

Cohn, Betsy, and Patricia Hynds. 1987. The manipulation of the religious issue. In *Reagan Versus the Sandinistas: The Undeclared War on Nicaragua.* Edited by Thomas W. Walker. Boulder, Colo.: Westview.

Collier, C. 1986. Foreign policy roles of the president and Congress. Congressional Research Service, Report No. 86-163 F, 16 September.

The colonel presents his case: His beliefs, his work and his grievances. 1987. *New York Times,* 10 July: A6.

Congressional Quarterly. 1982. *The Washington Lobby.* 4th ed. Washington, D.C.: Congressional Quarterly.

Congressional Quarterly. 1986. *Congressional Quarterly Almanac, 99th Congress, 1st session 1985.* Washington, D.C.: Congressional Quarterly.

Congressional Quarterly. 1987. *Congressional Quarterly Almanac, 99th Congress, 2nd session 1986.* Washington, D.C.: Congressional Quarterly.

Congressional Quarterly. 1992. *Weekly Report, June 13, 1992.* Washington, D.C.: Congressional Quarterly.

Congressional Record. 1986. Washington, D.C.: Government Printing Office. S2425–26.

Congressmen attacked over El Salvador stand. 1983. *New York Times,* 5 May: D23.

Conroy, Michael E. 1987. Economic aggression as an instrument of low-intensity warfare. In *Reagan Versus the Sandinistas: The Undeclared War on Nicaragua.* Edited by Thomas W. Walker. Boulder, Colo.: Westview.

Converse, Philip E. 1964. The nature of belief systems in mass publics. In *Ideology and Discontent.* Edited by David E. Apter. New York: Free Press.

Converse, Philip E., and Howard Schuman. 1970. Silent majorities and the Vietnam War. *Scientific American* 222: 17–25.

Copson, Raymond W. 1988. The Reagan doctrine: U.S. assistance to anti-Marxist guerrillas. *CRS Issue Brief,* 11 March.

Council for Inter-American Security. 1987. *West Watch.* 1986 review. Washington, D.C.: Council for Inter-American Security. (February–March).

Crabb, Cecil V. Jr., and Pat M. Holt. 1980. *Invitation to Struggle: Congress, the President and Foreign policy.* Washington, D.C.: Congressional Quarterly.

Dahl, Robert A. 1966. Further reflections on "the elitist theory of democracy." *American Political Science Review* 60: 296–305.

Dahl, Robert A. 1971. *Polyarchy: Participation and Opposition.* New Haven, Conn.: Yale University Press.

Dahl, Robert A. 1984. *Modern Political Analysis.* 4th ed. Englewood Cliffs, N.J.: Prentice-Hall.

Dallek, Robert. 1998. *Flawed Giant: Lyndon Johnson and His Times, 1961–1973.* New York: Oxford University Press.

Davidson, Roger H., and Walter J. Oleszek. 1990. *Congress and Its Members.* 3rd ed. Washington, D.C.: Congressional Quarterly.

Davis, M. Scott, and Christopher Kline. 1988. *The Role of the Public in Foreign Policy Making: An Overview of the Literature.* Washington, D.C.: Roosevelt Center for American Policy Studies.

Day 2: The president's knowledge and the ayatollah's money. 1987. *New York Times,* 9 July: A10–11.

DeBenedetti, Charles. 1990. *An American Ordeal: The Antiwar Movement of the Vietnam Era.* Syracuse, N.Y.: Syracuse University Press.

Decision Making Information. 1985. A survey of national attitudes towards Nicaragua, prepared for Republican National Committee. McLean, Va.: Decision Making Information [Wirthlin Group]. Mimeo.

Defense Department. 1971. *Pentagon Papers: The Defense Dept. History of U.S. Decision Making on Vietnam.* Boston: Beacon Press.

Deibel, Terry L. 1987. *Presidents, Public Opinion and Power: The Nixon, Carter and Reagan Years.* New York: Foreign Policy Association.

Destler, I.M., Leslie H. Gelb, and Anthony Lake. 1984. *Our Own Worst Enemy: The Unmaking of American Foreign Policy.* New York: Simon & Schuster.

Devine, Donald J. 1970. *The Attentive Public: Polyarchial Democracy.* Chicago: Rand McNally.

Dickinson, James R., and Maralee Schwartz. 1986. NCPAC is gunning for the "Ortega 33." *Washington Post,* 20 February: A14.

Diskin, Martin. 1987. The manipulation of indigenous struggles. In *Reagan Versus the Sandinistas: The Undeclared War on Nicaragua.* Edited by Thomas W. Walker. Boulder, Colo.: Westview.

Drew, Elizabeth. 1991. Letter from Washington. *The New Yorker,* 4 February: 82–90.

Drew, Elizabeth. 1995. *On the Edge: The Clinton Presidency.* New York: Simon & Schuster.

Duscha, Julius. 1971. The political pro who runs defense. *New York Times Magazine,* 13 June.

Duscha, Julius. 1973. Campus Press Freedom and Responsibility. Washington, D.C.: American Association of State Colleges and Universities.

Eagleburger, Lawrence. 1992a. Intervention at the London Conference on the Former Yugoslavia. In *U.S. Department of State Dispatch,* 3, 7 September.

Eagleburger, Lawrence. 1992b. Identifying War Criminals. In *U.S. Department of State Dispatch,* 52.

Eckstein, Harry. 1975. Case study and theory in political science. In *Handbook of Political Science.* Edited by Fred Greenstein and Nelson Polsby, 7: 79–138.

Economist, 1994. Can Bombs Save Bosnia? London: The Economist Newspaper Ltd., 12 February: 15.

Edwards, George C. III. 1976. Presidential influence in the House: Presidential prestige as a source of presidential power. *American Political Science Review* 70: 101–13.

Edwards, George C. III. 1978. Presidential electoral performance as a source of presidential power. *American Journal of Political Science* 22: 152–68.

Edwards, George C. III. 1980. *Presidential Influence in Congress.* San Francisco: Freeman.

Edwards, George C. III. 1981. Congressional responsiveness to public opinion: The case of presidential popularity. In *Public Opinion and Public Policy.* Edited by Norman R. Luttbeg. Itasca, Ill.: Peacock.

Edwards, George C. III. 1983. *The Public Presidency: The Pursuit of Popular Support.* New York: St. Martin's.

Edwards, George C. III. 1985. Measuring presidential success in Congress: Alternative approaches. *Journal of Politics* 47: 667–85.

Edwards, George C. III. 1986. The two presidencies: A re-evaluation. *American Politics Quarterly* 14: 247–63.

Edwards, George C. III. 1989. *At the Margins: Presidential Leadership of Congress.* New Haven: Yale University Press.

Edwards, George C. III. 1990. *Presidential Approval: A Sourcebook.* Baltimore: Johns Hopkins University Press.

Engelberg, Stephen. 1985. Thousands join protest in Washington. *New York Times,* 21 April: 22.

Erskine, Hazel. 1970. The polls: Is war a mistake? *Public Opinion Quarterly* 34: 134–50.

Euchner, Charles C. 1990a. The presidency and interest groups. In *The Presidents and the Public.* Edited by Harold F. Bass Jr., Dom Bonafede, and Charles C. Euchner. Washington, D.C.: Congressional Quarterly.

Euchner, Charles C. 1990b. Public support and opinion. In *The Presidents and the Public.* Edited by Harold F. Bass Jr., Dom Bonafede, and Charles C. Euchner. Washington, D.C.: Congressional Quarterly.

Excerpts from address of Weinberger. 1984. *New York Times,* 29 November: A5.

Falcoff, Mark. 1987. Contra-dictions: Public leadership and opinion in Central America. *Public Opinion* 10(4): 45–51.

Farkas, Steve, Robert Y. Shapiro, and Benjamin I. Page. 1990. The dynamics of public opinion and policy. Paper presented at the annual meeting of the American Association for Public Opinion Research, Lancaster, Penn.

Federal Information Systems. 1991. Washington, D.C.: March 5.

Federal Information Systems. 1991. Washington, D.C.: February 10.

Felton, John. 1984. On foreign aid, more stumbling blocks. *Congressional Quarterly Weekly Report* 42: 2418.

Felton, John. 1985a. Congress sought to place limits early on U.S. covert assistance to "contras." *Congressional Quarterly Weekly Report* 43: 710–11.

Felton, John. 1985b. House, in dramatic shift, backs contra aid. *Congressional Quarterly Weekly Report* 43: 1139–40.

Felton, John. 1986a. After House defeat, Reagan to push "contra" aid. *Congressional Quarterly Weekly Report* 44: 648–53.

Felton, John. 1986b. Reagan loses ground on "contra" aid program. *Congressional Quarterly Weekly Report* 44: 535–37.

Felton, John. 1989. Hill gives contra package bipartisan launch. *Congressional Quarterly Weekly Report* 47: 832–36.

Fiorina, Morris. 1981. *Retrospective Voting in American National Elections.* New Haven, Conn.: Yale University Press.

Fisher, Louis. 1978. *White House-Congress Relationships: Information Exchange and Lobbying.* Congressional Research Service Report No. 78-147 GOV. Washington, D.C.: Library of Congress.

Fitzgerald, Francis. 1972. *Fire in the Lake.* Boston: Little, Brown.

Flaherty, Peter. 1986. *Memo to key supporters: Contra aid victory!* Washington, D.C.: Citizens for Reagan.

Fleisher, Richard, and Jon R. Bond. 1983. Assessing presidential support in the House: Lessons from Reagan and Carter. *Journal of Politics* 45: 745–58.

Foreign Policy Association. 1990. *Foreign Policy Bulletin,* New York: Foreign Policy Association.

Foster, H. Schuyler. 1983. *Activism Replaces Isolationism.* Washington, D.C.: Foxhall.

Foyle, Douglas C. 1996. The influence of public opinion on American foreign policy decision making: Context, beliefs, and process. Ph.D. dissertation, Political Science Department, Duke University, Durham, N.C.

Foyle, Douglas C. 1999. *Counting the Public in: Presidents, Public Opinion, and Foreign Policy.* New York: Columbia University Press.

Franck, Thomas M., and Edward Weisband. 1979. *Foreign Policy by Congress.* New York: Oxford University Press.

Franke, Richard Herbert, and James D. Kaul. 1978. The Hawthorne experiments: First statistical interpretation. *American Sociological Review.* 43: 623–43.

Fraser, Cleveland R., John C. Green, and James L. Guth. 1988. The right wing of the eagle:

The foreign policy attitudes of Republican party activists. Paper presented at the International Studies Association, St. Louis, Mo.

Fraser, Cleveland R., John C. Green, and James L. Guth. 1989. The left wing of the eagle: The foreign policy attitudes of Democratic party activists. Paper presented at the American Political Science Association, Atlanta, Ga.

Free, Lloyd A., and Hadley Cantril. 1968. *The Political Beliefs of Americans.* New York: Simon & Schuster.

Friends Committee on National Legislation. 1970. 1969 legislative report—Vietnam. Washington, D.C.: Friends Committee on National Legislation.

Frireman, Ken. 1986. Reagan's efforts were a major factor in aid turnaround. *Miami Herald,* 27 June.

Fritz, Sara. 1986a. Contras lobby angers swing-vote Democrats. *Los Angeles Times,* 19 March: 12.

Fritz, Sara. 1986b. Democrats swinging over to Reagan's contra stand. *Los Angeles Times,* 15 April: 4, 24.

Fuerbunger, Jonathan. 1987. Contra aid accord set by Congress and White House. *New York Times,* 21 December: A1, 17.

Gelb, Leslie H. 1982. Reagan backing covert actions, officials assert. *New York Times,* 14 March: A1, A12.

George, Alexander. 1979. Chapter in *Diplomacy: New approaches in history, theory, and policy.* Edited by Paul Gordon Lauren. New York: Free Press.

Gibbons, William Conrad. 1987. *The U.S. Government and the Vietnam War, Executive and Legislative Relations.* 4 vols. Princeton, N.J.: Princeton University Press.

Ginsberg, Benjamin. 1986. *The Captive Public: How Mass Opinion Promotes State Power.* New York: Basic Books.

Gitlin, Todd. 1987. *The Sixties: Years of Hope, Days of Rage.* New York: Bantam.

Glennon, John P. ed. 1992. *Foreign Relations of the United States, 1964–1968: Volume I: Vietnam 1964.* Washington, D.C.: United States Government Printing Office.

Gompert, David C. 1996. The United States and Yugoslavia's wars. In *The World and Yugoslavia's Wars.* Edited by Richard H. Ullman. New York: Council on Foreign Relations, pp. 122–44.

Goulding, Phil G. 1970. *Confirm or Deny: Informing the People on National Security.* New York: Harper & Row.

Graber, Doris A. 1968. *Public Opinion, the President, and Foreign Policy: Four Case Studies from the Formative Years.* New York: Holt, Rinehart, and Winston.

Graber, Doris A., ed. 1982. *The President and the Public.* Philadelphia: Institute for the Study of Human Issues.

Graham, Thomas W. 1988. The pattern and importance of public knowledge in the nuclear age. *Journal of Conflict Resolution* 32: 319–34.

Graham, Thomas W. 1989. The politics of failure: Strategic nuclear arms control, public opinion, and domestic politics in the United States—1945–1980. Ph.D. dissertation, M.I.T., Cambridge, Mass.

Gravel, Mike, ed. 1971–72. *The Pentagon Papers: The Defense Department History of United States Decisionmaking on Vietnam.* Boston: Beacon Press.

Gutman, Roy. 1988. *Banana Diplomacy: The Making of American Policy in Nicaragua, 1981–1987.* New York: Simon & Schuster.

Gutman, Roy. 1992. "Serbian Guards Executed Prisoners, Survivor Says," *Los Angeles Times.* 5 August: A14.

Haig, Alexander. 1984. *Caveat: Realism, Reagan, and Foreign Policy.* New York: Macmillan.

Halberstam, David. 1972. *The Best and the Brightest.* New York: Penguin.

Halloran, Richard. 1984. U.S. will not drift into a Latin war, Weinberger says. *New York Times,* 29 November: A1.

Harmon, Katherine Newcomer, and Marsha L. Brauen. 1979. Joint electoral outcomes as cues for congressional support of U.S. presidents. *Legislative Studies Quarterly* 4: 281–99.

Heith, Diane T. 1998. White House use of public opinion polls: Staffing the White House public opinion apparatus. *Public Opinion Quarterly* 62(2): 165–89.

Herring, George C. 1986. *America's Longest War: The United States and Vietnam, 1950–1975.* 2d ed. New York: Knopf. Distributed by Random House.

Hersh, Seymour. 1983. *The Price of Power: Kissinger in the Nixon White House.* New York: Summit Books.

Hibbs, Douglas A. 1982a. On the demand for economic outcomes: Macroeconomic performance and mass political support in the United States, Great Britain, and Germany. *Journal of Politics* 44: 426–62.

Hibbs, Douglas A. 1982b. The dynamics of political support for American presidents among occupational and partisan groups. *American Journal of Political Science* 26: 312–32.

Hilsman, Roger. 1987. *The Politics of Policy-Making in Defense and Foreign Affairs.* Englewood Cliffs, N.J.: Prentice-Hall.

Hinckley, Ronald H. 1986. Domestic public opinion and U.S. national security issues. Second Quarterly Report to NSC Crisis Management Center. Washington, D.C.: National Security Council.

Hinckley, Ronald H. 1988a. Polls and policymakers: The case of the National Security Council. Paper presented at the meeting of AAPOR: May.

Hinckley, Ronald H. 1988b. Public attitudes toward key foreign policy events. *Journal of Conflict Resolution* 32: 295–318.

Hinckley, Ronald H. 1992. *People, Polls, and Policymakers: American Public Opinion and National Security,* New York: Lexington Books.

Hodgson, Godfrey. 1976. *America in Our Time.* Garden City, New York: Doubleday.

Hoffman, David. 1985. Reagan launches new initiative for "contra aid." *Washington Post,* 5 April: A1, A22.

Hoffmann, Stanley, 1996. Yugoslavia: Implications for Europe and for European Institutions. In *The World and Yugoslavia's Wars.* Edited by Richard H. Ullman. New York: Council on Foreign Relations, pp. 97–121.

Holmes, Jack E. 1985. *The Mood/Interest Theory of American Foreign Policy.* Lexington, KY. University Press of Kentucky.

Holsti, Ole R. 1984. *American Leadership in World Affairs: Vietnam and the Breakdown of Consensus.* Boston: Allen & Unwin.

Holsti, Ole R. 1987. A leadership divided: The foreign policy beliefs of American leaders, 1976–89. In *The Domestic Sources of American Foreign Policy.* Edited by Charles W. Kegley Jr. and Eugene Wittkopf. New York: St. Martin's.

Holsti, Ole R. 1988a. The domestic and foreign policy beliefs of American leaders. *Journal of Conflict Resolution* 32: 229–48.

Holsti, Ole R. 1988b. Public opinion and foreign policy: A wish list. Paper presented at International Society of Political Psychology Seminar, New York.

Holsti, Ole R. 1992. Public opinion and foreign policy: Challenges to the Almond-Lippmann consensus. Mershon Series: Research programs and debates. *International Studies Quarterly* 36: 439–66.

Holsti, Ole R. 1996. *Public Opinion and American Foreign Policy.* Ann Arbor: University of Michigan Press.

Holsti, Ole R., and James N. Rosenau. 1984. *American Leadership in World Affairs: Vietnam and the Breakdown of Consensus.* Boston: Allen & Unwin.

Holsti, Ole R., and James N. Rosenau. 1986. The foreign policy beliefs of American leaders: Some further thoughts on theory and method. *International Studies Quarterly* 30: 473–84.

Holsti, Ole R., and James N. Rosenau. 1990. The structure of foreign policy attitudes: American leaders, 1976–1984. *Journal of Politics* 52: 94–125.

Holsti, Ole R., and James N. Rosenau. 1993. The structure of foreign policy beliefs among American opinion leaders—after the Cold War. *Millennium* 22: 235–78.

Honomichl, Jack J. 1989. How Ronald Reagan took America's pulse. *Advertising Age,* 23 January: 1.

Horton, John. 1985. The real intelligence failure. *Foreign Service Journal* 62(2): 22–5.

Hughes, Barry B. 1978. *The Domestic Context of American Foreign Policy.* San Francisco: Freeman.

Hurwitz, Jon. 1989. Presidential leadership and public followership. In *Manipulating Public Opinion.* Edited by Michael Margolis and Gary A. Mausar. Pacific Grove, Calif.: Brooks/ Cole.

Hurwitz, Jon, and Mark Peffley. 1987. How are foreign policy attitudes structured? A hierarchical model. *American Political Science Review* 81: 1099–1120.

Hurwitz, Jon, and Mark Peffley. 1988. Toward a theoretical approach to the study of foreign policy opinionation. Paper presented at Workshop on Public Opinion and Foreign Policy, International Society of Political Psychology, New York City.

Hurwitz, Jon, and Mark Peffley. 1990. Americans respond to changes in Soviet-American relations: The impact of recent events on foreign policy belief systems. Mershon Center, Columbus, Ohio. Mimeo.

Hurwitz, Jon, Mark Peffley, and Paul Raymond. 1989. Presidential support during the Iran-Contra affair: An individual-level analysis of presidential reappraisal. *American Politics Quarterly* 17: 359–85.

Ippolito, Dennis S., Thomas G. Walker, and Kenneth L. Kolson. 1976. *Public Opinion and Responsible Democracy.* Englewood Cliffs, N.J.: Prentice-Hall.

Issacson, Walter. 1993. *Kissinger: A Biography.* New York: Simon & Schuster.

Issacson, Walter. 1997. *The Wise Men: Six Friends and the World They Made.* New York: Simon & Schuster.

Iyengar, Shanto, and Donald Kinder. 1987. *News That Matters.* Chicago: University of Chicago Press.

Jacobs, Lawrence R. 1992. Institutions and culture: Health policy and public opinion in the U.S. and Britain. *World Politics* 44: 179–209.

Jacobs, Lawrence R., and Robert Y. Shapiro. 1995. The rise of presidential polling: The Nixon White House in historical perspective. *Public Opinion Quarterly* 59(2): 163–95.

Jacobs, Lawrence R. and Robert Y. Shapiro. 2000. *Politicans Don't Pander: Political Manipulation and the Loss of Democratic Responsiveness.* Chicago: University of Chicago Press.

Jentleson, Bruce W. 1992. The pretty prudent public: Post post-Vietnam American opinion on the use of military force. *International Studies Quarterly* 36(1): 49–74.

Jentleson, Bruce W., and Rebecca L. Britton. 1998. Still pretty prudent: Post-Cold War American public opinion on the use of military force. *Journal of Conflict Resolution* 42(August): 395–487.

Johnson, Lyndon B. 1964. *My Hope for America.* New York: Random House.

Johnson, Lyndon B. 1971. *The Vantage Point: Perspectives of the Presidency, 1963–1969.* New York: Holt, Rinehart and Winston.

Johnson, Lyndon B. 1997. *Lyndon B. Johnson's Vietnam Papers: A Documentary Collection.* Edited by David M. Barrett. College Station: Texas A&M University Press.

Johnson, Victor. 1989. Congress and contra aid. In *Latin America and Caribbean Con-*

temporary Record, 1987–1988. Edited by Abraham F. Lowenthal. New York: Holmes & Meier.

Johnston, David. 1990. Poindexter is found guilty of all five criminal charges for Iran-Contra cover-up. *New York Times,* 8 April: A1.

Johnston, Sir Russell. 1993. *The Yugoslav Conflict: Chronology of Events from 30th May 1991–8th November 1993.* Paris: Information Document of the Defence Committee of the Western European Union, November 29.

Kalt, Joseph P., and Mark A. Zupan. 1984. Capture and ideology in the economic theory of politics. *American Economic Review* 74: 279–300.

Karnow, Stanley. 1983. *Vietnam: The War Nobody Won.* New York: Foreign Policy Association.

Karnow, Stanley. 1991. *Vietnam, a History.* Rev. and updated ed. New York: Penguin Books.

Katz, Andrew Z. 1997. Public opinion and foreign policy: The Nixon Administration and the pursuit of peace with honor in Vietnam. *Presidential Studies Quarterly* 28(Summer): 496–513.

Kau, James B., and Paul H. Rubin. 1979. Self-interest, ideology, and logrolling in congressional voting. *Journal of Law and Economics* 22: 365–84.

Kegley, Charles W. Jr., and Eugene R. Wittkopf. 1979. *American Foreign Policy: Patterns and Process.* New York: St. Martin's.

Kegley, Charles W. Jr., and Eugene R. Wittkopf., eds. 1987. *The Domestic Sources of American Foreign Policy.* New York: St. Martin's.

Kegley, Charles W. Jr., and Eugene R. Wittkopf. 1991. *American Foreign Policy: Patterns and Process.* 4th ed. New York: St. Martin's.

Kellerman, Barbara. 1984. *The Political Presidency: Practice of Leadership from Kennedy through Reagan.* New York: Oxford University Press.

Kelley, Stanley. 1983. *Interpreting Elections.* Princeton, N.J.: Princeton University Press.

Kennan, George F. 1951. *American Diplomacy, 1900–1950.* New York: Mentor Books.

Kenney, George. 1992. See no evil, make no policy. *The Washington Monthly* 24(November): 33–35.

Kenworthy, Eldon. 1987. Selling the policy. In *Reagan versus the Sandinistas: The Undeclared War on Nicaragua.* Edited by Thomas W. Walker. Boulder, Colo.: Westview.

Kernell, Samuel. 1977. Presidential popularity and negative voting. *American Political Science Review* 71: 44–66.

Kernell, Samuel. 1978. Explaining presidential popularity. *American Political Science Review* 72: 506–22.

Kernell, Samuel. 1986. *Going Public: New Strategies of Presidential Leadership.* Washington, D.C.: Congressional Quarterly.

Key, V. O. 1961. *Public Opinion and American Democracy.* New York: Knopf.

Key, V. O. 1966. *The Responsible Electorate: Rationality in Presidential Voting, 1936–1960.* Cambridge, Mass.: Harvard University Press.

Kinzer, Stephen. 1986. Nicaraguan rebel chief gives up fight. *New York Times,* 17 May: 3.

Kissinger, Henry. 1979. *The White House Years.* New York: Little, Brown.

Kissinger, Henry. 1982. *Years of Upheaval.* New York: Little, Brown.

Kissinger, Henry. 1996. No glossing over Bosnia troubles, *Houston Chronicle,* 8 September: O1.

Kissinger, Henry. 1999. *Years of Renewal.* New York: Simon & Schuster.

Klingberg, Frank L. 1979. Cyclical trends in American foreign policy moods and their policy implications. In *Challenges to America: U.S. Foreign Policy in the 1980s.* Edited by Charles W. Kegley Jr. and Patrick McGowan. Beverly Hills, Calif.: Sage.

Klingberg, Frank L. 1983. *Cyclical Trends in American Foreign Policy Moods: The Unfolding of America's World Role.* Lanham, Md.: University Press of America.

Knudsen, Baard Bredrup. 1984. Europe and contemporary schools of thought in U.S. foreign policy: From alliance to alienation? Paper presented at the International Studies Association, Atlanta, Ga.

Knudsen, Baard Bredrup. 1985. From ideology to foreign policy "schools of thought" to policy preferences: American foreign policy elites and Europe. Paper presented at the International Studies Association, Washington, D.C.

Kornbluh, Peter. 1987. *Nicaragua: The Price of Intervention*. Washington, D.C.: Institute for Policy Studies.

Krosnick, Jon A., and Donald R. Kinder. 1990. Altering the foundations of support for the president through priming. *American Political Science Review* 84: 497–512.

Kull, Steven. 1993. *U.S. Public Attitudes on Intervention in Bosnia*. Washington D.C.: Program on International Policy Attitudes.

Kull, Steven. 1999. Expecting more to say: The American public on its role in government decision making. Washington, D.C.: Center on Policy Attitudes, May 10.

Kull, Steven, and I. M. Destler. 1999. *Misreading the Public: The Myth of a New Isolationalism*. Washington, D.C.: Brookings Institution Press.

Kull, Steven and Clark Ramsay. 1994. *U.S. Public Attitudes on Involvement Bosnia*. College Park, MD: Center for International Security Studies.

Kusnitz, Leonard A. 1984. *Public Opinion and Foreign Policy: America's China Policy, 1949–79*. Westport, Conn.: Greenwood.

Ladd, Everett Carll. 1983. Public opinion on Central America. *Public Opinion Quarterly* 6(4): 20.

Ladd, Everett Carll. 1987. Where the public stands on Nicaragua. *Public Opinion Quarterly* 10(3): 2–4, 59–60.

Laird, Melvin R. 1962. *A House Divided; America's Strategy Gap*. Chicago: H. Regnery Co.

LaMay, Craig. 1991. By the numbers. In *The Media at War*. Edited by Craig LaMay, Martha FritzSimon, and Jeanne Sahadi. New York: Columbia University, Freedom Forum Media Studies Center.

Lamert, James B. 1992. Effective Public Opinion. In *Public Opinion, the Press, and Public Policy*. Edited by D. Kannamer. Westport, CT: Praeger.

Langley, Monica. 1986. But in Florida, Rep. MacKay takes heat for opposing rebels. *Wall Street Journal,* 13 October: 34.

Lanoue, David J. 1989. The "Teflon Factor": Ronald Reagan and comparative presidential popularity. *Polity* 21: 481–501.

Layne, Christopher, and Ted Galen Carpenter. 1990. Time for Congress to vote on the issue of war in the Gulf. Foreign Policy Briefing No. 5, Cato Institute, 14 December.

Lazarsfeld, Paul F., Bernard Berelson, and Hazel Gaudet. 1968. *The People's Choice*. New York: Columbia University Press.

LeoGrande, William M. 1984. *Central American and the Polls*. Washington, D.C.: Washington Office on Latin America.

LeoGrande, William M. 1987. The contras and Congress. In *Reagan versus the Sandinistas: The Undeclared War on Nicaragua*. Edited by Thomas W. Walker. Boulder, Colo.: Westview.

LeoGrande, William M. 1990. Did the public matter? The impact of opinion on congressional support for Ronald Reagan's Nicaragua policy. Paper presented at the Conference on Public Opinion and U.S. Foreign Policy: The Case of Contra Funding, Princeton University, Princeton, N.J.

LeoGrande, William M. 1993. The controversy over contra aid, 1981–90: An historical narrative. In *Public Opinion in U.S. Foreign Policy: The Controversy Over Contra Aid*. Edited by Richard Sobel. Lanham, Md.: Rowman & Littlefield.

LeoGrande, William M., and Philip Brenner. 1993. The House divided: Ideological polarization over aid to the Nicaraguan contras. *Legislative Studies Quarterly,* 18.

Lepper, Mary Milling. 1971. *Foreign Policy Formulation: A Case Study of the Nuclear Test Ban Treaty of 1963.* Columbus, Oh.: Charles E. Merrill.

Letters to the Editor. 1988–89. *Foreign Policy* 73: 171–85.

Levering, Ralph B. 1978. *The Public and American Foreign Policy, 1918–1978.* New York: Morrow.

Lewis-Beck, Michael S., and Tom W. Rice. 1982. Presidential popularity and presidential vote. *Public Opinion Quarterly* 46: 534–37.

Lichter, S. Robert, Stanley Rothman, and Linda S. Lichter. 1986. *The Media Elite: America's New Power Brokers.* Bethesda, Md.: Adler and Adler.

Linsky, Martin. 1986. *Impact: How the Press Affects Federal Policy Making.* New York: W.W. Norton.

Lippman, Thomas, W. 1994. Perry suggests air strikes might go beyond Sarajevo. Washington, D.C., *The Washington Post,* 14 February: A20.

Lippmann, Walter. 1922. *Public Opinion.* New York: Harcourt, Brace and Company.

Lippmann, Walter. 1955. *Essays in the Public Philosophy.* Boston: Little, Brown.

Lipset, Seymour Martin. 1985. Feeling better: Measuring the nation's confidence. *Public Opinion* 8(2): 6–9, 56–58.

Lipset, Seymour Martin, and William Schneider. 1983. *The Confidence Gap.* Baltimore: Johns Hopkins University Press.

Lipset, Seymour Martin, and William Schneider. 1987. The confidence gap during the Reagan years, 1981–1987. *Political Science Quarterly* 102: 1–23.

Lockerbie, Brad, and Stephen A. Borrelli. 1990. Question wording and public support for contra aid, 1983–1986. *Public Opinion Quarterly* 54: 195–208.

Lord, Carnes. 1984. In defense of public diplomacy. *Commentary* 77: 42–50.

Los Angeles Times. 1996. America in the Eye of the Hurricane. 8 September.

Lowi, Theodore J. 1969. *The End of Liberalism.* New York: W. W. Norton.

Lowi, Theodore J. 1985. *The Personal President: Power Invested, Promise Unfulfilled.* Ithaca, N.Y.: Cornell University Press.

Lunch, William L., and Peter W. Sperlich. 1979. American public opinion and the war in Vietnam. *Western Political Quarterly* 32: 21–44.

Luttbeg, Norman R., ed. 1981. *Public Opinion and Public Policy.* 3rd ed. Itasca, Ill.: Peacock Publishers.

McCormick, James M. 1992. *American Foreign Policy and Process.* Itasca, Ill.: F. E. Peacock Publishers.

McCormick, James M., and Eugene R. Wittkopf. 1990. Bipartisanship, partisanship, and ideology. Congressional-executive foreign policy relations, 1947–1988. *Journal of Politics* 52: 1077–1100.

McManus, Doyle. 1986. U.S. resumes funding for rebel leader Pastora. *Los Angeles Times,* 12 March: 1.

McNamara, Robert S. 1986. *Blundering into Disaster: Surviving the First Century of the Nuclear Age.* New York: Pantheon Books.

McNamara, Robert S., with Brian VanDeMark. 1995. *In Retrospect: The Tragedy and Lessons of Vietnam.* New York: Times Books.

McNamara, Robert S., James G. Blight, and Robert K. Brigham, with Thomas J. Biersteber and Herbert Y. Schandler. 1999. *Argument without End: In Search of Answers to the Vietnam Tragedy.* New York: Public Affairs.

McNeil, Frank. 1988. *War and Peace in Central America: Reality and Illusion.* New York: Scribner.

Maass, Arthur. 1983. *Congress and the Common Good.* New York: Basic Books.

MacKuen, Michael Bruce. 1983. Political drama, economic conditions, and the dynamics of presidential popularity. *American Journal of Political Science* 27:165–92.

Madison, James, Alexander Hamilton, and John Jay. 1937. *The Federalist Papers.* Introduction by Edward Mead Earle. New York: Modern Library.

Maggiotto, Michael A., and Eugene R. Wittkopf. 1981. American public attitudes toward foreign policy. *International Studies Quarterly* 25: 601–31.

Margolis, Michael, and Gary A. Mausar. 1989. *Manipulating Public Opinion: Essays on Public Opinion as a Dependent Variable.* Pacific Grove, Calif.: Brooks/Cole.

Market Opinion Research. 1988. *Americans Talk Security: A Survey of American Voters' Attitudes Concerning National Security Issues.* National Surveys 4 and 5, April and May. Detroit: Market Opinion Research.

Markus, Gregory B. 1982. Political attitudes during an election year. *American Political Science Review* 76: 538–60.

Marra, Robin F., Charles W. Ostrom Jr., and Dennis M. Simon. 1990. Foreign policy and presidential popularity: Creating windows of opportunity in the perpetual election. *Journal of Conflict Resolution* 34: 558–623.

"Martial Problems." 1994. *The Economist,* 3 December: 15.

Martin, Jeanne. 1976. Presidential elections and administration support among congressmen. *American Journal of Political Science* 20: 483–89.

Matthews, Donald R., and James A. Stimson. 1975. *Yeas and nays: Normal decision-making in the U.S. House of Representatives.* New York: John Wiley & Sons.

Mayhew, David R. 1974. *Congress: The Electoral Connection.* New Haven, Conn.: Yale University Press.

Maxwell, Kenneth. 1994. Review of *Public Opinion in U.S. Foreign Policy. Foreign Affairs* 73(2): 160.

Medding, Peter Y. 1989. Elitist democracy: An unsuccessful critique of a misunderstood theory. *Journal of Politics* 31: 641–64.

Merry, Robert W. 1986. Reagan's risky tack ties defeat of contra aid to Soviet takeover or U.S. invasion of Nicaragua. *Wall Street Journal,* 5 March: 64.

Miller, Warren E. 1967. Voting and foreign policy. In *Domestic Sources of Foreign Policy.* Edited by James N. Rosenau. New York: Free Press.

Miller, Warren E., and Donald Stokes. 1963. Constituency influence in Congress. *American Political Science Review* 57(March): 45–56.

Moffett, George. 1985. Reagan changes course in Central America policy. *Christian Science Monitor,* 5 April: 1.

Monroe, Alan. 1979. Consistency between public preferences and national policy decisions. *American Politics Quarterly* 7: 3–19.

Monroe, Alan. 1998. Public opinion and public policy, 1980–1993. *Public Opinion Quarterly* 62(1): 6–28.

Moore, David W. 1992. *Superpollsters: How They Measure and Manipulate Public Opinion in America.* New York: Four Walls Eight Windows.

Morgan, Edward P. 1994. *The Sixties Experience: Hard Lessons about Modern America.* Philadelphia: Temple University Press,

Moyers, Bill. 1968. One thing we learned. *Foreign Affairs* 46(4): 657–64.

Mueller, John E. 1970. Presidential popularity from Truman to Johnson. *American Political Science Review* 64(1): 18–34.

Mueller, John E. 1973. *War, Presidents and Public Opinion.* New York: Wiley.

Mueller, John E. 1994. *Policy and Opinion in the Gulf War.* Chicago: University of Chicago Press.

Nacos, Bridgette, Robert Shapiro, and Pierangelo Isernia. 2000. *Decisionmaking in a Glass*

House: Mass Media, Public Opinion and American and European Foreign Policy in the Twenty-first Century. Lanham, MD: Rowman & Littlefield.

National Security Council. 1985a. Action memorandum: Subject: Coordinating our Nicaraguan resistance strategy. Washington, D.C.: National Security Council.

National Security Council. 1985b. Intelligence document: Subject: Timing and the Nicaraguan resistance vote. Washington, D.C.: National Security Council, NSC/ISC Control No. 400300.

National Security File. 1967. Vietnam Box 75. Folder Title 2EE 1965–67, Primarily McNamara Recommendations re: Strategic Actions [1967]. McNamara to LBJ-11/19/67. Austin, TX: Lyndon Johnson Presidential Library.

Nelson, Michael, ed. 1990. *The Presidency and the Political System.* 3rd ed. Washington, D.C.: Congressional Quarterly.

Neuman, Johanna. 1990. Baker resurrects an old line on wars, 'In one word, jobs.' *USA Today,* 14 November.

Neustadt, Richard E. 1960, 1964. *Presidential Power.* New York: New American Library.

Neustadt, Richard E. 1980. *Presidential Power: The Politics of Leadership from FDR to Carter.* New York: Wiley.

Neustadt, Richard E. 1990. *Presidential Power and the Modern Presidents: The Politics of Leadership from Roosevelt to Reagan.* New York: Free Press.

The new bid to Nicaragua. 1985. *New York Times,* 6 April: 18.

The New York Times Staff. 1971. *The Pentagon Papers,* New York: Bantam Books.

Nincic, Miroslav. 1988. *United States Foreign Policy.* Washington, D.C.: Congressional Quarterly.

Nixon, Richard M. 1962. *Six Crises.* Garden City, New York: Doubleday.

Nixon, Richard M. 1978. RN: *Memoirs of Richard Nixon.* New York: Warner Books.

Nixon, Richard M. 1980. *The Real War.* New York: Warner Books.

Nixon, Richard M. 1985. *No More Vietnams.* New York: Avon Books.

Nixon: I erred on Viet bombing. 1988. *Chicago Tribune,* 11 April: 7.

Oberdorfer, Don. 1983. Washington's role troubles Congress. *Washington Post,* 3 April: A1, A13.

Oberdorfer, Don, and Patrick Tyler. 1983. U.S.-backed Nicaraguan army swells to 7,000 men. *Washington Post,* 8 May.

O'Donnell, Kenneth P., and David F. Powers, with J. McCarthy. 1972. *Johnny We Hardly Knew Ye: Memories of John Fitzgerald Kennedy.* Boston: Little, Brown.

O'Neill, Thomas P., with William Novak. 1987. *Man of the House.* New York: Random House.

Opinion outlook: Views on national security. 1986. *National Journal* 18: 1224.

Ostrom, Charles W. Jr., and Brian L. Job. 1986. The president and the political use of force. *American Political Science Review* 80: 541–66.

Ostrom, Charles W. Jr., and Dennis M. Simon. 1985. Promise and performance: A dynamic model of presidential popularity. *American Political Science Review* 79: 334–58.

Ostrom, Charles W. Jr., and Dennis M. Simon. 1989. The man in the teflon suit? The environmental connection, political drama, and popular support in the Reagan presidency. *Public Opinion Quarterly* 53: 353–87.

Ostrom, Charles W. Jr., Brian L. Job., Robin F. Marra, and Dennis M. Simon. 1990. Foreign policy and presidential popularity: Creating windows of opportunity in the perpetual election. *Journal of Conflict Resolution* 34(4): 588–624.

Page, Benjamin I. 1983. The effects of public opinion on policy. *American Political Science Review* 77: 175–90.

Page, Benjamin I. 1984. Presidents as opinion leaders. *Policy Studies Journal* 12: 649–61.

Page, Benjamin I. 1988. Foreign policy and the rational public. *Journal of Conflict Resolution* 32: 211–47.

Page, Benjamin I., and Robert Y. Shapiro. 1983. Effects of public opinion on policy. *American Political Science Review* 77: 175–90.

Page, Benjamin I., and Robert Y. Shapiro. 1984. Presidents as opinion leaders: Some new evidence. *Policy Studies Journal* 12: 649–61.

Page, Benjamin I., and Robert Y. Shapiro. 1989. Educating and manipulating the public. In *Manipulating Public Opinion*. Edited by Michael Margolis and Gary A. Mausar. Pacific Grove, Calif.: Brooks/Cole.

Page, Benjamin I., and Robert Y. Shapiro. 1992. *The Rational Public: Fifty Years of Trends in Americans' Preferences*. Chicago: University of Chicago Press.

Page, Benjamin I., Robert Y. Shapiro, and Richard A. Brody. 1972. Policy voting and the electoral process: The Vietnam War issue. *American Political Science Review* 66: 979–95.

Page, Benjamin I., Robert Y. Shapiro, and G. Dempsey. 1987. What moves public opinion? *American Political Science Review* 81: 23–43.

Parenti, Michael. 1986. *Inventing Reality: The Politics of the Mass Media*. New York: St. Martin's.

Parry, Robert, and Brian Barger. 1986. CIA gave political aid to contras. *Washington Post,* 14 April: A20.

Parry, Robert, and Peter Kornbluh. 1988. Iran-contra's untold story. *Foreign Policy* 72: 3–30.

Pastor, Robert A. 1975. Coping with Congress's foreign policy. *Foreign Service Journal* 52(12): 15–18, 23.

Pastor, Robert A. 1980. *Congress and the Politics of U.S. Foreign Economic Policy*. Berkeley: University of California Press.

Pastor, Robert A. 1985. The cry-and-sigh syndrome: Congress and trade policy. In *Making Economic Policy in Congress*. Edited by Allen E. Schick. Washington, D.C.: American Enterprise Institute.

Pastor, Robert A. 1988. *Condemned to Repetition: The United States and Nicaragua*. Princeton, N.J.: Princeton University Press.

Pastor, Robert A. 1990a. Nicaragua's choice: The making of a free election. *Journal of Democracy* 1(3): 13–25.

Pastor, Robert A. 1990b. Interbranch politics and U.S. foreign policy. Emory University, Atlanta, Ga. Typescript.

Pastor, Robert A. 1992. *Whirlpool: U.S. Foreign Policy Toward Latin America and the Caribbean*. Princeton, N.J.: Princeton University Press.

Pastor, Robert A. 1993. The war between the branches: Explaining U.S. policy toward Nicaragua, 1979–89. In *Public Opinion in U.S. Foreign Policy: The Controversy Over Contra Aid*. Edited by Richard Sobel. Lanham, Md.: Rowman & Littlefield.

Patterson, Bradley H. Jr. 1988. *The Ring of Power: The White House Staff and Its Expanding Role in Government*. New York: Basic Books.

Peltzman, Sam. 1984. Constituent interest and congressional voting. *Journal of Law and Economics* 27: 181–210.

Perry, William. 1994. U.S. objectives are not secret. *Washington Post,* 17 March, p. 22.

Perry, William. 1995. For the record. *Washington Post,* 17 March: A26.

Phillips, Don, and Helen Dewar. 1989. Hill approves nonmilitary contra aid. *Washington Post,* 14 April: A1.

Poggioli, Sylvia. *Scouts without compasses: An NPR reporter on the disinformation trap in former Yugoslavia*. Cambridge, Mass.: Nieman Reports, Fall 1993.

Poll: Americans divided on Nicaraguan intervention. 1985. *Miami Herald,* 31 March: 4A.

Popkin, Samuel L. 1991. *The Reasoning Voter*. Chicago: University of Chicago Press.

Powlick, Philip J. 1991. The attitudinal bases for responsiveness to public opinion among American foreign policy officials. *Journal of Conflict Resolution* 35: 611–41.

Powlick, Philip J. 1995. The sources of public opinion for American foreign policy officials. *International Studies Quarterly* 39: 427–52.

President Reagan's address on Central America to the joint session of Congress. 1983. *New York Times,* 28 April: A12.

President's news conference on foreign and domestic issues. 1988. *New York Times,* 25 February: A16.

Pressman, Steven. 1985. Massive lobbying campaign waged over aid for "contras." *Congressional Quarterly Weekly Report* 43: 715–16.

Priest, Dara. 1991. "Pennsylvania mourns 15 second victims." *Washington Post,* 28 February: A33.

Pritchard, Anita. 1986. An evaluation of *CQ* presidential support scores: The relationship between presidential election results and congressional voting decisions. *American Journal of Political Science* 30: 480–95.

Putnam, Robert D. 1988. Diplomacy and domestic politics: The logic of two-level games. *International Organization* 42: 427–60.

Putnam, Robert D., and Nicholas Bayne. *Hanging Together: Cooperation and Conflict in the Seven-Power Summits.* Cambridge, Mass.: Harvard University Press.

Quinn-Judge, Paul. 1994. 25,000 GIs suggested for peace in Bosnia; joint chiefs head issues new figure. *The Boston Globe,* 10 March.

Raymond, Walter Jr. 1988–89. Letter to the editor [responding to Parry/Kornbluh article]. *Foreign Policy* 73: 171–76.

Raymond, Walter Jr. 1983. Private sector support for Central American program. National Security Council Memorandum. Washington, D.C.: National Security Council.

Reagan, Ronald. 1983. Central America: Defending our vital interests. *Current Policy,* Washington, D.C.: U.S. Department of State. 482.

Reagan, Ronald. 1984. *Public Papers of the President of the United States: Ronald Reagan 1983 Book I.* Washington, D.C.: United States Government Printing Office.

Reagan, Ronald. 1985. *Public Papers of the President of the United States: Ronald Reagan 1983 Book II.* Washington, D.C.: United States Government Printing Office.

Reagan, Ronald. 1986. *Public Papers of the President of the United States: Ronald Reagan 1984 Book I.* Washington, D.C.: United States Government Printing Office.

Reagan, Ronald. 1987. Reagan on contras: 'Strive and struggle.' *New York Times,* 8 October: A12.

Reagan, Ronald. 1988. *Public Papers of the President of the United States: Ronald Reagan 1985 Book I.* Washington, D.C.: United States Government Printing Office.

Reagan, Ronald. 1989. *Public Papers of the President of the United States: Ronald Reagan 1987 Book I.* Washington, D.C.: United States Government Printing Office.

Reagan, Ronald. 1990a. *An American Life.* New York: Simon & Schuster.

Reagan, Ronald. 1990b. *Public Papers of the Presidents of the United States: Ronald Reagan 1988 Book I.* Washington D.C.: United States Government Printing Office.

Reagan, Ronald. 1991. *Public Papers of the Presidents of the United States: Ronald Reagan 1988–1989 Book II.* Washington, D.C.: United States Government Printing Office.

Reagan, Ronald. 1998. *A Shining City: The Legacy of Ronald Reagan.* Edited by D. Eric Felton. New York: Simon & Schuster Trade.

Reeves, Richard. 1994. *Greensboro News and Record,* 12 December.

Reiter, Howard L. 1987. U.S. public opinion of the Nicaraguan war and implications for political strategy. Paper presented at the American Political Science Association, Chicago.

Reiter, Howard L. 1990. Unmobilized constituencies: Public opinion of the Nicaraguan war. *New Political Science* 18/19: 125–46.

RePass, David E. 1971. Issue salience and party choice. *American Political Science Review* 65: 389–400.

Richman, Alvin. 1987. U.S. state department information memoranda, 1986–87. Washington, D.C.: U.S. State Department.

Rielly, John E., ed. 1975. *American Public Opinion and U.S. Foreign Policy, 1975.* Chicago: Chicago Council on Foreign Relations.

Rielly, John E., ed. 1983. *American Public Opinion and U.S. Foreign Policy, 1983.* Chicago: Chicago Council on Foreign Relations.

Rielly, John E., ed. 1987. *American Public Opinion and U.S. Foreign Policy, 1987.* Chicago: Chicago Council on Foreign Relations.

Rielly, John E., ed. 1995. *American Public Opinion and U.S. Foreign Policy, 1995.* Chicago: Chicago Council on Foreign Relations.

Rielly, John E., ed. 1999. *American Public Opinion and U.S. Foreign Policy, 1999.* Chicago: Chicago Council on Foreign Relations.

Ripley, Randall B., and Grace A. Frankin. 1987. *Congress, the Bureaucracy and Public Policy.* 4th ed. Chicago: Dorsey.

Rivers, Douglas, and Nancy L. Rose. 1985. Passing the president's program: Public opinion and presidential influence in Congress. *American Journal of Political Science* 29: 183–96.

Roberts, Steven V. 1985a. Senate would aid rebels with $38 million. *New York Times,* 7 June: A1, A8.

Roberts, Steven V. 1985b. House reverses earlier ban on aid to Nicaraguan rebels, passes $27 million package. *New York Times,* 13 June: A1, A12.

Roberts Steven V. 1986a. Reagan is defeated on contra aid plan. *New York Times,* 21 March: A1, A12.

Roberts, Steven V. 1986b. Senate approves Reagan's request to help contras. *New York Times,* 28 March: A1.

Roberts, Steven V. 1988. Reagan, in speech, presses Congress on aid to contras. *New York Times,* 3 February: A1.

Rogers, David, and David Ignatius. 1985a. How CIA-aided raids in Nicaragua in '84 led Congress to end funds. *Wall Street Journal,* 6 March: 1, 20.

Rogers, David, and David Ignatius. 1985b. CIA internal report details U.S. role in contra raids in Nicaragua last year. *Wall Street Journal,* 6 March: 1, 20.

Roll, Charles W., and Albert H. Cantril. 1972. *Polls: Their Use and Misuse in Politics.* New York: Basic Books.

Rood, Mick. 1987. State News Service. Washington D.C.: 18 September.

Rosegrant, Susan, and Michael D. Watkins. 1996a. Getting to Dayton: Negotiating an end to the war in Bosnia. Kennedy School of Government Case Program, C125-96-1356 0.

Rosegrant, Susan, and Michael D. Watkins. 1996b. *The Gulf crisis: Building a coalition for war.* Kennedy School of Government Case Program, C16-94-1264.0.

Rosenau, James N. 1961. *Public Opinion and Foreign Policy: An Operational Formulation.* New York: Random House.

Rosenberg, Milton J., Sidney Verba, and Philip E. Converse. 1970. *Vietnam and the Silent Majority: A Dove's Guide.* New York: Harper & Row.

Rosenstone, Steven J., and John M. Hansen. 1993. *Mobilization, Participation, and Democracy in America.* New York: Macmillan.

Rosenthal, Andrew. 1989. The North trial papers: A window on the effort to circumvent Congress. *New York Times,* 14 April: A16.

Rovner, Mark. 1987. *Trouble at our Doorstep: Public Attitudes and Public Policy on Central America.* Washington, D.C.: Roosevelt Center.

Rusk, Dean, with Richard Rusk and Daniel S. Papp. 1990. *As I Saw It.* New York: W.W. Norton.

Russett, Bruce. 1990. *Controlling the Sword: Democratic Governance and National Security.* Cambridge, Mass.: Harvard University Press.

Schandler, Herbert Y. 1997. *Lyndon Johnson and Vietnam: The Unmaking of a President.* Princeton, N.J.: Princeton University Press.

Schattschneider, E. E. 1935. *Politics, Pressure, and the Tariff.* New York: Prentice-Hall.

Schattschneider, E. E. 1960. *The Semi-Sovereign People: A Realist's View of Democracy in America.* New York: Holt, Rinehart and Winston.

Schlozman, Kay Lehman, and John T. Tierney. 1986. *Organized Interests and American Democracy.* New York: Harper & Row.

Schmitt, Eric. 1991. U.S. battle plan: Massive air strikes. *New York Times,* 10 January: A17.

Schneider, William. 1979. Bang-bang Television. In *Eagle Entangled: U.S. Foreign Policy in a Complex World.* Edited by Kenneth A. Oye, Donald Rothchild, and Robert J. Lieber, Boston: Little, Brown.

Schneider, William. 1983. Rambo and reality: Having it both ways. *Eagle Resurgent? The Reagan Era in American Foreign Policy.* Edited by Kennett A. Oye, Donald Rothchild, and Robert J. Lieber. New York: Longman.

Schuman, Howard. 1972. Two sources of antiwar sentiment in America. *American Journal of Sociology* 78(3): 518–36.

Schwarz, John E., and Barton Fenmore. 1977. Presidential election results and congressional roll call behavior: The cases of 1964, 1968, and 1972. *Legislative Studies Quarterly* 2: 409–22.

Serafino, Nina. 1987. *U.S. Assistance to Nicaraguan Guerrillas: Issues for the Congress.* Washington, D.C.: Congressional Research Service, Library of Congress.

Serafino, Nina. 1989. *Contra Aid: Summary and Chronology of Major Congressional Action. 1981–89.* Washington, D.C.: Congressional Research Service, Library of Congress.

Serafino, Nina, and K. Larry Storrs. 1993. The Reagan administration's efforts to gain support for contra aid. In *Public Opinion in U.S. Foreign Policy: The controversy over contra aid.* Edited by Richard Sobel. Lanham, Md.: Rowman & Littlefield.

Sellers, D. 1986. Coalition targets foes of contra aid. *Washington Times,* 15 April.

Shaffer, William R. 1987. Ideological trends among southern U.S. Democratic senators. *American Politics Quarterly* 15: 299–324.

Shapiro, Margaret. 1985. Contra aid vote presages renewed U.S. role. *Washington Post,* 14 June: A18.

Shapiro, Robert Y., and Lawrence R. Jacobs. 1989. The relationship between public opinion and public policy: A review. In *Political Behavior Annual.* Edited by Samuel Long. Boulder, Colo.: Westview.

Shapiro, Robert Y., and Benjamin I. Page. 1988. Foreign policy and the rational public. *Journal of Conflict Resolution* 32: 211–47.

Shapiro, Robert Y., and Lawrence R. Jacobs. 1997. The myth of the pandering politicians. *The Public Perspective* 8(April/May): 3–5.

Shapley, Deborah. 1973. *Promise and Power: The Life and Times of Robert McNamara.* Boston: Little, Brown.

Shribman, David. 1984. Poll finds fewer than half in U.S. back Latin policy. *New York Times,* 29 April: A1.

Shultz, George P. 1995. *Turmoil & Triumph: My Years as Secretary of State.* New York: Simon & Schuster Trade.

Sigelman, Lee. 1980. Gauging the public response to presidential leadership. *Presidential Studies Quarterly* 10: 427–33.

Simon, Dennis M., and Charles W. Ostrom Jr. 1988. The politics of prestige: Popular support and the modern presidency. *Presidential Studies Quarterly* 18: 741–59.

Simpson, John. 1991. *From the House of War: John Simpson in the Gulf.* London: Arrow Books.

Small, Melvin. 1988. *Johnson, Nixon, and the Doves.* New Brunswick: Rutgers University Press.

Smalley, Robert M. 1985. Key points regarding American attitudes toward Nicaragua [information memorandum to the secretary of state]. Washington, D.C.: U.S. State Department. 16 May.

Smith, Hedrick. 1985. A larger force of Latin rebels sought by U.S. *New York Times,* 17 April: A1, A10.

Smith, Hedrick. 1989. *The Power Game: How Washington Works.* New York: Ballantine.

Smith, Tom W. 1985. The polls: America's most important problems: Part I. *Public Opinion Quarterly* 49(Summer): 264–74.

Smith, Wayne S. 1987. Lies about Nicaragua. *Foreign Policy* 67: 87–103.

Snyder, E. 1973. Proposal to establish a short term, ad hoc, multi-organizational, single purpose project to cut off war funds. Friends Committee on National Legislation. Mimeo.

Sobel, Richard. 1988. Public opinion about U.S. Central America policy. Paper presented at the Conference on the Future for Central America, University of Chicago.

Sobel, Richard. 1989. The polls—a report: Public opinion about United States intervention in El Salvador and Nicaragua. *Public Opinion Quarterly* 53: 114–28.

Sobel, Richard. 1990. "Staying power in Mideast." *Dallas Morning News,* 10 October.

Sobel, Richard, ed. 1993. *Public Opinion in U.S. Foreign Policy: The Controversy over Contra Aid.* Foreword by Everett C. Ladd. Lanham, Md.: Rowman & Littlefield.

Sobel, Richard. 1995a. Contra aid fundamentals: Exploring the intricacies and the issues. *Political Science Quarterly,* 110(2): 287–306.

Sobel, Richard. 1995b. "What people really say about Bosnia." *New York Times,* 22 November: A23.

Sobel, Richard. 1996. U.S. and European attitudes towards intervention in the former Yugoslavia: *Mourir pour la Bosnie?* In *The World and Yugoslavia's Wars.* Edited by Richard H. Ullman. New York: Council on Foreign Relations.

Sobel, Richard. 1998a. Portraying American public opinion toward the Bosnia crisis. *Harvard International Journal of Press/Politics,* 3(2): 16–33.

Sobel, Richard. 1998b. The polls—Trends. United States intervention in Bosnia. *Public Opinion Quarterly* 62(Summer): 250–78.

Sobel, Richard, et al. 1999. National and International Security. In *American Public Opinion and U.S. Foreign Policy.* Edited by John E. Rielly. Chicago Council on Foreign Relations.

Sobel, Richard, and Eric Shiraev, eds. In process. International Public Opinion and the Bosnia Crisis. Manuscript.

Spanier, John, and Eric M. Ulsaner. 1989. *American Foreign Policy-making and the Democratic Dilemmas.* Pacific Grove, Calif.: Brooks-Cole.

Spence, Jack. 1987. The U.S. media: Covering (over) Nicaragua. In *Reagan versus the Sandinistas: The Undeclared War on Nicaragua.* Edited by Thomas W. Walker. Boulder, Colo.: Westview.

Stanfield, Rochelle L. 1990. Centralized headache. *National Journal* 22: 189.

Starobin, Paul, and Jeremy Gaunt. 1986. Campaign charges: Activities of pro-contra groups come under scrutiny. *Congressional Quarterly Weekly Report* 44: 3096–97.

Stimson, James A. 1976. Public support for American presidents: A cyclical model. *Public Opinion Quarterly* 40: 1–21.

Stimson, James A. 1991. *Public Opinion in America: Moods, Cycles, and Swings.* Boulder, Colo.: Westview.

Survey Research Consultants International. 1990. *Index to International Public Opinion.* Westport, CT: Greenwood Press.

Szulc, Tad. 1963. Vietnam victory by end of '65, envisaged by U.S. *New York Times,* 30 October: 1.

Szulc, Tad. 1990. *Then and Now: How the World Has Changed Since WW II.* New York: Morrow.

Talbott, Strobe. 1995. American leadership and the new Europa: Implementing the Dalton Peace Agreement. *U.S. Department of State Dispatches* 6(50–52): 917–20.

Tananbaum, Duane. 1988. *The Bricker Amendment Controversy: A Test of Eisenhower's Political Leadership.* Ithaca, N.Y.: Cornell University Press.

Tatalovich, Raymond, and Byron W. Daynes. 1984. *Presidential Power in the United States.* Pacific Grove, Calif.: Brooks/Cole.

Taubman, Philip, and Raymond Bonner. 1983. U.S. ties to anti-Sandinistas are reported to be extensive. *New York Times,* 3 April: A1, A14.

Taylor, Andrew, and Lenore Webb. 1988. Chronology of Hill-Reagan tug of war over U.S. involvement with the contras. *Congressional Quarterly Weekly Report* 46: 806–7.

Taylor, Paul. 1986. Right expects boost from contra loss. *Washington Post,* 25 March: A9.

Taylor, Philip M. 1998. *War and the Media: Propaganda and Persuasion in the Gulf War.* Manchester, NY: Manchester University Press.

Thomas, Evan. 1990. No Vietnam: The lessons of Southeast Asia shape the president's strategy in the Gulf. *Newsweek,* 10 December: 24–31.

A tip to Bosnia's besiegers. 1994. *Washington Post,* 13 March: C6.

Truman, David B. 1951. *The Governmental Process.* New York: Knopf.

Tyler, Patrick E., and Bob Woodward. 1982. U.S. approves convert plan in Nicaragua. *Washington Post,* 10 March: A1.

U.S. Congress. 1983. House Committee on Foreign Affairs. Congress and U.S. policy toward Central America and the Caribbean. In *Congress and Foreign Policy—1982.* Edited by K. Larry Storrs, Nina M. Serafino, and Richard P. Cronin. Washington, D.C.: Government Printing Office.

U.S. Congress. 1984. House Committee on Foreign Affairs. Congress and the Central American-Caribbean region. In *Congress and Foreign Policy—1983.* Edited by K. Larry Storrs, Nina M. Serafino, Jonathan E. Sanford, and Richard P. Cronin. Washington, D.C.: Government Printing Office.

U.S. Congress. 1985. House Committee on Foreign Affairs. Congress and policy toward Central America. In *Congress and Foreign Policy—1984.* Edited by Steven R. Harper. Washington, D.C.: Government Printing Office.

U.S. Congress. 1987a. House Select Committee to Investigate Covert Arms Transactions with Iran and Senate Select Committee on Secret Military Assistance to Iran and the Nicaraguan Opposition. *Iran-contra affair.* 100th Congress, 1st Session, H. Rept. No. 100–433, S. Rept. No. 100–216. Washington, D.C.: Government Printing Office.

U.S. Congress. 1987b. House Select Committee to Investigate Covert Arms Transactions with Iran and Senate Select Committee on Secret Military Assistance to Iran and the Nicaraguan Opposition. *Testimony of Robert C. McFarlane [and others].* Hearing. 100th Congress, 1st Session, H. Rept. No. H961–35, S. Rept. No. S961–6. Washington, D.C.: Government Printing Office.

U.S. Congress. 1987c. House Select Committee to Investigate Covert Arms Transactions with Iran. U.S. Department of State, Office of the Inspector General, Audit Report No. 7PP-008, Special Inquiry into the Department's Contracts with International Business Communications and Its Principals, July 1987. *Iran-contra investigations: Testimony of George P. Shultz and Edwin Meese, III. Hearing.* 100th Congress, 1st Session, H. Rept. No. H961–48, S. Rept. No. S961–12. Washington, D.C.: Government Printing Office.

U.S. Congress. 1988a. House Committee on Foreign Affairs. The battle over Nicaragua. In *Congress and Foreign Policy—1985–86.* Edited by Anne L. Potter. Washington, D.C.: Government Printing Office.

U.S. Congress. 1988b. Senate Committee on Foreign Relations and the House Committee on

Foreign Affairs. *Inter-American relations: A collection of documents, legislation, description of inter-American organizations, and other material pertaining to inter-American affairs.* 100th Congress, 2nd Session, S. Rept. No. 100–168. Washington, D.C.: Government Printing Office.

U.S. Congress. 1989a. House Committee on Foreign Affairs. Congress and policy toward Central America and Panama. In *Congress and Foreign Policy—1988.* Edited by Maureen Taft-Morales and Mark P. Sullivan. Washington, D.C.: Government Printing Office.

U.S. Congress. 1989b. House Committee on Foreign Affairs. Congress and U.S. policy toward Nicaragua in 1987. In *Congress and Foreign Policy—1987.* Edited by Linda Robinson. Washington, D.C.: Government Printing Office.

U.S. Congress. 1990a. Joint Session of the Two Houses—Address by the President of the United States. Washington, D.C. 11 September.

U.S. Congress. 1990b. House Committee on Foreign Affairs. Congress and policy toward Central America in 1989. In *Congress and Foreign Policy—1989.* Edited by Mark P. Sullivan and K. Larry Storrs. Washington, D.C.: Government Printing Office.

U.S. Departments of Commerce, Justice, State, the Judiciary, and Related Agencies Appropriations Acts of 1984, 1985 and 1986 (P.L. 98-166, P.L. 98-411, and P.L. 99-180).

U.S. Department of State. 1994. *Bosnia and Croatia: The Challenge of Peace and Reconstruction.* Washington, D.C.: U.S. Department of State, 5(14): 4 April.

U.S. General Accounting Office. 1987a. Letter to Representatives Jack Brooks and Dante B. Fascell [on alleged lobbying and propaganda activities of the Office for Public Diplomacy], B-229069. September 30.

U.S. General Accounting Office. 1987b. Report to congressional requesters—Contracting: [The Department of] State's administration of certain public diplomacy contracts. Prepared in response to the March 31, 1987, request of Rep. Jack Brooks and Rep. Dante B. Fascell. GAO/NSAID-88-34, October.

U.S. House of Representatives. 1985. Permanent Select Committee on Intelligence of the House of Representatives. *Compilation of intelligence laws and related laws and executive orders of interest to the national intelligence community,* 99th Congress, 1st Session. Washington, D.C.: Government Printing Office.

U.S. House of Representatives. 1988. Committee on Foreign Affairs. *Congress and Foreign Policy—1985–86.* Washington, D.C.: U.S. House of Representatives Committee on Foreign Affairs.

U.S. must be ready to use its power, Shultz declares. 1984. *New York Times,* 10 December: 1.

U.S. Senate. 1984. Committee on Foreign Relations. National bipartisan report on Central America. Hearing. 98th Congress, 2nd Session. S. Hearings. 98-872.

Valenti, Jack. 1975. *A Very Human President.* New York: Norton.

Wahlke, John C. 1989. Policy demands and system support: The role of the represented. In *Readings in American Government and Politics.* Edited by Randall B. Ripley and Elliott E. Slotnick. New York: McGraw-Hill.

Walker, Jack L. 1966. A critique of the elitist theory of democracy. *American Political Science Review* 60: 285–95.

Walker, Thomas W., ed. 1987. *Reagan versus the Sandinistas: The Undeclared War on Nicaragua.* Boulder, Colo.: Westview.

Watts, William. Americans look at the world: Internationalism on the rise. *The Gallup Report International 3* (July): 1.

Watts, William, and Lloyd A. Free, eds. 1985. *State of the Nation III.* New York: Universe Books.

Weekly compilation of presidential documents (Reagan administration). 1985. 21:8, 25 February.

Weinberger, Caspar W. 1990. *Fighting for Peace: Seven Critical Years in the Pentagon.* New York: Warner Books.

Weinraub, Bernard. 1986. Reagan condemns Nicaragua in plea for aid to rebels. *New York Times,* 17 March: 1.

Weissberg, Robert. 1976. *Public Opinion and Popular Government.* Englewood Cliffs, N.J.: Prentice-Hall.

Wicker, Tom. 1991. *One of Us: Richard Nixon and the American Dream.* New York: Random House.

Wirthlin, Richard B. 1986. Nicaragua and aid to the contras [memorandum to Donald T. Regan]. McLean, Va.: Decision Making Information [Wirthlin Group]. Mimeo.

Wise, David. 1968. The twilight of a president. *New York Times Magazine,* 3 November.

Wittkopf, Eugene R. 1981. The structure of foreign policy attitudes: An alternative view. *Social Science Quarterly* 62: 108–23.

Wittkopf, Eugene R. 1983. Elites and masses: A comparative analysis of attitudes toward America's world role. *Journal of Politics* 45: 303–34.

Wittkopf, Eugene R. 1986. On the foreign policy beliefs of the American people: A critique and some evidence. *International Studies Quarterly* 30: 425–45.

Wittkopf, Eugene R. 1987. Elites and masses: Another look at attitudes toward America's world role. *International Studies Quarterly* 31: 131–59.

Wittkopf, Eugene R. 1988. American foreign policy beliefs, preferences, and performance evaluations. Paper presented at the International Society of Political Psychology, New York City.

Wittkopf, Eugene R. 1990. *Faces of Internationalism: Public Opinion and American Foreign Policy.* Durham, N.C.: Duke University Press.

Wittkopf, Eugene R. N.d. Domestic sources of international orientation change: The role of public opinion in American foreign policy. In *Changing Course in Foreign Policy.* Edited by Charles F. Hermann, Margaret G. Hermann, and Richard Herrmann.

Wittkopf, Eugene R., and Michael A. Maggiotto. 1983. The two faces of internationalism: Public attitudes toward American foreign policy in the 1970s—and beyond? *Social Science Quarterly* 64: 288–304.

Wittkopf, Eugene R., and James M. McCormick. 1990. The cold war consensus: Did it exist? *Polity* 22: 627–54.

Wittkopf, Eugene R., and James M. McCormick. 1993. The domestic politics of contra aid: Public opinion, Congress, and the president. In *Public Opinion in U.S. Foreign Policy: The Controversy over Contra Aid.* Edited by Richard Sobel. Lanham, Md.: Rowman & Littlefield.

Woodward, Bob. 1991. *The Commanders.* New York: Simon & Schuster.

Woodward, Susan. 1995. *Balkan Tragedy: Chaos and Dissolution after the Cold War.* Washington D.C.: Brookings Institution.

Wright, Jim. 1990. Streams of hope, rivers of blood: A personal narrative about Central America and the United States. University of Texas at Fort Worth. Typescript.

Zaroulis, Nancy, and Gerald Sullivan. 1985. *Who Spoke Up: American Protest against the War in Vietnam, 1963–1975.* New York: Holt, Reinhart and Winston.

Zimmermann, Warren. 1996. *Origins of a Catastrophe: Yugoslavia and Its Destroyers.* New York: Times Books.

Index